SCHOOL LEADERSHIP AND
INSTRUCTIONAL IMPROVEMENT

SCHOOL LEADERSHIP AND INSTRUCTIONAL IMPROVEMENT

Daniel L. Duke

Lewis & Clark College

Random House   **New York**
This book was developed for
Random House by Lane Akers, Inc.

First Edition

987654321

Copyright © 1987 by Random House

Library of Congress Cataloging-in-Publication Data

Duke, Daniel Linden.
  School leadership and instructional improvement.

  Bibliography: p.
  Includes index.
  1. School management and organization—United States.
2. School supervision—United States. 3. Education—
United States—Aims and objectives. I. Title.
II. Title: Leadership and instructional improvement.
LB2805.D86   1986   371.2′00973   86-20294
ISBN 0-394-35474-5

Manufactured in the United States of America

ACKNOWLEDGMENTS

This book deals with leadership and improvement. Neither is possible without a great deal of support and guidance from others. In preparing to write *School Leadership and Instructional Improvement,* as well as during its actual writing, I became acutely aware of all the debts I owe. The length of the bibliography is partial testimony to the wisdom I have gained from others. Then there are all those colleagues who are too busy teaching and leading schools and school systems to have time to write for publication. I would like to name some of those individuals who have played an important role in helping me think about school leadership:

Orval Ause	Rich McCullough
George Benson	Don McElroy
Eric Bigler	Bill McGovern
Bob Blum	Joe Pascarelli
Jim Carlile	Barbara Roper
Harry Clemmons	Dick Sagor
Dea Cox	Cathy Schar
Al Davidian	Ben Schellenberg
Margaret Dutton	Pat Schmuck
Christie Ford	Judy Scott
Bev Gladder	Pam Shelley
Gerald Hesling	Linda Simington
Larry Hibbard	Syd Steinbock
Ken Hill	Ellen Stevens
Nancy Isaacson	Rick Stiggins
Jim Jamieson	Sue Sullivan
Vern Jones	Pete Taylor
Zeno Katterle	Mike Wallmark
Bill Korach	Bruce Weitzel
David Livingston	

There are also the students in my Lewis and Clark classes to be thanked. I think particularly of the contributions made by those aspiring school leaders who suffered through EdAd 502—The Supervision, Evaluation, and Development of Educational Staff. They tested my ideas and led me to rethink much of the content of this book.

Marty Herdener dedicated a substantial portion of a year to the preparation of this book. She not only typed and edited the first draft, she made fun of the damn thing! For her unwavering support and good spirits I am forever grateful. Gratitude also should be expressed to Lester Kaplan and Jean Akers, who did a superb job of copy editing, and to Lane Akers, who had faith that I was the person to write a textbook on school leadership.

Last, and most important, there are the members of my family. Their contributions ranged from hugs to agreeing to turn down the stereo. Joshua, Krista, and Jay shared their school experiences with me and, in so doing, reminded me why I was writing the book. Devan has not yet been to school, but she helped by checking my home office periodically to see that I was still breathing. My wife, Cheryl, consented to a year of my excused absences, unexcused absences, and tardies on the agreement that my next book would be a travel guide to Kauai.

My heartfelt appreciation to all.

Daniel L. Duke

CONTENTS

SCHOOL LEADERSHIP AND INSTRUCTIONAL IMPROVEMENT

INTRODUCTION

This book is written for school leaders and prospective school leaders. It is based on the belief that one of the most important commitments of a school leader is the continuous improvement of instruction.

Anyone familiar with the world of contemporary schooling knows that educators have more to do than time permits. Choices, therefore, must be made. Priorities must be specified. Which responsibilities are foremost? What tasks will be undertaken only if time allows? The situation in which school leaders find themselves is analogous to a battlefield surgery (M.A.S.H.) unit. Given limited time and increasingly fewer resources, a triage system often develops in which choices of where to devote energy are dictated by the likelihood of success: Patients with the greatest chance for survival receive help first. This book maintains that school leaders are likely to have the greatest positive impact on the lives and welfare of students when they devote energy to the improvement of instruction. Of course, other leadership efforts may benefit students as well. The odds of helping the young diminish the further leaders drift away from instructional concerns.

These concerns encompass three classic educational issues:

- *What* should be taught?
- *How* should it be taught?
- How can it be determined that students *have learned* what has been taught?

Since knowledge and the needs of students are always changing, these questions must be asked on a continuing basis. It is the school leader's primary duty to make sure that sufficient attention is focused on them.

Purposes of the Book

For some, a textbook symbolizes a comprehensive body of knowledge generally considered essential to a field of endeavor. For others, a textbook represents a source of security, a well-organized corpus of information to which to turn in an emergency. Still others regard a textbook as an archaic form of private instruction containing too much outdated information oriented too little to solving practical problems.

My intentions in this textbook are both modest and ambitious. I make no promise to cover all the material related to school leadership. I shall focus on

1

issues that bear directly on the quality of instruction in elementary and secondary schools. Regrettably, my experience and scholarly activity force me to limit my coverage to schools in the United States. Little will be found concerning the various noninstructional duties of school leaders. What is sacrificed in breadth I trust will be offset by the level of detail devoted to matters of instruction, curriculum, and evaluation. My intention is to provide as practical a resource as possible for individuals charged with the responsibilities of supervising instruction, helping teachers grow professionally, and creating productive learning environments for students.

The heart of this book is a model of instructional leadership involving seven key functions. By carefully examining each of these functions, the reader should develop a framework for thinking about how to allocate scarce time and energy to the pursuit of instructional improvement.

Context

For decades educational administration textbooks have attempted to describe and analyze a variety of roles and functions. Such activities as supervision and staff development shared space with budget preparation, school law, and maintenance of the physical plant. Emphasis was placed on the line of authority, district organizational structure, and general management theory. Why should a textbook for leaders now appear that focuses primarily on *instructional* issues? The answer requires an understanding of the historical context in which the book was written.

Contemporary educators in the United States have had to confront three recurring issues—excellence, equity, and efficiency. Interestingly, these issues have tended to be addressed independently rather than simultaneously. In fact, it could be argued that failure to treat all three issues at the same time has ensured their continuation as problems, for they are definitely interrelated. Concentrating resources on excellence is likely to beget concern over equity. Shifting resources to meet the educational needs of "at risk" youth is fated to generate questions about cost effectiveness, particularly among those who must bear the greatest burden for school finance. As schools scale down their operations, and concentrate on "the basics" in response to demands for greater efficiency, those who seek excellence again become discontented. Doubts arise over the viability of an educational system where schools can do no more than aim for minimum competence.

There is no reason to believe that tomorrow's educational leaders will escape having to deal with the same three issues. Their instructional concerns will continue to reside close to the heart of demands for excellence, equity, and efficiency.

For example, the push for educational excellence that followed the initial successes of the Soviet space program in the late fifties zeroed in on the need for better curricular content and instruction. Critics such as James Bryant Conant called for sweeping reforms in teacher preparation and supervision, school organization, and student grouping.[1] Conant was particularly concerned that the academically talented "top 15 percent" were being insufficiently challenged.[2]

A decade after the launching of Sputnik, national concern had shifted from educational excellence to educational equity. A national commission investigating the causes of racial violence in the United States indicted the schools for perpetuating racism and inequality.[3] At the same time the National Advisory Commission on Civil Disorders singled out the schools as a major key to opportunities for disadvantaged youth. Researchers studying the classroom experiences of minority youth, and later of female and handicapped students, began to identify ways in which teachers communicated lower expectations to these young people, thereby jeopardizing their chances of benefiting fully from schooling.[4] Efforts were made to prepare new teachers to deal more effectively with the requirements of students with special needs. Schools were called upon to host a variety of special programs, such as those supported by Title I (now Chapter I) and Title IX of the Elementary and Secondary Education Act, and Public Law 94–142. While many of the changes proposed during this time were aimed at developing new policies and securing additional resources for "at risk" youth, ultimately, the future of these youngsters was linked directly to what happened to them day to day in schools and classrooms. It was in the classroom that teachers were asked to deal with handicapped students and to acknowledge the value of cultural differences among their students.

An unprecedented amount of federal, state, and local money was committed to improving the life chances of disadvantaged youth during the late sixties. Money was provided for everything from teacher training to reading labs, multicultural curricula to bilingual education. As school enrollments began to decline in the seventies, however, taxpayers voiced growing frustration over the continued increase in school expenditures. Demands were made for greater efficiency in school operations and accountability in meeting educational goals. The steady decline in student performance on standardized tests of achievement during this period—despite the high level of funding for public schooling—further fueled public dissatisfaction. Innovative programs that were not directly related to the "basics" were axed, and educators were pressured into concentrating more time and energy on reading, writing, and arithmetic. School officials were urged to provide closer supervision of teachers and to remove incompetent teachers from classrooms.

The more the schools moved "back to basics," the more instruction was focused on ensuring minimum competence. This emphasis helped to foster concern that many students were being insufficiently challenged to develop their potential. In the early eighties a number of commissions and special reports warned the public that education in the United States was in desperate need of reform. The most publicized of these efforts was the report of the National Commission on Excellence in Education entitled *A Nation at Risk*. It called for increased course requirements for high school graduation, higher standards for student performance, more testing, a longer school year, and higher pay and incentives to attract talented teachers.[5] Table 1 presents a sampling of recommendations from other reports. These recommendations were important not

**Table 1   Calls for Instructional Improvement
in the Early Eighties**

Report or Study	Recommendations
John I. Goodlad. *A Place Called School* (New York: McGraw-Hill, 1984).	• More active involvement of students in learning • Minimum of 25 hours of instruction per student per week • Mentor programs • Mastery learning basis for instruction • Improvement of teaching skills • Continuous monitoring of student progress • Greater emphasis on student cooperation
Ernest L. Boyer. *High School: A Report on Secondary Education in America* (New York: Harper & Row, 1983).	• Higher expectations for teachers and students • Greater variety of teaching styles • More active involvement of students in learning • Less reliance on textbooks • Fewer students in classes requiring writing
Mortimer J. Adler. *The Paideia Proposal: An Educational Manifesto* (New York: Macmillan, 1982).	• High academic standards for *all* students • More active involvement of students in learning • Instructional balance between information dissemination, coaching, and Socratic questioning
Education Commission of the States. *Action for Excellence.* 1983.	• More homework • Smaller class size • Increased use of technology in classrooms • More frequent testing of student skill development

because they reflected a consensus concerning needed changes, but because they suggested a strong link between the future of American society and the quality of instruction in the nation's classroom.

Many reports went further to tie the quality of instruction to the nature of school organization and leadership. Virtually every report singled out the school principal as the key to successful reform. The Paideia Proposal called upon the principal to serve as the "head teacher," modeling good instructional practices for the faculty.[6] In *Action for Excellence,* the Education Commission of the States urged principals to serve as instructional leaders, directly overseeing matters of morale, discipline, and academic quality.[7] John Goodlad raised the possibility that experienced teachers also could serve as instructional leaders.[8] Ernest Boyer argued that principals should exercise more control over teacher selection and teacher rewards.[9]

As if the ferment generated by these national reports were not sufficient impetus for reform, several important bodies of research became available to large numbers of educators during the early eighties that served to intensify interest in instructional improvement and school leadership.

One body of research has been described variously as "teaching effects," "teacher effectiveness," and "process-product research." These studies investigated the possible relationships between specific teacher behaviors and student achievement. Teacher behaviors that were correlated with relatively large student gains in learning or with good student discipline were promoted as desirable instructional practice. By the early eighties, findings from these studies were being used as the basis for widespread staff development efforts and teacher training. Concerned educators could no longer legitimately claim that research offered them no practical guidance for helping teachers improve their classroom performance. In addition, researchers and critics who claimed that the quality of instruction accounted for little of the variance in student outcomes were clearly placed on the defensive. Teachers *could* make a difference.

Close on the heels of this research on teacher effectiveness came a series of studies on school effectiveness. Rather than focusing on the instructional practices of particular teachers, these studies investigated a wide assortment of school characteristics. Schools with steadily improving student achievement were compared to those with declining student achievement. The use of "wide-angle lens" approaches allowed researchers to identify differences not only in instructional practices but also in school organization and leadership practices. One study after another cited the importance of instructional leadership.[10]

Another group of studies sought to describe and understand the processes by which schools change and improve. Researchers looked at how innovations were planned, implemented, and evaluated. They studied failed experiments as well as successes. The quality of school leadership was found to be a key to successful innovation.[11] Where leaders devoted time and energy to involving members of the school community in planning changes, and where they provided recognition to teachers and set appropriate expectations, schools were more likely to experience productive change.

At the same time that the importance of school leadership was being acknowledged, the whole concept of leadership in general was regaining credibility. After the years of Watergate, military failures, and the Peter Principle, the eighties ushered in a time when calls were made for strong and enlightened leadership. James MacGregor Burns, the eminent historian, urged that the power of the President be strengthened.[12] The bestseller *In Search of Excellence* attributed much of the success of top corporations to executive vision, commitment, and style.[13] In *The Next American Frontier,* Robert Reich tied the renaissance of the United States economy to the regaining of corporate control by leaders with technical, rather than legal or financial, expertise.[14]

The message of the eighties is clear. Leadership is essential to the success of the nation as well as its institutions. To lead is not to deny the value of democratic governance or shared decision making, as had been suggested during the sixties. Enlightened leaders typically do not solve problems as much as see that problems get solved. To accomplish this critical function, today's leaders must not only know how to work effectively with people; they must understand the technical side of operations, too. In the sphere of education, school leaders must possess a working knowledge of instruction, curriculum, and evaluation as well as of group dynamics, management practices, and school law.

In 1984 the Phi Delta Kappa Commission on Public Confidence in Education asked a national sample of citizens to identify bases for confidence in the public schools. Preliminary analyses of the data found that "administrator effectiveness" (the quality of school leadership) was second only to "dedicated, competent teachers" and "special instructional and extracurricular programs" as a source of public confidence.[15] Individual responses specified the vital functions served by school leaders: supervision of teachers, problem-solving ability, and commitment to trust, respect, and a student-centered environment.

Who Is a School Leader?

School Leadership and Instructional Improvement is written for school leaders and aspiring school leaders. Does this mean that the audience is limited to building principals? Not at all. While it is correct to assume that the principal is the most obvious candidate for instructional leadership, other individuals may also fulfill the responsibilities. In one review of research on successful elementary programs, Russell Gersten, Douglas Carnine, and Susan Green report that trained supervisors and staff consultants may overcome the apathy or resistance of principals and produce instructional improvement.[16] Thomas Sergiovanni makes a persuasive case for the value of department chairpersons in the instructional improvement process.[17] Other administrators, including vice principals, administrative assistants, program directors, and grade-level or pod leaders, have important contributions to make. Last, but certainly not least, teachers serving perhaps as master teachers or on special assignment may function as instructional leaders.

As will be seen in the chapters that follow, the only essential ingredients for instructional leadership are a willingness to allocate a substantial portion of time to instructional improvement, a capacity to transcend the concerns of any particular classroom and focus on welfare of the entire school, and a clear vision of the nature of good instruction. Others besides the principal, of course, may possess these characteristics. If no person or group assumes the instructional leadership role, it is unlikely that the school will be a productive and stimulating environment for students or teachers.

Organization of the Book

Part I of the book, "Thinking about School Leadership," presents three prerequisites for effective leadership. Chapter 1 examines different concepts of leader effectiveness to provide a basis for judging the quality of instructional leadership. Once a leader is clear about the nature of effective leadership, he or she is ready to develop specific visions of successful practice at the individual and organizational level. These visions, introduced in Chapter 2, serve to guide leader actions on a day-to-day basis. Translating vision into reality requires time. Therefore, the third prerequisite of effective leadership involves understanding and controlling one's daily schedule of activities. How personal time is allocated often distinguishes effective school leaders from ineffective ones.

Part II, "Visions of Effectiveness," goes on to offer three sets of working models, having made the case that school leaders need such visions to guide their day-to-day practice. Chapter 3 presents a variety of models of good teaching. A leader intent on instructional improvement must have a good sense of what teaching, under ideal conditions, looks like. Similarly, Chapter 4 provides a model of instructional leadership. The seven functions of instructional leadership presented in this model are elaborated in Part III. Chapter 5 attempts to describe several visions of effective schools to readers in an effort to portray to them the context in which instructional improvement occurs.

Part III, "Dimensions of Leadership for Instructional Improvement," involves a detailed review of the components of instructional leadership. Chapters 6, 7, and 8 address the most important dimensions: teacher supervision, evaluation, and staff and professional development. Chapter 6 focuses on entire systems, while Chapters 7 and 8 cover the daily conduct of supervision and development in schools. Succeeding chapters discuss other key leadership issues, including instructional management and support (Chapter 9), resource management (Chapter 10), quality control (Chapter 11), and coordination and troubleshooting (Chapter 12). Each chapter in Part III includes diagnostic questions to help school leaders assess their own performance as well as their school's.

Leadership is obviously more than a set of functions and situations. For a full appreciation of the challenges facing contemporary school leaders, attention must be directed to the quality of leaders' lives. Part IV, "Personal Dimensions of School Leadership," opens with an analysis of the process by which individuals become school leaders. Chapter 13 investigates such areas as administrative training, selection, and socialization. The final chapter of the book considers the issues that face veteran school leaders. What are the forces that conspire to divert attention from instructional improvement? What are the ethical dilemmas that confound instructional leadership? How do effective leaders cope with the challenges of organizational complexity, ethical confusion, and personal meaning?

The journey on which we now embark is a strenuous one dotted with detours, but the destination—good instruction for the nation's youth—more than justifies its rigors.

NOTES

1. James B. Conant, *The American High School Today* (New York: McGraw-Hill, 1959).
2. Robert L. Hampel, "The American High School Today: James Bryant Conant's Reservations and Reconsiderations," *Phi Delta Kappan,* Vol. 64, No. 9 (May 1983), pp. 607–612.
3. *Report of the National Advisory Commission on Civil Disorders* (New York: Bantam Books, 1968).
4. Thomas L. Good and Jere E. Brophy, *Looking in Classrooms,* 3rd ed. (New York: Harper & Row, 1984).
5. National Commission on Excellence in Education. *A Nation at Risk: The Imperative for Educational Reform* (Washington, D.C.: U.S. Government Printing Office, 1983).
6. Mortimer J. Adler. *The Paideia Proposal: An Educational Manifesto* (New York: Macmillan, 1982).
7. Education Commission of the States. *Action for Excellence* (1983).
8. John I. Goodlad. *A Place Called School* (New York: McGraw-Hill, 1984).
9. Ernest L. Boyer. *High School: A Report on Secondary Education in America* (New York: Harper & Row, 1983).
10. Joan Shoemaker and Hugh W. Fraser, "What Principals Can Do: Some Implications from Studies of Effective Schooling," *Phi Delta Kappan,* Vol. 63, No. 3 (November 1981), pp. 178–182.
11. Seymour B. Sarason, *The Culture of the School and the Problem of Change* (Boston: Allyn & Bacon, 1971).
12. James MacGregor Burns, *The Power to Lead* (New York: Simon & Schuster, 1984).
13. Thomas J. Peters and Robert H. Waterman, *In Search of Excellence: Lessons from America's Best-Run Companies* (New York: Harper & Row, 1982).
14. Robert B. Reich, *The Next American Frontier* (New York: Times Books, 1983).
15. Lila N. Carol and Luvern L. Cunningham, "Views of Public Confidence in Education," *Issues in Education,* Vol. II, No. 2 (Fall 1984), p. 115.
16. Russell Gersten, Douglas Carnine, and Susan Green, "The Principal as Instructional Leader: A Second Look," *Educational Leadership,* Vol. 40, No. 3 (December 1982), pp. 47–49.
17. Thomas J. Sergiovanni, *Handbook for Effective Department Leadership* (Boston: Allyn & Bacon, 1984).

PART I

THINKING ABOUT SCHOOL LEADERSHIP

School administrators frequently complain that they are so heavily involved in reacting to circumstances that they have no time left for reflection. Meeting the needs of others is so compelling and immediate that school leaders may have little opportunity to chart their own course of action. One elementary principal likens her job to that of being a mother: "All you do is run around all day taking care of other people's needs!" The irony of this situation is that leaders often are selected precisely because they possess initiative—the capacity to determine what must be done and to see that it is accomplished.

How is it that individuals chosen because of their initiative become ensnared in a thicket of reaction? Part of the reason obviously concerns the complexity of contemporary school leadership, a domain characterized by a multiplicity of conflicting expectations, routine crises, and crowds. A second reason, however, is simply that school leaders allow themselves to lose the *habit* of reflection. Perhaps some never possessed it in the first place! By falling into the trap of thinking that immediate action is the essence of leadership and by failing to schedule time for contemplating what needs to be done, leaders unwittingly ensure that their lives will be an unending succession of responses conditioned by other people's frustrations, emergencies, and needs.

Because I believe that thought, rather than reaction, is the key to effective leadership, I have chosen to begin this book with two chapters of a philosophical nature. Chapter 1 examines a variety of conceptual foundations for thinking about the effectiveness of school leaders. Without a working concept of personal effectiveness, a school leader is likely to remain at the mercy of the moment.

Chapter 2 starts with an analysis of how school leaders spend their time. A critical factor in effective time management is having a clear vision of the way things ought to be. Such a vision permits leaders—who always have more to do than time available—to allocate time in ways that increase the likelihood that central goals will be achieved. The second part of Chapter 2 focuses on the value of vision for school leaders.

CHAPTER 1

THINKING ABOUT THE EFFECTIVENESS OF SCHOOL LEADERS

The ability of leaders to keep their heads when all about them are losing theirs is based on three key factors. First, leaders must have some basis for judging their own performance, for estimating whether or not they are functioning effectively. Second, they need visions of what their organizations would look like if they were operating successfully. Once leaders have such visions, they can develop and hone the third crucial ability of an effective leader—good time management. Knowing how to spend one's time in ways that increase, rather than reduce, the chances of realizing one's vision separates strong leaders from their less fortunate colleagues. The present chapter explores a variety of concepts of leader effectiveness and identifies one as the foundation upon which succeeding chapters will be based.

The Benefit of Having a Concept of Effectiveness

With all that leaders must do, why should they devote time to theorizing about their own effectiveness? There are at least four reasons.

In the first place, leaders with an understanding of the foundation upon which their effectiveness is based are in a much better position to resist efforts by others to use them to promote special interests. It is natural for people to attempt to influence leaders, and it is difficult for most leaders to avoid the public arena where they are subject to lobbying and possible manipulation. Having a clear concept of effectiveness based on a personal vision makes it easier for a leader to choose between competing demands.

Second, like everyone else, leaders need performance feedback. To continue to grow and to improve their effectiveness, leaders need information on how they were doing. A concept of effectiveness helps establish standards or criteria for judging a leader's actions. It helps in generating specific evaluation questions and planning professional development activities.

A third reason for theorizing about leadership is that it allows leaders to reflect on the meaning of their work. Issues of meaning often lie close to the heart of people's frustrations and anxieties.[1] Everyone has feelings of uncertainty regarding the worth of his or her efforts. The act of reflecting on one's effectiveness helps direct attention to deeper issues of personal and professional meaning, issues which are bound to influence the quality of leaders' lives and the lives of those around them.

A final reason for having a clear concept of leader effectiveness is that leaders must so often explain their behavior. They must account for their actions to a variety of people—constituents, opponents, interest groups, other leaders, subordinates, superiors. The task of justifying their actions is made less difficult by reference to a well-thought-out concept of effectiveness. People may reject a particular concept, but they cannot accuse the leader of acting in an arbitrary or capricious manner. Concerns and disagreements can be discussed in terms of competing concepts of effectiveness rather than the leader's personal characteristics.

This book groups some of the more well-known concepts of school-leadership effectiveness into four categories: traditional concepts, concepts derived from the field of scientific management, concepts based on leader interactions, and recent concepts based on research.[2] Before these are reviewed, however, a brief explanation is needed concerning use of the term *leadership*.

Leadership Versus Management

Textbooks on school administration do not reflect agreement on the best generic label for their subject. Some are addressed to managers, others to administrators, and still others to leaders. This book uses the word *leader* to expand the reference group for the book and to point out the functional distinction between leadership and management.

This book is written for a variety of role groups: principals, assistant principals, program directors, supervisors, department chairpersons, head teachers, and the like. Reference to the term *management* may be perceived to exclude those not occupying formally designated administrative positions. *Leadership* is less apt to be associated exclusively with a particular role or title. Many people are capable of exercising leadership, depending on their ability and the circumstances at hand. In fact, managers may, for some portion of their time, function as leaders. So, too, may classroom teachers.

How does leadership differ from management? In the military, a distinction is often drawn between the management of things and the leadership of people. Indeed, it would be hard to visualize an officer "managing" troops into battle or "leading" weapons and material. Some feel that school administrators are removed from people and, hence, more managerial in their orientation. James March, for example, characterizes school administration as primarily the *management* of accounts *about* people—financial accounts, pupil progress accounts, and personnel accounts.[3] But March fails to address the normative questions of whether school administration should or should not be focused on these "accounts." In other words, he neglects to base his analysis on a particular concept of effectiveness.

To say that leaders are more involved with providing direction to people than with managing accounts is to grasp only one of the crucial differences between leadership and management. A second distinction concerns the premises that guide the actions of leaders and managers. With a touch of historical irony, former President Richard M. Nixon, in his book *Leaders,* posits that managers "do the thing right" while leaders "do the right thing." [4] In other words, managers are concerned primarily with following established procedures correctly. Leaders are guided by a sense of "right" and a concern for consequences that transcend rules and regulations. Obviously, leaders may not make very effective managers and vice versa.

The concepts of effectiveness that will be reviewed in the following sections are all concerned to some extent with the consequences of a school leader's actions. These consequences typically, though not exclusively, involve people—students, patrons, teachers, school officials. De-emphasizing bureaucratic routines and nonhuman targets of action is not intended to devalue the importance of school management, only to suggest that effective management alone is unlikely to create or sustain the conditions necessary for continuous instructional improvement—the primary focus of this book.

CONCEPTS OF LEADER EFFECTIVENESS

Traditional Concepts

In the past, and to some extent even today, the public's image of a leader has been a male image. Sara Lightfoot maintains that the essence of traditional leadership can be captured by three roles—general, coach, and father.[5] The words evoke pictures of courage in the midst of crisis, directions delivered under pressure, and the security of the hearth. Of Lightfoot's three male stereotypes, the father probably comes closest to describing traditional school leadership, at least for the secondary level. Traditional elementary school leadership, on the other hand, may be better characterized by a mother image.

In the eyes of legal authorities, school "marms" and "masters" were, in fact, surrogate parents. *In loco parentis* status assured school leaders considerable discretion in dealing with their young charges. The notion that educators acted with the best interests of young people uppermost in their thoughts was not seriously challenged until the student rights movement of the late sixties.

How, then, might one have judged the quality of leadership provided by the surrogate fathers and mothers who ran the schools of the last century? The word *effectiveness* hardly seems appropriate. It is more likely that a school leader would have been judged on the basis of *goodness*. Was he or she a *good* leader? As David Tyack and Elizabeth Hansot have shown, traditional school leadership embodied moral qualities seldom stressed in contemporary discourse.[6] More important than results or efficiency was the leader's reputation for upright character. School leadership was a calling that demanded impeccable moral credentials. Heads of schools served as exemplars of virtue, not only for the young, but for entire communities.

Besides modeling virtue, traditional school leaders also had to *manage* it (to use Tyack and Hansot's phrasing). Managing virtue typically entailed the maintenance of orderly learning environments. In fact, order and discipline frequently became ends in themselves, rather than simply means to more productive learning. The school leader who saw to it that students behaved appropriately usually was certain to earn the respect of patrons, whether or not students demonstrated great academic achievement.

By the end of the nineteenth century, notions of the good or virtuous school leader had begun to yield to new concepts, ones heavily influenced by developments in American industry. The *scientific management movement* fostered images of leaders as technical experts. These images seemed to fit the needs of rapidly growing schools and school systems. One-room schools gave way to schools of several hundred students and many teachers. School leaders assumed responsibility for supervising staff members and enforcing complicated policies. They had less time to interact regularly with students or to teach. As Tyack and Hansot conclude:

> Whereas school leaders of the nineteenth century tended to see themselves as constituting an aristocracy of character, in the twentieth century they began to regard themselves as a distinct group of experts, certified by specialized training, linked into exclusively professional associations ... elaborating legal and bureaucratic rules, and turning to science and business as sources of authority for an emergent profession.[7]

Scientific Management—Goals and Efficiency

The notion of scientific management is closely linked with the work of Frederick W. Taylor.[8] Taylor studied the behavior of workers in an effort to eliminate wasted time, effort, and ultimately money. His "time and motion" studies fostered the belief that there typically was one way to accomplish organizational objectives that was most efficient. Key tasks for scientific managers were to determine the most efficient way of doing something and to ensure that employees followed it. To this day, few openly dispute the validity of certain central assumptions underlying scientific management:

- Organizations need goals in order to set specific work objectives for individual employees.
- Faced with alternative ways to achieve a work objective, the preferred way is the one that gets the job done for the least cost.

Though linked by Taylor and his disciples, goal accomplishment and efficiency may be separated for purposes of discussion and analysis. Conceivably, school leaders' performance may be judged on the basis of whether or not they function within their operating budget, regardless of whether key goals for the school are achieved. Alternatively, leaders' effectiveness may be based solely on the extent to which they accomplish intended goals, no matter what the cost. Of course, in the real world, goals and the cost of achieving them cannot be so neatly separated.

Many school districts utilize some form of Management by Objectives

(MBO) system for planning and for personnel evaluation. [9,10] The school board begins by approving annual goals for the district. Building principals then are expected to generate school goals that support the achievement of district goals. The principals, in turn, may require individual staff members to set personal goals aimed at the realization of school goals. Basing judgments of system, school, and individual effectiveness on the extent to which specified goals are accomplished appears to be quite rational and practical. But there are some problems.

First, are all goals to be weighted equally? A school leader, for example, may be expected to achieve a number of goals during a given year. What if some goals are achieved and others are not, or if certain complex goals are only partially achieved? What if a school in a district committed to raising student achievement in all basic skill areas registers increases only in mathematics? Or what if all the mathematics achievement of third-graders improves, while that of sixth-graders declines? Stallings and Kaskowitz have demonstrated, in fact, that there can be as much within-school as between-school variation in achievement test results. [11] No one disagrees that school leaders should try to achieve specific goals, but what is less clear is how information on progress toward the accomplishment of school goals can be used to assess or make inferences about the effectiveness of school leaders.

This concern is complicated further when the issue of comparing goals across schools or among individuals is considered. Which school leader should be evaluated more favorably—one who fully accomplishes a relatively modest goal or one who just misses achieving a very challenging goal? If accomplishing goals is the sole basis for judging the effectiveness of school leaders, some individuals may shun more meaningful targets in favor of "sure bets." The best interests of students may not always be well served if goal feasibility is the only criterion by which school leaders judge potential goals.

To think of goal feasibility is to reflect, in part, on the cost involved in achieving a goal. If leaders' effectiveness is somehow linked to goal attainment, their efficiency relates to goal attainment per unit cost. Efficiency can be improved either by maintaining costs while increasing goal attainment or by reducing costs while maintaining goal attainment. There is little evidence to indicate that building administrators are systematically and explicitly evaluated in terms of the efficiency of their performance, but this situation may change if resources for education continue to dwindle.

What if two principals head two schools of comparable size in which student performance, based on standardized test scores, is roughly equivalent? No one may notice unless one principal accomplishes the feat using half the staff employed by the other principal! Is the efficiency with which a school leader utilizes resources a legitimate criterion for assessing performance?

In theory, efficiency seems a useful basis for performance assessment. In practice, however, leaders in different schools are rarely presented with comparable groups of students or staff. Access to resources varies, and this includes materials, facilities, even community volunteers. It is also difficult to reach agreement on how to determine whether goals have been achieved or even which goals are most important. Unlike their private-sector counterparts, school leaders do not share a universally accepted goal—profit—or an agreed-upon basis for measuring it. Under the circumstances, then, efficiency seems of limited use as a basis for evaluating school leaders.

In sum, the impact of scientific management on notions of school leadership has been uneven. To be sure, school leaders cannot ignore such offspring of the concept as goal-based management and fiscal accountability. Some critics, like Raymond Callahan, have decried what they call the total capitulation of educators to the "cult of efficiency."[12] Others argue persuasively that school leaders successfully resisted wholesale adoption of the managerial models presented by Frederick Taylor and his disciples.[13] They recognize that schools are not factories, that some of the most meaningful goals cannot be expressed clearly or measured accurately, and that there are other worthy values besides efficiency. Many of the individuals who reject scientific management have been influenced directly or indirectly by the human relations movement.

Human Relations and Effectiveness

Originating during the thirties as a reaction, in part, to scientific management, the human relations movement focused on the quality of life in the workplace and the relations between workers and supervisors. The central interest was less in what organizations produce and how much it costs than it was in how organization members feel about what they are doing. Out of this movement emerged a new basis for judging a leader's performance—employee satisfaction.

With regard to schools, it seems reasonable to argue that dissatisfied teachers are less likely to produce student-achievement gains than those who feel good about their work. In fact, many observers of schools in the United States link the decline in student achievement during the sixties and seventies in part to deteriorating working conditions for teachers.[14] Teachers find themselves in unsafe schools striving to fulfill ambiguous expectations with diminishing resources. Morale plummets as retrenchment, caused by declining student enrollment, inflation, and other factors, spawns increased class sizes and teacher layoffs.

Roland Barth contends that principals should regard one of their main tasks as the creation of supportive environments within which teachers can work.[15] Other school leaders can also play a role. The development of teacher centers during the seventies demonstrated that teachers could provide each other with encouragement and opportunities for growth.

Teacher job satisfaction is sometimes associated with teacher involvement in school decision making. Teacher interest in playing a role in school governance is presumed to be high. Where teachers participate in making school decisions, they are more likely to feel a sense of "ownership" in the decisions and to spend the time necessary to implement the decisions successfully. When researchers in one study found that many teachers do not always take advantage of opportunities to participate in school decision making,[16] a closer look at the results found that teachers often are suspicious of official invitations to become involved. They felt that their time was being wasted since they sensed that the ultimate decision lay with the school administration. Involvement without influence is hardly an inducement to participate in school governance.

Samuel Bacharach and Stephen Mitchell have taken a critical look at much of the literature on job satisfaction.[17] They point out that despite the widespread belief that increased job satisfaction leads to increased productivity, few of the hundreds of studies done in the area provide confirmation. They speculate that increased productivity actually may be a cause, rather than a result, of job satisfaction. If such a hypothesis is correct, school leaders may be advised to devote more energy to raising student achievement than to improving teacher morale. On the other hand, some theorists contend that teacher job satisfaction is a legitimate goal in and of itself, whether or not student achievement improves.[18]

Wilbur Brookover and Lawrence Lezotte raise the possibility that high teacher job satisfaction may even be negatively related to student achievement.[19] In a study of elementary school effectiveness, Brookover and Lezotte discovered that schools in which the relations between teachers and principal were warm and friendly were more likely to be characterized by steadily declining test scores. Principals who maintained some social distance from their staffs were found in schools with improving test scores. Perhaps it is easier for leaders who refrain from fraternizing with teachers to enforce high expectations.

Brookover and Lezotte's research suggests that measuring teacher job satisfaction alone may not provide a complete picture of a school leader's effectiveness. In addition, it can be argued that the advent of teacher unions and collective bargaining has provided teachers with powerful mechanisms for correcting adverse working conditions without relying on school leaders. Alvin Gouldner has maintained, in fact, that the duty of leaders in situations where employee interests are well served by such formal mechanisms as unions may actually involve frustrating rather than satisfying the desires of workers.[20]

As the power of teacher unions has expanded, school leaders frequently have been placed in an awkward position. Besides serving teachers, they are also expected to be accountable to superiors and patrons. In some cases, meeting the needs of one group may mean countering the needs of another. Therefore, it is worthwhile to consider for a moment the use of employer satisfaction and patron satisfaction as alternative bases for judging the effectiveness of school leaders.

School administrators are appointed by and ultimately are responsible to a school board made up of elected or appointed representatives of the public. Day-to-day supervision of school administrators, however, is the function of the superintendent and his or her assistants. They evaluate school administrators and make recommendations regarding placement and contract renewal.

One study of principal evaluation reveals that principals are evaluated in terms of a variety of categories, ranging from communication skills and student management to personal appearance and emotional stability.[21] No two evaluation systems are identical. Interestingly, one evaluation criterion that rarely is referred to explicitly is loyalty. It can be assumed, however, that allegiance to district policies and personal support for the superintendent figure heavily in the actual process by which principals and other school leaders are evaluated. Few superintendents will tolerate principals who consistently circumvent their authority or who build up independent power bases in the community. To reduce the likelihood of such disloyal behavior, principals in larger districts typically are rotated between schools periodically.

Should a school leader conceive of effectiveness strictly in terms of employer satisfaction? Such a singular focus potentially can be limiting. Superintendents are not known to hold school leaders accountable for instructional improvement.[22] Their major concerns tend to be oriented more toward organizational maintenance than innovation. They ask questions like the following: Are parents accepting of the schooling their children receive? Has the principal kept the school free of controversy? Have potential crises been defused in a manner that protects district interests?

Few examples can be found of school leaders who have been dismissed or disciplined because of low student achievement or poor instruction.[23] When school leaders get into trouble, it is often because they fail to carry out central office directives or because they generate publicity as a result of mishandling an isolated incident. Perhaps, then, the ultimate indication of a school leader's effectiveness—at least for supervisors and patrons—is whether or not the individual appears to be "in control." Herein lies a problem, however. Equating the effectiveness of a school leader with being in control may place too high a premium on student discipline and personnel policy enforcement. Presumably, rules and policies are not ends in themselves, but means to better instruction and learning. If the superintendent, the school board, and the district's patrons are satisfied when schools run smoothly, then it may be the professional responsibility of school leaders to see that instructional improvement is not sacrificed for the sake of tranquility.

Basing a concept of leader effectiveness exclusively on patron satisfaction may involve another problem as well. As community demands for participation in school decision making have increased over the past few decades, it has become more difficult to identify the "will of the community." Cases involving efforts by special interests to remove certain books from school libraries and to modify sex education programs provide vivid illustrations of the problem. For all practical purposes, a community is really a pluralistic entity made up of various interest groups. School leaders increasingly are called upon to serve as brokers, advocates, lobbyists, and negotiators.[24] Some segments of the community, such as those with grown children or no children, demand greater efficiency. Minority parents urge school leaders to protect their children from discriminatory instructional practice. Right-wing groups exert pressure for curriculum change. There seemingly is no way that school leaders can satisfy all of their patrons. While a leader's concept of effectiveness may require that all patrons be assured a hearing, it clearly cannot be based exclusively on pleasing everybody.

Recent Trends in Leader Effectiveness

For various reasons, many of which have already been discussed, traditional concepts of leader effectiveness along with those derived from scientific management theory and those based on satisfying different groups fail to place sufficient emphasis on instructional improvement. A review of several contemporary trends in thinking about the effectiveness of school leaders will determine whether they pay greater attention to instructional issues. These trends may be characterized by key leader behaviors, student-outcome-based assessment, and situational competence.

Key Leader Behaviors.   In recent years a number of efforts have been made to identify specific behaviors associated with school leadership. This work fits into the larger context of competency-based education, a movement that has detailed specific behavioral outcomes for a variety of programs, including requirements for high school graduation and teacher certification. Some states, such as Georgia and Oregon, require that preparation programs for teachers, counselors, and school administrators be based on specific competencies. Competency-based education traces its roots, at least in part, to mastery learning and behavioral models of learning.

In the field of school administration, lists of competencies have tended to be based on the judgments of experts more than on systematic observations of school leaders who demonstrate a capacity for achieving concrete results. One of the most comprehensive undertakings of this kind was sponsored by the American Association of School Administrators (AASA).[25] Presented in the form of guidelines for programs training educational administrators, it specifies seven goals for leaders and seven competencies necessary to attain these goals. As the following list indicates, each competency is subdivided into a series of discrete skills.

SECTION ONE: LEADERSHIP OUTCOME GOALS

Successful administrator preparation programs must prepare school leaders who understand the *theoretical foundations and demonstrate the application* of each of the specific performance goal areas listed below. School leaders of tomorrow must:
1. Establish and maintain a positive and open learning environment to facilitate the motivation and social integration of students and staff.
2. Build strong local, state, and national support for education.
3. Develop and deliver an effective curriculum which expands the definitions of literacy, competency, and cultural integration to include advanced technologies, problem solving, critical thinking skills, and cultural enrichment for all students.
4. Develop and implement effective models/modes of instructional delivery that best utilize time, staff, advanced technologies, community resources, and financial means to maximize student outcomes.
5. Create programs of continuous improvement and evaluation of both staff and program effectiveness as keys to student learning and development.
6. Skillfully manage system operations and facilities to enhance student learning.

7. Conduct and utilize research as a basis of problem solving and program planning of all kinds.

SECTION TWO: COMPETENCIES AND SKILLS FOR GOAL ACCOMPLISHMENT

All students completing preparation programs should be able to demonstrate the competencies related to each of these seven goals. These competencies and their underlying skills and understandings include:

Competency 1—Designing, implementing, and evaluating a school climate improvement program that utilizes mutual staff and student efforts to formulate and attain school goals. This competency includes the following:
a. human relations, organizational development, and leadership skills;
b. collaborative goal setting and action planning;
c. organizational and personal planning and time management skills;
d. skills in participative management and variations in staffing;
e. climate assessment methods and skills;
f. skills in improving the quality of relationships among staff and students to enhance learning;
g. multi-cultural and ethnic understanding; and
h. group process, interpersonal communication, and motivation skills.

Competency 2—Understanding political theory and applying political skills in building local, state, and national support for education. This competency includes the following:

a. skills in developing school/community or public relations, coalition building, and related public service activities;
b. understanding the politics of school governance and operation;
c. developing political strategies to pass bond, tax, and other referenda;
d. lobbying, negotiating, collective bargaining, power, policy development, and policy maintenance skills to assure successful educational programs;
e. communicating and projecting an articulate position for education;
f. comprehending the role and function of mass media in shaping and forming opinions; and
g. conflict mediation and the skills to accept and cope with inherent controversies.

Competency 3—Developing a systematic school curriculum that assures both extensive cultural enrichment activities and mastery of fundamental as well as progressively more complex skills required in advanced problem solving, creative, and technological activities. This competency includes the following:

a. planning/futures methods to anticipate occupational trends and their educational implications;
b. application of taxonomies of instructional objectives and validation procedures for curricular units/sequences;
c. application of theories of cognitive development and the sequencing/structuring of curricula;
d. development/application of valid and reliable performance indicators for instructional outcomes;
e. utilization of computers and other technologies as instructional aids; and
f. development/utilization of available cultural resources.

Competency 4—Planning and implementing an instructional management system which includes learning objectives, curriculum design, and instructional strategies and techniques that facilitate high levels of achievement. This competency includes the following:

a. skills in curriculum design and the use of instructional delivery strategies;
b. using instructional and motivational psychology;
c. knowing alternative methods of monitoring and evaluating student achievement;
d. management of change to enhance the mastery of educational goals;
e. using computer management applications with the instructional program;
f. utilization of instructional time and resources; and
g. skills in cost-effectiveness analysis and program budgeting.

Competency 5—Designing staff development and evaluation systems to enhance effectiveness of educational personnel. This competency includes the following:

a. assessing system and staff needs to identify areas for concentrated staff development and new personnel resource allocation;
b. utilization of system and staff evaluation data in personnel policy and decision making;
c. appraisal of the effectiveness of staff development programming in terms of professional performance;
d. using clinical supervision as a staff improvement and evaluation strategy; and
e. assessment of individual and institutional sources of stress and methods of reducing them.

Competency 6—Allocating human, material, and financial resources to efficiently and accountably assure successful student learning. This competency includes the following:

a. facilities planning, maintenance, and operation;
b. financial planning and cash flow management;
c. personnel administration;
d. administering pupil personnel services and categorical programs;
e. knowledge of legal concepts, regulations, and codes for school operation; and
f. use of analytical techniques of management.

Competency 7—Conducting research and utilizing research findings in decisions to improve long range planning, school operations, and student learning. This competency includes the following:

a. research design and methods including gathering, analyzing, and interpreting data;
b. understanding of descriptive and inferential statistics;
c. use of evaluation and planning models and methods; and
d. selection, administration, and interpretation of evaluation instruments.

While the AASA competencies are aimed at educational leaders in general, James Lipham has developed a set of competencies designed more specifically for school principals.[26] The major categories of competencies include the following:

Instructional Improvement

Phase I.   Assessing Program Relevance
Phase II.   Planning Program Improvements
Phase III. Implementing Program Improvements
Phase IV.   Evaluating Program Change

Staff Personnel

Stage I.   Identification of New Staff
Stage II.   Assignment of Staff
Stage III. Orientation of Staff
Stage IV.   Staff Improvement
Stage V.   Evaluation of Staff

Student Personnel

Area I.   Student Values
Area II.   Student Involvement
Area III.   Student Guidance Services

Finances and Facilities

Area I.   Financial Resources
Area II.   School Plant Resources

Extraorganizational Relations

Area I.   Community Analysis
Area II.   Community Relations
Area III.   Relations with Educational Agencies

Each of the phases, stages, and areas in the inventory is divided into specific behaviors or competencies. For example, under Staff Personnel, the Assignment of Staff stage encompasses the items listed below:

- Assesses the degree of congruence between expectations for the role and the need-dispositions of the individual.
- Assigns new staff members to optimize the achievement of both organizational goals and the goals of individual staff members.
- Reassigns experienced staff members to positions and roles to permit the attainment of organizational and individual goals.
- Anticipates and coordinates individual and subunit goals and programs with school and school system goals and programs.

In a competency-based program, effectiveness represents the extent to which an individual masters or manifests the behaviors that are judged to be important for a particular sphere of responsibility. An assumption is made that school leaders who demonstrate competence in designated skills will be able to produce a variety of desirable outcomes for students, staff, and school. One strength of the "key behaviors" approach lies in its usefulness to those charged with the task of preparing future school leaders. Curricula can be built around the development of skills or behaviors. Evaluation, at least in theory, becomes a relatively straightforward matter of determining whether or not candidates have mastered these skills or behaviors.

Predictably, there are problems with this concept of effectiveness as well. Educational administration specialists share anecdotes about particular candidates who mastered every specific leadership skill, yet somehow failed to put them all together in a manner sufficient to convey the impression of leadership. Further, it is difficult to develop a list of key leader behaviors equally applicable to all the circumstances a school leader might confront. Certain skills needed to deal effectively with a school that has just experienced a prolonged teachers' strike may differ from those required to plan and open a new school.

Some fear that skill-based approaches may trivialize leadership by minimizing the complexity of the role. A recent paper on the aesthetics of leadership argues that effective leadership is less a matter of manifesting a set of behaviors than of being able to bring meaning to particular situations.[27] The perception that a leader is effective says as much about the perceiver as the leader. Leadership comes to be associated not with behaviors but with certain aesthetic properties, including the following:

- Direction—A sense of purpose or commitment greater than the self
- Engagement—A capacity for inspiring involvement
- Fit—The relationship between a leader and the context or times in which he or she is called upon to lead.
- Originality—The capacity to capture the public's imagination through uniqueness of style

Concepts of leader effectiveness that are based on the identification of key behaviors focus on the control of inputs. The chief "inputs," in this case, are leader capabilities and training. By teaching would-be school leaders the appropriate skills and by carefully limiting certification to those who master the skills, preparation programs presumably can reduce the likelihood that school systems will hire incompetent leaders. This process may bring on extensive monitoring of educational administration programs as well as legal challenges by individuals who are denied certification. In the case of legal challenge, the plaintiff may demand proof either that a particular competency is essential to effective school leadership or that the methods used to measure competency are valid and reliable.

Student-outcome-based Assessment   Unlike the preceding approach, outcome-based concepts of effectiveness take a relatively benign stance toward the training of school leaders. What counts is output. A school leader's effectiveness is based on how well students achieve. As long as student performance meets or exceeds expectations, school leaders are presumed to be doing their jobs well. It matters little if their individual behavior or styles vary.

The impetus behind the outcome-based approach comes largely from school-effectiveness research, referred to in the Introduction. The major challenges of outcome-based concepts of effectiveness are (1) to determine what constitutes student achievement and (2) to decide how to measure it. To date, these concepts have tended to be based on student achievement in reading, language, and mathematics as measured by conventional standardized tests.[28] For example, a school-effectiveness project in Santa Clara County, California, defines an effective school as one in which mean student achievement on third- and sixth-grade standardized tests of basic skills matches or exceeds prediction (as reported by the state using expectancy bands) for three consecutive years. Milwaukee's RISE Project specifies that a school is effective when at least 80 percent of its students perform at grade level on locally developed, nationally normed tests. Ron Edmonds expressed his outcome-based concept of effectiveness in a somewhat different manner, giving attention to the socioeconomic status of students as well as their academic achievement:

> To be effective a school need not bring all students to identical levels of mastery, but it must bring an equal percentage of its highest and lowest social classes to minimum mastery.[29]

There are several reasons why school leaders may wish to be assessed on the basis of student achievement. These reasons include convenience, objectivity, research legitimacy, and public support.

Basing judgments of leader performance on student achievement is convenient, if for no other reason than that many districts already require some type of standardized testing. For example, in many states and cities test data are aggregated over time and used to predict mean student achievement for the coming year. In places where data like these are available, school leaders can easily be evaluated by looking at student achievement relative to prediction.

Standardized tests of student achievement also may be favored because they seem much less subjective than criteria that entail perceptions, high-inference questions, or global assessment. In an era when performance evaluations are increasingly subject to legal review and litigation, school officials may find comfort in the relatively objective data afforded by standardized tests.

A third reason test data may be attractive as evaluation criteria is related to the previously mentioned body of research correlating student achievement with teacher and administrator behaviors and school characteristics. This research, while not without faults, commands widespread respect among professionals. The principal is often cited as a key factor in school effectiveness. School officials need only show principals this research and hold them accountable for getting the results it says they should get. Presumably, student achievement will increase.

Finally, significant portions of the general public seem to feel that student achievement as measured by standardized tests is a reasonable basis for judging whether schools and their employees are succeeding. A growing number of newspapers annually present comparative data on how local schools fare on mandated tests. Parents read the results and put pressure on the local school board to provide greater support to poor achieving schools.

Despite the possible benefits of relying on student-achievement data as a basis for assessing school leaders, there are compelling reasons for caution. These reasons include lack of consensus about the best way to utilize test data, limitations of the data base, and serious constraints on administrative efforts to boost test scores.

Current concepts of school effectiveness do not agree on the most appropriate way to use student-achievement data.[30] Edmonds, for example, relied on a criterion-referenced concept—one that seeks mastery of basic skills by equal percentages of the highest and lowest social classes of students. Other concepts of effectiveness are norm referenced and are based on school performance in relation to comparable schools. Brookover and Lezotte choose to contrast declining schools with improving schools, but are unclear about the extent to which decline or improvement must be sustained over time. The Santa Clara County Project specifies at least three consecutive years of predicted or better-than-predicted student achievement. Focusing on gains in achievement rather than on mastery of a specified level of achievement seems in some ways a fairer way to handle student data, since no two schools begin a year with the same aggregate of student abilities. A shortcoming of this approach, though, relates to the improbability that any school could continue indefinitely to produce increases in mean student achievement. What should happen when a school begins to level off? How can the maximum expected achievement for a school be reliably estimated? Is it reasonable to expect sustained improvement when student turnover is high?

A further problem with norm-referenced concepts of effectiveness is that they presume at any given time that some schools must be ineffective. Not all schools can simultaneously be improving in relation to the norm. If some schools must be ineffective, and if an effective school leader is one who leads an effective school, then some leaders must be ineffective. Yet, it remains to be determined whether particular ineffective schools actually may house some very able leaders. It is also conceivable that certain effective schools may not necessarily be administered by particularly effective leaders. As mentioned earlier, several researchers have found that the principal is not always the instructional leader in effective schools. The role may be performed by teachers or other supervisory personnel.[31]

For the sake of argument, let us assume that consensus did exist on a definition for a school leader's effectiveness in terms of student achievement. There might still be problems because school leaders generally do not exercise direct control over the teaching-learning process, nor do they usually build their faculties from scratch. The authority and discretion of principals are limited by the traditional loosely coupled nature of schools, teacher contracts, and school board policies. While William Martin and Donald Willower report that principals are the "focal point of organizational governance," they concede that principals' power is far from absolute.[32]

Consider, for example, the 1983–1984 teachers' contract in Portland, Oregon. Teachers insisted on a clause that specifically prevented the use of student achievement test data as a basis for teacher evaluation. Teachers elsewhere have bargained for similar provisions. Is it prudent or fair to hold school leaders accountable for student achievement when they, in turn, are unable to hold teachers accountable?

The analysis thus far assumes a somewhat narrow concept of outcome-based effectiveness—one based on student achievement as measured by standardized tests. Serious questions exist concerning the value of student test

scores. Larry Cuban argues that the real question is not how student performance on standardized tests can be raised but whether the broader mission of the
school system can be served by raising test scores.[33] Perhaps it would be wise to
recognize that schools must strive for a number of student behavior outcomes.
An expanded concept of student outcomes could encompass such factors as attendance rate, incidence of problem behavior, dropout rate, exposure to different subject matter, and post-graduate activities. Student achievement also
could be defined to include problem-solving abilities, creative endeavors, writing skill, oral proficiency, character development, and attitude toward learning.
The Jesuit Secondary Education Association has expanded its basis for assessing student achievement to include openness to growth, civic competence,
personal conduct as a religious and loving person, and commitment to doing
justice.[34]

Even if notions of what constitutes student achievement are broadened,
however, many of the criticisms of outcome-based assessment may still apply.
It may be that school leaders exercise too little direct control over the classroom
to be held accountable for any student outcome. After all, student performance
is the product of the efforts of many educators over a number of years. Physicians generally are not evaluated in terms of patient performance, except in
cases involving gross malpractice. They are held accountable for "good medical practice." Is there an equivalent to "good medical practice" to which school
leaders may be held accountable?

Situational Competence   A major contribution of recent research, particularly
studies of the principal's role in school effectiveness, has been the creation of
relatively clear concepts of "good educational practice" for school leaders. Besides key behaviors, this research has identified critical circumstances, or situations, with which school leaders must deal. The difference between more
effective and less effective school leaders centers on how they handle various
situations.

Concepts of school-leader effectiveness based on situational competence
are supported by contemporary leadership theory. Gary Yukl points out, for
example, that situational leadership theory challenges the key-leader-behavior
approach, which suggests that effective leaders use similar skills under various
conditions.[35] Different situations faced by leaders have been studied to determine which traits and behaviors are related to successful performance. The
skills needed to resolve an immediate crisis differ from those called for in long-
range planning or complex negotiations. The message is clear: Leaders must
learn to adapt their behavior to the requirements, constraints, and opportunities presented by the situation at hand.

A school leader's job deals with a series of situations, ranging from one-
time tasks, such as correcting a misbehaving student or resolving a parent-
teacher conflict, to ongoing responsibilities like evaluating staff and facilitating
the use of effective instructional methods. While few if any of these situations
can be managed simply by following a universally accepted set of directions,
rarely is a leader required to venture into totally uncharted water. Rather, in
managing different situations, school leaders—like physicians—can and should

be guided by notions of good practice as described in the theoretical and practical literature of their profession. A primary purpose of this book is to expose school leaders to the theoretical and practical literature related to instructional improvement.

Unlike physicians, whose cases are mostly unrelated to one another, a school leader's situations are generally connected to one another. The ultimate task for a principal, for example, is the overall leadership and management of the school, a large-scale situation. To meet this responsibility, principals must display an understanding of the special needs of their particular school and pursue a course of action designed to maximize the possibility of satisfying those needs. There must be consistency in their actions—both between the intentions that underlie their activities and the needs of their school and among the activities themselves. For example, a principal of a school with a high percentage of students reading significantly below grade level would probably not be able to justify hiring an additional music teacher instead of a remedial reading teacher, presuming a choice was available.

As a concept of school-leader effectiveness, then, situational competence necessitates looking at the extent to which (1) the handling of smaller responsibilities is consistent with good educational practice and (2) the overall handling of larger responsibilities (leading the school, department, grade level, and so on) are consistent with the needs of that particular unit. There is a potential problem with the situational-competence concept of effectiveness, however.

Similar to the criticism of the key-behavior approach, an argument may be made that close monitoring of school leaders to ensure compliance with good educational practice could stifle creative leadership. It is not uncommon for school leaders, for instance, to maintain that district and government red tape inhibit rather than enhance their performance. In a study of Chicago principals, a group of University of Illinois researchers report widespread circumvention of policies, short-circuiting of bureaucratic procedures, and "management by loophole."[36]

Although many school leaders may find it limiting, a concept of good educational practice is not inherently limiting to creative leadership. If notions of good practice come to be regarded as obstacles, it simply may mean that they have not been properly developed in the first place or that they need to be updated in light of recent research. Discrepancies between good practice and the current concept of competence also may exist because school leaders themselves fail to keep up with recent developments in their field. Chris Argyris and Donald Schön caution that "whatever competence means today, we can be sure its meaning will have changed by tomorrow."[37] Such is the nature of professions like school leadership.

SELECTING A CONCEPT OF EFFECTIVENESS

A variety of concepts of leader effectiveness have been presented in this opening chapter. Each has its strengths and shortcomings, as Table 1.1 indicates. What is important is less a matter of which concept of effectiveness a school

Table 1.1   Conceptions of the Quality of School Leadership

Basis for Judging Leadership Quality	Unresolved Issues in Judging Leadership Quality
Exemplification of virtue	• Is it enough for a school leader to inspire good behavior? To what extent is academic achievement fostered by an emphasis on virtue?
Goal attainment	• Are goals comparable in terms of importance or difficulty? • If goal attainment alone is valued, how can the selection of modest or easily achieved goals be prevented?
Efficiency	• Does it make sense to focus on efficiency when school leaders have little budgetary discretion and when agreement is rare concerning which school goals are most important?
Employee satisfaction	• Is there a positive relationship between teacher job satisfaction and student outcomes?
Employer satisfaction	• Can too much emphasis on loyalty result in minimizing the importance of changes in school practice?
Patron satisfaction	• Since there is no consensus among patrons, how is patron satisfaction with school leadership to be determined?
Key leader behaviors	• Can a leader master all the competencies associated with effective school leadership and yet still be ineffective? • Do key behaviors vary with different situations faced by leaders?
Outcome-based assessment	• What constitutes student outcomes? • How should student outcomes be measured?
Situational competence	• Is the handling of particular situations consistent with (1) good educational practice and (2) the needs of the school?

leader selects than that he or she devotes time and energy to selecting some basis for judging his or her effectiveness. Without a basis for judging effectiveness, the odds are slight that intentional efforts to improve one's leadership will succeed. Improvement under such conditions of uncertainty would be left purely to chance.

Although it has just been said that no particular concept of effectiveness is necessarily the best for everyone, nonetheless, this book will use *situational competence* as the basis for examining school-leader effectiveness. The reasons for choosing the situational-competence concept are fourfold:

First, it is flexible. Unlike some other concepts, no assumption is made that there is only one way for effective leaders to behave. Behavior is dictated by the characteristics of the particular leader and the particular situation. Situations vary over time and from level to level. There is thus no reason to believe that elementary school leadership is identical to secondary school leadership or that heading an English department is exactly the same as directing all fourth-grade teachers.

Second, the situational-competence concept assumes that leaders continually must reflect on how they handle various situations. Since notions of good practice inevitably change, prudent school leaders should be prepared to alter their behavior to accommodate such change. Ideally, groups of school leaders would convene periodically to consider the current state of knowledge regarding how to handle specific situations effectively.

Third, school leaders can draw on a steadily growing body of research on school effectiveness as they try to define situational competence. This research provides important insights on how school leaders respond to various situations in schools where student achievement is relatively high. In Chapter 4, an effort will be made to present a model of school leadership based on school-effectiveness research and the idea of situational competence.

Finally, the situational-competence concept is fair. It does not define effective leadership exclusively in terms of student outcomes. Just as physicians cannot guarantee that patients will improve, school leaders cannot provide complete assurance that students will learn or behave as expected. Too many factors beyond the school leader's control come into play. What school leaders can be accountable for, however, is handling critical situations according to prevailing notions of good educational practice. As indicated earlier, these notions can and should be linked to school-based research on student achievement.

Review Questions

1. Why is it important for school leaders to have a concept of effective performance?
2. What are the different concepts of leader effectiveness mentioned in this chapter?
3. What are the strengths and weaknesses of each concept of leader effectiveness?
4. Why was "situational competence" selected as the basis for this book?
5. Can you identify different situations faced by school leaders concerned about instructional improvement?

NOTES

1. Irvin D. Yalom, *Existential Psychotherapy* (New York: Basic Books, 1980), pp. 419–460.
2. Portions of this section are drawn from Daniel L. Duke and Michael Imber, "Should Principals Be Required to Be Effective?" *School Organization,* Vol. 5, No. 2 (April/June 1985), pp. 125–146.
3. James G. March, "American Public School Administration: A Short Analysis," *School Review,* Vol. 86, No. 2 (February 1978), p. 224.

4. Richard M. Nixon, *Leaders* (New York: Warner Books, 1982).
5. Sara Lawrence Lightfoot, *The Good High School* (New York: Basic Books, 1983), pp. 323–324.
6. David Tyack and Elizabeth Hansot, *Managers of Virtue* (New York: Basic Books, 1982).
7. *Ibid.,* p. 7.
8. Frederick W. Taylor, *Scientific Management* (New York: Harper, 1911).
9. Daniel L. Duke and Richard J. Stiggins, "Evaluating the Performance of Principals: A Descriptive Study," *Educational Administration Quarterly,* Vol. 21, No. 4 (Fall 1985), pp. 71–98.
10. E. Zappulla, *Evaluating Administrative Performance: Current Trends and Techniques* (Belmont, Calif.: Star, 1983).
11. Jane Stallings and D. Kaskowitz, "Follow Through Classroom Observation 1972–73" (Menlo Park, Calif.: Stanford Research Institute, 1974).
12. Raymond E. Callahan, *Education and the Cult of Efficiency* (Chicago: University of Chicago Press, 1962).
13. David B. Tyack and Robert Cummings, "Leadership in American Public Schools Before 1954," in Luvern L. Cunningham *et al.* (Eds.), *Educational Administration* (Berkeley: McCutchan, 1977).
14. Daniel L. Duke, *Teaching—The Imperiled Profession* (Albany, N.Y.: State University of New York Press, 1984).
15. Roland Barth, *Run School Run* (Cambridge: Harvard University Press, 1980), p. 208.
16. Daniel L. Duke, Beverly K. Showers, and Michael Imber, "Teachers and Shared Decision Making: The Costs and Benefits of Involvement," *Educational Administration Quarterly,* Vol. 16, No. 1 (Winter 1980), pp. 93–106.
17. Samuel Bacharach and Stephen Mitchell, "The Sources of Dissatisfaction in Educational Administration: A Role-Specific Analysis," *Educational Administration Quarterly,* Vol. 19, No. 1 (Winter 1983), pp. 101–128.
18. Michael Imber, "Increased Decision Making Involvement for Teachers: Ethical and Practical Considerations," *Journal of Educational Thought,* Vol. 17, No. 1 (April 1983), pp. 36–42.
19. Wilbur B. Brookover and Lawrence W. Lezotte, "Changes in School Characteristics Coincident with Changes in Student Achievement," Institute for Research on Teaching, Michigan State University, May 1979.
20. Alvin Gouldner, *Studies in Leadership* (New York: Harper & Brothers, 1950).
21. Daniel L. Duke and Richard J. Stiggins, "Evaluating the Performance of Principals: A Descriptive Study."
22. *Ibid.*
23. *Ibid.*
24. Paul V. Bredeson, "An Analysis of the Metaphorical Perspectives of School Principals," *Educational Administration Quarterly,* Vol. 21, No. 1 (Winter 1985), p. 37.
25. John R. Hoyle, "Programs in Educational Administration and the AASA Preparation Guidelines," *Educational Administration Quarterly,* Vol. 21, No. 1 (Winter 1985), pp. 71–93.
26. James M. Lipham, "Leadership of the Principal for Educational Improvement," paper presented at the Northwest Regional Educational Laboratory, 1982.
27. Daniel L. Duke, "The Aesthetics of Leadership," *Educational Administration Quarterly,* Vol. 22, No. 1 (Winter 1986), pp. 7–27.
28. For a thorough discussion of student-outcome-based assessment, see Daniel L. Duke and Michael Imber, "Should Principals Be Required to Be Effective?"
29. Ronald Edmonds, "Programs of School Improvement: An Overview," *Educational Leadership,* Vol. 40, No. 3 (December 1982), p. 4.
30. J. A. Frechtling, "Alternative Methods for Determining Effectiveness: Convergence and Divergence," paper presented at the annual meeting of the American Educational Research Association, New York, 1982.

31. Russell Gersten, Douglas Carnine, and Susan Green, "The Principal as Instructional Leader: A Second Look," *Educational Leadership,* Vol. 40, No. 3 (December 1982), pp. 47–49.
32. William J. Martin and Donald Willower, "The Managerial Behavior of High School Principals," *Educational Administration Quarterly,* Vol. 17, No. 1 (Winter 1981), pp. 69–90.
33. Larry Cuban, "Effective Schools: A Friendly But Cautionary Note," *Phi Delta Kappan,* Vol. 64, No. 10 (June 1983), pp. 695–696.
34. Vincent J. Duminuco, "Viewpoint," *The School Administrator* (March 1985), p. 80.
35. Gary A. Yukl, *Leadership in Organizations* (Englewood Cliffs, N.J.: Prentice-Hall, 1981), pp. 132–169.
36. Van Cleve Morris, Robert L. Crowson, Cynthia Porter-Gehrie, and Emanuel Hurwitz, Jr., *The Urban Principal* (Chicago: College of Education, University of Illinois at Chicago Circle, 1981).
37. Chris Argyris and Donald A. Schön, *Theory in Practice: Increasing Professional Effectiveness* (San Francisco: Jossey Bass, 1976), p. 157.

CHAPTER 2

TIME AND VISION

Why has a presumably practical book on school leadership begun with a somewhat theoretical discussion of various concepts of leader effectiveness? It has been said that nothing is as practical as a good theory. The appropriateness of this maxim for present purposes can be grasped if we acknowledge that school leaders do not have unlimited resources available to accomplish what is expected of them. Therefore, they must determine some basis for allocating scarce resources. A theory or concept of effectiveness provides guidelines to school leaders on how to utilize limited resources to achieve the maximum desired impact.

One of the most important resources of today's school leaders is their own time. In years past they could count on additional money and personnel when a new challenge arose. Years of declining enrollments and inflation, however, have produced citizens less willing to increase taxes to support local schools. A declining percentage of the voting public has children in school. If school leaders are to function more effectively in such a climate of fiscal restraint, they must be prepared to reassess how they currently spend their time.

This becomes even more crucial when we realize that most school leaders have more to do than time available. They rarely can accomplish all they are expected to accomplish, much less do it in a consistently excellent manner. Perhaps one of the greatest challenges facing contemporary school leaders is living with the realization that everything cannot be done as well as they would like. Writing from personal experience as well as from a scholar's view of the field, Roland Barth concludes that each of a school leader's responsibilities is "manageable, but the sum total forms an overwhelming load."[1] When the Educational Research Service surveyed nearly a thousand school principals in 1984, it found that insufficient time was a concern for the vast majority of them.[2] More than one in three indicated that lack of time for classroom observations and conferences with teachers were "major" problems. Approximately one in five added that lack of time to meet with students and keep current in their field were "major" problems.

Given the sheer number of activities in which school leaders are expected to engage, it is essential that priorities be designated. Ideally, a leader would choose to spend the most time performing those duties most likely to achieve the most desirable ends. In reality, however, many leaders are unclear about how they actually spend their time. Additionally, they often lack a vision of the most desirable ends to guide them in reallocating their time. They are uncertain about which of their responsibilities are most likely to have the greatest impact. *The difference between more effective and less effective school leaders may boil down to two factors: More effective leaders (1) possess—and are able to articulate—a vision of effective schooling and (2) allocate their time in ways that increase the likelihood of realizing that vision.* The present chapter looks in depth at how school leaders actually do spend their time. Subsequent chapters investigate how they *should* spend their time when instructional improvement is a high priority. The chapter closes with an analysis of the value of vision.

THE PRINCIPAL'S ROLE—AMBIGUITY AND COMPLEXITY

If the recent literature on the principalship is accurate, the role can be characterized by two trends—growing ambiguity and complexity. Ambiguity results, in part, from the fact that principals are expected to accomplish different things by different groups. It is difficult to steer a steady course through these multiple and often competing sets of expectations. And frequently, each set of expectations appears to be legitimate and reasonable. Clear choices between right and wrong are rare for principals.

In an effort to provide some guidelines to help resolve these problems of ambiguity, principals tend to develop—or request that others develop—rules, regulations, and standard operating procedures. Ironically, this attempt to reduce one problem spawns another. As rules, regulations, and procedures proliferate, complexity increases. Just remembering all the formal guidelines becomes a major challenge of the job.

Two job descriptions for principals illustrate the twin problems of ambiguity and complexity. They also suggest some fundamental differences in the nature of school leadership at the elementary and secondary level.

JOB DESCRIPTION

*North Marion Elementary School**

The educational service of the schools shall be organized under a unified plan as a division of the school system under the immediate direction of the superintendent but with specified duties and responsibilities assigned to the principals.

1. Principals shall be employed for an 11-month term.
2. A principal shall be responsible for knowing and administering the policies and programs of the school system as they apply to his school and to make available to his staff all regulations as they are enacted by the superintendent or board of education.
3. Within the limits of the State laws, the rules and regulations of the State Board

*My appreciation to Margaret Dutton of North Marion School District for sharing this job description.

of Education and the local district school board, and instructions from the superintendent, principals shall be the final administrative authority in their respective schools and make reports to the superintendent.

4. Principals shall keep those to whom they are responsible fully advised of the needs and conditions of their schools.

5. In accordance with general policies and plans, principals shall be responsible for the detailed organization of the program of their school, for the assignment of duties to staff members, and the administration and supervision of the instructional program.

6. Each principal shall make regular and thorough inspections of school property in his charge and shall direct those who are in charge of the care of his building.

7. Each principal shall assist in the development of the budget as required and shall keep such records and reports as are required. A principal shall submit lists of supplies and equipment needed for operation of his building to the superintendent.

8. A principal shall, in cooperation with the employee, prepare a work schedule for custodial workers assigned to his building, a copy of which shall be filed with the superintendent at the opening of the school year or whenever revised.

9. Each principal shall be responsible for taking all reasonable precautions to safeguard the health and general well being of his staff and the students in his school. In case of dire emergency affecting the health, safety, or welfare of the pupils, employees or property under his care, he shall have the authority to use his discretion, but shall report to the superintendent any action taken as soon as possible.

10. Principals shall be responsible for the accuracy of the regular attendance reports and insure that no unlawful attendance is reported therein. Also, they shall make such reports as are required by law and the superintendent.

11. A principal shall not absent himself from his building without leaving someone in charge to assume responsibilities.

12. Each principal shall handle all complaints affecting his school, investigate the same, refer to the superintendent cases which he cannot seem to adjust satisfactorily, and redress legitimate grievance where possible.

13. School principals shall visit classrooms to evaluate the efficiency and effectiveness of each member of the staff for whom he is responsible and report the same to the superintendent and recommend changes for improvement.

14. Each principal shall have the power to suspend pupils for cause for a period not to exceed ten days or until the parent or guardian of the pupil reports to the principal. All suspensions shall be reported to the superintendent in writing, indicating the reasons for the suspension.

15. Each principal shall report to the superintendent immediately, supplemented by a written memorandum, any serious infringement of property rights within his school that come to his attention and similarly any breach of contract affecting his school, or any serious injury to a pupil or staff member that may occur at any given time or place where the rights and responsibilities of the school may be involved.

16. Principals shall be responsible for the administration of a system of accounting for all student activity money.

17. Principals shall familiarize themselves with the school bus routes and with the laws, rules, and regulations governing transportation. Each principal shall cooperate with the contractor and drivers to maintain order and discipline in the buses at all times.

18. Principals shall, either personally or by delegation, write news items for local papers. These items should contain interesting accounts of significant activities that may have happened in the school.

19. Each principal shall be responsible for a written organizational plan for his building. The plan will designate second and third in authority and will fix responsibility for carrying out all of the school's programs and functions.

20. Each principal shall see that substitute teachers receive a copy of the "Duties of Substitute Teachers" as stated in the District Handbook.

21. Each principal shall hold meetings of teachers, plan the agenda for such meetings, and preside over the meetings for the purpose of organization and instruction.

22. Principals shall, when asked by the superintendent, make recommendations as to the hiring or dismissal of staff members.

23. Principals are responsible for providing a system for orderly registration for their respective schools. Arrangements should be made for duty teachers for opening day.

24. Principals shall keep a record of the fire drills held in their buildings, including time taken to vacate the building, date and hour of drill, and comments on the success of the drill. Fire drills will be held at least once each month in each building. At the opening of the year, these drills should be frequent enough to insure that teachers and pupils know what to do. No fire drill will be called in any building except through the principal. He will insure that a drill is not called

    a. when general tests or examinations are in progress
    b. at a time when large groups are in showers
    c. at times when programs are being presented or other activities which there is good reason not to disturb.

    Principals shall further work out alternate exits in case one or more exits may be blocked. The fire alarm in all schools is a long blast of the siren or alarm.

25. A principal shall obtain parental approval before any student is questioned by authorities of the law, or before any student is removed from the school premises by the police. Police questioning for the purpose of securing information shall be done only in the presence of the principal. No questioning which takes the form of interrogation shall be permitted. When a student is involved in a case of self-incrimination, and the parents cannot be contacted, the student shall be taken to his home in order that contact with the authorities will be made only through the parents.

JOB DESCRIPTION

*Lake Oswego High School**

Responsibility: The principal is designated as the chief officer of the school plant that he administers. As the administrative and supervisory head of the school, he assumes responsibility and carries administrative authority for the operation of the entire school program consistent with state law, policies of the Board of Directors, and administrative rules and regulations of the school district under the direction of the superintendent and his delegated assistants.

1. GENERAL ADMINISTRATIVE CHARGES:

The Principal:

a. Serves as an instructional leader by developing, maintaining, systematically evaluating, and improving programs that promote student learning, and responds to student and community needs.
b. Develops and executes a system of personnel selection, assignments, supervision and evaluation which encourages growth in staff performance.
c. Directs and supervises the implementation and observance of all Board policies, administrative rules, contractual agreements, school rules and policies.
d. Manages and assesses the effective operation of the school by implementing regulations and procedures, preparing and administering the budget, and providing for the utilization of all resources and facilities.
e. Develops and maintains a program for community-staff-student relations that promotes effective communication and participation and that fosters positive human relations and good morale.

DISTRICT OFFICE EXPECTATIONS:

The Principal:

a. Prepares and maintains accurate records and reports as required by law or by the board or superintendent.
b. Participates in district principals' meetings, athletic conference meetings, negotiations meetings, and such other meetings as required or appropriate.
c. Keeps the central office administrators informed on the operation, needs and problems of the school.

*My appreciation to William Korach of Lake Oswego School District for sharing this job description.

d. Works with all central office administrators in a cooperative effort to insure the development and maintenance of a high quality educational program.

e. Serves as a special resource to the board of education when appropriate.

f. Maintains liaison and articulation with other schools in the district.

g. Supervises curriculum, discipline, attendance, guidance, staff development and evaluation, student activities, and community relations to ensure that a consistent philosophy exists among these programs.

2. PERSONNEL EXPECTATIONS:

The Principal:

a. Interprets and implements district policy, contractual agreements, administrative rules and school regulations as they apply to the staff of Lake Oswego High School.

b. Directs the recruitment, employment, evaluation, promotion and retention of all teachers and noninstructional staff with the approval of the superintendent or his designated representative.

c. Assigns all building staff members, with the approval of the superintendent, to specific duties and responsibilities.

d. Strives to create school climate where student and staff morale is consistently high.

e. Hears and reviews all appeals in accordance with district policy and contractual agreements.

f. Recommends to the superintendent a staffing design which defines the role of principal, assistant principal, and the deans detailing specific expectations.

g. Prepares annual evaluation reports on all administrative, instructional and certified staff.

h. Delegates authority to responsible personnel to assume responsibility for the school in the absence of the principal.

i. Organizes and conducts faculty meetings, faculty council meetings, and department chairman meetings.

j. Becomes the primary evaluator of all staff members who are placed on an intensive supervision schedule where future employment is in question.

k. Assures the professional growth and effective performance of school staff by directing and implementing a goal-based staff development program.

l. Assures the rights of every individual within the school to be treated fairly and equally without regard to sex, race, national origin, age or handicap.

3. COMMUNITY EXPECTATIONS:

The Principal:

a. Assures effective community-staff-student relations that promote communication and participation by identifying needs, planning, implementing, monitoring and evaluating the school-community relations activities.

b. Supervises all community oriented publications, so as to keep parents well informed of all student programs and activities.

c. Writes a monthly parent newsletter, attends all Laker Club meetings, attends all school board meetings and generally assists in all school district efforts to promote good community relations.

d. Organizes and assists the efforts of the high school citizen advisory committee.

e. Encourages publicity about school activities by the local newspapers.

f. Maintains a cooperative relationship liaison with community law enforcement, social and welfare agencies.

4. INSTRUCTIONAL PROGRAM EXPECTATIONS:

The Principal:

a. Serves as the instructional leader of the school in its primary function as an educational institution.

b. Supervises the continual development, evaluation and revision of the curriculum.

c. Maintains an appropriate balance of emphasis between the school's academic, activity and athletic programs.

d. Contributes to the development of effective school programs by participating in professional conferences, joining professional organizations and keeping up with current readings in the field.

5. PUPIL EXPECTATIONS:

The Principal:

a. Provides a student guidance and counseling program with specific expectations.

b. Assures that students receive a quality education by monitoring and evaluating staff.

c. Provides a positive learning climate in the school by establishing and maintaining appropriate student behavior.

d. Supports the efforts of student government so as to insure the continuous opportunity for student input into the decision making process.

e. Assures that the utilization of the school and grounds meet health and safety standards for all students.

6. MANAGEMENT EXPECTATIONS:

The Principal:

a. Assures the systematic implementation of program planning, budgeting, evaluation, record-keeping, and financial and property accounting by being informed and directing others in the system's procedures.

b. Builds and administers the annual budget.

c. Assures that all funds allocated to the building are accounted for by maintaining a system of internal control.

d. Approves or rejects all requisitions for the expenditure of funds.

e. Provides for the maintenance of building and grounds facilities by planning, establishing priorities, budgeting, monitoring and evaluating maintenance and improvement work performed at the school.

7. DELEGATION OF RESPONSIBILITIES EXPECTATIONS:

In a large high school it is impossible for the building principal to function without delegating many of his responsibilities. This does not mean that his responsibilities are abrogated, only that another administrator is charged with specified shared responsibilities. These shared responsibilities are outlined under the administrative job descriptions that follow.

The job descriptions reflect the expectation that principals interact routinely with central office supervisors, teachers, classified personnel, students, parents, and members of the community. Principals may be called upon to develop rules, enforce rules, determine if rules have been broken, mete out punishment, and provide expert testimony. They are expected to evaluate their staff and, at the same time, assist individuals in growing professionally. They should create a supportive environment for student learning and also handle serious discipline problems. These and other functions can generate considerable confusion among principals concerning the ultimate locus of their loyalties. Such confusion may diminish their effectiveness. As Arthur Blumberg and William Greenfield conclude,

> The principal's general work situation is ambiguous and as such is likely to produce much psychological stress for the individual and, in some instances, may severely impair the principal's ability to perform to the level of his/her expectations.[3]

The job descriptions also reveal several differences in expectations between elementary and secondary principals. The high school principal, for example, typically is responsible for a larger, more complex organization. High school students—being more mature—are capable of creating more serious behavior problems. Parents tend to be less directly involved in secondary education than in elementary education. High school principals must supervise and evaluate a broader range of specialists and coordinate a much more extensive student activities program. Elementary principals are more apt to work alone, unaided by administrative assistants.

Many traditional textbooks on educational administration suggest that the roles of elementary, middle level, and high school principal are more similar than different. This book contends that these roles share many of the same functions, but that differences in span of control, age of students, complexity of curriculum, and community expectations must also be appreciated. It is not clear that principals who are effective at one level will necessarily be effective at another level. For this reason, separate analyses will be done of how elementary, middle level, and high school principals spend their time.

THE JOB OF ELEMENTARY PRINCIPAL

To find out how elementary principals spend their time, researchers have tended to observe them in action for short periods of time and to question them about it in surveys. One of the few attempts to take a truly in-depth look at the job has been Harry Wolcott's year-long study of Ed Bell.[4] Applying the intensive data-collection techniques of the anthropologist, Wolcott pursued Bell into formal meetings, classrooms, conferences, and after-school activities. *The Man in the Principal's Office* is as close to a complete record of the life of an elementary principal as the literature affords. Among the unique features of the account is an attempt to chart the seasonal shifts in activity of an elementary principal.

Wolcott divides Bell's seasonal functions into six major categories: orienting, meeting, and dealing with problems of pupils, evaluating teachers, preparing for the next school year, and performing contingent activities. Table 2.1 suggests that Bell's most intense and sustained activities were faculty and school district meetings and handling pupil problems.

In addition to looking at Ed Bell's yearly cycle of activities, Wolcott examined his daily routines. As Table 2.2 indicates, Bell spent less than one-fourth of his time alone and noninteractive. Most of his days typically consisted of prearranged meetings, deliberate but not prearranged meetings, and chance encounters. However, despite—or perhaps because of—the almost constant interaction with people, the principalship can be a very lonely position. The portrait Wolcott paints of Bell reveals a busy person with little opportunity to develop or sustain meaningful professional relationships.

How representative is Ed Bell's work life? Several studies have been conducted in which the daily activities of different elementary principals have been monitored for brief periods. For example, John Kmetz and Donald Willower observed five elementary principals in different types of districts for one week in 1981.[5] The principals worked an average of 41.7 hours on the job, and an additional eight evening hours per week. They averaged 122.3 discrete activities per day (the range was 87.6 to 149.2), suggesting a workload characterized by variety and brevity, an unrelenting pace, and fragmentation.[6] Unscheduled meetings accounted for the largest percentage of time ($\bar{X} = 32.5\%$), followed by desk work ($\bar{X} = 18.6\%$), scheduled meetings ($\bar{X} = 10.3\%$), and phone calls ($\bar{X} = 8.0\%$). The remaining time was divided among a number of activities—brief verbal encounters, tours of the building, trips, monitoring student behavior, observing, making announcements, and teaching.

Kmetz and Willower also analyzed all correspondence that the five principals handled during a week. Incoming correspondence accounted for 63 percent of the 916 items processed. The largest group of people originating it was teachers, followed by vendors.

Table 2.1 Seasonal Activities of An Elementary School Principal

Duration and Intensity of Activity by Month

Activity	SEPT.	OCT.	NOV.	DEC.	JAN.	FEB.	MAR.	APR.	MAY	JUNE	JULY	AUG.
Orienting												
New staff	───											- -
New pupils and parents	- -	- -	- -		- -	- -	- -	- -	- -			- -
Student teachers, supervisors	- -	- -	- -	- -		- -	- -	- -	- -			- -
Meeting												
Public relations (open house, room desserts, new parents)	───		───				───	───				
Faculty and school district	- -	- -	- -	- -	- -	- -	- -	- -	- -			- -
Regional, state, national									- -			
School-related socials (parties, farewells)	- -			- -				- -	- -			
Pupil problems	- -	- -	- -									
Teacher evaluations		───				───						
Preparing for next school year												
Budget projection			- -		- -	- -	- -	- -	- -			- -
Interviewing						───	───	───	- -		- -	- -
Assignments, ordering supplies	───											
Contingent activities												
In-service training								───	- -			
Workshops/summer school							───	───	- -		───	───
Personal vacation				───							───	───

Key: Intermittent activity - - - - Intense activity ───────

SOURCE: Harry F. Wolcott, *The Man in the Principal's Office* (New York: Holt, Rinehart & Winston, 1973), p. 183.

Table 2.2   Distribution of the Principal's Time During an "Average" School Day, 8:00 A.M.–5:00 P.M. (Based on a Sample of 12 Two-Hour Periods of Observation During a Two-Week Period)

Activity of Principal	Observed Day-to-Day Range (in percentages)	Percent of Time in an "Average" Day
Prearranged meeting or conference	13–35	26
Deliberate but not prearranged encounter	24–29	25
Casual or chance encounter	10–28	15
Telephoning	7–10	9
Talking on intercom	6–15	1
Alone and stationary (e.g., working in his office)	13–24	15
Alone and enroute (e.g., going to a meeting, walking down the hall)	7–14	9
	Total	100

SOURCE: Harry F. Wolcott, *The Man in the Principal's Office* (New York; Holt, Rinehart & Winston, 1973), p. 89.

As in the case of Ed Bell, the workday of the elementary principals in this study was dominated by personal contacts, not paper processing. Over 70 percent of their time—representing more than 86 percent of their total number of activities—was spent in face-to-face encounters, phone calls, and brief interactions during monitoring and touring. Meetings tended to take place in the principals' offices.

When the principals' activities were analyzed for purpose, it was found that almost 54 percent (38.6 percent of the workweek) concerned organizational maintenance—personnel matters, student services, school plant concerns, public relations, and safety. Curriculum and instruction, including teacher observations and conferences, encompassed over 12 percent of the activities (27.1 percent of the workweek). Student discipline accounted for 24.4 percent of the activities (23.6 percent of the workweek). Thus, activities generally associated directly with instructional improvement occupied roughly a quarter of the principals' time.

A somewhat more extensive study—this time of elementary and secondary principals in Chicago—produced similar results. Four researchers from the University of Illinois at Chicago Circle "shadowed" 24 principals periodically from 1977 to 1980.[7] They observed that activities involving instructional leadership, including classroom observation and teacher supervision, were not the predominant focus of the principalship. Instead, major segments of time were devoted to checking out what was going on, serving as the school spokesperson, disseminating information to staff members, and handling disturbances.

Elementary principals in the Chicago study spent even more time interacting with people than their counterparts in the Kmetz and Willower study—83 percent.[8] Students accounted for an average of 22 percent of this interaction time, and teachers another 18 percent. The variations among individual elementary principals, however, were substantial. For example, time spent with students ranged from 8 percent to 35 percent, time with teachers from 10 percent to 24 percent.

Additional data gave further details on the work life of Chicago elementary principals. Over two-thirds of their interaction time resulted from contacts they themselves initiated. Face-to-face interactions made up an average of 66 percent of the typical workday, though the length of each contact was brief. Face-to-face contacts of two principals averaged 1 minute 54 seconds and 3 minutes 12 seconds, respectively.[9] Almost half the principals' workday was spent in the office, while less than 10 percent was spent in classrooms.

In both of the preceding studies, the data on the range of responses of all principals are equally interesting. No two principals spent time in exactly the same way. While the mythical "average" elementary principal appears to be tied to his or her desk for much of the day and condemned to a relentless succession of brief interactions with a variety of people, certain individuals managed to dedicate substantial portions of their time to classroom observation and teacher supervision. A few were even able to teach students on a regular basis. Exceptional principals such as these—defying the conventions of school leadership—will be discussed in Chapter 4.

THE JOB OF MIDDLE-LEVEL PRINCIPAL

Relatively little research is available on how principals of middle-level schools (junior high and middle schools) spend their time. The major source of information is a national survey commissioned by the National Association of Secondary School Principals in 1981.[10] Nearly 1500 middle-level principals completed questionnaires regarding various aspects of their work. The findings indicate that the typical middle-level principal puts in a workweek of over 50 hours. Like their elementary counterparts, they spend their time in a variety of activities. Figure 2.1 reflects respondents' judgments of how their time is and should be spent.

Other than in the area of personnel, it appears that middle-level principals are not spending time the way they would prefer. They see managerial duties and discipline taking time away from activities such as program development and planning. When asked to identify major roadblocks preventing them from doing their jobs, 86 percent cited the time taken up by administrative detail (the most prevalent response among a set of 23 functions).[11]

Jerry Valentine and Thomas Moeller surveyed 260 Missouri middle-level schools to investigate possible relationships between how principals spend time and how effective they see themselves.[12] Effectiveness was defined subjectively by principals themselves. Areas where they felt they spent the most time and were most effective included:

- Informing teachers of budgetary allocations
- Maintaining written policies concerning school rules and regulations for students and teachers
- Providing supervisory assistance at school activities

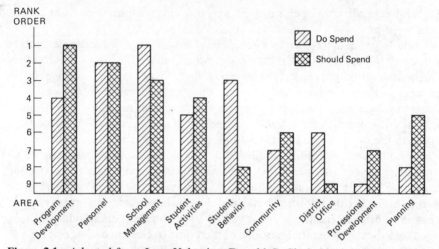

Figure 2.1   Adapted from Jerry Valentine, Donald C. Clark, Neal C. Nickerson, Jr., and James W. Keefe, *The Middle Level Principalship,* Vol. 1 (Reston, Va.: National Association of Secondary School Principals, 1981), p. 36. Reprinted with permission.

- Maintaining written evaluations of school staff
- Maintaining an up-to-date file of purchase invoices

Areas where principals perceived they spent the least time and were least effective included:

- Working with teachers in designing and using instruments to evaluate the instructional program
- Working with teachers on understanding and using information in student cumulative records
- Disseminating occupational/educational information to students
- Discussing the services provided by system-wide subject matter specialists with teachers
- Developing a staffing plan based on school needs and financial resources

In reviewing their findings, Valentine and Moeller concluded that middle-level principals perceived they devoted the most time and were most effective in activities associated more with the managerial aspects of administration than with instructional-leadership functions.[13] The study gave no indication of whether or not Missouri principals preferred this distribution of their time.

THE JOB OF HIGH SCHOOL PRINCIPAL

National concern over quality of American secondary education during the early eighties subjected the high school principalship to intense scrutiny. The consensus that emerges is that, like elementary and middle-level principals, high school principals typically must subordinate functions associated with instructional improvement to routine managerial activities.

William Martin and Donald Willower reported a study in which they interviewed and then observed five high school principals for a week in the fall.[14] The principals worked an average of 42.2 hours on the job each week and an additional 11 hours in the evening, slightly longer than the workweek reported earlier for elementary principals. An average of 149.2 tasks were performed each day by the principals—again, larger than the figure for elementary principals. Table 2.3 presents a breakdown of the types of tasks undertaken by the five high school principals.

The data indicate that unscheduled meetings accounted for the greatest percentage of time, over one-quarter of each school day. Scheduled meetings and desk work also occupied substantial percentages of time. Less than 3 percent of the high school principals' time was spent observing teachers. Virtually the same percentage was reported in the Kmetz and Willower study of elementary principals.

Face-to-face contacts took up 53.8 percent of the principals' time on the job. These contacts tended to be initiated by the principals and to occur in their offices. As with their elementary counterparts, high school principals live in a world where the primary mode of communication is the spoken word. It is also a world where opportunities for reflection are few and where interpersonal relations are characterized by brief encounters affording little occasion for in-depth discussion.

When Martin and Willower analyzed the various tasks performed by high school principals, they found that over a third of their time (36.5 percent) was occupied with matters of organizational maintenance, including scheduling classes, arranging transportation, providing information to parents, and dealing with student attendance. Activities related to the school's academic pro-

Table 2.3   Analysis of Task Performance (the Chronological Record)

Type of Activity	Number of Activities	Total Time*	Average Duration*	Percentage of Time
Desk work	254	2394	9.4	16.0
Scheduled meetings	117	2601	22.2	17.3
Unscheduled meetings	1221	4122	3.4	27.5
Exchanges	1355	1355	1.0	9.0
Phone calls	393	868	2.2	5.8
Personal	133	767	5.8	5.1
Tours	88	1158	13.2	7.7
Monitoring	82	828	10.1	5.5
Trips	11	327	29.7	2.2
Announcing	61	103	1.7	0.7
Observing	8	363	45.4	2.4
Processing	5	103	21.2	0.7
Teaching	2	18	9.0	0.1

SOURCE: William J. Martin and Donald J. Willower, "The Managerial Behavior of High School Principals," *Educational Administration Quarterly,* Vol. 17, No. 1 (Winter 1981), p. 72. Reprinted by permission of Sage Publications, Inc.
* All times were computed in minutes.

gram—such as curriculum development, implementation of new teaching strategies, and pupil services—accounted for 17.4 percent of their time. The remainder of their time was allotted to pupil control (23.8 percent), administration of the extra-curricular program (14.7 percent), and miscellaneous activities (7.6 percent).

The general impressions we get from the Martin and Willower study are confirmed in the previously cited work of Morris, Crowson, Porter-Gehrie, and Hurwitz.[15] In examining the workweek of a sample of Chicago secondary principals, they concluded that the job of principal consists largely of brief interactions with a variety of people. The variation among individuals, however, was substantial. One principal, over a five-day period, engaged in 148 face-to-face contacts totaling 789 minutes, for an average of 5 minutes and 20 seconds per contact. Another principal engaged in 434 interactions totaling 1085 minutes, for an average of only 2 minutes and 30 seconds per contact. While principals' contacts (about 60 percent) tended to be with teachers, administrative aides, students, and office clerks, the variation among individuals again was noteworthy. The percentage of the workday spent interacting with teachers ranged from 13 percent to 30 percent, with students from 8 percent to 24 percent. Variations also were found in the location of contacts. For example, principals spent from 28 percent to 58 percent of their workday in their own office and from 3 percent to 14 percent in classrooms.

A CLOSER LOOK AT THE PRINCIPAL'S JOB

The preceding analyses of how elementary, middle-level, and high school principals spend their time prompt several observations. Where data are reported in ranges as well as averages, it appears that individual principals vary considerably in how, with whom, and where they spend their time. Since the variety among the Chicago principals occurred within the same school system in the preceding study, it appears that these individuals exercise substantial discretion over their use of time. Such a realization is an important justification for this book. If principals, as well as other school leaders, had no control over what they did, there would be little reason to explore more effective ways of allocating time. Since principals apparently spend their time in different ways, though, and since schools are characterized by different levels of achievement, it is reasonable to assume that some relationship exists between principals' use of time and school effectiveness. Chapter 4 explores this relationship in detail.

James Hager and L. E. Scarr asked the principals in their Lake Washington (WA) School District to specify how they actually spend their time and how they would like to spend their time ideally.[16] Principals were asked to assign percentages to five general categories of activity—operations, staff and program development, community relationships, student services, and evaluation. Detailed time logs were maintained to verify how time actually was spent. Discrepancies between the two sets of responses suggest that, despite considerable discretion, many principals still fail to spend time in ways they judge most desirable. Table 2.4 contains a breakdown of the data by category and administrative level.

The data indicate that Lake Washington principals, and most likely school leaders elsewhere, would prefer to spend more time doing staff and program development and evaluation, activities closely associated with instructional improvement. To do this would mean reducing time spent in student services, primarily discipline, and general administrative operations. The process of altering the pattern is not a simple or easy one. Staff and students grow accustomed to the established routines of principals. To accomplish a shift in work priorities, school leaders must first understand why their current use of time is less than ideal. Such an understanding may be informed by a clear vision of a well-run school. Simple dissatisfaction with the *status quo* alone is unlikely to produce lasting changes.

Before addressing the crucial matter of a school leader's vision it is necessary to look at how school leaders other than principals spend their time.

LEADERS IN SUPPORTING ROLES

While principals typically are the most visible school leaders, other individuals may exert major influence over what goes on in schools. Unfortunately, few studies of how these persons spend their time are available. Still, it is important to consider the work accomplished by assistant administrators, department chairs, and other leaders in supporting roles.

In 1970 the National Association of Secondary School Principals (NASSP) published one of the most extensive analyses of the assistant principalship to date.[17] In 16 schools across the United States assistant principals were "shadowed" for a week. Researchers also conducted interviews with colleagues and students. Perhaps the most interesting finding of the study was that the assistant principalship does not conform to any one set of job characteristics. Only

Table 2.4 Analysis of Administrator's Actual Versus Ideal Use of Time

	Actual Use of Time (%)	*Ideal Use of Time* (%)
Elementary Principals		
Operations	13	09
Staff/program development	24	35
Community relationships	16	14
Student service	21	12
Evaluation	26	30
Secondary Principals		
Operations	14	10
Staff/program development	17	27
Community relationships	14	15
Student services	40	24
Evaluation	15	24

SOURCE: Based on data reported by James L. Hager and L. E. Scarr, "Effective Schools—Effective Principals: How to Develop Both," *Educational Leadership,* Vol. 40, No. 5 (February 1983), p. 39.

two functions, in fact, were shared by virtually all the subjects—attendance and discipline. Carefully spelled out job descriptions covering the assistant principal's duties were practically nonexistent.

In all but two cases, assistant principals spent a majority of their time working with teachers and students. Nearly three out of four of their activities involved face-to-face encounters with one other person. Much of their work arose in response to events initiated by others. Assistant principals exercised relatively little control over the nature of their work.

As described in the NASSP study, the assistant principalship does not appear to be centrally concerned with instructional improvement:

> Clearly, the focus of his operation is the school building and grounds and, to a lesser extent, an ill-defined "community." It is the people who work and learn within this setting with whom the assistant principal must deal. His is a position of judge and jury, of confidant, arbiter, and confessor. He polices and protects, encourages and represses, ministers unto and punishes.
>
> Only to a slight extent does he deal with abstractions except as they concern live, busy people. His is not a position to encourage dreaming; and only to a slight extent, long-range planning. He works almost exclusively with the here and now.[18]

The authors of the study concluded that there was little in the experience of dealing with the small problems and crises of the assistant principalship that prepared them for the role of principal.

Assistant principals are found most often in secondary schools, where the size of the student body and the complexity of the tasks require a team of administrators. Larger elementary schools also may employ an assistant principal or part-time administrative assistant. Where several assistant principals are present, some degree of specialization among them is likely to occur. Assistant principals may focus on curriculum, discipline, guidance, or operations. It is unclear whether or not districts expect assistant principals eventually to gain experience in all specialty areas.

Large urban secondary schools sometimes employ full- or part-time deans of students to handle student behavior problems and attendance. Indeed, the area of school discipline has witnessed a greater proliferation of specialized roles than perhaps any other part of the school program.[19] Assisting deans and assistant principals may be security personnel, campus supervisors, attendance officers, detention center supervisors, community liaisons, social workers, and special counselors.

Next to principals and assistant principals, department chairs are probably the most frequently mentioned school leaders. Since most elementary schools are not departmentalized, chairs are usually found in middle-level and high schools. These individuals would seem well able to exercise instructional leadership, since they possess subject matter expertise and interact regularly with the same group of teachers. But for a variety of reasons, department chairs do not always function as instructional leaders. For one thing, they are not always selected on the basis of leadership skill, subject matter knowledge, or instructional competence but often because of seniority. Union contracts may prohibit a chair from undertaking certain key functions, such as teacher evaluation.

In his comprehensive *Handbook for Effective Department Leadership,* Thomas Sergiovanni lists the competencies associated with supervisory roles in general. They include the following:

I. Educational Leadership
- setting instructional goals
- designing instructional units
- developing and adapting curricula
- evaluating and selecting learning materials
- evaluating the utilization of learning resources
- producing learning materials
- supervising in a clinical mode
- planning for individual growth

II. Supervisory Leadership
- building a healthy climate
- team building
- resolving conflict
- making decisions
- planning and organizing meetings
- recruiting and selecting personnel
- assigning personnel
- bringing about change

III. Organizational Leadership
- revising existing structures
- assimilating programs
- monitoring new arrangements
- developing a staffing plan
- informing the public
- student discipline
- policies and procedures

IV. Administrative Leadership[20]

Thomas Weaver and Jeffry Gordon used these competencies as a basis for a survey of department chairs. Chairs identified 13 crucial skill areas for which they felt a need for further training:

- Setting instructional goals
- Team building
- Resolving conflict
- Assigning personnel
- Bringing about change
- Revising existing structures, policies, and procedures
- Planning for individual growth
- Building a healthy climate
- Making decisions
- Program planning
- Supervising in a clinical mode

- Recruiting and selecting personnel
- Developing a staffing plan[21]

Effectiveness is at least partly a function of both technical skill and opportunities to exercise that skill. In the preceding discussion of the principal's role, we learned that some principals feel they lack the time and opportunity to perform the tasks they deem most important. Weaver and Gordon's study indicates that department chairs may lack sufficient skill to perform important tasks. Both of these issues need to be addressed by policymakers and by those engaged in the preparation of school leaders. Ultimately, though, changes will occur only when school leaders themselves decide they must acquire new skills and alter the way they spend time.

Besides principals, assistant principals, and department chairs, there are other school leaders in a variety of full-time and part-time roles, including program directors, building-based staff-development specialists, project heads, and grade-level leaders. Some districts have implemented differentiated staffing schemes in an effort to create more teacher-leadership opportunities and to recognize the expertise of particularly talented teachers. These efforts were strongly encouraged by the National Commission on Excellence in Education, which recommended the creation of more leadership roles for teachers as a way to prevent the continued exodus of gifted teachers.[22]

In one such example of differentiated staffing—the Greenwich (Connecticut) Public Schools—91 out of a total of 630 teachers function in some leadership capacity.[23] Four teacher leaders are in charge of district-wide programs such as staff development. Sixteen teachers are based in elementary and junior high schools and function as either part-time assistant principals or department chairs. Five teachers serve as division chairs in the high school. Finally, 66 are designated senior teachers and have a variety of administrative responsibilities, ranging from department chair to program head. The second and third groups are expected to evaluate teachers in their department or division. All those with extended responsibility receive a special stipend.

A study of how individuals prepare for the school principalship found that most had some experience, while still a teacher, in a differentiated role or quasi-administrative post.[24] Such positions apparently provide a valuable set of on-the-job experiences that serve to socialize prospective principals and provide district officials with data on leadership potential. These arrangements have an added benefit in permitting districts to save money, since teacher leaders typically are paid less than full-time administrators. At present little is known about how teacher leaders actually spend their workday or about their overall impact on school effectiveness.

THE VALUE OF VISION

The information available on how school leaders spend their time suggests that they are more involved in managerial work than instructional improvement activities. James March states that "much of the job of an educational administrator involves the mundane work of making a bureaucracy work," a chore he claims is "filled with activities quite distant from those implied by a conception of administration as heroic leadership."[25] The typical workday, at least for full-time school administrators, tends to be filled with brief encounters and interruptions. And it appears that many school leaders would prefer to be engaged in activities more closely related to the "technical core" of schooling—instruction, curriculum, and evaluation.[26]

Why *do* many school leaders have so little opportunity to lead? There are several possible explanations. It may be that school administrators are not expected to lead. In other words, the chief functions of principals and other administrators may be perceived to be managerial in nature. An alternative but not incongruent explanation is that school administrators as a group lack a clear understanding of what instructional leadership entails. It is this quandary that this book is concerned about.

An essential requirement of leadership is vision. This is what seems to get lost when school leaders reluctantly become bogged down in managerial routines. Vision permits a leader to see beyond his or her immediate situation, to comprehend why things must be done in a certain way. Vision enables a leader to make decisions about how best to spend time, not just randomly responding to the demands of others. Vision prods school leaders to be proactive rather than reactive.

The term *vision* has become prominent in the literature on leadership fairly recently. Two popular analyses of successful businesses and their executives—*In Search of Excellence*[27] and *Corporate Cultures*[28]—have isolated vision as a key ingredient. What is currently implied by the term *vision* was probably captured previously by such terms as *initiative* and *sense of direction*.

To many, the notion of vision remains just that—a notion, placed in the same airy class of impracticalities as theory, model, and idea. Yet to those who recognize its value, few things are as useful as a good vision. It compels a leader to focus on what is truly important. Vision can shift the focus of attention from maintenance and survival to improvement and growth. As a result, leaders may find it easier to set clear objectives and inspire others to extraordinary performance.

Vision is like a Lamaze class. It provides a leader with a clear sense of what to expect. Just as a pregnant woman learns what the birthing process will be like, a leader with vision may anticipate the sacrifices necessary to reach a desired goal, thereby reducing the element of surprise and minimizing disappointment.

When a team of University of Texas researchers studied the characteristics of more-effective and less-effective elementary and secondary principals, they found that vision was a central feature of the former group.[29] When asked, "What is your vision for this school—your long-range goals and expectations?", more effective principals listed a variety of goals related to meeting the learning needs of all students, helping teachers adjust to changing school populations, raising test scores, and the like. Less-effective principals "usually responded with a long pause and then a nonspecific statement, such as, 'We have a good school and a good faculty, and I want us to keep it that way'.... In short, the less-effective principals had no vision for their schools; they focused on maintaining tranquility in the here and now."[30]

Educators, of course, may be guided by different types of vision. For example, Atlanta superintendent Alonzo Crim speaks of his school system and his city as a "community of believers."[31] Far from being abstract, this vision connoted a working commitment to high expectations for students, adult volunteers in the schools, school-business partnerships, and community service projects for students. Crim's vision allowed him to make tough decisions on how to allocate scarce resources. It allowed him to direct and concentrate the energies of Atlanta's educators and citizens as well as his own.

Since this book deals with school leadership, three types of vision seem particularly appropriate for discussion: visions of effective teaching, effective instructional leadership, and effective schools. While there is unlikely to be one best set of visions, they should at least be compatible with each other. It makes little sense, for instance, to be guided by a vision of teaching as creative artistry at the same time one is striving to create an ideal school based on norms of conformity and predictability. Without compatible visions to guide them, school leaders are likely to spend much of their time in activities of questionable value to instructional improvement and student learning. The next part of the book introduces a variety of possible visions of teaching, leadership, and schools.

STUDY QUESTIONS

1. If you have access to a school leader, observe how he or she spends time. Into what meaningful categories can the leader's workday be divided? What percentage of time is spent on issues related to instruction, curriculum, and evaluation?

2. What are similarities and differences in how elementary, middle-level, and high school principals spend their time?

3. Interview five school leaders. Ask them how they actually spend their time and how they would like to spend their time.

4. Visit five schools and make an inventory of all the opportunities teachers have to exercise school leadership. How do teachers feel about these activities?

5. Ask an educator to articulate his or her vision of the ideal school. How does this vision compare to your own? How would you undertake to realize your vision?

NOTES

1. Roland Barth, *Run School Run* (Cambridge: Harvard University Press, 1980), p. 175.
2. Educational Research Service, "A Special Report: Polling the Principals," *Principal,* Vol. 64, No. 4 (March 1985), p. 61.
3. Harry F. Wolcott, *The Man in the Principal's Office* (New York: Holt, Rinehart & Winston, 1973).

4. *Ibid.*
5. John T. Kmetz and Donald J. Willower, "Elementary School Principals' Work Behavior," *Educational Administration Quarterly,* Vol. 18, No. 4 (Fall 1982), pp. 62–78.
6. *Ibid.,* p. 72.
7. Van Cleve Morris, Robert L. Crowson, Cynthia Porter-Gehrie, and Emanual Hurwitz, Jr., *Principals in Action* (Columbus, Ohio: Charles E. Merrill, 1984).
8. *Ibid.,* p. 33.
9. *Ibid.,* p. 38.
10. Jerry Valentine, Donald C. Clark, Neal C. Nickerson, Jr., and James W. Keefe, *The Middle Level Principalship,* Vol. I (Reston, Va: The National Association of Secondary School Principals, 1981).
11. *Ibid.,* p. 43.
12. Jerry W. Valentine and Thomas E. Moeller,"The Relationship between Programmatic Characteristics of Middle Level Schools and the Competencies of the Principals of Those Schools" (unpublished paper).
13. *Ibid.,* p. 51.
14. William J. Martin and Donald J. Willower, "The Managerial Behavior of High School Principals," *Educational Administration Quarterly,* Vol. 17, No. 1 (Winter 1981), pp. 69–90.
15. Morris, et al., *Principals in Action,* pp. 51–65.
16. James L. Hager and L. E. Scarr, "Effective Schools—Effective Principals: How to Develop Both," *Educational Leadership,* Vol. 40, No. 5 (February 1983), pp. 38–40.
17. David B. Austin and Harry L. Brown, Jr., *Report of the Assistant Principalship* (Washington, D.C.: National Association of Secondary School Principals, 1970).
18. *Ibid.,* p. 76.
19. Daniel L. Duke and Adrienne M. Meckel, "Disciplinary Roles in American Schools," *British Journal of Teacher Education,* Vol. 6, No. 1 (Janury 1980), pp. 37–50.
20. Thomas J. Sergiovanni, *Handbook for Effective Department Leadership,* 2nd ed. (Boston: Allyn & Bacon, 1984).
21. Frances Weaver and Jeffry Gordon, "Staff Development Needs of Department Heads," *Educational Leadership,* Vol. 36, No. 8 (May 1979), pp. 578–580.
22. National Commission on Excellence in Education, *A Nation at Risk: The Imperative for Educational Reform* (Washington D.C.: U.S. Government Printing Office, 1983).
23. Arthur E. Wise, Linda Darling-Hammond, Milbrey W. McLaughlin, and Harriet T. Bernstein, *Case Studies for Teacher Evaluation: A Study of Effective Practices* (Santa Monica, Calif.: Rand, 1984), pp. 101–102.
24. Daniel L. Duke, Nancy S. Isaacson, Richard Sagor, and Patricia A. Schmuck, "Transition to Leadership: An Investigation of the First Year of the Principalship," (a presentation made at the annual convention of the American Educational Research Assocation, 1985).
25. James G. March, "American Public School Administration: A Short Analysis," *School Review,* Vol. 86, No. 2 (February 1978) p. 233.
26. *Ibid.,* p. 225. Also see Roland Barth, *Run School Run,* p. 180.
27. Thomas J. Peters and Robert H. Waterman, *In Search of Excellence* (New York: Harper & Row, 1982).
28. Terrence E. Deal and Allan A. Kennedy, *Corporate Cultures* (Reading, Mass.: Addison-Wesley, 1982).
29. William L. Rutherford, "School Principals as Effective Leaders," *Phi Delta Kappan,* Vol. 67, No. 1 (September 1985), pp. 31–34.
30. *Ibid.,* p. 32.
31. Alonzo A. Crim, "A Community of Believers," *Daedalus,* Vol. 110, No. 4 (Fall 1981), pp. 145–162.

PART II

VISIONS OF EFFECTIVENESS

It is one thing for researchers to isolate particular elements of effective teaching or schooling and quite another for school leaders to articulate such images. As indicated in Chapter 2, an image or vision grasps the complex relationships between separate elements. It serves as an ideal toward which to aspire. And the pursuit—rather than the achievement—of a vision is what is most important to the health of any organization. For this reason, it must be dynamic. It must evolve as needs, capacities, and resources change.

The three chapters in this section offer visions that will be valuable to those interested in instructional improvement. Chapter 3 reviews some current visions of teaching before presenting an integrated conceptualization that will guide subsequent segments of the book. Chapter 4 addresses the issue of school leadership. Specifically, it attempts to identify the key situations in which a school leader must be capable in order to promote continuous instructional improvement. The result is a working model of instructional leadership. Chapter 5 puts teaching and leadership into an organizational context. Several visions of effective schools, based on case studies, are presented to increase the reader's ability to recognize how assorted pieces of the instructional puzzle fit together in a real context. There is, after all, little benefit to practitioners in considering teaching or leadership apart from the actual setting in which it occurs.

CHAPTER 3

VISIONS OF EFFECTIVE TEACHING

School leaders, particularly principals, spend relatively little time observing in classrooms and working with teachers to improve instruction. Chapter 2 indicated that some leaders are quite unhappy with this state of affairs. How does it happen that people in positions of leadership—people presumably with some control over their daily schedules—are unable to allocate their time in ways they want?

This book contends that many leaders unconsciously permit themselves to become absorbed in non-instructional matters because they believe they have little constructive advice to offer teachers. A principal or department chair is unlikely to protect time to visit classes if all he or she can provide s a tip or two on student discipline or room appearance. When this is the case, contact with teachers actually can become aversive, reminding leaders of how inadequate or outdated their knowledge is of instructional theory, curriculum development, student assessment, and the like. Small wonder so many leaders adopt any excuse not to work with teachers.

For school leaders to feel that they can contribute to teacher growth and instructional improvement, it is vital that they cultivate a vision of effective teaching. Such a vision is more than a teaching strategy or method: It is a complex image of what a classroom looks and feels like when students are learning. A vision includes a sense of the planning that precedes instruction and of the outcomes when that instruction proves effective. It encompasses a rationale or a set of reasons for particular teacher actions or decisions. In short, a vision of teaching equips a leader to recognize the extent to which students are benefiting from instruction and to make constructive suggestions for increasing the benefits.

No one vision of teaching has been found universally best. Alan Tom describes four distinct images of teaching: teaching as a craft, teaching as an art, teaching as an applied science, and—his preference—teaching as a moral craft.[1] Bruce Joyce and Marsha Weil identify 25 discrete "models of teaching," each with distinct goals, methods, and theoretical bases;[2] the appropriateness of a given model varies with the nature of the school, the concerns of the community, the capabilities of the students, and the skills of the teachers. The following section will briefly describe several of the more popular contemporary visions of teaching and then try to combine some of the major aspects of these separate visions into an integrated vision of teaching excellence.

A POTPOURRI OF VISIONS

A vision takes no prescribed form. Those concerned with instruction have sometimes expressed their vision in terms of teacher characteristics, at other times, with the teaching process. We shall tend toward the latter course, since visions of teaching, more than visions of teachers, seem to be more useful to school leaders. Still, it is unlikely that any vision of effective teaching can be complete without some reference to teacher capabilities.

To aid in the identification of "effective professional teachers," the Teacher Education Conference Board of New York developed a list of ten important teacher characteristics:

1. Diligence in keeping oneself current and increasing one's mastery with respect to the body of knowledge and skill taught;
2. Commitment to continual personal growth through intellectual activity;
3. Awareness of societal expectations, institutional goals, and professional responsibilities;
4. Receptivity to advances in pedagogical practices;
5. Conscientiousness and proficiency in planning and preparation for teaching encounters, based on knowledge of the outcomes to be sought and the most efficient means of achieving them;
6. Artistry in managing and performing instructional functions effectively;
7. Concern for students as individuals, based on mutual respect;
8. Dependability as participant in faculty planning and decision making;
9. Dedication to furthering the effectiveness of the teaching profession.
10. Generosity in contributing talents to community welfare and improvement.[3]

These characteristics are all necessary for formulating any vision of teaching. The issue of teacher capability is all the more important at a time when fewer talented young people are opting for careers in education.[4] School leaders no longer can count on a wide selection of bright new teachers to assist them in educational reform efforts. More will be said in Part III about the need for school leaders to be able recruiters of new teachers.

Adler's Threefold Vision of Teaching

Perhaps no other vision of teaching relies so heavily on the availability of multi-talented and literate instructors as Mortimer's Adler's. His "Paideia Program" calls on teachers to acquire skill in three types of teaching—didactic instruction, coaching, and Socratic questioning.[5] Each is intended to cultivate a distinct area of learning. Adler and his group prescribe a common curriculum for all students that serves as the focus of instruction.

The goal of didactic instruction, which may include written or oral forms, is the acquisition of organized knowledge. But there is a challenge inherent in this approach. To promote genuine knowledge, lectures and textbooks must actively engage students in the instruction. Didactic instruction that forces students to remain passive does little more than contribute additional material to memory.

Teachers who seek to actively engage the minds of students as they acquire new information don't just have to rely on formal lectures. They can share knowledge informally or give students written materials. When teachers do lecture, Adler's program urges them to consider the following guidelines:

1. To encourage active listening, blend questions with the introduction of new knowledge.
2. Demonstrate lively interest in the subject.
3. Introduce some element of "wonder" at the beginning of the lecture.
4. Avoid sharing information that is either too challenging or not challenging enough for students.
5. Ensure that question-and-answer periods after lectures allow for two way inter-action.
6. Commence lectures with an overview of what students can expect to learn and the reasons why they should learn it.
7. Cover only as much material as students are able to absorb.[6]

The second element of Adler's vision of teaching involves coaching or su-pervised practice. Coaching may entail such activities as "walking" a student through the solution to a problem or providing continuous feedback on pro-nunciation as the student tries to deliver a message in a new language. The in-tention here is to stimulate the development of learning *skills*—reading, writing, speaking, listening, problem solving, calculating, exercising critical judgment, and the like. Since the most effective coaching occurs between two people, teachers should provide ample opportunities for one-on-one interac-tions while other students work on their own. In certain instances, coaching may involve demonstrating or modeling a skill. A key to coaching is sensing when a student is ready to take the risk involved in trying to exhibit a skill in public. Teacher sensitivity in delivering criticism and respecting student effort will help promote coaching, particularly with reluctant learners. Timing is an-other critical feature of successful coaching—it does little good to provide per-formance feedback to students long after the performance.

Socratic questioning is the third component of Adler's vision. Discussions of books (not textbooks) and works of art that both teacher and students have experienced are used to pursue the goal of enlarged student understanding of ideas and values. Seminars are recommended as an ideal setting for Socratic questioning. Teachers and students converse informally, sharing opinions and debating issues. Unlike didactic instruction, Socratic questioning does not pre-sume that teachers possess all the answers. The teacher's role, according to Adler, is to prime "the pump of discussion by asking leading questions and pursuing the answers given to them by asking more questions."[7] Since it is dif-ficult to ask leading questions while simultaneously monitoring the direction in which the discussion is going, Adler recommends that there be two discussion leaders. Seminars at the secondary level should occur no more than once or twice a week and should last a minimum of 90 minutes. Effective seminar lead-ers are able to accomplish three central tasks:

- Ask a series of questions that define the discussion and give it direction
- Examine the answers by trying to draw out the reasons for them or their impli-cations

- Engage the participants in two-way talk when their views appear to be in conflict[8]

Adler's vision of teaching requires teachers who possess a repertoire of instructional skills, sound judgment regarding student understanding of material, the capacity to communicate effectively to individuals and groups, and expertise in a subject matter area. The next vision focuses on the ability of teachers to motivate students to learn.

Teaching for Support, Success, and Self-esteem

Like Adler's approach, motivational teaching begins with teachers who are skilled. In a summary of research on motivational teaching, Raymond Wlodkowski identifies four essential teacher qualities: expertise, empathy, enthusiasm, and clarity.[9] This approach presumes that good organization, effective classroom control, and thorough coverage of subject matter are not sufficient to ensure that students benefit from instruction—teachers must also be able to make the learning experience interesting and meaningful.

Referring to motivational teaching as an "experiential approach," Horowitz contends that teachers indirectly promote students' acquisition of knowledge through experiences that capture their imagination.[10] Others stress the direct connection between academic achievement and teacher efforts to boost students' self-esteem,[11] providing them with opportunities to succeed, treating them with respect and warmth, and permitting them a measure of independence.

Perhaps no exponent of motivational teaching has achieved greater visibility than William Purkey. Purkey's approach, known as invitational teaching, is rooted in perceptual psychology. As Purkey and colleague John Novak state,

> Rather than viewing people as objects to be stimulated, shaped, modified, reinforced, and conditioned, or as captives of unconscious urges or unfulfilled desires, the perceptual tradition views people as they see themselves, others, and the world. It takes as its starting point the notion that each person is a conscious agent: he or she experiences, interprets, constructs, decides, acts, and is ultimately responsible for his or her actions.[12]

Purkey's vision of invitational teaching consists of three major skill areas; being ready, being with, and following through. The first encompasses all activities related to preparing oneself and the learning environment. The learning environment that is truly inviting to students is a "clean, comfortable, and safe setting in which people [students] who work in schools feel welcome and at ease."[13] Students do not feel they are facing an obstacle course intended to eliminate the unfit. Thus, in preparing themselves to be "inviting," teachers are counseled to examine their presuppositions about students—stereotypes, prejudices, beliefs about motives, and the like. It is unlikely that a teacher will be effectively inviting if he or she believes that a student's background or race may prevent him or her from taking full advantage of instruction.

Once prepared, teachers should focus on being *with* their students, a task that obviously entails more than simply occupying common physical space. Effectively being *with* students is largely a function of a teacher's communications skill—both verbal and nonverbal. Teachers need to send attractive invitations to students—invitations to take part in learning, invitations to express concerns, invitations to take risks without fear of losing support. An environment full of such invitations is likely to foster student feelings of acceptance, which in turn can stimulate self-esteem and, eventually, achievement. Purkey and Novak delineate seven critical elements of being with students. These are summarized in Table 3.1.

The third skill area in invitational teaching is following through. When an invitation fails to produce desired results—for example, when students do not become fully engaged in a discussion—teachers must examine the reasons why and initiate strategies to increase the probability of future success. Purkey and Novak are concerned that teachers may quit trying to reach students after a few attempts and convince themselves that the problem resides solely with the students. While invitational teachers may not achieve success in every instance, they never give up on a student.

The vision of teaching of Purkey, Novak, and other motivation specialists goes beyond instructional technique to encompass all types of interaction between teachers and learners; it values respect for human beings over concern for efficiency and effectiveness. Motivational teaching is based on the capacity of teachers to promote academic achievement by stimulating the interest of stu-

Table 3.1 Keys to "Being With" Students for Invitational Teaching

Skill Area	*Skill Indicators*
Developing trust	Eliminate surprises Follow through on agreements Watch body language Share feelings honestly
Reaching each student	Avoid random patterns of interaction with students Set aside time to listen to individual students Encourage students to write messages to the teacher Know something positive to say about each student
Reading situations	Attend carefully to what students say Look beyond students' overt behavior
Making invitations attractive	Don't say one thing while meaning another Don't rush students to respond Make praise realistic
Ensuring delivery	Communicate invitations clearly Follow up to make sure students "receive" an invitation
Negotiating	Inquire about rejected invitations Generate alternative courses of action
Handling rejection	Don't take rejection personally

SOURCE: William Watson Purkey and John M. Novak, *Inviting School Success,* 2nd ed. (Belmont, Calif: Wadsworth, 1984), pp. 58–69.

dents and by communicating their own caring to them. Madeline Hunter's vision of teaching also recognizes the role of motivation in academic achievement, but it places far greater emphasis on lesson design and instructional expertise.

☆ Hunter's Clinical Teaching

Madeline Hunter's vision of teaching has gained wide acceptance around the United States as a sound basis for teacher professional development. Supporters claim that the skills involved in her Clinical Teaching workshops should be part of every pre-service teacher-training program. Known variously as Target Teaching, the UCLA model, and ITIP (Instructional Theory in Practice), Clinical Teaching is based on two central beliefs.[14] First, teachers are decision makers. Second, research-based data on factors affecting student learning can help teachers make sound instructional decisions. The key is knowing under what conditions to use which research-based findings—or what Hunter calls "propositional knowledge."

From various studies of teaching Hunter has derived a set of propositions.[15] These propositions encompass "principles of learning" regarding student participation, motivation, reinforcement, retention, and transfer of learning. In addition, there are propositions dealing with teaching to objectives, determining the correct level of difficulty of material, and monitoring and adjusting instruction. The heart of Clinical Teaching, however, is the well-designed lesson.

Lessons should start with an introductory statement—or *anticipatory set*—concerning the new learning to be presented. This is the time when teachers should engage student interest and link the current lesson with previous learning. Next comes the specification of instructional objectives for the lesson and their purpose in the overall scheme of student development. The body of the lesson contains the information or new learning targeted for student acquisition. Following this input, teachers provide modeling in the form of skill demonstration, illustrations of the finished product, and the like. Then it is time to check whether or not students understand the new material. If they do, teachers should provide students with opportunities to demonstrate their understanding while receiving immediate feedback—or what Hunter calls "guided practice." The lesson continues with some activity in which students share their impressions of what they have learned, and concludes with independent practice, in the form of either seatwork or homework.

With the increasing popularity of Clinical Teaching has also come criticism.[16] Some claim that the prescribed format of Hunter's lessons stifles creativity. Others say the approach is really designed as a basis for evaluating teachers. Hunter contends that Clinical Teaching is designed to free teachers so they can innovate; if the principles of her approach are used to evaluate teachers, it is only because school leaders have misunderstood her intentions.

Clinical Teaching places primary emphasis on the capacity of teachers to use research-based propositions in making decisions about the design and delivery of instruction. The vision of teaching based on Benjamin Bloom's mastery learning model has a similar emphasis.

Bloom's Teaching for Mastery

Mastery learning derives from the conceptual work of John Carroll. Carroll maintained that students will master instructional objectives to the extent that they are both permitted and willing to invest the time necessary to learn the content.[17] Therefore, the time it takes each student to learn will vary depending on such factors as prior student achievement and attitudes. The important implication of this model, of course, is that given enough time most students can learn most content. Bloom designed his model to provide students with adequate opportunities (time) and incentives to learn. It has four key elements:

- Cues—teacher efforts to explain and present learning activities clearly
- Reinforcements—praise, blame, encouragement, rewards, and punishments used to sustain learning
- Feedback and correctives—provisions for assuring that prerequisite content has been mastered before moving on to new content
- Participation—student engagement in learning tasks[18]

Bloom's vision of teaching is guided by the belief that students should not be exposed to content for which they are unprepared. Since students are presumed to learn at different rates, teaching for mastery requires considerable instructional flexibility. It can be accomplished through individualized instruction and teacher tutoring; those who subscribe to Bloom's vision are not apt to rely heavily on large-group or "massed" instruction. Coverage of content is less important than mastery of content. As a result, teaching for mastery requires the continuous monitoring of student progress. Arbitrary barriers to progress, such as student grouping by age and use of cumulative tests, must be modified or eliminated.

Various forms of teaching for mastery are used in elementary and middle level schools throughout the United States. One form—Individually Prescribed Instruction—provides teachers with individualized curriculum materials based on highly specific behavioral objectives.[19] Students work independently while the teacher monitors their progress and provides personalized assistance. Johnson City, New York, has gained national recognition for its comprehensive mastery learning program and impressive improvements in student achievement. An observer would see a Johnson City teacher who has been trained to teach for mastery perform in the following ways:

- Assesses precognitive skills formally or informally
  - Anticipates special problems and corrects them
  - Provides opportunities for students to review, relearn, or learn the necessary precognitive skills
  - Creates a positive learning environment, models caring and trust, and assures students they will work together to learn
  - Provides appropriate cues and overview of task or unit
  - Connects new learning with prior learning and gives reasons for studying the task or unit
  - Beams instruction using alternative learning approaches; creates images; uses

appropriate audiovisuals; uses clear verbal instruction; and models learning by thinking aloud

- Provides appropriate opportunities for student participation and simulation activities
- Provides guided practice; circulates in the room; asks questions to determine understanding; has students help students; and provides opportunities for small-group and individual discussions
- Continually assesses formally and informally how well students are learning
- Uses assessment to determine which objectives still need to be learned, what correctives will be needed, and what teaching strategies should be altered
- Provides a variety of correctives; has students helping students; provides special help sessions; and uses alternative learning approaches and materials appropriate for each individual
- Creates opportunities for students to have in-depth, high-level cognitive experiences and opportunities for independent inquiry
- Allows students to continue to next task or unit after demonstrated performance
- Provides opportunities for students to demonstrate new levels of achievement and alters grades to reflect new understandings
- States unifying ideas and specific objectives for each unit; estimates and publishes the amount of time necessary to learn each unit
- Identifies each objective as a concept, procedure, or fact, and designs appropriate instructional strategies to teach the different types of objectives
- Gives formative tests that are aligned and matched with the stated objectives
- Gives individual correctives that reflect an analysis of what each student needs to learn
- Creates inquiry activities and exercises to foster in-depth, high-level cognitive experiences[20]

While Bloom and his disciples have focused on ways to individualize instruction, other researchers have concentrated on direct instruction, or the delivery of instruction to groups of students. Much of the data supporting the direct-instruction vision of teaching derive from the so-called teacher-effectiveness or process-product research. It is an increasingly popular approach.

✗ Direct Instruction

It seems hard to believe that prior to the late 1950s those who studied teachers and teaching tended to avoid looking at student outcomes. With the rise of teacher-effectiveness research, however, observers began to identify specific teacher behaviors that were highly correlated with increases in student learning. Several excellent summaries of this research are available,[21] and all acknowledge the vital role of direct instruction in the acquisition of basic skills.

Direct instruction is defined as "an academic, teacher-centered focus with little student choice of activity that utilizes large groups, factual questions, and controlled practice."[22] The basic format for direct instruction is quite similar to Hunter's model of a lesson. The teacher controls the pace, sequence, and content of direct instruction. In addition, the direct instruction model requires great care in expressing expectations, conducting group question-and-answer sessions, and managing student behavior. Considerable empirical research backs up the need for care in each of these areas.

It should come as no surprise that teachers tend to get from students what they expect to receive. This tendency has been referred to as the "self-fulfilling prophecy." Direct instruction is well suited to the continuous communication of teacher expectations. Good and Brophy maintain that teachers' expectations affect the way they treat their students, and that, over time, the way they treat students affects the amount that students learn.[23] The researchers identify a set of basic teacher expectations, including the following:

- Teachers should expect all students to meet at least the minimum specified objectives.
- Teachers should expect students to enjoy learning.
- The teacher should assume good intentions and a positive self-concept.
- The teacher should expect to be obeyed.[24]

One aspect of direct instruction where teacher expectations have been found particularly influential is questioning. The question is one of the basic tools of teaching—the equivalent of a saw to a carpenter. The way a teacher conducts question-and-answer sessions can have a considerable impact on student achievement.[25] For example, teachers may emphasize the slowness of some students to grasp content by asking them fewer questions, asking them less challenging questions, and waiting a shorter time for them to reply. Over time these students may begin to think of themselves as less capable. Faced with the frustration of trying to provide answers in a few seconds, they may cease trying completely, thereby confirming low teacher expectations.

Susan Barnes has extracted six recommendations from teacher-effectiveness research that are aimed at minimizing the likelihood that teacher questioning will inhibit student learning. She urges teachers to:

- Vary the level of difficulty of questions for all students
- Probe, rephrase, and prompt in order to draw out responses
- Wait for some response (no response should not be an option)
- Provide an answer to the question
- Ask process questions (How did you get that answer?)
- Stress students' understanding of the meaning of questions[26]

Classroom management is another aspect of direct instruction that has received considerable attention. One reason why direct instruction often is preferred to small-group and individualized instruction is because teacher control of student behavior is easier in a large-group format. Students are less likely to spend great amounts of time *off task*. If there is one consistent finding in teacher-effectiveness research, it is that student achievement is directly related to the amount of time students are engaged in learning—or *on task*.[27]

To say that control of student behavior is easier with direct instruction than with other methods is not to say, of course, that it is easy. Teachers must develop skill in articulating clear behavioral expectations, monitoring student conduct in all parts of the room, and providing consequences for disruptive behavior. Effective classroom managers create routines for handling various situations—such as distributing materials or dealing with students' entering class late—that could occupy large amounts of instructional time. They make certain that students understand what is expected of them during transitions between different phases of lessons. Perhaps most important, teachers are careful to reinforce students when they behave appropriately. Research strongly suggests that excessive reliance on punishment when students misbehave can be counterproductive.[28]

Besides teacher expectations, questioning, and classroom management, the teacher-effectiveness research addresses other issues: teacher praise and feedback, homework, student grouping strategies, and teacher modeling. While the heart of this body of research is direct instruction, it also makes reference to the benefits of cooperative learning among students and independent work. The major limitation of teacher-effectiveness research is that student achievement on standardized tests in basic skill areas has tended to be the sole student outcome used to judge which teachers are most effective. There is less certainty concerning effective teacher behaviors associated with higher-order cognitive learning and content besides elementary reading, language arts, and arithmetic.

It should also be noted that direct instruction has been associated with the least effective as well as the most effective teaching of basic skills.[29] The implication here may be that the costs of doing direct instruction poorly are greater than the costs of doing some other approach to instruction poorly.

DEVELOPING AN INTEGRATED VISION OF TEACHING EXCELLENCE

To say that no one approach to teaching is invariably the best is not to justify every teacher simply doing whatever he or she wants. Teachers have access to research and others' professional experience to inform them of preferred courses of action. One value of having a vision of teaching is that it guides us in selecting data relevant to continuous instructional improvement. This process inevitably produces adjustments in our visions and our thinking, as we sift through new data and experience. Without a vision, we can only make arbitrary guesses about how best to meet the needs of students. The lack of a vision may help explain why some educators find themselves vulnerable to instructional fads. Not knowing what they are striving to achieve, it is hard for them to reject a new sales pitch.

Five visions of teaching have so far been presented. Each has a great deal to recommend it. For the purposes of this book, however, certain key features of each vision have been integrated. The intention is not to create an "ultimate" vision of teaching, but to identify common situations in which teacher skill and judgment appear to be crucial to student achievement and development. Such a *situational* vision is consistent with the notion of situational competence advanced in Chapter 1 as a worthy basis for assessing the quality of school leadership. This integrated vision is referred to as a vision of teaching excellence—rather than, say, a vision of teaching effectiveness—because excellence connotes unlimited potential for growth. While many visions seem to be based on mastery of minimum competencies, this one recognizes the continuing need for professionals to grow.

Over and above others mentioned in this chapter, one central assumption underlies this our vision. Without talented teachers—professionals possessing subject matter expertise, communications skills, pedagogical abilities, and sound judgment—it is unlikely that any vision of teaching can be seriously pursued. Years ago it may have been unnecessary to worry about the quality of those entering and remaining in the teaching profession, but such is no longer the case. There is strong evidence that the profession is attracting less capable college graduates.[30] Many states, in fact, have resorted to testing prospective teachers to make certain they possess basic literacy skills. Because of this, the recruitment, selection, and retention of talented teachers should be a major focus of concern for school leaders. This will be discussed further in Chapters 6 and 7.

Assuming, then, that we have bright teachers capable of growing professionally, our vision encompasses six central teaching situations: planning, instruction, classroom management, progress monitoring, clinical assistance, and care giving. These situations call for more than a specific skill or set of behaviors. They represent professional spheres of responsibility requiring sound judgment and frequent introspection and encompass professional norms and organizational expectations. Figure 3.1 presents this vision of teaching excellence.

Planning is an obvious starting point. Without careful planning, teachers are unlikely to accomplish all that is expected of them. Why? Teachers have a brief period of time and limited resources to reach students. Therefore, they must be clear about the content of their lessons and their daily instructional objectives. Lessons need to be well organized to fit the time and resources available. Plans also are useful to guide the periodic assessment of students to determine whether content is being learned. By deciding on objectives and assessment procedures in advance, teachers are more likely to provide instruction that is focused and clear. Objectives must be determined in accordance with district and state curriculum guidelines. Planning should always take into account the abilities and backgrounds of the individual students who make up the class.

Instruction—or the delivery of subject matter—is the second key teaching situation, and it encompasses a variety of modes. At different times teachers may be called upon to introduce new content, review and re-teach previously introduced material, and demonstrate skills and procedures. Instruction also entails communicating clear expectations regarding the quality of academic work, giving reasons why students need to learn certain content, and modeling proper attitudes toward learning. Good instruction demands facility in pacing, questioning, and reiterating key points. Capable teachers know the value of alerting students to what is coming and providing time to practice new skills

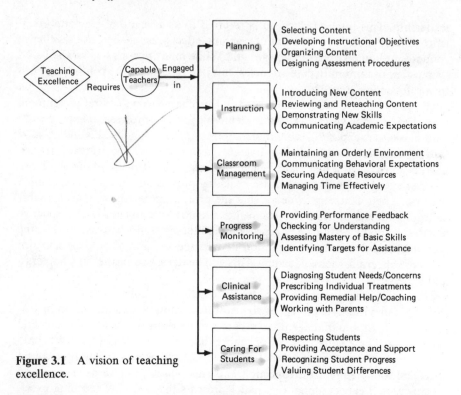

	Planning	⎰ Selecting Content ⎱ Developing Instructional Objectives ⎰ Organizing Content ⎱ Designing Assessment Procedures

Teaching Excellence — Requires — Capable Teachers — Engaged in

Planning
{ Selecting Content
Developing Instructional Objectives
Organizing Content
Designing Assessment Procedures }

Instruction
{ Introducing New Content
Reviewing and Reteaching Content
Demonstrating New Skills
Communicating Academic Expectations }

Classroom Management
{ Maintaining an Orderly Environment
Communicating Behavioral Expectations
Securing Adequate Resources
Managing Time Effectively }

Progress Monitoring
{ Providing Performance Feedback
Checking for Understanding
Assessing Mastery of Basic Skills
Identifying Targets for Assistance }

Clinical Assistance
{ Diagnosing Student Needs/Concerns
Prescribing Individual Treatments
Providing Remedial Help/Coaching
Working with Parents }

Caring For Students
{ Respecting Students
Providing Acceptance and Support
Recognizing Student Progress
Valuing Student Differences }

Figure 3.1   A vision of teaching excellence.

and information. It is essential that teachers possess a repertoire of instructional strategies to help them address the unique demands of particular subjects, instructional objectives, and groups of students.

To make certain that a minimum of instructional time is lost, good classroom management is vital. Classroom management has been defined as "the provisions and procedures necessary to create and maintain an environment in which instruction and learning can occur."[31] This includes all teacher efforts to ensure an orderly classroom, the development of rules and consequences for disobedience, and monitoring of student conduct. Once rules have been developed, they must be taught to students in the form of behavioral expectations. Disorderly classrooms often are those in which students are unclear about how they are expected to behave. Classroom management encompasses more than just the handling of student behavior, however. Teachers must make certain that students have the resources needed to benefit fully from instruction. These resources range from writing instruments and paper to books written at an appropriate level of difficulty. Teachers also must manage time effectively so that students have maximum exposure to instruction. This task involves making smooth transitions between instructional activities and minimizing interruptions.

To determine whether instructional objectives are being achieved, student progress must be closely monitored. Considerable instructional time may be wasted if a teacher checks student learning infrequently. Some students may not have understood certain key concepts or skills necessary to benefit from subsequent instruction. By failing to check student understanding, teachers may proceed to cover subject matter for which these students are unprepared. The vision of teaching excellence presented here holds that students should receive continuous feedback on their performance. Through classroom questions, homework, tests, and one-on-one contacts, teachers can determine on a regular basis whether students are understanding lesson material and mastering essential objectives. When particular students have not understood or mastered material, teachers must see that remedial assistance is provided, so that they do not fall further behind their classmates or become disinterested.

Helping students may require teachers to provide assistance of a clinical nature. This necessitates dealing with the needs of an individual, rather than a group. To diagnose student needs and prescribe appropriate instructional treatments, teachers may have to investigate a student's background and school history. Contact with his or her parents may be needed to obtain information and enlist support at home for remedial or corrective strategies. Clinical assistance may involve instruction, coaching, and counseling outside of the regular classroom context. Contemporary schools typically provide a variety of referral opportunities for students requiring extraordinary assistance. These include resource rooms, school psychologists, Chapter 1 programs, and special learning centers. Needless to say, however, the quality of help provided from such referrals depends on the accuracy of the original diagnosis and the ability of regular teachers to make appropriate adjustments in classroom instruction.

The final component of the integrated vision of teaching excellence presented here relates to the affective dimensions of instruction—how students are cared for. Without the sense that they are cared for, many students may be unable to take full advantage of learning opportunities, however rich and plentiful. Caring is manifested in different ways. Do teachers respect students as people, avoiding techniques like public embarrassment and arbitrary punishment? Do they communicate acceptance and support to students? Such communication is not always accomplished with words. Setting aside time to listen to students often is a powerful nonverbal way of conveying acceptance.

Recognizing and reinforcing students when they perform well or try hard is another important aspect of caring. Some teachers too easily fall into the habit of taking student achievement for granted. When they do comment on student performance, it is usually critical. "Catching" students doing well seems to be much more effective practice than interceding only during inappropriate or inadequate performance.

Another key element in a caring environment is the valuing of difference. Today's teachers frequently confront classes made up of students from different races, ethnic groups, family circumstances, and socioeconomic levels. Some may possess handicaps or communicate in a language other than English. Teachers are in a key position to influence the way students view their differences. For the sake of healthy development, it is critical that students are encouraged to regard their differences as sources of strength rather than shame or self-consciousness.

This is the integrated vision of teaching in brief—a vision informed by a variety of contemporary models and research. The primary purpose of this book, however, is not to describe a vision of teaching but to inquire about the nature of school leadership needed to pursue such a vision. The next chapter reviews the recent research on instructional leadership in an effort to generate a vision of school leadership compatible with the goal of continuous instructional improvement.

STUDY QUESTIONS

1. Identify a vision of teaching not discussed in the chapter. Discuss its positive and negative aspects.
2. Try to express your own vision of teaching in writing. Reflect on your own experiences, including effective teachers with whom you have studied.
3. Many studies of teaching effectiveness report that "direct instruction" is preferable to other approaches. Why do you think "direct instruction" is so successful?
4. Select one teaching-effectiveness study to read. What method is used to investigate teaching effectiveness? How is effectiveness defined? What are the implications of the findings for school leadership?
5. Are you able to distinguish among different visions of teaching? Select several teachers to observe. How would you describe their approach to teaching? Try to avoid using judgmental terms. Describe what you see as objectively as possible.

NOTES

1. Alan R. Tom, *Teaching as a Moral Craft* (New York: Longman, 1984), pp. 120–144.
2. Bruce Joyce and Marsha Weil, *Models of Teaching* (Englewood Cliffs, N.J.: Prentice/Hall International, 1980).
3. "The Effective Teacher," Position Paper, Teacher Education Conference Board, October, 1981.
4. For a thorough discussion of the declining quality of prospective teachers, see Daniel L. Duke, *Teaching–The Imperiled Profession* (Albany, N.Y.: State University of New York Press, 1984).
5. Mortimer J. Adler, *The Paideia Program* (New York: Macmillan, 1984).
6. *Ibid.*, pp. 51–54.
7. *Ibid.*, p. 18.
8. *Ibid.*, p. 23.
9. Raymond J. Wlodkowski, *Enhancing Adult Motivation to Learn* (San Francisco: Jossey-Bass, 1985), p. 17.
10. R. Horowitz, "Effects of the Open Classroom," *Educational Environments and Effects: Evaluation, Policy, and Productivity,* Herbert J. Walberg (Ed.), (Berkeley: McCutchan, 1979).
11. William Watson Purkey, *Self-Concept and School Achievement* (Englewood Cliffs, N.J.: Prentice-Hall, 1970).
12. William Watson Purkey and John M. Novak, *Inviting School Success,* 2nd ed. (Belmont, Calif.: Wadsworth, 1984), p. 22.
13. *Ibid.*, p. 57

14. Madeline Hunter, "What's Wrong with Madeline Hunter?" *Educational Leadership,* Vol. 42, No. 5 (February 1985), p. 57.
15. Madeline Hunter, *Mastery Teaching* (El Segundo, Calif.: Tip, 1983).
16. Madeline Hunter, "What's Wrong with Madeline Hunter?"
17. John B. Carroll, "A Model of School Learning," *Teachers College Record,* Vol. 64, No. 4 (Spring 1963), pp. 723–733.
18. Geneva D. Haertel, Herbert J. Walberg, and Thomas Weinstein, "Psychological Models of Educational Performance: A Theoretical Synthesis of Constructs," *Review of Educational Research,* Vol. 53, No. 1 (Spring 1983), pp. 79–82.
19. Joyce and Weil, *Models of Teaching,* pp. 447–453.
20. Stephen F. Hamilton and Albert Mamary, "Assessing the Effectiveness of Program Delivery," *NASSP Bulletin,* Vol. 67, No. 465 (October 1983), pp. 42–43.
21. Carolyn Denham and Ann Lieberman (Eds.), *Time to Learn* (Sacramento: California Commission for Teacher Preparation and Licensing, 1980); Barak Rosenshine, "Teaching Functions in Instructional Programs," *The Elementary School Journal,* Vol. 83 (1983), pp. 335–351.
22. Janet Kierstead, "Direct Instruction and Experiential Approaches: Are They Really Mutually Exclusive?" *Educational Leadership,* Vol. 42, No. 8 (May 1985), p. 25.
23. Thomas L. Good and Jere E. Brophy, *Looking in Classrooms,* 3rd ed. (New York: Harper & Row, 1984), p. 94.
24. *Ibid.,* pp. 112–119.
25. *Ibid.,* pp. 104–105.
26. Susan Barnes, *Synthesis of Selected Research on Teaching Findings* (Austin, Tex.: Research & Development Center for Teacher Education, 1981).
27. Charles W. Fisher, David C. Berliner, Nikola N. Filby, Richard Marliave, Leonard S. Cohen, and Marilyn M. Dishaw, "Teaching Behaviors, Academic Learning Time, and Student Achievement: An Overview," *Time to Learn,* Carolyn Denham and Ann Lieberman (Eds.) (Sacramento: California Commission for Teacher Preparation & Licensing, 1980).
28. Good and Brophy, pp. 213–218.
29. Thomas L. Good and Douglas A. Grouws, "Teaching Effects: A Process-Product Study in Fourth-Grade Mathematics Classrooms," *Journal of Teacher Education,* Vol. 28 (May–June 1977), pp. 49–54.
30. Duke, *Teaching—The Imperiled Profession,* pp. 8–22.
31. Daniel L. Duke (Ed.), *Classroom Management,* The Seventy-eighth Yearbook of the National Society for the Study of Education (Chicago: University of Chicago Press, 1979), p. xii.

CHAPTER 4

A VISION OF
INSTRUCTIONAL
LEADERSHIP

Those who observe and write about schools have advocated certain styles of leadership for decades, but only in recent years have researchers attempted to link school leadership to specific indicators of effectiveness. The school-effectiveness studies that began appearing in the 1970s suggested that leadership in schools with high or steadily improving student test scores differed from leadership in schools with low or steadily declining student test scores. Initially, these reports did little more than proclaim that school leadership was a factor to be considered in explaining differences among schools in student achievement. Subsequent efforts were directed at identifying more precisely what leaders in effective schools actually did to influence the quality of learning and teaching. Thanks in large part to this research, it is now possible to isolate a set of key leadership functions associated with good instruction. This chapter will trace the evolution of recent research on instructional leadership and develop a vision of such leadership that is compatible with the vision of effective teaching presented in the last chapter.

EARLY SCHOOL-EFFECTIVENESS STUDIES

Researchers conducting the first studies of school effectiveness were disturbed by the fact that two schools of similar size and student makeup could experience substantially different levels of student achievement. Such a situation seemed to contradict the prevailing belief that schools could do little to counter the impact of student background on achievement. Selecting small samples of schools—typically elementary schools serving inner-city children—these researchers tried to identify consistent differences between more effective and less effective schools. Relying primarily on case-study methodology, they conducted on-site observations and interviews. Since they had few preconceived ideas of what factors might differentiate these schools, they were usually not in a position to collect in-depth descriptive data on any particular factors or to indicate how these factors actually influenced student achievement. Instead they tended to generate lists of somewhat general characteristics of effective schools. Virtually every one of the school-effectiveness studies, however, cited some aspect of school leadership as a critical characteristic.

For example, Wilbur Brookover and Lawrence Lezotte investigated six elementary schools with improving test scores and two elementary schools with declining test scores.[1] They found that the improving schools differed from the declining schools in terms of school structure, climate, and leadership. Principals of improving schools were more likely to be instructional leaders and disciplinarians. They assumed responsibility for evaluating the achievement of instructional objectives. Principals of declining schools appeared to be more permissive and to stress informal relationships with teachers. They placed more emphasis on public relations than their counterparts in improving schools. Brookover and Lezotte also noted that principals and teachers in improving schools were more likely to *believe* that students were capable of meeting academic expectations, even though the actual levels of student achievement were higher in the declining schools!

There have been a number of excellent reviews of the early school-effectiveness studies. Several of them focus specifically on the findings related to school or instructional leadership. Table 4.1 summarizes the conclusions of three reviews.

While the terms used differ somewhat, the reviews tend to agree on certain common characteristics of school leadership in effective elementary schools. Generalizations should be made with caution, however. It is uncertain to what extent the findings apply to secondary schools or even to suburban elementary schools. The basis for judging school effectiveness in these studies is quite narrow—student performance on standardized tests of basic skills achievement. Finally, none of them directly address the issue of causation.[2] As a result, it is not known whether the configurations of leadership characteristics presented in Table 4.1 have created effective schools or been created by them. In other words, the studies do not prove which came first, student achievement or

Table 4.1   Reviews of Findings Related to School Leadership in Early School-Effectiveness Studies

Principal Characteristics Associated with Effective Schools		
Kroeze	*Shoemaker and Fraser*	*Sweeney*
Goal emphasis	Assertive, achievement-oriented leadership	Coordination of instructional programs
Coordination and organization	Orderly, purposeful, and peaceful school climate	Emphasis on achievement
Power and discretionary decision making	High expectations for staff and pupils	Frequent evaluation of student progress
Human relations	Well-designed instructional objectives and evaluation system	Orderly environment Establishment of instructional strategies Support for teachers

SOURCES: David J. Kroeze, "Effective Principals as Instructional Leaders: New Directions for Research," *Administrator's Notebook,* Vol. 30, No. 9 (1984).
Joan Shoemaker and Hugh W. Fraser, "What Principals Can Do: Some Implications from Studies of Effective Schooling," *Phi Delta Kappan,* Vol. 63, No. 3 (November 1981), pp. 178–182.
James Sweeney, "Research Synthesis on Effective School Leadership," *Educational Leadership,* Vol. 39, No. 5 (February 1982), pp. 346–252.

able leadership. Despite these concerns, this early school-effectiveness research strongly suggested that leadership was at least one important factor in the quality of teaching and learning in schools.

EFFORTS TO CONCEPTUALIZE INSTRUCTIONAL LEADERSHIP

Following the first generation of school-effectiveness studies came a series of attempts to specify and validate the exact nature of leadership behaviors associated with relatively high levels of student achievement. Two terms have been used as convenient labels for these behaviors—*instructional management* and *instructional leadership*. The latter term will be used in this book to describe what Wynn DeBevoise calls "those actions that a principal takes, or delegates to others, to promote growth in student learning."[3]

The typical approach to conceptualizing instructional leadership has been for researchers to review first-generation school-effectiveness studies and identify frequently cited characteristics of principals from effective schools. Lists of these are then used to generate items for rating scales or surveys of instructional leadership. These instruments, in turn, are administered to various groups—including teachers and school administrators—and further refined. The result is a set of reasonably valid and reliable tools for measuring the extent to which particular school leaders are perceived to manifest characteristics associated with instructional leadership. Table 4.2 presents the main categories of instructional leadership behaviors described by four groups of researchers.

One of the most popular instruments for assessing instructional management behavior is the Instructional Management Rating Scale (IMRS) of Philip Hallinger and his colleagues.[4] The IMRS is based on descriptions of instructional management behavior derived from principal questionnaires, school documents related to curriculum and instruction, and research studies of school effectiveness. It contains 71 items organized into ten subscales representing distinct job functions related to instructional management. Figure 4.1 provides a graphic representation of instructional management. Specific behaviors are divided into one of three key dimensions—mission definition, management of curriculum and instruction, and school climate promotion.

When Hallinger and his colleagues administered the IMRS in one California school district, they were surprised to find that it saw principals engaged in frequent instructional management activity. Hallinger speculated that this finding probably was the result of central office policies and procedures specifically designed to promote instructional management. These included the following:

- The superintendent made explicit his expectation that principals were to be highly involved in instructional leadership activities.
- Elementary schools each were assigned a vice principal to relieve the principals of noninstructional duties.
- Many teachers and all principals received in-service training in instructional strategies, lesson design, and classroom management.

Table 4.2 Efforts to Identify Instructional Leadership Skills

Hallinger et al.	Jackson, Logsdon, Taylor	Patterson	Daresh and Liu
Defines the mission	Establishes school goals and standards	Helps individual staff	Provides staff development
Frames goals		Helps groups of teachers	Conducts teacher supervision and evaluation
Communicates goals			
Manages curriculum and instruction	Establishes positive school climate and expectations for success	Is concerned about professional growth of teachers	Facilitates instruction
Knows C & I	Establishes curriculum and instruction that emphasize the basic skills	Develops curriculum	Acquires resources and maintains facilities
Coordinates curriculum		Supports staff improvement	Resolves student problems
Supervises and evaluates			
Monitors progress	Establishes coordination linkages and parent-community support	Conducts staff conferences on curriculum	
Promotes school climates		Conducts special-purpose conferences	
Sets standards		Counsels pupils	
Sets expectations		Helps staff understand pupils and central office	
Protects time		Is concerned with teacher suggestions, problems, and requests	
Promotes improvement			

SOURCES: Philip Hallinger, Joseph Murphy, Marsha Weil, Richard P. Mesa, and Alexis Mitman, "Identifying the Specific Practices, Behaviors for Principals," *NASSP Bulletin*, Vol. 67, No. 463 (May 1983), pp. 83–91.
Shirley A. Jackson, David M. Logsdon, and Nancy E. Taylor, "Instructional Leaadership Behaviors," *Urban Education*, Vol. 18, No. 1 (April 1983), pp. 59–70.
J. P. Patterson, *A Descriptive Analysis of the Instructional Leadership Activities of Elementary Principals*, doctoral dissertation, University of Oregon, 1977.
John C. Daresh and Ching-Jan Liu, "High School Principals' Perceptions of Their Instructional Leadership Behavior," a paper presented at the annual conference of the American Educational Research Association, 1985.

Figure 4.1   Instructional Management Function

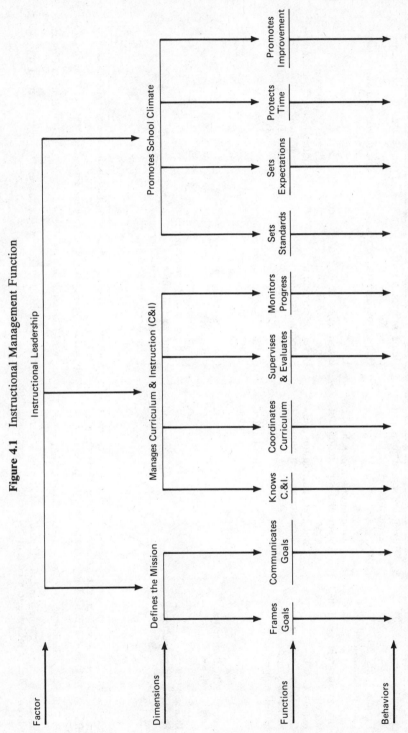

SOURCE: Philip Hallinger, Joseph Murphy, Marsha Weil, Richard P. Mesa, and Alexis Mitman, "Identifying the Specific Practices, Behaviors for Principles," *NASSP Bulletin*, Vol. 67, No. 463 (May 1983), p. 86.

- All principals received training in supervision and teacher evaluation. Practices in these areas were monitored by district office personnel.
- Principals were involved in the process of curriculum realignment.
- School goals of the principals were collected by the district office.
- District-wide proficiency standards were developed and linked to the testing instruments used by the district.
- Administrative promotions were based, in part, on instructional expertise.[5]

The IMRS was also used to assess the instructional management behavior of a parochial high school principal and his administrative team.[6] This study found that instructional management can be provided by others besides the principal. A key function of the principal is to see that instructional management responsibilities are judiciously delegated. While this particular principal relied heavily on his assistant principals, he did not seem to make great use of department chairs for instructional management purposes.

A second effort to assess instructional leadership behaviors was undertaken by Shirley Jackson, David Logsdon, and Nancy Taylor.[7] They initially developed a 41-item School Instructional Climate Survey (SICS), based on findings drawn from the school-effectiveness research. Survey questions were grouped into the following categories: (1) establishing school goals and standards, (2) establishing a positive school climate and expectations for success, (3) establishing a curriculum and instruction that emphasize the basic skills, and (4) establishing coordination linkages and parent-community support. The SICS was administered to 97 teachers and eight principals in eight urban elementary schools. Half of the schools were defined as instructionally effective, the other half as instructionally ineffective. To be effective, a school had to have at least half of its students at or above the 50th percentile on achievement tests in basic skills (California Test of Basic Skills).

Seven items related to school leadership were found to differentiate effective and ineffective schools. In effective schools, the principal was likely to be found in the halls interacting with students. He or she was available to assist teachers in problem solving, and was prepared to provide constructive feedback after classroom observations. Student achievement in basic skills was given recognition, discipline policies were clearly defined and reasonable, and school facilities were clean. In the ineffective schools, principals rarely met with individual teachers to discuss how best to accomplish instructional objectives. They seemed generally more permissive and less likely to monitor teacher performance closely. The researchers concluded:

> Not a "pal," this administrator [the effective principal] is a leader who expects and demands achievement regardless of student background, provides needed services and training, monitors test scores, and rewards success.[8]

J. P. Patterson developed an instrument to measure elementary teacher ratings of principal's instructional leadership. The Instructional Leadership Survey (ILS) contains ten research-based subscales, including the following:

- Helps individual staff
- Helps groups of teachers

- Concern for professional growth of teachers
- Curriculum development
- Staff improvement
- Conducts staff conferences on curriculum
- Conducts special-purpose conferences
- Counseling of pupils
- Helps staff understand pupils and central office
- Concern with teacher suggestions, problems, and requests[9]

Charles Smith and Rodney Muth used the ILS to survey samples of eight teachers from 19 elementary schools in a large city.[10] Composite scores on the ILS were divided into high, medium, and low clusters. When these scores were compared to student achievement as determined by the state's standardized basic skills test, it was found that nine of the ten principals with the highest scores came from the schools with the highest student achievement. Of the nine lowest-ranked principals, eight came from schools with the lowest student achievement.

In another study of instructional leadership, John Daresh and Ching-Jen Liu focused on the behavior of high school principals.[11] They developed a three-part survey consisting of a section for background information, a "Perception of School Quality Inventory" (PSQI), and an "Instructional Leadership Behavior Questionnaire" (ILBQ). The ILBQ contained 30 statements designed to identify the extent to which principals believed that they were involved in five areas of instructional leadership—staff development, teacher supervision and evaluation, instructional facilitation, resource acquisition and building maintenance, and student problem resolution.

Data were collected from principals and selected department chairpersons in a stratified random sample of 107 Ohio high schools. Based on responses to the PSQI, schools were divided into these categories: effective, average, and not effective. Statistically significant differences were found in the perceived behavior of principals in "effective" and "average" schools in the areas of staff development, teacher supervision and evaluation, and resource acquisition and building maintenance. Statistically significant differences between principals in "effective" and "not effective" schools were found for all five areas of instructional leadership. In addition, the study reported no significant relationships between the instructional leadership behaviors of "effective" school principals and school size, years of experience as a principal, and number of assistant principals.

Studies like these have given us a clearer idea of what principals and other educators think are the behaviors associated with instructional leadership. While no consensus emerged on the exact nature of instructional leadership, certain general areas of administrative responsibility appeared consistently. The next task for researchers was to determine what instructional leadership actually looked like on a daily basis and what it really meant to a school and community. Several efforts of the past decade have provided us with this type of in-depth understanding of instructional leadership.

DESCRIPTIVE STUDIES

One of the first attempts to put a group of exceptional principals under the microscope was made by Arthur Blumberg and William Greenfield.[12] They identified eight "out-of-the-ordinary" principals and conducted intensive, open-ended interviews with each of them. Six of the eight also participated in an extensive group interview. The result is a collection of eight portraits of principals, each reflecting considerable uniqueness. Blumberg and Greenfield saw no single model of the exceptional principal, but they did identify some common characteristics for all or most of the eight principals:

- Principals were highly goal-oriented and had a keen sense of goal clarity.
- Principals were characterized by a high degree of ontological security (in other words, they knew themselves, their capabilities, and what they were about).
- Principals displayed a high tolerance for ambiguity.
- Principals tended to test the limits of both the interpersonal and organizational systems they encounter.
- Principals were sensitive to the dynamics of power.
- Principals approached problem situations from a highly analytical perspective.
- Principals behaved in ways that enabled them to be in charge of the job and not let the job be in charge of them.[13]

Judith Little and Thomas Bird analyzed interviews with and observational data on school administrators in five "successful" secondary schools and came to a similar conclusion—no single pattern of behavior seemed to characterize successful instructional leaders.[14] Little and Bird observed a total of 17 administrators, including principals and assistant principals, and identified four distinct "patterns or images of leadership." Each reflected different assumptions about teaching, teachers, schools, and the proper role of school leaders.

Some administrators, for example, saw their chief function as a matter of "letting good teachers teach." They concentrated their energy on ensuring smooth operations and an orderly environment. Other administrators focused on the improvement of teaching, which they both expected and supported. They often advocated a particular model of teaching. Still other administrators operated as staff developers, involving themselves directly in training teachers, conducting seminars, observing in classrooms, and helping teachers resolve instructional problems. The fourth group of administrators devoted primary attention to cultivating productive relations among staff members. By encouraging faculty interaction and mutual assistance, they hoped to foster a collective capacity for improvement.

While no one model of instructional leadership emerged from the findings, this study—like the Blumberg and Greenfield one—did find certain leader-related factors in the success of all five schools. For instance, administrators in each school encouraged professional norms of collegiality and experimentation. Teachers felt supported in their efforts to assist one another and secure enough to test new ideas. Furthermore, relations between administrators and teachers were described in terms of mutual trust and respect. On a less positive note, Little and Bird found that the instructional potential of team leaders and department chairs was not tapped sufficiently, but this was partly because these people were reluctant to assume leadership roles.

There have been several in-depth studies aimed at describing the instructional leadership behavior of individual principals. In one such investigation, extensive interviews were conducted with an Oregon elementary principal and her superiors to determine the extent to which her activities conformed to a model of instructional leadership proposed by this author. The model proved to be a useful framework for describing her behavior and accounting for her widely acknowledged success with students and staff. Among her key activities were the following:

- Recruitment of talented staff members
- Carefully planned in-service education
- Informal supervision of teachers, including daily classroom visits
- Formal "clinical" supervision, including pre-observation conferences, structured classroom observation, and post-observation conferences
- Instructional support for teachers in the area of student discipline
- Coordination of school activities, with attention to minimizing the disruption of instruction
- Support for teachers in matters involving parents
- Recognition of student accomplishments
- Ensuring that teachers obtained necessary resources in a timely manner
- Coordination of school improvement and new projects
- Participation in efforts to coordinate relations between schools in the district
- Troubleshooting to determine staff and student concerns on a regular basis
- Management of "school climate"[15]

In another case study, this time of an elementary principal in a rural midwestern community, researchers found that instructional leadership may involve indirect as well as direct influence.[16] Preliminary analysis of how the principal spent his time suggested that he was not an instructional leader. He spent relatively little time in classrooms or otherwise working directly with teachers. Interviews with teachers, however, revealed that the principal was generally perceived to play an important role in supporting effective instruction. This role was described in terms of managerial tasks and maintenance of school climate. It encompassed such functions as personal confidante, procurator, problem solver, building organizer, and district liaison. Besides fulfilling what teachers thought of as vital responsibilities, the principal possessed certain crucial personal attibutes that contributed to his effectiveness. For example, teachers felt he respected their professional judgments and was always willing to listen. They also felt he was open to criticism and trustworthy.

Reflecting on all these descriptive studies, it is apparent that instructional leadership is a relatively complex phenomenon involving a mixture of activities directly or indirectly related to instructional improvement. No one pattern of behaviors characterizes all successful instructional leaders. Thus, it may be useful to think of instructional leadership in terms of key situations that must be handled competently for effective teaching to be possible. Such a concept of instructional leadership is clearly consistent with the general notion of situational competence introduced in Chapter 1. The next section will attempt to construct a model of instructional leadership based on situational competence.

AN INTEGRATED VISION OF INSTRUCTIONAL LEADERS

Though no single set of behaviors characterizes all successful instructional leaders, the research suggests that instructional leaders must see to it that certain predictable functions or situations are handled appropriately. What constitutes "appropriateness," of course, may vary from one setting to the next. For example, it is unlikely that day-to-day supervision would be identical for elementary and secondary teachers, teachers in small rural and large urban schools, or a highly experienced faculty and a group of novices. But effective instructional leadership at any level and in any setting demands some provision for teacher supervision. Part III of this book contains a comprehensive review of these insights derived from professional practice and systematic inquiry. Exactly how they can be applied most productively, however, is a matter best left to school leaders themselves, based on their judgment of local needs, available resources, and other considerations.

The scholarship presented so far in this chapter points to seven situations that instructional leaders must be prepared to deal with (see Figure 4.2):

- Teacher supervision and development
- Teacher evaluation
- Instructional management and support
- Resource management
- Quality control
- Coordination
- Troubleshooting

Handling each of these situations well requires far more than a particular skill or set of competencies. The situations constitute complex configurations of intentions, activities, people, and interrelationships. They call for a variety of technical skills and professional judgments, adapted to the particular needs of

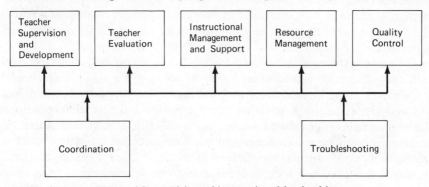

Figure 4.2 A vision of instructional leadership

the moment. Since these needs are ever-changing, no single prescription for dealing with a given situation will suffice. And while each situation is somewhat discrete, all may occur simultaneously, blurring the lines between, say, teacher evaluation and troubleshooting. Though certain situations are managerial in nature, their successful handling may depend on the type of vision and imagination associated with leadership.

The most critical situation that the instructional leader must deal with is the supervision and development of teachers. It is in this context that the actual improvement of instruction is most likely to occur. Supervision entails the direct monitoring of instruction and the collection of data that may be useful in setting targets for improvement. It calls for considerable personal contact between teachers and instructional leaders; conferences and classroom observations play central roles in this process. Personal attributes of the instructional leader—such as the capacity to listen carefully and to inspire trust—are critical to the success of supervision.

Development involves efforts to improve the performance of individual teachers as well as entire staffs. Goal setting is often an important component of professional and staff development. Instructional leaders may sometimes serve as trainers of teachers. In other cases, they see to it that teachers are provided with opportunities to receive training elsewhere. Development has become a major concern recently because of the aging of many faculties and the drop in demand for new teachers.

While improvement is the primary purpose of supervision and development, accountability is the primary purpose of teacher evaluation. Instructional leaders often are required by law to evaluate teachers. To perform this task conscientiously and constructively, the instructional leader must be guided by a working concept—or vision—of effective teaching. Teacher evaluation constitutes a system, complete with formal policies and guidelines, contractual requirements for documentation, and provisions for correction of inadequate performance. While many educators express a desire to separate the supervision and evaluation of teachers, a total divorce is unlikely, given current time constraints, laws, and administrative practices.

Many studies of instructional leadership point to the importance of instructional management and support. This involves the development and implementation of school policies related to instruction and the creation of a school climate conducive to instructional improvement; school discipline plans and efforts to reduce classroom interruptions fall into this category.

Effective instruction requires resources—time, personnel, materials, and textbooks. Resource management encompasses such functions as class and student scheduling, development of the school calendar, teacher recruitment and assignment, textbook adoption, and acquisition and allocation of instructional materials. Instructional leaders must be extra careful that scarce resources are not used to serve private desires or parochial interests instead of the welfare of all students. In a time of fiscal constraint, today's instructional leaders cannot resolve many instructional problems simply by requesting additional resources. Deciding how best to utilize valuable resources has become a crucial dimension of instructional leadership.

To determine whether resources are being used effectively, various mechanisms for quality control are needed. Research stresses the key role of instructional leaders in assessing whether school goals are being achieved. They may be called upon to review test results, evaluate school programs, adjust expectations and performance standards, and monitor the progress of individual students. Quality control also extends to assessment of student and staff performance.

Two functions of instructional leaders—coordination and trouble-shooting—cut across all of the preceding five situations. Coordination includes activities designed to eliminate duplication of services, clarify goals and expectations, and reduce the tendencies of sub-units of the school to work at cross-purposes. To promote coordination, leaders must maintain close contact with parents, patrons, and central office personnel as well as various members of the school staff. While coordination may call for the development of organizational processes, procedures, and structures, ultimately it depends on the interpersonal skills of instructional leaders—explaining what must be done, monitoring to see that it is done, and following through on corrective strategies if it is not done correctly.

Troubleshooting refers to anticipating instructional problems and dealing with them before they get too great. It is reasonably safe to assume that every school experiences various kinds of problems on a continuing basis. While preventing problems is a worthy focus of attention, leaders also need to devote time and energy to managing them. They need information about the nature of the problems, the circumstances that spawned them, and the resources available to resolve them. Troubleshooting for the purpose of instructional improvement may demand grade-level meetings, staffings, course evaluations, parent contacts, curriculum reviews, and a host of other processes designed to detect early warning signals.

This vision of instructional leadership, consisting of seven key situations that instructional leaders must deal with effectively, is the heart of this book. The next part of the book has some descriptive chapters on each of these seven areas. The vision derives in large part from recent research on school effectiveness. It is tied directly to the vision of teaching excellence developed in Chapter 3. Figure 4.3 presents a graphic representation of this relationship. It is important to note that the relationship between instructional leadership and teaching excellence (symbolized by the central line with two arrows) is characterized by a continuing interaction. In other words, instructional leadership constantly influences teaching and teaching constantly influences instructional leadership.

Before we take an in-depth look at the activities of instructional leaders, it may be useful to consider the contexts in which they work—schools. As we break down effective instruction and leadership into various components we must remember that effective schools are greater than the sum of their parts. What do these exceptional schools look like? How does it feel to visit one? What elements of effective schooling might be overlooked if we focused only on instruction and leadership? These and related issues will be addressed in Chapter 5.

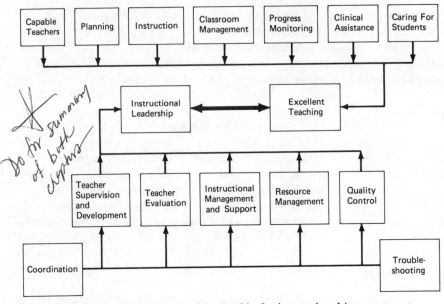

Figure 4.3 A model of school leadership for instructional improvement

---

STUDY QUESTIONS

1. Pretend that you have been asked to visit several schools in your area and to judge which one is most effective. How would you proceed? What would you look for? Develop a list of questions to ask while you visit each school. What would you want to know about school leadership?

2. Ask five teachers to comment on the kinds of leadership activities that they feel, based on their own experience, help teachers improve instruction.

3. Look at the diagram of the dimensions of instructional leadership. Based on what you know of the work of a school principal, what activities are not represented on the diagram?

4. How, specifically, can department chairpersons contribute to instructional leadership? Why are some department chairpersons reluctant to assume these responsibilities?

NOTES

1. Wilbur B. Brookover and Lawrence W. Lezotte, "Changes in School Characteristics Coincident with Changes in Student Achievement," Institute for Research on Teaching, Michigan State University, 1979.

2. Brian Rowan, David Dwyer, and Steven Bossert, "Methodological Considerations in Studies of Effective Principals," Far West Laboratory for Educational Research and Development, 1984.

3. Wynn De Bevoise, "Synthesis of Research on the Principal as Instructional Leader," *Educational Leadership,* Vol. 41, No. 5 (February 1984), p. 15.

4. Philip Hallinger, "Assessing the Instructional Management Behavior of Principals," paper presented at the annual meeting of the American Educational Research Association, 1983.
5. *Ibid.*
6 Karen S. Gallagher, Michael Riley, and Patrick Murphy, "The Instructional Management Behavior of the High School Principal," paper presented at the Annual Convention of the American Educational Research Association, 1985.
7. Shirley A. Jackson, David M. Logsdon, and Nancy E. Taylor, "Instructional Leadership Behaviors: Differentiating Effective from Ineffective Low-Income Urban Schools," *Urban Education,* Vol. 18, No. 1 (April 1983), pp. 59–70.
8. Ibid, p. 70.
9. J. P. Patterson, *A Descriptive Analysis of the Instructional Leadership Activities of Elementary Principals,* doctoral dissertation, University of Oregon, 1977.
10. Charles R. Smith and Rodney Muth, "Instructional Leadership and School Effectiveness," paper presented at the annual meeting of the American Educational Research Association, 1985.
11. John C. Daresh and Ching-Jen Liu, "High School Principals' Perceptions of Their Instructional Leadership Behavior," paper presented at the annual meeting of the American Educational Research Assocation, 1985.
12. Arthur Blumberg and William Greenfield, *The Effective Principal* (Boston: Allyn & Bacon, 1980).
13. *Ibid.,* pp. 246–249.
14. Judith Warren Little and Thomas D. Bird, "Is There Instructional Leadership in High Schools? First Findings from a Study of Secondary School Administrators and Their Influence on Teachers' Professional Norms," paper presented at the Annual Meeting of the American Educational Research Association, 1984.
15. JoAnn Mazzarella, "Instructional Leadership: Profile of an Elementary School Principal," *Oregon School Study Council Bulletin,* Vol. 26, No. 3 (November 1982).
16. Lynne M. Hannoy and Kelline W. Stevens, "The Indirect Instructional Leadership Role of a Principal," paper presented at the Annual Meeting of the American Educational Research Association, 1984.

CHAPTER 5

VISIONS OF EFFECTIVE SCHOOLS

All leaders work within a set of contexts. To fully appreciate the demands of leadership, it is necessary to understand these contexts, for at the same time that leaders are shaping their organizations, their organizations are shaping them.

Leaders work in a sociocultural context. They are shaped by the prevailing norms, beliefs, values, and conventions of a particular community or society. Communities, however, are not static entities but change over time. Therefore, it is also important to understand the temporal context in which leaders function. Each time has its own concerns, exigencies, and priorities. Finally, most leaders work within an organizational context. Organizations are collections of people that mobilize resources to achieve certain goals.

This book addresses leaders who will be working in U.S. schools in the last part of the twentieth century. The conduct of these leaders will differ in significant ways from that of hospital directors, Japanese school heads, and U.S. principals during the Depression. This chapter attempts to portray some of the specific organizational contexts in which contemporary school leaders work. More precisely, it will present vignettes of schools widely recognized as effective in an attempt to encourage practicing administrators and aspiring school leaders to appreciate the diversity and complexity of settings in which successful teaching and learning take place.

No One School Is Best

It has become popular in recent years for researchers to study a number of schools and identify common characteristics that may help account for their particular success or lack of success. The implication is that it may be possible to isolate one best way to organize the teaching and learning process.

For example, the Phi Delta Kappa Commission on Discipline identified and surveyed schools reputed to have good discipline.[1] Over 500 schools were contacted in an effort to compile a body of descriptive data on practices associated with good discipline. The Commission isolated 13 "common characteristics of well-disciplined schools," which included items like the following:

- Most of the educators viewed their school as a place where staff and students come to work and to experience the success of doing something well.
- These schools focused on causes of discipline problems rather than symptoms.

In recent years similar lists of common characteristics have been generated for "effective" schools,[2] "good" high schools,[3] "exceptional" urban elementary schools,[4] and "successful" schools for young adolescents.[5] These lists typically overlap. Still, it is unlikely that two schools achieving the same general results will look, sound, and feel exactly the same. Every school has a unique history, collection of students and staff, and community setting. Most schools—along with other organizations—have relatively distinct cultures.[6]

CASE STUDIES OF ACTUAL SCHOOLS

To illustrate the variety among schools that are referred to as exemplary or effective, this chapter will present several brief case studies of actual schools. Since schools are dynamic, the ones described here are apt to have changed substantially by the time the accounts are read. The real value of case studies lies in their capacity to foster visions of what schools can and perhaps should look like. School leaders need such visions to inspire others to pursue large-scale improvement in school performance.[7]

A Negative Vision

Visions need not always be positive to be useful. Sometimes it may be instructive to study a school that is failing to function well. Here is a case study of a school where instructional improvement was a low priority.

Millard Fillmore Middle School (a pseudonym) is located in the middle of a city of roughly half a million people. Though it borders several middle-class neighborhoods, Fillmore draws many students from less affluent sections of the city. The school served as a K-8 school for several decades until the Board decided seven years ago to switch to a middle school format. At the point when a case study was commissioned, Fillmore enrolled 600 youngsters in grades six, seven, and eight.[8] Black and Asian adolescents made up close to half the student body.

The principal of Fillmore, a 16-year incumbent, requested that two outside consultants each spend a month studying the school to recommend areas for improvement. He was concerned about several different issues. First, student achievement on standardized tests of reading and mathematics ability was going steadily downhill. Traditionally one of the district's top middle schools, Fillmore actually had slipped in recent years below the mean for district sixth, seventh, and eighth grade achievement. Parents registered alarm over declining achievement and over some disciplinary incidents of increasing severity. During the past two years, three incidents in particular had provoked angry parent reactions. Twelve students were suspended for drinking at a school-sponsored dance, the student body president was apprehended for possessing marijuana, and a female student had been accosted in a restroom by a male student. Parents expressed concern over the safety of their children.

Disappointment with Fillmore became the order of the day. Many Fillmore parents—including a Board member—had hoped the school would become a model of interracial harmony and academic excellence when it became a middle school. Feeling that their high social and academic expectations for the school were not being met, many parents began to request that their children be transferred to other middle schools in the district. Over 65 requests for transfer had been processed the summer before the case study was commissioned.

Why was Fillmore not working effectively? To find out, it was necessary to collect a variety of information from many sources. Each teacher was observed for at least one period. Interviews were scheduled with almost every staff member, including support personnel and secretaries. A structured questionnaire was administered to four groups of students—high achievers, those with behavior problems, underachievers, and "average" students. Seven years of minutes of faculty meetings and the parent advisory council were reviewed. The result was a richly detailed description of Fillmore, its history, and how people felt about it. The account suggested seven possible factors contributing to the school's problems.

The first factor was the general lack of instructional support from school administrators. This manifested itself in various ways. Teachers, for example, complained that the principal spent too much time in his office and too little time in classrooms. Even when he communicated positive observations, he tended to rely on written memos rather than drop-in visits and face-to-face communication. Teachers did not regard the principal or any of his administrative assistants as authorities on good teaching practice. Ironically, Fillmore boasted an Instructional Support Team, which seemed to be anything but that. Many teachers complained that the team—consisting of the principal, assistant principal, head counselor, student behavior specialist, and integration specialist—was rarely available to provide assistance. Instead of meeting before or after school, it met during school hours, precisely the time when teachers might require its services to cover classes, diagnose learning problems, or observe teaching. When the team did provide help, only a small group of favorites were the beneficiaries. This situation served to polarize the faculty.

The faculty was further fragmented over the absence of any plan for continuing staff development. Staff members were supposed to regard themselves as middle school teachers, but no one was able to articulate what the unique mission of a middle school teacher was. Aside from a workshop given seven years before, no effort had been made to develop or sustain a working concept of a middle school or a middle school teacher. In the absence of any integrating staff-development activity, teachers who had once been elementary teachers clustered together and talked about teaching "the whole child," while former junior high teachers closed ranks and stressed course content. School leadership had failed to utilize staff development—or any other mechanism—to foster a shared sense of mission for Fillmore teachers.

A third problem was the mediocre quality of instruction in most classrooms. Though teachers insisted they were a talented group prevented from doing a better job by uncooperative students and by administrative obstacles, observations revealed an overreliance on seatwork, large amounts of time lost in transitions between class activities, no provisions for continuous monitoring of student progress, and uninspiring lectures. Teachers were not held accountable for instructional objectives, lesson plans, or wise use of preparation periods. Few opportunities were provided for teachers to share ideas. When they did interact, their talk was more likely to center on student conduct or complaints about paperwork than on instruction.

The principal was not perceived to delegate authority very much or very effectively. For instance, his appointees to the Instructional Support Team were not generally regarded as the most knowledgeable instructional experts at Fillmore. When teachers submitted creative ideas for school improvement to him, he rarely responded. The situation had gotten so bad that a group of female teachers met to consider filing a formal grievance. They argued that the principal did not value the advice or expertise of women faculty members. The fact that all but one member of the Instructional Support Team were male seemed to strengthen their case.

A fifth factor contributing to Fillmore's ineffectiveness concerned the lack of follow-through when faculty members identified problems requiring attention. The minutes of faculty meetings included continual references to such problems as teacher failure to show up for nonclass duties and scheduling. The principal invited staff members to share their concerns during faculty meetings, but he failed to act decisively upon the problems once they were raised. As a result, many teachers refused to share their concerns. They were convinced nothing would be done.

These and many other problems at Fillmore can be traced, at least in part, to failures of instructional leadership. The principal and his assistants provided no clear sense of direction and no set of high expectations to motivate staff members. Teachers did not feel that their talents were recognized or used effectively by these leaders. Staff development was virtually nonexistent. Inadequate instruction was systematically overlooked or at least tolerated by the principal. Staff concerns were not handled expeditiously by the Instructional Support Team.

There is a happy ending to this particular case study. Following the official report on the deteriorating status of Fillmore Middle School, the principal and assistant principal were reassigned and the Instructional Support Team was disbanded. Within one year of these changes, the achievement of Fillmore students had begun to climb again (relative to other district middle schools), parent requests for transfer had dwindled, and major discipline incidents had disappeared. New leadership brought with it a commitment to improved instruction, ongoing staff development, intensive classroom supervision, disciplinary consistency, teacher involvement in decision making, and a willingness to respond quickly to teacher concerns. Interestingly, both reassigned administrators did fine in their new posts, an indication that sometimes the match between leadership and context is the problem rather than the leaders themselves. Success stories like Fillmore's are becoming more common, but no two stories are likely to be the same. In the case of Milwaukee's RISE project, a whole group of inner-city schools were able to raise student achievement dramatically without sacrificing the unique identities of individual schools.

Milwaukee "Rises" to the Occasion

In 1979 the Milwaukee School Board directed the Superintendent, Lee McMurrin, to develop a plan for raising achievement in 18 elementary and two middle schools that had scored lowest on annual tests administered by the district.[9] The result was Project RISE (Rising to Individual Scholastic Excellence), a district-coordinated effort to enable at least four-fifths of the students in each participating school to perform at the appropriate grade level on locally developed, nationally normed achievement tests of basic skills. All schools were located in the central city and served a predominantly low-income and minority student population.

In just three years virtually every one of the 20 schools had achieved or exceeded the target for improved student achievement. What is equally impressive is that the turnaround was accomplished without additional monies, changes in administrators and teachers, or shifts in student composition. What had happened in Milwaukee?

The success of Project RISE cannot be explained by any single factor. By design, each participating school had a somewhat different experience. District officials recognized that educational improvement would be most likely to occur when it was school-based. The district's role was to create an overriding goal, to expose participants to research advising how to raise the achievement of inner-city students, and to provide technical assistance when necessary. Each school was expected to develop its own school improvement plan.

Looking back on the first five years of Project RISE, Maureen McCormick-Larkin, a curriculum supervisor with the Milwaukee Public Schools, saw certain similarities among the RISE schools that achieved the greatest gains. First she noted substantial shifts in staff attitudes. Three factors made this possible: focused staff development, networking with teachers in effective schools outside of Milwaukee, and the elimination of homogeneous student grouping. And so teachers came to realize that all students could achieve, despite their past academic record or socioeconomic background. In addition, their attitudes toward themselves changed. By assuming leadership roles in staff development for non-RISE teachers, by planning their own in-service activities, and by publicizing their schools' accomplishments to the community, teachers gained a vital sense of professional competence and personal efficacy.

A second set of changes involved school management and organization. Principals reported assuming a greater role as instructional leaders. They noted that teachers were becoming deeply involved in schoolwide planning and decision making and supported their efforts. For example, teachers expressed a desire to eliminate "pullout" programs because they disrupted instruction. By supporting this and other teacher requests, principals came to be seen in a new light.

Teacher involvement in planning and decision making occurred in school-effectiveness committees and on grade-level teams. Participation in these groups did much to improve coordination across classrooms and to reduce teacher isolation. Teachers also were able to develop and enforce consistent expectations for student behavior and to assume responsibilities previously assigned to pullout programs.

Changes also occurred in school practices and policies. The support of parents was actively solicited, and parents were kept informed of any changes in school operations. For instance, homework policies were developed in each school as a means of supplementing and reinforcing classroom instruction. Parents were asked to see to it that students spent sufficient time on homework assignments. When students failed to complete assignments, they had to make up work either during lunch or before or after school in a "homework center." Other new school policies covered interruptions, grade-level performance standards, and expectations for student conduct.

The final set of changes noted by McCormick-Larkin concerned classroom practices. Teachers participated in the development of instructional strategies to ensure that every student was taught the entire grade-level curriculum. Grade-level objectives were organized into units of instruction. Most lessons included a whole-class component geared to grade-level expectations and a small-group component based on the actual level of performance of particular students. Individual instruction, previously provided by pullout programs, was delivered in-class by support teachers. Lessons tended to be highly structured, involving a review of the previous lesson, a homework check, a developmental lesson, a check for understanding, monitored seatwork, and a related homework assignment.

The similarities across top-performing RISE schools suggest that, despite their unique experiences, each school had improved within a common community and district context. These contexts were characterized by widespread parental support and district commitment. District officials have been careful to protect RISE schools from additional and possibly conflicting innovations and expectations. Parents have insisted that their children be provided with an education that will permit them to advance steadily through the school system. High-quality instruction has come to be expected by both groups.

Effectiveness Amidst Desegregation—Louisville's Byck School

Dann C. Byck Elementary School in Louisville, Kentucky, achieved national prominence when it was selected as an "exceptional urban elementary school" by a Phi Delta Kappa study group.[10] Its fame was remarkable since it was earned during a period of tremendous local upheaval and change. Louisville was forced to merge school systems and impose a widescale busing program to respond to court-ordered desegregation. In addition, the district experienced a teacher strike, major administrative changes, and substantial community dissatisfaction.

As principal Matt Benningfield and instructional coordinator Janice Walker recall, Byck School had reached the end of a cycle in 1975. Years of federally supported programs such as Head Start and Follow Through, along with special curriculum projects, had produced a successful urban elementary school serving low-income blacks. The school was orderly and achievement oriented, the staff well trained and committed. Then things began to change. First, faculty morale plummeted when they learned that computer-set instructional goals for individual students could not be adjusted to accommodate unforeseen events and personal crises. Intermediate teachers grew dissatisfied when they began receiving fewer resources than primary teachers.

Six weeks before the beginning of the 1975–1976 school year, a federal judge ordered the implementation of a busing plan to facilitate the desegregation of newly merged Louisville and Jefferson County school systems. The National Guard was called out to help police ensure a peaceful transition. Despite its presence, anti-busing demonstrators managed to disrupt activities at many school sites.

As a result of the desegregation plan Byck found itself with an enrollment of about 84 percent white students, 15 percent black students, and 1 percent students of other races. No longer were there the federal funds that had been available when Byck was an all-black school. In addition, the faculty experienced changes. From a group with equal numbers of black and white teachers, the faculty shifted to conform to the mandated ratio of 20 percent black and 80 percent white teachers. Merging two school systems also meant absorbing different instructional programs, evaluation procedures, and textbooks.

Five years after the turmoil of merger and desegregation, a Phi Delta Kappa study team visited Byck Elementary School and found that the school had become a success again. But success is always relative. The achievements of 1980, with a heterogeneous student body and few federally supported programs, were different from those of the previous period. Byck had developed into a model of shared decision making, with staff, parents, and students joining administrators in developing school policies and programs. Test scores rose, but not at the expense of good relationships between teachers and students. Instruction reflected creativity, vitality, and enthusiasm. Parents and teachers alike noted with pride the positive self-images shown by most Byck students. Students learned to get along with peers from different neighborhoods and cultures. As a result, many parents elected to have their children remain at Byck, even after their assigned years for busing had elapsed.

Whereas the dramatic reversals of Project RISE schools originated with the efforts of district officials, Byck's renaissance derived more from local initiative. Faced with a potential crisis when school opened in 1975, Byck staff members refused to insulate themselves or become defensive. They continued to encourage extensive parental involvement, thereby moderating the fears of parents whose children were attending Byck for the first time. The principal remained open to shared decision making rather than adopting an authoritarian style in the face of system-wide unrest. As a result of these responses to crisis, Byck was in a position during the 1976–1977 school year to focus on substantive changes in instruction and curriculum. The pros and cons of different strategies were debated openly. Parents freely discussed their apprehensions and concerns. Out of these exchanges came a variety of innovations, including a special transition class for youngsters who needed to bring themselves up to certain achievement levels to function within the county-wide continuous progress system.

In addition, the Byck staff participated in a self-study during the 1976–1977 school year. This experience produced unity in a staff disoriented by turnover and transfer. Through the self-study teachers began to understand the principal's style, goals, and philosophy. They came to appreciate his commitment to continuing in-service, close monitoring of student progress, and quick intervention to resolve student problems. It was evident that the faculty had become unified around Byck's vision when they were willing to accept slightly larger classes in order to create a new position—that of instructional coordinator. Teachers elected someone from their own ranks to fill the role.

During the years that followed, Byck developed mechanisms for efficient instructional planning and resource acquisition. The instructional coordinator began to share instructional-leadership responsibilities with the principal. The staff lobbied the Board of Education to win approval for a criterion-referenced pre-test that they needed as a diagnostic tool. Slowly, these and other activities and experiences began to yield a set of shared beliefs, or what might be thought of as a common Byckian culture. This culture was characterized by:

> ... openness, personal responsibility for instruction, concern for the welfare of students (your own as well as others), a willingness to invest personal time, open dealings with parents, professional growth, sharing of instructional strategies and materials, trusting colleagues to do a good job, and maintaining high expectations for students.[11]

Perhaps more than anything else, it was the emergence of this culture that explained the success of Byck Elementary School. The culture represented a positive response to crisis, a desire to rise to the challenge of change rather than resist. The culture derived in large part from the able leadership of Benningfield, but only because he was willing to share that leadership and foster a sense of collective responsibility. The Byck story demonstrates that schools need not become passive victims of external events. With appropriate leadership, a school may actually influence the greater community and become a model of cooperation and achievement in the midst of turmoil.

A Successful Rural Middle School

In her book *Successful Schools for Young Adolescents,* Joan Lipsitz presents detailed descriptions of four "developmentally appropriate" middle-grade schools. These exemplary schools promote healthy social as well as academic growth. One of Lipsitz's case studies is Western Middle School in Alamance County, North Carolina.

Built in 1978, Western has over 700 students in grades six, seven, and eight. The school is divided structurally into four "houses," one for each grade and a fourth for a mixed-age combination. The staff consists of 39 teachers, an assistant principal, guidance counselor, music teacher, four teachers for exceptional students, a half-time speech teacher, a librarian, a home-school coordinator, and a part-time nurse.

To understand Western, one must understand the setting in which it is located. Lipsitz describes the Alamance County School District, outside of Burlington, as a "stable, conservative, mostly rural area of factory workers, farm workers, professionals, small businessmen, and teachers."[12] Over 70 percent of the parents own their own houses, and about the same percentage of students live with both parents. The community insists on playing an active role in school life; for example, they exerted pressure to prevent planners from making Western Middle School a fully "open-space" facility. Teachers are part of the community, not just figuratively but literally. Many were raised in Alamance County, so they understand the context in which their students grow up.

The story of Western is also, to a large extent, the story of Wilma Parrish, the principal. She enthusiastically proclaims that Western is "proud country," and her students echo the slogan. The members of the Western community indeed have a great deal about which to be proud. Students score above the national norm in reading. The average daily attendance is between 97 and 98 percent. Behavior problems, acts of vandalism, and suspensions are well below the numbers for other middle schools in the vicinity. Black and white students interact frequently and without animosity. Not surprisingly, Parrish's frequent polls of parental feelings about Western typically find high levels of satisfaction.

To create a successful program at Western, Parrish drew heavily on her own instincts about what constitutes good schooling. She does not hesitate to play the role of chauffeur when a student is reluctant to come to school, secretary when a teacher needs dittoing, or cheerleader when community support is required. Greatly influenced by the work of William Purkey, Parrish displays a sensitivity to the emotional needs of young adolescents. For example, she recognizes the importance of never embarrassing her students. She insists they be treated with understanding and respect—enhancing students' self-image is a major goal at Western.

Parrish estimates she spends about 35 percent of her time engaged in instructional supervision and 30 percent in long-range curriculum planning. To devote so much time to instructional leadership, Parrish must delegate or share many of her other responsibilities. For instance, she uses a teacher committee to assist in allocating her annual discretionary budget. Teachers also play a major role in determining their yearly assignments. As a result, teachers at Western may be found teaching in two-teacher teams, larger team arrangements, and self-contained classrooms. Teachers also help decide where students will be placed each year.

One responsibility Parrish has not delegated is the articulation of a vision for what Western can become. She keeps a list of essential components of middle schools which guides her staff-development efforts. Unlike her counterpart at Fillmore Middle School in the opening vignette, Parrish knows where the school should be heading and sees to it that her staff knows as well. Lipsitz reports a "remarkable consensus" about the purposes and goals of Western Middle School.

The curriculum at Western is divided into three segments—a core, including language arts, reading, social studies, science, health, and mathematics; unified arts, consisting of physical education, career education, band, and music; and "exploratory," a program of short courses covering high-interest topics. Despite the objections of some parents to "exploratory," Parrish maintains that it provides essential enrichment for her students. Equipped with a guiding image of a well-developed adolescent, she is able to deal with challenges to Western's program in an informed, professional manner. She recognizes that intellectual growth typically must be subordinated to self-exploration and self-definition during early adolescence. Abstract ideas should have little claim on instructional time. Stress should be placed on the concrete—facts, skills, activities.

Western Middle School strongly reflects the values of the setting in which it is located, but at the same time, the vision of its principal and staff ensures that students will not become victims of parochialism or parental prejudice. The balance struck between community concerns and professional perspective could be achieved only in an atmosphere of mutual trust. The pervasive trust that characterizes relations between Western and parents is testimony to the hard work and commitment of both groups. They have learned that trust, like a successful marriage, requires more than good intentions.

A Suburban High School of Excellence

West Linn, Oregon, is a community in transition and so is its school district. Once a mill town made up primarily of blue collar workers, West Linn is rapidly becoming an executive "bedroom" for nearby Portland. With this shift have come demands for a school system second to none, and nowhere has the pressure for academic excellence been felt more strongly than at West Linn High School. Principal Dick Sagor and his staff have been equal to the challenge, however—in 1984 West Linn received national recognition from the Department of Education as a "school of excellence."

Perhaps no one is more proud of the feat than Dea Cox, West Linn's avuncular superintendent. When Cox took the helm of the district, he confronted a state of fragmentation. Teachers were angry at the Board of Education for lack of support. The community had voted down several budgets. Cox's predecessor had been forced to resign. To respond to the crisis, Cox adopted two strategies. First, he acknowledged that school systems are political entities rather than the rational models found in textbooks. He set about to build public support and local coalitions. The second course of action was what Cox, with a gleam in his eye, calls his "people strategy." He sought out the very best people he could find to administer and staff West Linn's schools, and he adamantly refused to hire "second-raters."

In a span of six years, Cox replaced all eight building principals with talented Ph.D.s from around the country. He also let it be known that tenuring a teacher in West Linn was a $1,000,000 commitment of district resources, and he did not intend that these decisions would be made lightly. To get tenure in West Linn, teachers would have to be more than merely acceptable.

Cox's beliefs are reflected in the leadership of Dick Sagor. Sagor is careful to cultivate and nurture good community relations. He recognizes the need, for example, to maintain a strong extra-curricular program while pushing for greater academic emphasis. Like a savvy field officer, he knows when to seize ground and when to hold the line. And so in the mid-eighties, when local as well as national concern was focused on science, mathematics, and computers, Sagor realized that he could add substantially to these areas of the curriculum, but he chose not to press for expansion of the social studies or art programs.

Sagor devotes great attention to staff building. He recruits for many positions on a national basis, traveling yearly to distant locales to enlist talented educators. He also lures talented veterans from neighboring districts, a practice he justifies on the grounds that free agency of teachers will compel all districts to pay more for quality instructors. When teachers come to West Linn High, they are immediately involved in an induction class which meets weekly for breakfast (at Sagor's expense) in the principal's spacious office. These sessions are designed to socialize newcomers to school and district expectations. Sagor refuses to leave the socialization process to chance.

Recognizing that one person cannot provide all the motivation for improvement in a high school with over a thousand students, Sagor has carefully increased the leadership capabilities of department chairs. They are expected to oversee curriculum change and encourage staff development of department members. Department meetings have been replaced by Curriculum Improvement meetings, an indication that the purpose of meetings is more than the sharing of routine information.

Besides department chairs, Sagor is helped by a team of skilled assistant administrators who handle much of the teacher supervision and evaluation process. By delegating authority, Sagor not only displays his faith in his staff, he also frees himself to do what he does best—generate and nurture ideas. One such idea resulted in a highly touted staff-development project called "A Day in the Life." Teachers volunteer to spend an entire day shadowing a student, trying to understand what a day in school is like from an adolescent's perspective. The teacher-observers then share their perceptions with Sagor and their colleagues. These sessions sometimes reveal less-than-inspiring instruction and unchallenging course content, and so pave the way for improvement efforts.

When Sagor is not dreaming up new programs, he is apt to be roaming around West Linn's corridors, greeting students and paying casual visits to classrooms. Occasionally he stops a student and asks, "What's this school all about?" It is important to Sagor that students realize that academic achievement is the school's primary reason for being. Staff members exert considerable energy to create what Sagor calls "an academic ethos." All administrators, including the principal, are expected to teach a class, for example. Teachers and students talk about curriculum and instruction. Student academic achievement receives widespread recognition, both in school and the community. West Linn's accomplishments are memorialized in Sagor's annual "State of the School" address and in his end-of-the-year informational brochure to patrons.

West Linn's story is that of a good high school that got better. Its success derives from community pressure, the practical wisdom of the superintendent, the vision of the high school principal and his team of instructional leaders, and the talents of its staff. The final case study describes a high school that rose to prominence from humbler origins.

The Rescue of Ribault High School

Once an all-white high school, Ribault High School in Jacksonville, Florida, was integrated in 1970 as a result of court-ordered desegregation.[13] The transition was a turbulent one marked by racial tension among students, a brief school closure, and the exodus of white families. Within two years of desegregation, there were almost no whites left at Ribault. The school functioned reasonably well until a change in leadership occurred. The new principal allowed problems such as rule breaking, drug use, and poor academic performance to increase without taking decisive action. When Florida introduced statewide proficiency testing in 1977, only one junior in five at Ribault passed the mathematics competency section—scores were close to the bottom in the state. And community discontent mounted.

As in the case of West Linn, a new superintendent—Herb Sang—precipitated change. Deciding to make Ribault a pilot school, Sang replaced the principal and started meeting with parents, students, and community leaders to shape the high school's future. Walter Harris, the new principal, responded to popular concerns by making Ribault a safe and orderly environment. He first tackled the unglamorous jobs—securing the parking lot and restricting access to strangers, cleaning up and monitoring restrooms, implementing a schoolwide dress code. Students who did not comply with the new regulations were expelled.

Only when order was restored did Harris shift his attention to instruction and curriculum. At the end of his first year at Ribault—with the superintendent's blessing—Harris announced to all teachers that they would have to reapply for their jobs. Harris knew that some teachers were not fully committed to working with Ribault's students, and he was determined that they would transfer elsewhere. Most teachers expressed strong support for the plan, which resulted in the hiring of 54 new teachers (about two-thirds of the staff) who *wanted* to work at Ribault.

By the fall of 1978 Harris was prepared to address the issue of academic achievement. Recognizing that adolescents respond well to competition, Harris encouraged a "let's win the big game" atmosphere around the Florida Assessment Test. Beginning several weeks before the test, pep rallies were held for all juniors taking the test. The superintendent was present to symbolize the importance of the occasion. Students were exhorted to do well on the test, not just for their own benefit, but for the sake of their school. The type of school pride usually reserved for athletic contests was generated for the pursuit of academic honor.

Ribault teachers also played an active role in preparing for the test. For example, the chair of the Mathematics Department and a compensatory education teacher made a careful item analysis of the previous year's test results, pinpointing where Ribault students performed well and where they did not. This information was used to guide instruction. Uplifted by the emerging "Ribault spirit," teachers rose to the occasion and held after-school and Saturday tutoring sessions for students preparing to take the test. Even the 20-minute homeroom period was used for test preparation. Answers to sample questions were read over the intercom, the numbers of correct answers per class were tallied, and the totals by homeroom were broadcast the following day.

The improvement of Ribault students on the test was dramatic. By 1980, Ribault's overall passing percentage on the mathematics section of the state test was above county and statewide figures. And the impact of the new spirit of achievement went beyond test performance—more students began to take algebra and geometry instead of basic math. Students and parents became proud to be associated with Ribault. Parent attendance at the annual open house climbed from 300 in Harris's first year, to 1,125 in 1980—the highest percentage in the county.

What factors cause a school to take a problem—in this case, low test performance—and redefine it as an opportunity for school improvement? In Ribault's case, the explanation begins with the quality of leadership—at both the school and district level. The willingness of staff members to give unselfishly of their free time to help students succeed played both a symbolic and a substantive role. Parent encouragement was another key ingredient to success. By creating a culture in which orderly conduct and academic achievement were expected, Ribault's staff and patrons helped rescue a high school on the verge of disaster.

Understanding Exceptional Schools

In the beginning of this chapter we pointed out that most leaders function in three contexts: a community setting, a historical time, and an organizational culture. In each of the case studies leaders were influential, but their influence cannot be neatly separated from these greater contexts. Community expectations varied somewhat from Milwaukee to West Linn and from Alamance County to Louisville, but they were always influential. Timing also was a factor; school effectiveness meant one thing in an era when the public clamored to go "back to basics" and another several years later when national commissions urged a push toward excellence. Finally, the cultures of the schools described in this chapter reflected certain unique features. The folksy, "downhome" environment of Western Middle School contrasts sharply with urbane, affluent West Linn High.

This chapter has tried to show that the job a particular school is doing cannot be appreciated apart from context. Walter Harris's vision for Ribault High was perfectly suited to the needs and aspirations of black parents in Jacksonville, Florida, in 1977. That same vision probably would not have proved useful for Leonard Covello during the 22 years he served as principal of New York City's Benjamin Franklin High School. Covello envisioned a school that was community centered rather than subject centered or student centered.[14] In the context of East Harlem in the thirties, Franklin needed to provide a sense of community identity for a neighborhood of 200,000 that had never before had its own high school. To meet the challenge, Covello saw to it that students and teachers studied local issues and local conditions, lobbied for public housing, worked on projects to beautify their environment, and published a community newspaper. Raising test scores was not the highest priority for Franklin High during this era of community formation.

Not only does the mission of a school vary with its context, but so, too, does the nature of school leadership. In one of the few studies to look at the relationship between school leadership and context, Philip Hallinger and Joseph Murphy found that instructional leadership in schools identified as effective varied with the socioeconomic status of the community.[15] Each of the seven California elementary schools in the study boasted at least three consecutive years of student achievement above expectations in third- and sixth-grade reading and mathematics. Two of the schools were located in low-income communities, three in middle-income communities, and two in upper-middle-income communities. Instructional leadership varied according to the type of community in a number of areas, including school goal setting, curriculum coordination, teacher supervision and evaluation, professional development, expectations and standards, and incentives for learning.

By now it should be apparent that the preparation of school leaders is a complex and complicated endeavor. While it is important for school leaders to have some vision of what teaching and schooling should look like, no *one* vision will be universally appropriate. Similarly, no single model of instructional leadership will fit every setting. This does not mean that the preparation of instructional leaders is futile. Part III of the book provides a detailed analysis of the situations in which instructional leaders should function competently no matter what the context. And while the precise nature of this competence will certainly vary, as Hallinger and Murphy note, these are situations that must be confronted by all school leaders.

STUDY QUESTIONS

1. Find a retired school administrator and ask him or her to reflect on how concepts of the ideal school have changed over the years.
2. Compare the visions of the ideal school of A. S. Neill (Summerhill), Mortimer Adler (*The Paideia Proposal*), and Sara Lightfoot (*The Good High School*).

3. Interview several people who attended schools outside the United States. Try to determine differences in schooling that can be attributed to cultural factors.

4. Providing an objective account of a school is extremely difficult, since it is impossible for observers to separate themselves totally from their own cultures. Try to develop a descriptive case study of a local school. Attempt to avoid making judgments about what you see and hear. Have someone else read your account and look for hidden biases and assumptions.

NOTES

1. William W. Wayson, *et al., Handbook for Developing Schools with Good Discipline* (Bloomington, Ind.: Phi Delta Kappa, 1982).
2. David A. Squires, William G. Huitt, and John K. Segars, *Effective Schools and Classrooms: A Research-Based Perspective* (Alexandria, Va.: Association for Supervision and Curriculum Development, 1984).
3. Sara Lawrence Lightfoot, *The Good High School* (New York: Basic Books, 1983).
4. *Why Do Some Urban Schools Succeed?* (Bloomington, Ind.: Phi Delta Kappa, 1980).
5. Joan Lipsitz, *Successful Schools for Young Adolescents* (New Brunswick, N.J.: Transaction Books, 1984).
6. Seymour Sarason, *The Culture of the School and the Problem of Change* (Boston: Allyn & Bacon, 1971).
7. Arthur Blumberg and William Greenfield, *The Effective Principal* (Boston: Allyn & Bacon, 1980), p. 201.
8. The author is indebted to Vernon Jones for his involvement in the case study.
9. This account is based on personal conversations with Maureen McCormick-Larkin and two articles: Maureen McCormick-Larkin, "Ingredients of a Successful School Effectiveness Project," *Educational Leadership*, Vol. 42, No. 6 (March 1985), pp. 31–37; and Maureen McCormick-Larkin and William J. Kritek, "Milwaukee's Project RISE," *Educational Leadership*, Vol. 40, No. 3 (December 1982), pp. 16–21.
10. This account is based on Matt Benningfield and Janice Walker, "Dann C. Byck Elementary School" in *Why Do Some Urban Schools Succeed?* (Bloomington, Ind.: Phi Delta Kappa, 1980).
11. *Ibid.,* p. 127.
12. Joan Lipsitz, *Successful Schools for Young Adolescents,* p. 29.
13. Material for this case study is drawn largely from Alan Weisberg's "Five Urban High Schools" (Palo Alto, Calif.: Bay Area Research Group, 1981).
14. For an entertaining account of Covello and Franklin High School, see David Tyack and Elisabeth Hansot, *Managers of Virtue* (New York: Basic Books, 1982), pp. 207–211.
15. Philip Hallinger and Joseph Murphy, "Instructional Leadership and School Socioeconomic Status: A Preliminary Investigation," *Administrator's Notebook*, Vol. 31, No. 5.

PART III

DIMENSIONS OF LEADERSHIP FOR INSTRUCTIONAL IMPROVEMENT

Having developed a clear vision for instructional improvement, it is time to get to the heart of the matter. What are the situations and issues that school leaders who are concerned about instruction must deal with? What guidelines can research give them? What questions should school leaders ask to assess just how ready a school is for instructional improvement?

The chapters in this part of the book derive from the model of instructional leadership developed in Chapter 4. Chapters 6, 7, and 8 cover the critical and related areas of teacher evaluation, supervision and development. Chapter 6 opens with an analysis of teacher evaluation systems. Chapter 7 takes a close-up look at evaluation and supervision and reveals some of the reasons why the daily practice of these activities may not always reflect official statements. Chapter 8 focuses on staff development for school-wide improvement. The remaining four chapters address, respectively, the areas of instructional management and support, resource management, quality control, coordination and troubleshooting.

Part III should be viewed less as a collection of prescriptions for "curing" instructionally ailing schools than as a map of the actual territory of instructional improvement. Diagnostic questions are used throughout this portion of the book to illustrate the kind of in-depth inquiry successful instructional leadership requires. There are no quick and easy solutions to instructional problems. As we've seen in Chapter 5, each school is unique, the product of a particular culture, community, and organizational history. This part of the book aims at identifying important issues and obstacles along the route to effective schooling.

CHAPTER 6

THE ELEMENTS OF TEACHER SUPERVISION AND EVALUATION SYSTEMS

Generally when school leaders assume a new position, they encounter an existing system for teacher evaluation and possibly for supervision and development. In many cases, these systems are based on district policies, state laws, and contractual obligations. Most have provisions for teacher goal setting, conferencing, classroom observations, end-of-year evaluations, procedures for assistance and discipline, and due process rights of teachers. School leaders, of course, influence the implementation of these provisions. It is becoming more and more apparent, however, that this influence is maximized when leaders fully understand the nature of the entire system—including its purposes, underlying assumptions, and relationships to other systems.

This chapter takes a broad look at the processes by which teachers are evaluated, supervised, and helped to grow. It identifies critical considerations in the design and improvement of supervision and evaluation systems, and closes with an analysis of several fundamental problems with current systems.

A State of Confusion

Discussion of teacher evaluation, supervision, and development is marked by considerable confusion. Key terms are defined in different ways by different authorities, and frequently their meanings overlap. In reality it is often impossible to determine where supervision stops and evaluation or development begins.

Evaluation is commonly understood to be a judgment about whether something or someone is good or bad, acceptable or unacceptable, appropriate or inappropriate. When the term is used in the context of school personnel decisions, it has come to mean a formal process by which judgments are made about the extent to which desired outcomes have been achieved. Evaluation specialists distinguish between *summative* evaluation and *formative* evaluation. The former represents a final judgment affecting a person's employment status, while the latter is an interim judgment intended to provide constructive, growth-promoting information to the person or persons being evaluated.

To the layman, supervision conjures up images of foremen on assembly lines overseeing the activities of workers. When applied to school settings, however, the terms can take on a variety of meanings. Some administrators think of supervision as a process of monitoring teacher performance through conferences and observations. Others maintain that supervision encompasses all activities intended to improve teacher performance, including staff development and professional growth opportunities. Opinion is divided on the desired relationship between supervision and evaluation. While one contingent argues that the two should be completely separate, another claims that information gotten from supervisory contacts is vital to the evaluation of teachers. In recent years some theorists have begun to define supervision in very broad terms. Carl Glickman, for example, regards supervision as "the glue of a successful school."[1] He adds that this glue represents "the process by which some person or group of people is responsible for providing a link between individual teacher needs and organizational goals so that individuals within the school can work in harmony toward their vision of what the school *should* be."[2] According to this definition, supervision would include teacher evaluation as well as teacher development.

To proceed with our analysis, we shall consider supervision to represent all efforts to monitor teacher performance. Evaluation is the process by which the acceptability of teacher performance is judged. Teacher development refers to those activities designed to promote professional growth as well as to correct deficiencies.

Organization theorists regard evaluation and supervision, along with rewards and sanctions, to be the basic components of an organization's control structure. These four mechanisms are found, to varying degrees, in all organizations. They are designed to ensure that (1) organizational goals are accomplished, and (2) to prevent entropy, the tendency within any complex entity for individuals and sub-units to go their own way.

School administration experts acknowledge these two basic purposes, but they see additional reasons for undertaking supervision and evaluation. To be successful, school leaders must have a clear understanding of *all* these purposes.

WHY SUPERVISE AND EVALUATE?

In a fantasy world where individuals' self-interests correspond exactly to the interests of the organizations employing them, supervision and evaluation might not be essential. But contemporary schools are anything but a fantasy world. The necessity of supervision and evaluation is acknowledged in district policies and teacher contracts. Richard Manatt reports that 26 states require teachers to be evaluated.[3] California mandates that all principals must be certified in clinical supervision, while other states require prospective administrators to take courses in supervision and evaluation. A central purpose of supervision and evaluation is accountability—providing assurances to the public that professional incompetence and malpractice will be detected and corrected.

Besides accountability, specialists have recognized several other potential purposes for supervision and evaluation (see Table 6.1). The most important of them is professional improvement.

"Improvement" encompasses everything from the diagnosis of needs for professional growth to the identification of performances worthy of special recognition. The literature suggests that improvement goals are frequently subordinated to accountability by wary school leaders.[4] This book contends that in a setting of effective instructional leadership, supervision and evaluation must serve the purpose of both improvement and accountability. For supervision and evaluation to focus exclusively on the "management of incompetence," to use Ed Bridges's phrase, is to invest too much time and energy in too few teachers. Assuming the majority of teachers are reasonably competent, the logical way to maximize the impact of supervision and evaluation is to place primary emphasis on the improvement of individual and school performance.[5]

Diagnostic Question 1.1

Do supervision and evaluation systems serve the purposes of improvement as well as accountability?

It is important to recognize that serving both accountability *and* improvement can create a variety of dilemmas for school leaders. In an ideal world, the two probably would be handled by totally separate systems. The role strain placed on school leaders who are asked both to protect patrons from teacher

Table 6.1 Purposes of Teacher Evaluation and Supervision

Bolton	*Borich*	*Darling-Hammond, Wise, and Pease*
Improvement of instruction	Diagnostic	Accountability
Rewarding superior performance	Formative	Individual
Modification of assignment	Summative	Organizational
Protection of individuals and the organization		Improvement
Validation of the selection process		Individual
Promotion of individual growth and self-evaluation		Organizational

SOURCES: Dale L. Bolton, *Selection and Evaluation of Teachers* (Berkeley: McCutchan, 1973).
Gary D. Borich, *The Appraisal of Teaching* (Reading, Mass.: Addison-Wesley, 1977), p. 31.
Linda Darling-Hammond, Arthur E. Wise, and Sara R. Pease, "Teacher Evaluation in the Organizational Context: A Review of the Literature," *Review of Educational Research,* Vol. 53, No. 3 (Fall 1983), p. 302.

incompetence and to help teachers grow is analogous to that experienced by counselors who are required to discipline as well as counsel students. On occasion, fulfilling one set of responsibilities is bound to undermine the other. In the immediate future, however, it is unlikely that accountability and improvement can be totally divorced. Resources are too scarce to permit an increase in the number of school leaders. And as long as the same individuals are expected both to help teachers improve and to monitor for poor performance, a certain amount of conflict can be expected. Under such circumstances, how can school leaders create the best possible systems for supervision and evaluation?

THE ELEMENTS OF GOOD SUPERVISION AND EVALUATION

Considerable effort has been devoted to identifying the elements of good systems for supervising and evaluating teachers. Some of these efforts focus on structural features, while others concentrate on how key individuals perceive these structural features. For example, in a comprehensive review of research on teacher evaluation, Darling-Hammond, Wise, and Pease hypothesize four "minimal conditions for the successful operation of a teacher evaluation system":

- All actors in the system have a shared understanding of the criteria and processes for teacher evaluation.
- All actors understand how these criteria and processes relate to the dominant symbols of the organization; that is, there is a shared sense that they capture the most important aspects of teaching. . . .
- Teachers perceive that the evaluation procedure enables and motivates them to improve their performance; and principals perceive that the procedure enables them to provide instructional leadership.
- All actors in the system perceive . . . that the procedure achieves a balance between control and autonomy for the various actors in the system.[6]

While these criteria relate to people's understandings and perceptions of the evaluation system, those identified in a Rand study of four innovative school districts are concerned more with the actual structure of the evaluation system. All four districts—Salt Lake City (Utah), Lake Washington (Wash.), Greenwich (Conn.), and Toledo (Ohio)—shared the following practices:

- They provide top-level leadership and institutional resources for the evaluation process.
- They ensure that evaluators have the necessary expertise to perform their task.
- They enable administrators and teachers to collaborate to develop a common understanding of evaluation goals and processes.
- They use an evaluation process and support systems that are compatible with each other and with the district's overall goals and organizational context.[7]

Ed Bridges and Barry Groves combine aspects of both structure-based and perception-based criteria in their District Evaluation Practices Inventory

(DEPI). The instrument is divided into eight major categories associated with effective evaluation practice:

- "Excellence in Teaching" is a high priority in the district.
- The district has adopted and published reasonable criteria for judging the competence of teachers.
- Sound procedures are used for determining whether teachers meet each criterion.
- Assistance and a reasonable time to improve are provided.
- Supervisors have requisite competencies and district has taken steps to ensure supervisors have these competencies.
- The necessary resources are provided.
- Supervisors are held accountable.
- A fair hearing prior to dismissal is provided.[8]

These and other lists of the key elements of good supervision and evaluation systems overlap in a number of areas. Similar ways that people perceive and make sense of these systems will be discussed in Chapter 7. This present chapter is devoted to an analysis of essential structural components. Five such components can be identified:

- A guiding vision of teaching or set of performance standards
- Procedures for collecting high-quality data on teaching performance
- Mechanisms for delivering useful feedback to teachers
- Resources for helping teachers improve their performance
- Procedures for handling inadequate teacher performance

A GUIDING VISION

No matter how sound the procedures are for supervising and evaluating teachers, they are unlikely to contribute much to instructional improvement if they are unsupported by a coherent vision of good teaching practice. Chapter 3 presented a variety of possible visions. In practice, the form that a vision of teaching frequently takes is a set of competencies or performance standards. Figure 6.1 is an example of a set of performance standards for the David Douglas School District in suburban Portland, Oregon. Each standard is accompanied by several behavioral indicators to guide in the appraisal of teaching performance.

Diagnostic Question 1.2

Is the system of teacher supervision and evaluation based on a sound vision of teaching?

Visions of teaching—whatever the form they take—may vary in quality. For example, performance standards are most likely to be useful in improving

DAVID DOUGLAS SCHOOL DISTRICT NO. 40
PROFESSIONAL COMPETENCY APPRAISAL CHECKLIST

Teacher's Name _____ School _____

Grade/Subject _____ School Year 19 ___ 19 ___ Principal _____ Evaluator _____

Year of: Teaching (including current year) _____ Probation _____ This District _____ This School _____

O — Outstanding	PRE-EVALUATION INTERVIEW DATE	PRE-OBS. CONF. DATES	OBSERVATION DATES	POST-OBS. CONF. DATES
VG — Very Good				
G — Good				
NI — An area where improvement is needed				
SI — Substantial improvement needed	POST-EVALUATION INTERVIEW DATE			
II — Assistance given, but improvement insufficient at this time				
TT — Recommended to teach other teachers				

Forms required: *1 — E-5; *2 — E-3, E-5; *3 — E-3, E-4A, E-4B, E5

Staff member's goal(s), if any _____

_____

Evaluator's goal(s) for staff member, if any _____

_____

PERFORMANCE STANDARDS AND INDICATORS	O	VG	G	NI *2	SI *3	II *3	TT *1
I. *The Staff Member Demonstrates Satisfactory Preparation Competencies*							
1. Is prepared academically for assignment							
2. Participates with assignment-related organization							
II. *The Staff Member Effectively Uses Performance Skills Needed in His/Her Assignment*							
1. Plans and organizes							
2. Creates and innovates							
3. Encourages students to learn and develop							
4. Adapts procedures to meet varying student needs/interests							
5. Encourages independent learning activities							
6. Chooses appropriate instructional materials							
7. Utilizes appropriate evaluative methods							
8. Gives individual help and attention							
9. Explains and gives directions clearly							
III. *The Staff Member Exercises Appropriate Management Ability*							
1. Handles discipline skillfully both in and out of assignment area							
2. Attends to details and routines							
3. Accepts and follows through in work assignments							
4. Manages confidential information							
IV. *The Staff Member Maintains Productive Working Relationships*							
1. Shows empathy for and relates well to students							
2. Works well with peers							
3. Works well with administrators and supervisors							
4. Works well with community							
V. *The Staff Member Exhibits Acceptable Personal Competencies*							
1. Uses language carefully							
2. Dresses appropriately for assignment							
3. Is tactful and calm							

Evaluator's summary _____

_____

Teacher remarks, if any _____

_____

This is to certify that we have read and discussed the above report.

Signed _____ Principal _____ Date

Signed _____ Teacher _____ Date

Signed _____ Evaluator (if other than Principal) _____ Date

Figure 6.1

instruction when they are (1) clearly stated, (2) based on the latest research, (3) developed as a result of teacher involvement, (4) widely publicized, and (5) reviewed on a regular basis. Furthermore, it makes sense to link performance standards to teacher job descriptions. In some districts, both performance standards and job descriptions have a tendency to be forgotten during the process of supervision and evaluation. Where performance standards and job descriptions no longer reflect what teachers are expected to do, the process of supervision and evaluation can begin to resemble the actions of a rudderless vessel. The destination of effective instruction may still be reached, but more because of luck than design.

In a comprehensive review of the literature on performance assessment, Richard Stiggins and Nancy Bridgeford provide additional guidance for the development of performance standards. They suggest that performance standards may interfere with evaluation practice if and when they,

- Focus on personal characteristics rather than instructional skills
- Call for inferences about teaching behavior that compromise reliability
- Are too general to provide diagnostic information
- Are unclear or unrelated to professional practices of teachers[9]

The last item is, in some ways, the most crucial. If performance standards are vague or unrelated to practice, it may be because experienced teachers have not participated in their development. The extent to which teachers are involved in the specification of performance standards may be a function of the concept of teaching held by district administrators. Teaching may be regarded as labor, craft, art, or profession.[10] If it is considered a true profession—as it is in this volume—teachers should play a major role in developing and periodically revising the performance standards that guide the supervision and evaluation of their teaching. Professionals, by definition, are in the best position to determine the standards by which the technical aspects of their work are judged. Also, it is difficult to imagine a better form of professional development for educators than generating or revising performance standards for effective teaching.

Diagnostic Question 1.3

Do teachers play a key role in developing and periodically reviewing performance standards of effective teaching?

QUALITY DATA ON TEACHING

Once a working vision of teaching has been developed, procedures must be established for gathering high-quality data related to actual teaching performance. Data may be needed for a variety of supervisory and evaluative purposes.

For example, data may be required to determine if (1) professional improvement goals have been met, (2) performance standards have been mastered, or (3) plans of assistance have been fulfilled. The quality of supervision and evaluation is unlikely to be any better than the quality of data collected on teaching performance. The quality of data, in turn, is related to three key factors:

- The variety of sources of relevant information
- The frequency with which information is collected
- The care with which information is collected

Variety of Sources

Traditionally, supervisors have relied on direct observation of teaching as their primary source of data, but there are, in fact, a number of different ways to collect observational data. In addition, important data may be gathered by surveying student opinion, reviewing documents related to lessons, looking at evidence of student achievement, and asking teachers to reflect on their own performance. Let us first consider different ways of collecting observational data.

Diagnostic Question 1.4

Are data on teaching performance drawn from a variety of sources?

Observation techniques may be divided into two general categories—wide-angle lens techniques and microscope techniques. As the names suggest, the first set attempts to look at teaching holistically, while the latter focuses on predetermined aspects of classroom activity. The decision about which to use depends on the observer's familiarity with the teacher and the teaching situation as well as the expressed needs of the teacher. For example, a wide-angle lens approach may be useful in getting to "know" a new teacher or in observing an experienced teacher who has mastered all the basic performance standards. A microscope technique may be useful when a teacher voices a specific concern or when a supervisor believes that improvement is needed in a certain area of teaching.

Three types of wide-angle lens techniques are (1) verbatim notes, (2) videotapes, and (3) the recording of impressions. Verbatim notes call on observers to write down as much of what they see and hear as possible.[11] Obviously, this technique can present problems in a rapidly paced class discussion or lecture. The observer may be compelled to adopt some shorthand or symbol system, or to use a *selective verbatim* approach. One form of selective verbatim involves time-sampling, where the observer writes down everything that occurs at specific intervals (such as every five minutes).

Easier on the hand and often more useful in post-observation discussions with teachers are videotapes of lessons. Videotapes provide as objective a record as possible of classroom activity. The only limitations of the technique are the limits of the camera's aperture and sound pickup capacity. Videotaping from the rear of the classroom usually loses the faces and sometimes the voices of students. Videotaping from the front of the classroom may miss some teacher moves and comments. During seatwork a camera is unlikely to gather as much useful data as an observer moving about the classroom.

A third wide-angle lens technique involves the recording of impressions. The application of this technique may range from the traditional and often maligned anecdotal notes of supervisors to the systematic and elaborate commentary of highly skilled ethnographers. Elliot Eisner has developed an impression-gathering approach he refers to as "educational criticism." Of this approach he says,[12]

> What critics do or should try to do is not translate what cannot be translated but rather to create a rendering of a situation, event, or object that will provide pointers to those aspects of the situation, event, or object that are in some way significant.

The recording of impressions is an attempt by observers to attach meaning or value to what they do and do not see, hear, and feel. The observer cannot attribute meanings or values to observed behavior without giving some sense of the context in which it takes place. This is both the strength and the weakness of the technique. Purely objective data lack sensitivity to contextual issues. For instance, a class may go for 40 minutes without a single student interruption. This factual observation is relatively useless, however, unless we know whether students were spellbound by the lecturer's magical use of words or terrified by his or her menacing tone and reputation for sarcastic retorts to student remarks. While such elaboration can be vital to understanding a lesson, it is still the opinion of an observer. By recording only subjective impressions, observers fail to establish a true picture of classroom activity to which they along with teachers can refer in cases of disputed judgments.

Microscope techniques are very useful sources of relatively objective data. There are literally hundreds of instruments available for collecting specific kinds of data.[13] Observers and teachers also may design their own devices for collecting microscope data. To simplify selection of the most appropriate technique, it is helpful to think in terms of two sets of categories. The first set is based on the type of focused data that is collected by an observer, the second set on what is being observed.

Types of data gathered by microscope techniques include frequency counts, checklists, rating scales, and diagrams. Frequency counts may involve tabulating such items as the number of times students interrupt, the number of recall questions asked by a teacher, or the number of times a teacher provides positive reinforcement. The usefulness of frequency counts can be enhanced by collecting supplementary data that permit ratios and percentages to be reported. Thus, we can report the number of student interruptions per minute, the percentage of all teacher questions that require student recall of facts, and the ratio of positive reinforcement to negative reinforcement per unit of time (that is, a class period). Figure 6.2 shows an instrument designed by Good and Brophy for counting the number of times a teacher gives praise to individual students.

Checklists permit observers to note whether or not certain behaviors take place, but the frequency of such behaviors is not recorded. For example, the observer and teacher may agree on the elements of a good lesson. They may

---

FORM 4.3. Individual Praise

USE: Whenever the teacher praises an individual student
PURPOSE: To see what behaviors the teacher reinforces through praise, and
to see how the teacher's praise is distributed among the students.
Whenever the teacher praises an individual student, code the student's
number and each category of teacher behavior that applies
(consecutively).

BEHAVIOR CATEGORIES	STUDENT NUMBER	CODES
1. Perseverance or effort, worked long or hard	14	1. **3**
	23	2. **3.4**
2. Progress (relative to the past) toward achievement	6	3. **3**
	18	4. **3**
3. Success (right answer, high score), achievement	8	5. **1**
4. Good thinking, good suggestion, good guess or nice try	8	6. **1**
	8	7. **1**
5. Imagination, creativity, originality		8. ___
6. Neatness, careful work		9. ___
7. Good or compliant behavior, follows rules, pays attention		10. ___
8. Thoughtfulness, courtesy, offering to share; prosocial behavior		11. ___
		12. ___
9. Other (specify)		13. ___
		14. ___
NOTES:		15. ___
all answers occurred during social studies discussion.		16. ___
		17. ___
		18. ___
		19. ___
		20. ___
Was particularly concerned about #8, a low-achieving male.		21. ___
		22. ___
		23. ___
		24. ___
		25. ___

Figure 6.2 Adapted from Thomas L. Good and Jere E. Brophy, *Looking in Classrooms* 3rd ed. (New York: Harper & Row, Publishers, 1984), p. 126. With permission of the publisher.

determine that a good lesson consists of an introduction, a specific objective, new information, student practice, and a closing review. Using this list, the observer checks each element included in a particular lesson by the teacher. In many cases, checklists must be supplemented with additional information to be very useful. Two teachers may both provide introductions to their lessons, but one introduction may be highly motivating and clear, while the other is dull and confusing. Checklists often miss such important distinctions. Figure 6.3 shows the form that checklists frequently take.

A third type of microscope data involves rating scales. Rather than simply noting the presence or absence of a given behavior, as is done on a checklist,

---

QUESTIONS TO HELP ANALYZE A LESSON[1]

*1.3 STUDENTS ARE CAREFULLY ORIENTED TO LESSONS

TEACHER BEHAVIORS	ANSWER	
	YES	NO
1. Was learning (skills/knowledge) to be acquired clearly stated to students?		
2. Were the students shown how the learning related to previous learning they had experienced or to needs in their lives?		
3. Did the teacher identify resource material for the lesson?		
4. Did the teacher identify major steps in tasks?		
5. Did the teacher list checkpoints to measure progress?		
6. Did the teacher point out next activity to be done?		

1.4 INSTRUCTION IS CLEAR AND FOCUSED

1. Did the teacher give an adequate explanation of the learning before students were expected to put it into practice?		
2. Did the teacher model the learning and its application for the students?		
3. Did the teacher allow time for practice?		
4. Did the teacher check regularly to make sure that all students understood the learning?		
5. Were the teacher's questions and directions relevant to the objectives?		
6. Was the practice directly related to the learning?		
7. Did the teacher provide/allow time for closure to the lesson?		
8. Did the teacher close the lesson by having students identify what the session's learning was?		
9. Did the students leave the class knowing and understanding what the learning for that session was?		
10. Did the teacher assign homework based on the day's learning?		

[1]This checklist was developed as a research synthesis by the Northwest Regional Educational Laboratory, Portland, Oregon.

Figure 6.3

114   *Dimensions of Leadership for Instructional Improvement*

Stanford Teacher Competence Appraisal Guide

		0	1	2	3	4	5	6	7
		UNABLE TO OBSERVE	WEAK	BELOW AVERAGE	AVERAGE	STRONG	SUPERIOR	OUTSTANDING	TRULY EXCEPTIONAL
		0	30%	15%	15%	15%	15%	15%	10%	10%

AIMS

1. Clarity of aims. — The purposes of the lesson are clear.
2. Appropriateness of aims. — The aims are neither too easy nor too difficult for the pupils. They are appropriate, and are accepted by the pupils.

PLANNING

3. Organization of the lesson. — The individual parts of the lesson are clearly related to each other in an appropriate way. The total organization facilitates what is to be learned.
4. Selection of content. — The content is appropriate for the aims of the lesson, the level of the class, and the teaching method.
5. Selection of materials. — The specific instructional materials and human resources used are clearly related to the content of the lesson and complement the selected method of instruction.

Figure 6.4

PERFORMANCE	6. Beginning the lesson.	Pupils come quickly to attention. They direct themselves to the tasks to be accomplished.						
	7. Clarity of presentation.	The content of the lesson is presented so that it is understandable to the pupils. Different points of view and specific illustrations are used when appropriate.						
	8. Pacing of the lesson.	The movement from one part of the lesson to the next is governed by the pupils' achievement. The teacher "stays with the class" and adjusts the tempo accordingly.						
	9. Pupil participation and attention.	The class is attentive. When appropriate, the pupils actively participate in the lesson.						
	10. Ending the lesson.	The lesson is ended when the pupils have achieved the aims of instruction. There is a deliberate attempt to tie together the planned and chance events of the lesson and relate them to the immediate and long-range aims of instruction.						
EVALUATION	11. Teacher-pupil rapport.	The personal relationships between pupils and the teacher are harmonious.						
	12. Variety of evaluative procedures.	The teacher devises and uses an adequate variety of procedures, both formal and informal, to evaluate progress in all of the aims of instruction.						
	13. Use of evaluation to improve teaching and learning.	The results of evaluation are carefully reviewed by teacher and pupils for the purpose of improving teaching and learning.						

the observer assesses its quality, using numerical ratings. Though usually less reliable than checklist data, ratings are an important source of information on observer judgment. Figure 6.4 gives us an example of a rating scale, the Stanford Teacher Competence Appraisal Guide. Observers are asked to rate teachers on a number of dimensions in relation to other teachers they have observed.

Diagrams provide a fourth type of microscope data. Observers attempt to represent pictorially what they see or hear. The basis for observational diagrams is typically a seating chart, with squares for each desk or chair. Students are given numbers when the observer does not know them by name. The observer may diagram such things as teacher and student movement around the room and patterns of verbal interaction. Figure 6.5 is a diagram of teacher position and student interaction during a class segment. It can easily be seen that

Each square depicts one student in the classroom. The teacher's position is marked with sequential numbers, 1, 2, 3, etc. Each time the teacher talks with a student, the observer marks the number of the teacher's position in the square denoting a specific student. For example, when this teacher was standing in position 1, she talked to students R, D, E, J, N, and S. From position 2, she talked to students P, R, T, X, and W. From position 3 she talked with students A, B, C, G, L, and R.

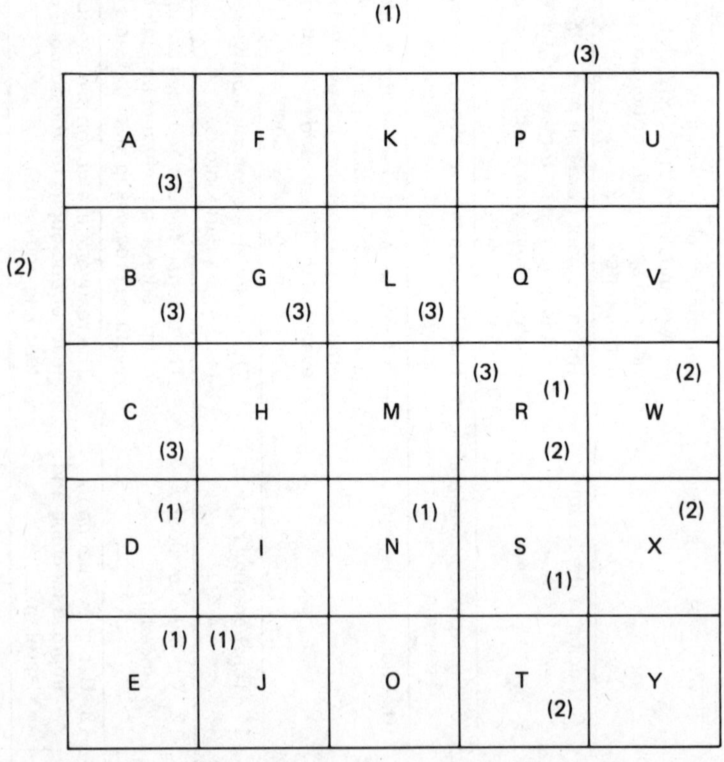

(1)

(3)

A (3)	F	K	P	U
B (3)	G (3)	L (3)	Q	V
C (3)	H	M	R (3)(1)(2)	W (2)
D (1)	I	N (1)	S (1)	X (2)
E (1)	J (1)	O	T (2)	Y

(2) is marked on the left side, row 2.

Figure 6.5 Reprinted with permission from the *NASSP Bulletin,* Vol. 67, No. 463, May 1983.

the teacher worked from three different locations and failed to interact with 11 of the 25 students.

Microscope techniques may be thought of in terms of the object as well as the form of data collection. Observers may choose to concentrate on some aspect of teacher behavior, student behavior, or teacher-student interaction. In addition, observers may focus on aspects of the lesson, including content and organization. It should be noted that everything of value to instructional improvement may not be equally accessible to observation. For example, observers cannot "see" students learning or teachers deciding. They must make inferences based on what students and teachers do that is audible or observable. Therefore, a student may give the right answer to a teacher question, but for the wrong reason. To reduce the likelihood of collecting misleading data on teaching performance, observers should rely on other sources of information besides classroom observation. One such source is student input.

Teachers frequently express concern that students will not be objective in their judgments of teaching performance. But if appropriate questions are asked, students can provide information of vital interest to those concerned with instructional improvement. After all, students spend much more time with teachers than adult observers. In addition, they are often in the best position to determine if instruction is effective. In a unique study comparing the quality of student and observer judgments of instruction, a group of University of Wisconsin researchers discovered that "students' reports of their understanding of the lesson and their cognitive processes during classroom instruction may be more reliable and more valid indicators of students' classroom learning than observers' judgments of student attention."[14] Involving students in assessing teaching performance also has the advantage of legitimizing student opinion and increasing the likelihood of student participation in other aspects of classroom life.

Students can provide helpful information on the following topics related to instructional improvement:

- Course content
  Organization
  Relevance
  Relationship to previous learning
  Difficulty
- Instruction
  Clarity of presentation
  Opportunity for assistance from teacher
  Student involvement in class discussions
  Ability of teacher to sustain interest
  Pacing of lessons
- Student characteristics
  Motivation
  Satisfaction
  Understanding of content

Some school districts routinely collect student opinions on instruction. Figure 6.6 is a checklist used to collect anonymous student opinions in Milpitas

Student Opinion Form
Milpitas United School District
Milpitas, California

STUDENT OPINION FORM TO BE RETURNED DIRECTLY TO THE TEACHER

Circle Period: 1   2   3   4   5   6   7

Directions:
This is an attempt by your teacher to improve the class by
listening to your reactions. Please respond to each statement below by checking in one of the columns to the right.
Be as honest as possible. Do not sign your name.

	MOST OF THE TIME	SOME-TIMES	HARDLY EVER	NO OPINION
1. This teacher has helped me be interested in the subject.				
2. I try to participate in this class.				
3. This teacher begins class promptly without wasting time.				
4. This teacher seems to know the subject we're studying.				
5. This teacher is well organized.				
6. Homework is worthwhile and not just busy-work.				
7. The amount of homework we get is right for this kind of class.				
8. I am graded fairly in this class.				
9. This teacher avoids treating certain students as favorites.				
10. This teacher is reasonable in what students are expected to do.				
11. This teacher shows understanding and concern for students.				
12. This teacher respects the expression of different opinions.				
13. This teacher talks too much about personal problems that shouldn't be brought to the classroom.				
14. This teacher explains lessons clearly.				
15. I have opportunities to express myself in class.				
16. This teacher spends too much time talking.				
17. This teacher seems to understand how much I know and helps me learn.				
18. This teacher uses different ways and aids to help me learn.				
19. This teacher goes over our written work and returns it to us.				
20. This teacher listens and tries to understand what we're saying.				
21. This teacher keeps the class under control enough to allow us to learn.				
22. This teacher tries to make the course interesting.				
23. This class is a place I like to be.				

Figure 6.6

(Calif.) United School District. It has several characteristics of a well-designed instrument for gathering student input:

- Instructions are clear.
- Language is free of technical terms and jargon.
- Form can be completed quickly.
- Items use first person singular and plural to personalize responses.

Al Davidian, former principal of Klamath Falls High School in Oregon, used a different procedure for gathering student data. Using an "item bank" of student-evaluation questions, he produced a personalized student-evaluation instrument for each teacher. As principal, he could choose six questions from the item bank. The chairperson of the teacher's department was allowed to choose eight items. The teacher then could choose as many as 16 items. Only teachers got to see student data from their own classes. Davidian and the department chairs received aggregate data for groups of teachers on a computer printout.

Joyce Epstein reports that data from parents may also be helpful for certain aspects of supervision and evaluation.[15] When she compared teacher evaluations done by elementary principals in Maryland with ones done by parents of students in these teachers' classrooms, she found that the two were modestly correlated. Parents tended, however, to focus more on the quality of teacher communications with the home, parental involvement in classroom activities, and classroom discipline—it is likely that parents have access to data on teacher performance to which school leaders are not always privy.

Besides student judgments, parent data, and classroom observations, information on the content of lessons can be invaluable to the process of instructional improvement. In practice, however, this area is very often neglected because supervisors lack expertise in particular subject matter areas. For this reason, it makes sense to involve fellow teachers, subject matter specialists, and department chairs in collecting data related to curriculum matters. The following list includes some of the documents or "artifacts" that may be of value in this process:

- Course goals and objectives
- Lesson plans and outlines
- Assignments
- Tests and quizzes
- Student class notes
- Teacher handouts

A fourth source of data is student achievement. There are, of course, reasons why it may not be appropriate to use student achievement data to conduct summative evaluations of teachers. No two teachers work with exactly the same group of students, so it is difficult to compare teaching performance across teachers or even for the same teacher from one year to the next. In reviewing the literature, Darling-Hammond, Wise, and Pease report low reliability for the use of student test scores as a measure of teaching effectiveness.[16] They also note that curriculum innovation may be inhibited when teachers are judged solely on the basis of student test performance. A teacher opinion poll in 1979 indicated that only 11 percent of teachers felt that student test scores were valid measures of teacher effectiveness.[17] And some teacher contracts, such as the one in Portland, Oregon, expressly prohibit the use of student achievement data to evaluate teachers.

Despite these concerns, student achievement cannot be totally ignored as a valuable source of data on teacher performance. Dramatic changes in the achievement of an individual student may infer a significant interaction, either negative or positive, between the student and a teacher. Years of relatively poor student performance in class may raise serious questions about a particular teacher's competence. Moreover, in two studies of California principals, Naftaly Glasman found that most principals shared student test data with teachers and believed that this procedure contributed to improved teacher performance.[18]

The real value of student achievement data seems to lie in its usefulness for formative purposes. Without accurate knowledge of how students are performing, teachers may be unable to modify instruction successfully. Besides test scores, teachers can get information from systematic reviews of student homework, responses to questions in class, and seatwork. "Debriefing" students at the end of a learning experience also may be helpful. A technique was developed for getting students to reconstruct a completed lesson, unit, or course in their own words. These debriefing data indicated how much students had learned that teachers intended them to learn.[19] Supervisors concerned about student achievement in particular classes should always make some direct contact with students as well as review the teacher's gradebook and actual examples of student work.

A fifth source of data on teaching performance is teachers themselves. In case studies of teacher evaluation, Stiggins and Bridgeford report that 53 percent of the teachers desired more opportunity for self-evaluation.[20] It is important for supervisors to know how teachers "make sense" of their own teaching. While there are obvious reasons why teacher self-evaluations would not be used to make decisions related to employment, such information may be very useful in supervision and evaluation that is directed toward improvement. In a comprehensive review, J. Gregory Carroll concludes that self-ratings "appear to be most helpful for comparisons with and interpretations of other sources of data, such as student ratings, student achievement, classroom observations, and videotape feedback."[21]

Several techniques are available for collecting self-evaluation data. Allan Glatthorn recommends that some teachers keep a reflective journal of "experiences, feelings, and reactions during the supervisory process."[22] Also, a variety of self-assessment instruments are available to teachers to stimulate reflection; Figure 6.7 is one such form. A third technique calls for teachers to watch videotapes of themselves and record their reactions. In addition, teacher self-reflection can be stimulated through opportunities to observe colleagues teaching. Given the limitations of access to supervisors and observers in most schools, teachers may find it essential to engage regularly in systematic self-evaluation.

Frequency

The quality of data used for teacher supervision and evaluation is related not only to the variety of information available, but also to the frequency with which it is collected. Teachers and supervisors have long acknowledged the limitations of making judgments of teaching performance based on only a single annual visit. Contemporary contracts often specify the minimum number of formal classroom observations that must be conducted prior to evaluating a teacher. Typically, between one and three observations are required. In cases

---

SELF-APPRAISAL OF TEACHING[1]

Teacher _____ Course _____

Term _____ Academic Year _____

Thoughtful self-evaluation can help improve teaching effectiveness. This questionnaire is designed for that purpose. You are asked to look at your own performance in teaching.

At your option, questions 12 and 13 may be added. Use the back of this form for any written comments you might want to express. These might record any unusual circumstances that relate to the course and to your teaching it.

Directions:

Rate yourself on each item, giving the highest score for unusually effective performances. Place in the blank space before each statement the number that most nearly expresses your view:

Highest			Average			Lowest	Don't Know
7	6	5	4	3	2	1	X

_____ 1. Have the major objectives of your course been made clear?

_____ 2. How do you rate agreement between course objectives and lesson assignments?

_____ 3. Are class presentations well planned and organized?

_____ 4. Are important ideas clearly explained?

_____ 5. How would you judge your mastery of the course content?

_____ 6. Is class time well used?

_____ 7. Have you encouraged critical thinking and analysis?

_____ 8. Have you encouraged students to seek your help when necessary?

_____ 9. Have you encouraged relevant student involvement in the class?

_____ 10. How tolerant are you of student viewpoints that differ from your own?

_____ 11. Considering the previous 10 items, how would you rate your performance in this course as compared to others in the department who have taught the same course?

_____ 12.

_____ 13.

_____ Composite rating.

[1]R.I. Miller, *Evaluating Faculty Performance* (San Francisco: Jossey-Bass, 1972), p. 37. Reprinted with permission of publisher.

Figure 6.7

where multiple observations are called for, observers usually conduct them at different points in the year. An alternative practice which may yield higher-quality data involves visiting the same class two or three days in a row. Such an arrangement reduces the likelihood that a teacher can put on a star performance, and permits the observer to determine instructional continuity from one day to the next.

Diagnostic Question 1.5

Have provisions been made for the frequent collection of data on teaching performance?

Judith Little and Thomas Bird report that teachers claim they lack faith in an observer who has made fewer than four visits.[23] To obtain more classroom data, there are two possible solutions: (1) more informal "drop-in" visits to supplement formal—and time-consuming—observations (some school leaders create convenient excuses to visit classrooms daily, delivering messages, newsletters, attendance sheets, and the like) and (2) an increase in the number of observers. Little and Bird calculate that a high school principal working alone with a faculty of 80 would need two years to observe every teacher once, presuming he or she conducted one observation a week.[24] With the aid of two assistant principals, the task could be accomplished in 27 weeks. Using department chairs would further reduce the time required to observe every teacher. While contracts and state laws often limit the kinds of individuals who can evaluate teachers, there are few restrictions on those who may simply observe in class and provide teachers with descriptive information.

Closely related to the issue of frequency is the duration of classroom observations. Observers may visit teachers frequently, but fail to remain long enough to see a lesson develop or to determine whether students understand what they are being taught. A reasonable expectation for a formal observation is that an observer remain for at least 40 minutes or a full class period. Enough time should be set aside, in other words, for an observer to determine whether specific instructional objectives have been accomplished. Observers who arrive late and leave early unintentionally foster the impression that lessons lack an integrity of their own. Many teachers resent such insensitivity and subsequently reject any data that derive from abbreviated visits.

Care

A third key to the quality of information on teaching performance is the care with which it is collected. Observers may spend considerable time collecting data from a variety of sources, but if they are collected in a careless manner using invalid and unreliable techniques, the results are unlikely to lead to instructional improvement. The guidelines for collecting high-quality evaluative data on teaching performance are basically the same as those followed by any conscientious researcher. Dale Bolton has identified several criteria that should be used to judge the value of observation instruments:

- *relevance*—the extent to which the instrument measures a factor that is considered important
- *reliability*—the consistency or reproducibility of the measure, i.e., whether the instrument maintains its stability from one application to the next.
- *validity*—whether the instrument measures the behavior, object, or event it was intended to measure
- *fidelity*—the degree to which the response to the instrument parallels the true or actual performance
- *ease of administration*—the practicality of the instrument in evaluation, i.e., scoring ease[25]

An observer who ignores these criteria when selecting an evaluation technique or instrument may wind up focusing on a relatively insignificant or uncharacteristic aspect of teaching. The observer may also allow subjective feelings to influence data collection, thereby reducing the likelihood that another observer would come up with similar findings. Or else the observer may think he or she is gathering data on a particular aspect of teaching, when in fact he or she is really finding out about a completely different dimension. Finally, the observer may select an instrument that is too time-consuming or difficult to analyze to be practical.

Diagnostic Question 1.6

Have provisions been made to periodically check the quality of data collected on teaching performance?

As Good and Brophy indicate in their highly useful guide to classroom observation, the major obligation of an observer is to collect *descriptive* data.[26] Descriptive data should be as free of judgments and impressions as possible. "Four students were asked questions requiring factual responses" is a descriptive statement. "The teacher asked too many factual questions" is a judgment. Descriptive data require minimal use of colorful adjectives and adverbs. As will be discussed later, descriptive data permit both observer and teacher to participate as equals in post-observation interpretations of the data. When observers record only their subjective impressions, there is no objective account of events to which both observer and teacher can refer in cases of disagreement.

One way to minimize the chances of collecting biased data is to use different observers periodically. Two observers—perhaps a regular supervisor and a teacher trained in classroom observation—both may observe the same lesson and compare notes to check the reliability of their data. Alternatively, observers can compare their descriptive notes with a videotape of the lesson. Whatever the procedure, observers are urged to check the quality of their data collection on a regular basis. The consequences for teachers of collecting erroneous data are simply too great to tolerate in any system of supervision and evaluation dedicated to accountability *and* improvement.

FEEDBACK ON INSTRUCTION

Once high-quality data related to teaching performance have been collected, they should be shared, analyzed, and interpreted in a timely manner. The longer teachers must wait to review information, the less likely they are to benefit from it. The feedback phase of supervision and evaluation is often the most neglected component of the entire process.

Methods of sharing data range from simply leaving a copy of observation notes with a teacher to the compilation of information into tables, charts, and graphs. Whatever the form, data should be left, whenever possible, in their most descriptive state. This provision allows the teacher to initiate analysis of the data. When observers arrive at post-observation conferences with data already analyzed, teachers are placed at a disadvantage. They may be intimidated by the observers and therefore reluctant to challenge the analyses. They may also be so impressed by the observers' analyses that they fail to develop and refine their own analytical skills. In either case, teachers are less likely to grow professionally than when observers permit them to try to make sense of the data first.

Diagnostic Question 1.7

Are data on teaching performance shared, analyzed, and interpreted in a timely manner?

Diagnostic Question 1.8

Are teachers permitted to analyze observation data before observers?

There are various ways to make sense of data on teaching performance, depending on the amount and form of available data. In the case of data on the content of lessons, analysis may focus on such criteria as accuracy, difficulty, relevance to student interests, and relationship to district curriculum guidelines. Regarding observations of teacher and student behavior, analysis may entail the search for patterns or tendencies during a lesson. For example, does the teacher tend to ask certain types of questions to certain types of students? Does off-task behavior tend to occur in a certain section of the classroom? Does a teacher tend to deliver praise in a routine and uninspired way?

Another kind of analysis involves the identification of trends over time. In these cases, teachers and observers review data from several observations to determine if certain behaviors occur with regularity. Some teachers, for instance, typically waste substantial portions of instructional time on transitions from one phase of a lesson to another. Other teachers may tend more to criticize inappropriate student behavior than to reinforce appropriate student behavior.

Detecting discrepancies between different sources of data constitutes yet another type of analysis. For example, what a teacher plans to do during a lesson—based on a pre-observation conference between the teacher and an observer—may differ from what the teacher actually does. Or a teacher's perception of how well students understand a complex concept may not correspond to the perceptions of the students themselves. In some cases, an observer may judge a class to be too noisy when, in fact, both students and teacher feel the noise level is entirely appropriate given the nature of the lesson.

There are a variety of ways to approach the analysis of data, but analysis alone will not always lead to improved teaching performance. It is the interpretation of analyzed data that is often the key to successful feedback. Data interpretation addresses the question "So what?" So a teacher tends to ask challenging questions to more able students? Is this a problem? To answer the question, the teacher or the observer should have some knowledge of research on teaching effectiveness. With this knowledge, he or she may infer that the teacher's questioning practices jeopardize the development of higher-order thinking skills in less able students. It is not sufficient for school leaders to be capable collectors and analyzers of data on teaching performance—they also must be able to relate their findings to research on good instructional practice. Since this research is constantly accumulating and changing, school leaders must stay current through reading and other forms of professional development.

Diagnostic Question 1.9

Are data on teaching performance analyzed in light of the latest research on effective practice?

The value of feedback may be further enhanced when it is balanced, focused, and frequent. Researchers have found that teachers are more likely to benefit from feedback when it has an appropriate mixture of praise and criticism.[27] Furthermore, experiments with videotaping and microteaching suggest that teachers are more likely to improve performance when they are exposed to feedback on a limited range of concerns.[28] Most people have difficulty attending to a large number of suggestions, no matter how valid or well intentioned. Finally, the more often teachers receive feedback, the more helpful it is likely to be.[29] Frequent feedback also is less apt to induce anxiety and defensiveness.

By creating situations where teachers expect to receive feedback on a regular basis, school leaders can minimize much of the fear and uncertainty surrounding supervision and evaluation.

HELPING TEACHERS IMPROVE

Up to this point, discussion has focused on how to make teachers more aware of what is occurring in their classrooms and of what their own instructional strengths and weaknesses are. Effective systems of supervision and evaluation also pinpoint areas for professional growth. If, however, a teacher is made aware of the need to change without being given the opportunities and resources necessary to improve, supervision and evaluation are likely to fail. A critical element, therefore, is some mechanism for providing assistance to teachers who are prepared to improve their professional performance.

Diagnostic Question 1.10

Do provisions exist for helping individual teachers and groups of teachers improve their professional performance?

Assistance for teachers may assume a variety of forms, but may be divided into two general categories—*professional development* and *staff development*. Professional development refers to efforts to assist individual teachers to become better teachers, taking account of their idiosyncratic needs, talents, deficiencies, assignments, and aspirations. Staff development refers to efforts to assist groups of teachers to better meet the organizational needs of their schools and school systems. In some cases, professional-development goals and staff-development goals may not be compatible.

With regard to professional development, assistance may focus on the mastering of fundamental performance standards or the acquisition of advanced skills and knowledge. The first target seems most appropriate for probationary or nontenured teachers, while the second pertains chiefly to experienced teachers. Selected veterans may be helped even beyond their present level of excellence in certain instructional areas, and thus become potential resources for colleagues and community.

Staff development is geared more to the improvement of schools than to the growth of individuals. Sometimes this form of assistance is intended to help teachers meet existing organizational expectations. For example, a principal may review all annual teacher evaluations for several years and discover that many faculty members are deficient in the teaching of writing—a district curriculum focus. Staff-development opportunities might then be provided to teachers so that they could learn the best ways to teach writing in various subject matter areas. In other instances, a new board policy or piece of legislation may necessitate providing assistance to *all* teachers in a school. Public Law 94-

142 required massive efforts by school leaders to train regular classroom teachers in how to work with mainstreamed handicapped students. Staff development will be discussed at greater length in Chapter 8.

Whatever the nature and purpose of teacher assistance, school leaders can select from a variety of methods and resources, including the following:

- Supervisor-directed assistance
- Independent study
- Peer assistance
- External assistance

Traditionally, supervisors—such as school principals—identified areas in which teachers needed improvement and then provided personal assistance. The limitations of such a system are obvious. Most supervisors probably are unable to stay abreast of the latest developments in all areas of instruction and curriculum, and even if they could, they may not be able to impart this knowledge effectively to all teachers. Sometimes, the fact that a supervisor makes job-related decisions affecting the employment status of teachers can interfere with the assistance process. To minimize such problems, some school districts, like Lake Washington (Wash.), employ full-time supervisors who are not allowed to function as evaluators. These people are trained in specific instructional strategies, and they provide assistance by invitation from a teacher or a principal.

Another way that teachers have traditionally received assistance is through independent study. Many adults prefer the privacy of working alone. They may fear public scrutiny or simply feel that they can move more quickly on their own. Again, there can be limitations to such a course of action. For certain improvements to occur, for instance, the involvement of other people is essential. People have difficulty seeing themselves as others see them. The presence of colleagues can foster a productive interchange of ideas and stimulate healthy professional competition.

Recent years have witnessed the growth of a variety of peer-assistance programs. Peers typically have the local knowledge and practical experiences so crucial to professional growth. One example of a peer-assistance program is the Toledo (Ohio) Public Schools' Intern Program.[30] This program places new teachers under the supervision of expert veteran teachers during their first year; the experienced teachers are released from classroom duties so that they can supervise, assist, and evaluate the interns. A second example is peer coaching. As Beverly Showers describes it, peer coaching calls for teams of teachers to "study the rationale of . . . new skills, see them demonstrated, practice them, and learn to provide feedback to one another as they experiment with the skills."[31] James Popham argues that peers should not only provide assistance to each other, but also that they should work in groups to evaluate the performance of fellow teachers.[32] He draws on the higher education model that calls for *ad hoc* faculty review committees to appraise the cases for promotion brought forth by individual instructors.

In some instances, though, even colleagues are unable to provide the assistance needed by certain teachers. External help may then be necessary. Sources of such help are college and university courses, district-sponsored and independent workshops, and special consultants. While such opportunities for growth get mixed reviews from teachers, they are sometimes capable of providing a crucial change in perspective which, in turn, can facilitate teacher development and reduce vulnerability. Many districts now provide the resources—such as tuition reimbursement and release time—to permit teachers to take advantage of these and other external sources of assistance. Some teacher-training institutions, such as Oregon State University and the University of Northern Colorado, have inaugurated *warranty programs* for their graduates. These programs call for the college or university to assume responsibility for assisting all education graduates whose teaching competence does not match district expectations after a period of employment.

It is vital that school leaders realize that no single form of assistance is apt to meet the needs of all teachers, or even the needs of the same teacher over time. For this reason, a variety of forms of assistance should always be at the disposal of those responsible for supervision and evaluation.

Diagnostic Question 1.11

Are a variety of kinds of assistance available for teacher growth and development?

REMEDIATION AND DISCIPLINE

No matter how good the supervision and evaluation process, it is reasonable to expect that some teachers will be unable to benefit from the usual forms of professional assistance. A profession involving more than two million practitioners is bound to have its share of marginally competent and troubled individuals. To protect the welfare of students and the integrity of the teaching profession, formal mechanisms must therefore exist for remediating serious problems with teaching performance and for disciplining those whose performance fails to improve. These mechanisms also must protect the due process rights of teachers whose property interests may be threatened by unsatisfactory supervision and evaluation.

Edwin Bridges and Barry Groves identify five general categories of teacher failure that may necessitate corrective action:

- Technical failure—The teacher's expertise falls short of what the task requires.
- Bureaucratic failure—The teacher fails to comply with school/district rules and regulations or directives of superiors.
- Ethical failure—The teacher fails to conform to standards of conduct presumably applicable to members of the teaching profession.
- Productive failure—The teacher fails to obtain certain desirable results in the classroom.

- Personal failure—The teacher lacks cognitive, affective, or physical attributes deemed instrumental in teaching.[33]

State law and district policy frequently define the specific conditions warranting disciplinary action and the procedure to be followed. Some type of formal *plan of assistance* may be called for as a final step prior to termination of a teacher's contract. Plans of assistance should be very clear and specific regarding the deficiency in need of correction, the corrective program to be followed, the evidence that will be used to determine whether the deficiency has been satisfactorily corrected, and the length of time allotted for the corrective program. Nancy Hungerford, an attorney with experience as a district personnel official, recommends that the same format be followed for all plans of assistance. Figure 6.8 illustrates this format in a case involving inadequate instructional planning and student assistance.

As can readily be seen, Hungerford's form leaves little to chance. The teacher is expected to develop a record-keeping system, lesson plans, and procedures for monitoring student progress. Dates when various phases of the plan are to be completed are specified, along with the time for a final evaluation of teacher performance. The preciseness of the plan gives the teacher a clear idea of what must be done to correct the deficiency, and the interim checkpoints and conferences ensure that he or she will receive continuous help. This plan of assistance, therefore, provides protection for the teacher without sacrificing accountability or rigor.

The Salt Lake City school system has developed a special team known as the "Remediation Team"[34] to aid as well as monitor teachers on plans of assistance. When informal efforts to correct a teacher's deficiencies fail, the principal may file a "Referral for Remediation" with the Superintendent. The Superintendent, in turn, designates a central office administrator as "learning specialist." This person assembles and chairs a Remediation Team consisting of four individuals, including the referring principal, a teacher whose subject matter area or grade level matches that of the teacher receiving assistance, and another teacher to ensure that the person's due process rights are protected. Two months are allocated initially for completing the plan of assistance, and if this period is insufficient, an additional three months may be set aside. During this second phase, the Remediation Team can call on a retired teacher or a teacher on leave to spend every school day with the deficient teacher providing intensive assistance. After five months the referring principal must determine whether or not the deficiency has been satisfactorily corrected.

For purposes of accountability, a system of teacher supervision and evaluation should provide formal mechanisms for correcting serious teacher deficiencies. In the event that corrective efforts are unsuccessful, there must be provisions for removing the teacher. Disciplinary action may range from reassignment to contract termination. Bear in mind that ultimately a faculty is no better than its weakest member, since only one incompetent teacher can undo the capable efforts of many others. Teacher remediation and discipline are probably the least popular, but among the most essential, functions of school leaders.

Diagnostic Question 1.12

Has provision been made for placing teachers with serious deficiencies on formal plans of assistance?

SAMPLE PLAN OF ASSISTANCE[1]

I. Statement of Area Needing Improvement

The teacher fails to adequately plan and facilitate instruction so that students receive instruction appropriate to their pre-existing skill level, so that students receive individual help with concepts they do not understand, and so that students receive adequate feedback concerning their progress in mastering the material.

II. Program to be Followed:

1. By _____ , the teacher will have reviewed with Counselor _____ the results of the entrance math exam given to all 9th-graders the previous spring and will have developed a record keeping system showing each of her students' progress in meeting the District minimal competencies in math.

This record-keeping system will be submitted to the principal by _____ .

2. Following _____ , weekly lesson plans will be developed for both the 9th and 10th-grade classes, listing for each day:
   — The math skill(s) to be taught
   — Number of students functioning below competency level in that skill, according to the spring exams.
   — Specific activities, demonstrations, illustrations that will be used to teach the concept.
   — Supplementary work that will be assigned to those students who have already mastered this particular concept.
   — How mastery of the skill will be evaluated (in-class paper checking, assignment handed in, chalk board performance, etc.)

Lesson plan will be submitted to the principal each Friday at or before 8 a.m. for the following week. The principal and teacher will meet each Friday at 2:45 p.m. to review the lesson plans, unless another time is arranged with the approval of the principal. The principal will observe to determine if the lesson plans for that particular day are being carried out as planned, and will provide feedback as to the effectiveness of the planned teaching activities, demonstrations, etc.

3. The teacher will develop a system for feedback and evaluation of student performance that includes the following components:
   — Completion of sample exercises in class as each skill is being taught so that students can determine if they are completing the problems correctly.
   — Teacher observation through board work, calling for answers, observing papers as students work so that teacher can identify those students who do not understand a concept.
   — Assigned daily work either graded in class (by student himself, fellow students, or volunteer helpers) or returned within two class days.
   — Review exercises assigned and reviewed in class prior to each major exam.
   — Progress reports home to parents of any student who receives grades of D or F on any major exam.

The principal, through review of lesson plans and through observation, will check to determine if this system is being followed.

The teacher will keep a grade book that lists each daily assignment, how corrected, grades reported, and the date when papers were returned.

The teacher will keep a file of review exercises assigned and progress reports sent home to students.

III.   Monitoring System

The teacher's progress in meeting expectations listed above will be monitored by (1) principal review of weekly lesson plans; (2) principal review of teacher's grade book and file, as required in #3 above; (3) principal review of teacher's competency record keeping; and (4) at two formal and two informal observations prior to _____ .

An interim progress conference will be held by _____ .

IV.   Final Evaluation:

A final evaluation of the teacher's progress in making the required improvements will be made by _____ .

Figure 6.8   Reprinted with permission of Nancy Hungerford.

TROUBLESHOOTING SUPERVISION AND EVALUATION

The elements of the supervision and evaluation process discussed here are typically set forth in formal systems of rules, regulations, and guidelines. School leaders should know these systems well. No system, however, operates in practice exactly the way it does on paper. Decades of experience with supervision and evaluation have revealed that there are certain areas that must be addressed as part of any attempt to improve supervision and evaluation. Four areas of concern in particular must be confronted if instructional improvement is to become a reality: the subordination of improvement, loose coupling, annualism, and prolonged emphasis on adequacy.

Accountability Versus Improvement

Earlier it was acknowledged that the attempt to use supervision and evaluation for both accountability and improvement creates many challenges for school leaders. Perhaps the greatest challenge revolves around the issue of trust. Trust is needed if teachers are to take the risks that often are prerequisites to growth. Yet how can teachers take risks when job loss can be a result of failure? Perhaps because of dilemmas like this, many school leaders simply abandon serious efforts to improve the performance of all teachers. Instead, they concentrate on a few very weak teachers, attempting to correct their deficiencies or else removing them. By stressing accountability over improvement, these school leaders ensure that supervision and evaluation address the needs of relatively few teachers. As a result, the system gets the reputation—and deservedly so—of being problem oriented rather than growth oriented. School leaders and teachers come to regard each other as adversaries. So for teachers in general to regard supervision and evaluation positively, school leaders must ensure that the goal of instructional improvement is pursued with vigor.

Loose Coupling

A second problem involves the lack of coordination between different parts of the supervision and evaluation system. For example, in theory, supervision and evaluation should be guided by research-based performance standards. But in practice, these performance standards may never be referred to when supervisors communicate with teachers about instruction—thus, the performance standards, cease to be a useful component of the system. In theory, teachers should establish improvement goals related to school and district goals. In practice, teacher goals often are unrelated to these superordinate goals. In theory, teacher evaluations at the end of the school year should be based, to some extent, on progress toward stated goals, classroom observations, and performance standards. In practice, these evaluations frequently are highly generalized statements that make no reference to annual goals, classroom observations, or performance standards. In theory, one year's set of teacher evaluations should serve as a basis for the succeeding year's goal-setting and staff-development activities. In practice, school leaders typically file and forget teacher evaluations. It is no wonder that educators often are skeptical about the value of supervision and evaluation. Before abandoning these processes, it is essential to determine whether or not they have been implemented appropriately or, in other words, whether or not the various parts of the system are connected and coordinated.

Annualism

Most systems of supervision and evaluation are designed to function during a school year, which normally runs from September through early June. Teachers are supposed to set goals in the fall and report on their progress in the spring. Classroom observations are supposed to take place throughout the late fall and winter, and teachers who receive negative evaluations generally must be notified by March or April that their contracts will not be renewed. Teacher evaluations must be submitted by late May or early June.

A school year (approximately 9½ months), however, may not afford sufficient time for meaningful supervision and evaluation. Such a brief period, for instance, discourages teachers from selecting challenging goals for improvement. Substantial instructional growth may demand several years of systematic study, practice, and feedback. In addition, a supervisor may be unable to observe a teacher in each desired area of performance during a single school year. It probably makes more sense to focus on only a few performance standards each year. This is the arrangement used by the Beaverton (Ore.) School District. It takes a Beaverton teacher three years to complete a supervision and evaluation cycle.

How necessary is it to evaluate every experienced teacher every year? College professors, as a rule, are reviewed every two or three years. Oregon requires tenured teachers to be evaluated biennially, a system that permits teachers to pursue relatively risk-free professional growth during nonevaluation years. For the same reasons that school systems seek to establish long-range goals, develop multi-year budgets, and negotiate two-and three-year contracts, school leaders may wish to extend the time period for completing a cycle of supervision and evaluation.

Adequacy or Excellence

A fourth problem with systems of supervision and evaluation is that they tend to make little provision for the cultivation of teaching virtuosity or excellence. Instead, they focus on determining whether all teachers meet the same minimum standards or competencies. Meaningful distinctions are not drawn between novice and experienced teachers, elementary and secondary teachers, or teachers of different subjects. Like standard models, all teachers are held accountable for the same performance standards for the duration of their careers in the district. Formal systems of supervision and evaluation rarely include opportunities for talented teachers to amplify on skills that are not expected of other teachers. These systems cannot easily accommodate teachers who develop unique qualities or who specialize in particular spheres of performance. New York's Teacher Education Conference Board has concluded that "teachers' collective effectiveness as a faculty may be greater where among them they possess a variety of strong features than where all are moderately competent in everything."[35]

A case can be made that, in practice, supervision and evaluation systems serve more to ensure adequacy—some would say mediocrity—than to promote excellence. While adequacy is a reasonable goal for probationary or nontenured teachers, it seems too limiting for experienced professionals. What is needed are systems of supervision and evaluation that make distinctions among the different kinds of teachers.[36] For example, why continue to evaluate a tenured teacher using the performance standards by which probationary teachers are judged? Veteran teachers should be expected to move beyond adequate performance and to develop areas of special talent. Supervisors, of course, should check every few years to make certain that these veteran teachers are still adequate in the "basics," but it is demeaning and unprofessional to do so annually. It is difficult to imagine that systems of supervision and evaluation will foster widespread interest in professional improvement as long as they are based on the belief that all teachers must look the same.

In their comprehensive review of research on teacher supervision and evaluation, Darling-Hammond, Wise, and Pease conclude that,

> Teacher evaluation is an activity that must satisfy competing individual and organizational needs. The imperative of uniform treatment for personnel decisions may result in standardized definitions of acceptable teaching behavior. However, research on teacher performance and teaching effectiveness does not lead to a stable list of measurable teaching behaviors effective in all teaching contexts ... If teacher evaluation is to be a useful tool for teacher improvement, the process must strike a careful balance between standardized, centrally administered performance expectations and teacher-specific approaches to evaluation and professional development.[37]

The focus of discussion thus far has been on systems of teacher supervision and evaluation. The term *system* implies formality, predictability, and logical connections between means and ends. The day-to-day experience of supervision and evaluation, however, is very personal and idiosyncratic. To be effective, instructional leaders must understand what this experience is like for individual teachers. The next chapter shifts focus from the properties of systems to the attributes and interrelationships of individuals.

STUDY QUESTIONS

1. Ask a teacher to describe the system by which he or she is supervised and evaluated. Then ask the teacher's supervisor to describe the same system. Do they share the same set of perceptions? If not, what factors may account for different perceptions?

2. Collect several different observation instruments and use them to collect classroom data. Critique them, using the criteria of validity, reliability, ease-of-use, relevance, and fidelity.

3. Identify several different teaching situations, such as large-group lecture, guided practice, and class discussion. For each situation, specify criteria you would use to judge the quality of teaching.

4. Develop a list of differences in the duties of elementary and secondary teachers. How can systems of supervision and evaluation accommodate these differences?

5. Using the format for a Plan of Assistance shown in Figure 6.8, develop a plan for a teacher who is unable to maintain control of student behavior during class discussions.

6. Compile an inventory of resources for teacher assistance available in your own school district. What additional resources might be useful?

NOTES

1. Carl D. Glickman, *Supervision of Instruction* (Boston: Allyn & Bacon, 1985), p. 4.
2. *Ibid.*, pp. 4–5.
3. Richard Manatt, "Teacher Performance Evaluation—Practical Application of Research," Occasional Paper 82–1 (Ames, Iowa: Iowa State University, 1982).
4. For an in-depth account of misguided supervision, see Arthur Blumberg, *Supervisors & Teachers: A Private Cold War*, 2nd ed. (Berkeley: McCutchan, 1980).
5. If the majority of teachers are not "reasonably competent," then the problem must be addressed by looking at recruiting, selection, and tenuring practices as well as teacher preparation programs.
6. Linda Darling-Hammond, Arthur E. Wise, and Sara R. Pease, "Teacher Evaluation in the Organizational Context: A Review of the Literature," *Review of Educational Research*, Vol. 53, No. 3 (Fall 1983), p. 320.
7. Arthur E. Wise, Linda Darling-Hammond, Milbrey W. McLaughlin, and Harriet T. Bernstein, *Case Studies for Teacher Evaluation: A Study of Effective Practices* (Santa Monica, Calif.: Rand, 1984), p. xi.

8. Edwin Bridges and Barry Groves, *Managing the Incompetent Teacher* (Eugene, Ore.: ERIC Clearinghouse on Education Management, 1984), pp. 71–74.
9. Richard J. Stiggins and Nancy J. Bridgeford, "Performance Assessment for Teacher Development," *Educational Evaluation and Policy Analysis,* Vol. 7, No. 1 (Spring 1985), p. 95.
10. Darling-Hammond, Wise, and Pease, p. 290.
11. For a good guide to taking verbatim notes, refer to James M. Cooper, *Developing Skills for Instructional Supervision* (New York: Longman, 1984), pp. 88–90.
12. Elliot W. Eisner, *The Educational Imagination* (New York: Macmillan, 1979), p. 197.
13. For examples of available instruments, refer to James M. Cooper, *Developing Skills for Instructional Supervision,* pp. 92–109; and Thomas L. Good and Jere E. Brophy, *Looking in Classrooms,* 3rd ed. (New York: Harper & Row, 1984).
14. Penelope L. Peterson, Susan R. Swing, Kevin D. Stark, and Gregory A. Waas, "Students' Cognitions and Time on Task during Mathematics Instruction," *American Educational Research Journal,* Vol. 21, No. 3 (Fall 1984), pp. 487–515.
15. Joyce L. Epstein, "A Question of Merit: Principals' and Parents' Evaluations of Teachers," paper presented at the annual meeting of the American Educational Research Association, 1984.
16. Darling-Hammond, Wise, and Pease, p. 307.
17. National Education Association, *Teacher Opinion Poll* (Washington, D.C.: National Education Association, 1978).
18. Naftaly S. Glasman, *Evaluation-Based Leadership* (forthcoming), p. 145.
19. Daniel L. Duke, "Debriefing: A Tool for Curriculum Research and Course Improvement," *Journal of Curriculum Studies,* Vol. 8, No. 2 (1977), pp. 157–163.
20. Richard J. Stiggins and Nancy J. Bridgeford, "Performance Assessment for Teacher Development," p. 92.
21. J. Gregory Carroll, "Faculty Self-Evaluation," *Handbook of Teacher Evaluation* Jason Millman (Ed.) (Beverly Hills, Calif.: SAGE, 1981), p. 181.
22. Allan A. Glatthorn, *Differentiated Supervision* (Alexandria, Va.: Association for Supervision and Curriculum Development, 1984).
23. Judith Warren Little and Thomas D. Bird, "Is There Instructional Leadership in High Schools? First Findings from a Study of Secondary School Administrators and Their Influence on Teachers' Professional Norms," paper presented at the Annual Convention of the American Educational Research Association, 1984, p. 23.
24. *Ibid.*
25. Dale L. Bolton, *Selection and Evaluation of Teachers* (Berkeley: McCutchan, 1973), p. 112.
26. Good and Brophy, *Looking in Classrooms,* pp. 47–62.
27. F. F. Fuller and B. A. Manning, "Self-confrontation Reviewed: A Conceptualization of Video Playback in Teacher Education," *Review of Educational Research,* Vol. 43, No. 4 (Fall 1973), pp. 469–528.
28. *Ibid.*
29. June E. Thompson, Sanford M. Dornbusch, and W. Richard Scott, "Failures of Communication in the Evaluation of Teachers by Principals," Technical Report No. 43 (Stanford: Stanford Center for Research and Development in Teaching, 1975).
30. The Toledo system is described in detail in Arthur Wise, *et. al., Case Studies for Teacher Evaluation: A Study of Effective Practices.*
31. Beverly Showers, "Teachers Coaching Teachers," *Educational Leadership,* Vol. 42, No. 7 (April 1985), p. 44.
32. W. James Popham, "The Evaluation of Teachers: A Mission Ahead of Its Measures," paper presented at the annual meeting of the American Educational Research Association, 1985.

33. Edwin M. Bridges and Barry Groves, *Managing the Incompetent Teacher,* pp. 6–7.
34. A full description of the Salt Lake City system is contained in Arthur E. Wise, *et al., Case Studies for Teacher Evaluation: A Study of Effective Practices.*
35. Teacher Education Conference Board, "The Effective Teacher" (Albany, N.Y.: Teacher Education Conference Board, 1981), p. 3.
36. Several systems that differentiate among teachers are reported in Darling-Hammond, Wise, and Pease, "Teacher Evaluation in the Organizational Context: A Review of the Literature," p. 311.
37. *Ibid.,* pp. 320–321.

CHAPTER 7

PERSONAL DIMENSIONS OF SUPERVISION AND EVALUATION

My first two years of teaching were very nearly my last. I became increasingly disillusioned with the system in which I was working. Teacher evaluations were one of my frustrations. I couldn't understand how principals (I had four in the first two years) could write such positive reports on a teacher that they didn't even know. Anyone can look good for 30 minutes and I was no exception. Principals visited my classroom twice, made glowing comments and then left, never to be seen again (at least not for another year).

Evaluations seemed to be done perfunctorily and with quick deliberation. Instructional improvements were never discussed, professional growth was never mentioned, and concerns were never brought up. During my entire first two years of teaching, no one ever questioned my techniques or challenged my methods. I knew that I was not doing the best job that I could. If I was such a great teacher I would have hated to see a terrible one! I think that the evaluation process had little impact on my teaching because improvement was never discussed. I decided to try a different school and give teaching one more year. If things were the same, I would leave teaching without regrets.

As it happened, the school that I transferred to very closely resembled my ideal. I was presented with models of excellent teaching and constantly challenged to improve my instructional skills. Informal observations took place almost daily and feedback was given often.

Evaluation took on a completely new meaning. I was well aware that my principal knew exactly what was going on in my class. I respected my principal's knowledge of methods and could sense that evaluations would be taken seriously.

Lesson plans were only a small part of the pre-conference discussion. For the first time, I was asked about my philosophy of teaching and the plans I had for professional growth. The atmosphere was informal and the meeting focused on my perceived needs and concerns.

Formal observations started on time and lasted at least 30 minutes. The punctuality impressed me (other principals had come late and left early). I received the impression that time was important and that my lesson planning was not taken for granted.

Feedback on the observations was quick and specific. Positive comments made a difference because I knew that they were honest and spoken by a person who knew what he was talking about.

Mary Yeager
Elementary Teacher
Portland Public Schools

The teacher who wrote this account captured in words what many educators feel. The experience of supervision and evaluation is not necessarily what formal documents would lead us to expect. Despite rhetoric to the contrary, many districts have failed to pursue the goal of teacher improvement in a serious way.[1] In addition, individual school leaders and teachers might neglect to follow good supervision and evaluation practices. One empirical study of the experiences of 12 urban elementary teachers disclosed that even guidelines for peer supervision were frequently ignored:

> For example, pre-observation conferences were conducted cursorily, if at all. Teachers claimed there was little time in their busy schedules to allow for thoughtful planning. Although teachers were trained to use a variety of instruments, many of those developed contained insufficient data from which to draw meaningful generalizations. In-depth analyses occurred only in approximately 20 percent of the conferences ... In the post-observation conferences, teachers seldom pursued the kind of thorough weighing of alternatives that was practiced in their coursework.[2]

The point to be made here should be obvious. Developing supervision and evaluation systems that are logically sound and legally safe and that look good on paper will not ensure instructional improvement. The human element plays a key role. Kenneth Strike and Barry Bull put forth the case clearly:

> ... it is not enough for evaluation procedures to produce rules that are "correct." A good system is also humane in its treatment of individuals, is nonalienating, produces cooperative working relations in the schools, and is effective in increasing the professional skills of the teaching staff.[3]

What factors, then, contribute to humane, growth-producing experiences with supervision and evaluation? This question served as the basis for a field study by Stiggins and Duke.[4] Having heard mostly complaints about supervision and evaluation, we set out to identify teachers who had actually improved their performance, understanding, or attitudes as a result of these processes. Over 50 case studies were developed of teachers in Oregon and Hawaii. When the case studies were content-analyzed, five clusters of factors were found associated with growth-producing supervision and evaluation.[5]

The first group of factors had to do with the evaluation context. Factors included the amount of time dedicated to supervision and evaluation, the clarity of district policies, recent history of local labor-management relations, the nature of the local teachers' contract, and the nature of state laws related to evaluation. Michael Knapp has concluded that supervision and evaluation systems sometimes fail to function as intended because they "rest on an idealized image of school management that ignores the powerful effects of organizational and contextual forces on management activity."[6]

The second and third groups dealt with performance information and feedback. This included a number of items discussed in the preceding chapter, such as clarity of performance standards, variety of data sources on teaching, and frequency of data collection and feedback. These factors related to the structural dimensions of supervision and evaluation. Experts like Blumberg argue that supervision and evaluation will never adequately serve the goal of improvement so long as leaders avoid basic changes in these structural elements.[7]

Structural changes are unlikely to yield qualitative improvements, though, without consideration of the key actors—teachers and supervisors. The final two groups of items associated with successful supervision and evaluation in the case studies involved the attributes of teachers and supervisors. This chapter takes a careful look at these attributes. It then examines the predictable occasions during the school year when teachers and supervisors interact and tries to identify ways to make these interactions as productive as possible.

IMPORTANT TEACHER ATTRIBUTES

Traditional literature on supervision and evaluation tends to overlook the importance of teacher attributes. The implication is clear—supervisors are responsible for the success or failure of these processes. But social learning theory tells us, that influence is reciprocal. Supervisors do influence teachers, but they, in turn, are influenced by teachers. Any school leader who has tried to work with a defensive and hostile teacher knows the impact that teacher disposition can have on the success of the supervision and evaluation experience.

Duke and Stiggins found that key teacher attributes affecting the outcome of this experience include level of competence, personal expectations, openness to criticism, orientation to change, and familiarity with the school. Most of these attributes probably reflect the overall level of development of the individual teacher. Before examining key teacher attributes, it may be useful to consider the nature and implications of a *developmental perspective*.

Adult Development

A *developmental perspective* implies that people tend to experience similar stages of growth, each characterized by predictable concerns and behavioral responses. Traditionally, development was regarded as a process that stopped when an adolescent became an adult. Specialists began to discover, however, that adults continue to develop. All people who reflect back on their early twenties will probably recognize that qualitative changes have occurred in the way they view their world, their lives, and their jobs. What is meaningful in a person's forties is apt to differ from what was important in his or her twenties. Stages of development, of course, do not neatly correspond to ten-year increments, and they are likely to differ for men and women, and from culture to culture.

As indicated earlier, Fuller used a developmental perspective to study how persons become teachers. As a result of this research, Fuller proposed that teachers experience three "stages," or clusters of concerns, as they move through the first years of their career.[8] Early concerns—referred to as "survival concerns"—relate to classroom control, mastery of content, and evaluations by supervisors. The idealism and identification with students that marked their pre-service preparation fade quickly in the face of real jobs filled with real responsibilities.

As survival concerns are addressed and successfully overcome, teachers begin to confront concerns with the teaching situation itself: inadequate resources, teaching assignments, and conflicting expectations. What is important about this stage is that teachers are still focused on themselves and their performance, not on students.

Eventually, many teachers are able to resolve concerns with their own teaching situation and shift attention to students. At this point, teachers wonder about meeting students' socio-emotional needs and ensuring that students learn what is required to advance.

Fuller criticized those who work with teachers but who ignore these stages of concern. Efforts to help teachers grow and improve performance are much more likely to succeed when they are geared to the appropriate level of concern of particular teachers. For example, it would be unwise to dwell on raising student academic performance until teachers have mastered classroom management and control. School leaders are therefore warned against assuming that all teachers share the same central concerns.

Competence

Teachers differ in areas other than their level of concern. For instance, they possess varying degrees of expertise in instruction and content. Teachers who are more competent may be less threatened by supervision and evaluation activities. H. S. Pambookian found that teachers who received favorable evaluations were more likely to change than those who received very low ratings.[9] At the same time, highly competent individuals can present a formidable challenge for supervisors, who may lack a sufficient level of expertise to contribute directly to teacher growth. Under such circumstances, the supervisor may need to locate other sources of assistance or play a more inquiring and less authoritative role.

Personal Expectations

In writing about people in the helping professions, Arthur Combs, Donald Avila, and William Purkey note that, "The success of a helper will depend not only on what he knows, but even more on the kind of person he is and how effectively he has learned to behave in his important task."[10] Personal expectations play a key role in determining behavior. Some people tend to accept relatively low levels of performance for themselves. They may be convinced that trying harder will not yield greater results and collect various excuses to explain why they should not put forth their best efforts.

Other people have high expectations for themselves. They often appear dissatisfied with their performance, and some accuse them of being perfectionists. Wittrock and Lumsdaine reviewed research on teacher attributions and found that this type of person tends to regard student outcomes as the result of teacher expertise and effort.[11] Such teachers refrain from making excuses about low student achievement. Furthermore, they tend to benefit more from feedback on their teaching than colleagues who are prone to blame low student achievement on student characteristics or other factors.

Of course, a point may be reached where high personal expectations are no longer functional. Teachers who never are able to appreciate their accomplishments or who interpret every student difficulty in terms of their own personal failure may become overly stressed and obsessive. And supervisors who concentrate solely on problems perhaps unwittingly reinforce these unproductive feelings—wise supervisors know when it is prudent to dwell on a teacher's accomplishments.

Openness to Criticism

Closely related to personal expectations is a person's openness to criticism. Those who find it difficult to hear criticism may actually fear the loss of acceptance or affection. Abraham Maslow observed that the need for acceptance precedes the need to feel competent.[12] If teachers feel that supervisors or colleagues will withdraw personal support as a result of discovering deficits in their teaching performance, they are likely to avoid situations in which they are judged or evaluated.

These feelings have been captured well by a junior high principal relating her experience supervising a new teacher. She speaks to the teacher:

> . . . there is a risk in sharing negative information. Often when people are told both positive and negative things, they hear only the negative, as we saw when you listed the positive and negative things I said about you. Hearing negative things makes people feel as though their whole person is condemned, that they are completely wrong or bad. Such feelings can be overwhelming and immobilizing.[13]

To encourage teachers to be more open to criticism, supervisors may need to establish a climate of safety. This might involve making a clear distinction between interactions that are associated with professional development and those intended for evaluative purposes. The latter may never feel safe for many teachers as long as one potential outcome is job loss.

Orientation to Change

Teachers who view change in positive terms are obviously more inclined to benefit from supervision and evaluation than those who desperately cling to the *status quo.* A positive orientation to change doubtless is closely related to other factors, such as personal expectations and openness to criticism. Competence probably plays a role as well, since a teacher may desire to change but lack the capacity to do so.

That adults are capable of change is an idea that has received relatively little attention from researchers until recently. We are beginning, however, to understand some of the conditions that contribute to positive change in adults. Robert Sutherland notes the importance of insight,[14] that unexpected flash of realization that yields understanding where previously there had been uncertainty. Insight can be stimulated by others, but ultimately it must come from within. Having someone listen as we reflect on our performance can be most useful for generating insights.

Change also derives from cognitive dissonance—discrepancies between what is and what should be. Fuller and Bown reasoned that teachers would be more likely to change if they perceived a difference between what they were doing and what they desired to do.[15] Sometimes these differences are not so apparent, however. Supervisors can facilitate change by helping teachers articulate their instructional goals and recognize how they actually conduct themselves in class. In addition, supervisors can help teachers to recognize that change is normal and important. As Combs, Avila, and Purkey imply, the expectation that change is necessary for professional effectiveness should be reinforced early on in a person's career:

> To become an effective teacher . . . is just that—a process of becoming. It is a matter of growth and occurs in gradual fashion over an extended period of time. This is a discovery that is often disappointing to beginners in the helping professions. With much enthusiasm and goodwill, they enter upon their training experience and expect that becoming an expert . . . is only a matter of learning the necessary tricks of the trade . . . People *grow* to be effective helpers and growth takes time.[16]

While change is essential for professional growth, supervisors must realize that all people have a limited capacity for change. Sometimes supervisors become resentful when they present teachers with new ideas that are obviously worthy of adoption, only to encounter resistance. These supervisors may have overlooked other things going on in teachers' lives at the moment. If, for example, teachers already have been asked to alter their performance in several areas, they are apt to be unreceptive to the new ideas, no matter how promising. Human energy is finite. The sensitive supervisor must try to assess current teacher commitments before pressing for further change.

Organizational Familiarity

Golfers use the term "local knowledge" to describe the advantage that comes from familiarity with a particular golf course—its terrain, playing conditions, and troublespots. Similarly, teachers who have considerable experience in a certain school may be in a better position than newcomers to take advantage of supervision and evaluation. Experience helps individuals who are oriented to change and open to feedback know what questions to ask. They also have a sense of how much change a given school can tolerate and where to enlist support for change.

Little has been written about the possible advantages of organizational familiarity. Typically, it is assumed that seasoned veterans have a greater investment in preserving the *status quo* than newcomers. It is likely, however, that many experienced teachers are prepared, or even anxious, to change. Supervisors need only to be careful not to imply that the change is desired because of past failures. In most cases, it is more productive for supervisors—or "change agents"—to assume that the vast majority of teachers have done the best that they could under the circumstances.

IMPORTANT SUPERVISOR ATTRIBUTES

If more were known about how to identify personality traits, school leaders could select teachers with the characteristics already identified in the preceding section. Supervision and evaluation undoubtedly would be made far simpler and more rewarding with teachers who all were open to criticism and willing to change. Unfortunately, we do not know how to reliably identify such traits as openness to criticism and orientation to change. Even if we did, there is no guarantee that the teaching profession would attract sufficient numbers of candidates with these traits. School leaders should therefore assume that part of their work will involve dealing with people who lack some or all the characteristics associated with positive supervision and evaluation experiences. What are the attributes that school leaders should possess if they are to stand the greatest chance of working effectively with all types of teachers?

Duke and Stiggins identified a variety of important characteristics for supervisors, including

- Communication skill
- Credibility
- Technical skill
- Trust
- Patience[17]

Let us look more closely at each of these qualities.

Communication Skill

The heart of supervision and evaluation is interaction between two people, and interaction necessitates communication. Many school leaders take communication for granted. They presume they are capable of communicating effectively, and are quite surprised when they learn that teachers feel communication problems exist in their school. Communication problems sometimes result from role interference, as exemplified by the reluctance of a subordinate to disclose personal problems to a superior. School leaders do not have any control over their assigned role or how others react to it. But they are in a position to see that their directions are clear, that they listen carefully, and that they provide honest information.

In an insightful account of several principals engaged in group inquiry, Barry Jentz and Joan Wofford relate the experiences of Lew, an elementary principal who discovered that effective communication does not come automatically.[18]

When Lew, an experienced principal, began to reflect on his actions, he realized that he was operating on some assumptions that contrasted sharply with his views on effective leadership. For example, he felt that his faculty respected him, but he believed that an effective leader should be liked as well. He slowly became more and more aware that he was saying one thing and doing another with his teachers. Lew sensed that his credibility suffered as a result of this.

These issues came to a head in an incident involving Jane, a fourth-grade teacher about whom Lew had a number of concerns. Jane was a rigid disciplinarian, too rigid for Lew. She backed students into corners with her ultimatums. She also seemed to have unreasonably high behavioral expectations for most students. Rather than communicate these concerns to Jane, Lew had begun to avoid her. He admitted having difficulty expressing negative feelings to those he did not like and who he thought did not like him.

To overcome his reluctance to face difficult interactions, Lew developed certain communication skills. First, he tried "listening nonliterally," a process that required hearing what Jane really was saying instead of using the time when she spoke to prepare his own responses. "Translating back," or paraphrasing, came next. To make certain he had heard what Jane intended him to hear, Lew tried to verbalize what he thought she said. In this way, he learned that Jane felt he did not back up his teachers when they made disciplinary referrals. Following an honest discussion of his own disciplinary practices, Lew was able to share with Jane the widespread perception among the faculty that she was a negative person. Using a technique called "putting yourself on the map," Lew told Jane that other teachers felt she did not respect them or him and that he agreed with them. Jane was shocked to learn Lew's true feelings as well as his perceptions of her colleagues' feelings.

As a result of his attempt to communicate more effectively, Lew entered into a new, less superficial relationship with Jane. He realized that his previous avoidance behavior had been based on the unexpressed belief that Jane could not change, learn, or grow. In fact, Jane was prepared to admit that she might need to alter some of her practices as long as she felt that Lew had understood her own concerns over his actions.

If one key goal of communication is understanding, then listening becomes a central part of the process. Like Lew, effective supervisors learn how to listen and, more important, how to let another person *know* they are listening. Thomas Gordon refers to this skill as "active listening."[19] Active listening requires the listener to refrain from diverting attention from the speaker's concerns. Diversion can occur when the listener asks "why" questions or steals the show with a personal anecdote. Active listening also requires clarification of confusing terms. Supervisors who find themselves talking most of the time during interactions with teachers may well need to work on their listening skills.

Communication also occurs nonverbally. Andrew Halpin has drawn attention, for example, to the "muted language" of hands and eyes, gesture, time use, and status symbols.[20] For example, when a supervisor gestures with her hand for a teacher to hurry up and finish a message, she is communicating impatience. If such gestures are common, they may cause the teacher to avoid contact altogether. How people organize and allocate time also can convey potent nonverbal messages, as anyone who has had to wait for someone who is late for an appointment knows. A supervisor who misses a conference without notifying a teacher or who comes late to a lesson and leaves early risks communicating to teachers a low regard for their work.

The words we choose also can either facilitate or confound communication. Supervisors who use esoteric terms or technical jargon unknown to teachers are unlikely to promote effective interactions. Judith Little found that successful schools tend to have a "shared language" that teachers and administrators use to discuss the complexities of teaching.[21] One reason for the success of Madeline Hunter's instructional-improvement efforts has been the care taken by trainers to develop a common vocabulary that enables teachers to discuss with each other the technical aspects of instruction and that permits supervisors to describe what they see in classrooms in ways that teachers can understand.

Diagnostic Question 1.13

Do school leaders exhibit skill in interpersonal communication, including active listening, appropriate nonverbal communication, and use of a "shared language"?

Credibility

Credibility is defined as the quality of being worthy of belief. School leaders who lack credibility may have to resort to coercive strategies to accomplish their goals. They may find it particularly difficult to undertake supervision and evaluation activities in a constructive and effective way.

If credibility is so important, how does a school leader acquire it? Unfortunately no prescription can be written for those who desire credibility. The quality is associated with a variety of characteristics, and different people value different sources of credibility. For some, the knowledge that a school leader was once a teacher is enough to establish credibility and command respect. For others, the leader must continue to teach part-time to retain credibility. Supervisors who can model the teaching behaviors they wish others to acquire frequently are more credible than supervisors who cannot. In some instances, however, supervisors may be more believable when they do not have all the answers. A supervisor who is a superstar can be easily dismissed by teachers as an exceptional human being. One who tries and fails on occasion may engender greater feelings of identification and empathy. Relatively few great coaches were ever themselves outstanding athletes. Knowledge of the game often is more important than technical skill.

One crucial source of credibility for instructional leaders springs from the capacity to articulate a vision of teaching excellence. Supervisors who can recognize good teaching when they see it and explain to teachers what they observe may be perceived as credible despite a lack of long teaching experience. Another source of credibility can be firsthand knowledge of the students with whom a teacher is working. All the instructional advice in the world may be useless if teachers sense that supervisors do not know their students. The more supervisors can relate their observations and suggestions to the needs and characteristics of particular students, the more believable their advice is likely to be.

Diagnostic Question 1.14

Are school leaders perceived by teachers as credible sources of knowledge regarding instructional improvement?

Technical Skill

School administrators trained many years ago are frequently amazed that supervision and evaluation have become so technically complex. It is no longer sufficient in most cases for supervisors simply to jot down a few general impressions of teacher performance at the close of each school year. They should be proficient in conferencing, goal setting, diagnosing instructional needs, and observing in classrooms. They should be prepared to help teachers improve performance or to locate those who can.

Stiggins and Bridgeford report that supervisors often lack two sets of critical skills: "skills in evaluating teaching performance; and skills in communicating with teachers about the evaluation process and results."[22] To correct these deficiencies, supervisors must learn and practice supervision and evaluation techniques, remain up-to-date on new research related to instructional effectiveness, and share experiences and insights with other supervisors. Technical competence is unlikely to be achieved by taking a single course or by the process of trial and error

---

Diagnostic Question 1.15

Do school leaders possess technical skill in conferencing, goal setting, instructional diagnosis, and classroom observation?

Trust

It is hard to imagine going downtown and encountering a friendly, smiling police officer who says, "Hello! I'm here to help you. Would you mind telling me about any laws you've broken lately?" In a sense, though, teachers find themselves in a similar position when supervisors ask them to disclose their problems and classroom concerns. Unless they trust the supervisor, they are unlikely to share possibly incriminating information, no matter how improvement oriented the supervision and evaluation system is *supposed* to be.

In his massive "Study of Schooling," John Goodlad found that a major factor differentiating "more and less renewing schools" was the degree of trust characterizing principal-teacher relations.[23] Writing about organizations in general, Donald Schön, observed that they constitute cooperative systems "in which individuals depend on the predictability of one another's responses."[24] Surprise may be useful for motivational purposes, but it is the enemy of trust.

The capacity to inspire trust is one of the most crucial attributes a school leader can possess. Those with this capacity can deliver even the most pointed criticism without destroying their relationships with others. Those lacking in the attribute find that even the most well-intentioned advice is interpreted negatively by others. The factors that produce trust in school settings have not been studied systematically, but it is likely that trust is related to one or more of the following:

- Supervisors' intentions (Do the supervisor and the teacher agree on the purpose of supervision and evaluation?)
- How supervisors handle evidence of performance from sources other than the classroom (e.g., hearsay, complaints)
- The consistency with which supervisors apply evaluation standards and regulations
- The extent to which teacher and supervisors see themselves as partners in the instructional improvement effort[25]

Trust is fragile. It can be undermined by a variety of supervisory actions. For example, Robert Donmoyer has noted that principals who cultivate personal closeness as a strategy to advance their own interests risk losing trust.[26] In their study of instructional leaders, Little and Bird warn that differential application of evaluation criteria can have negative consequences.[27] Some teachers are put off by gratuitous praise, particularly when they know the supervisor has spent insufficient time in class. Others become suspicious when supervisors take teachers' concerns and alter them in light of their own interests or abilities. School leaders committed to effective supervision and evaluation must realize the adverse consequences of any behavior that causes teachers to suspect their motives.

Diagnostic Question 1.16

Are relations between teachers and school leaders characterized by trust and honesty?

Patience

The last critical attribute is one of the least discussed. Some may regard any discussion of patience in the context of a complex, fast-paced organization like a school as unrealistic. They consider patience a luxury that is difficult to practice in crowded, deadline-driven environments. Successful supervisors, however, manage to create a feeling of calm and order, even in the midst of chaos. They recognize that teachers with many instructional concerns cannot address them all simultaneously. They also understand that the most serious problem is not always the best one to tackle first. Teachers, like others, sometimes need to experience success before confronting major dilemmas.

Patience can be communicated by actions as well as words. For example, when supervisors respond to outpourings of teacher concerns by listing them and working out a long-range plan for addressing each one in sequence, they are modeling patience. When supervisors refrain from panic in the face of crisis, they likewise are modeling patience. Much of the literature on leadership points to its symbolic value. Those who are close to difficult situations—like teachers—can become overwhelmed on occasion. Having a school leader who symbolizes patience and calm and to whom teachers can turn during times of trouble can be critical to instructional improvement.

Diagnostic Question 1.17

Are school leaders able to approach supervision and evaluation with patience?

THE CYCLE OF SUPERVISION AND EVALUATION

It is one thing to articulate the important attributes of teachers, school leaders, and systems of supervision and evaluation, and quite another to understand how they all interact during the annual cycle of events that bring teachers and school leaders together. In this section we shall briefly look again at each of these events—planning, goal setting, pre-observation conferences, classroom observations, post-observation conferences, programs of assistance, and annual evaluations—and try to incorporate suggestions from Chapter 6 and the first part of Chapter 7 into a series of guidelines for those engaged in supervision and evaluation.

Planning

Effective supervision and evaluation do not begin in September. They start in May and June of the preceding school year and continue through the summer. For example, when supervisors meet with teachers in the spring to review their annual performance evaluations, they can also use the occasion to set goals for the coming year. Such an arrangement extends the time available to teachers to think about and work on instructional improvement, thereby reducing the limitations of "annualism." Teachers can use the summer to undertake professional development activities related to their goals, and supervisors can use the time to locate resources and materials for assisting teachers when school begins again. Potential resources include local university courses, workshops, conferences, consultants, peer coaches, videotape equipment, and central office assistance.

Once all annual teacher evaluations have been completed, supervisors need to review them collectively before filing them. If a substantial proportion of the evaluations reveal similar areas of concern, supervisors should consider planning staff-development activities that address them for the coming year.

Besides locating professional-development resources and planning staff-development activities, supervisors may spend time during the summer reviewing and updating job descriptions, rereading the teacher contract, identifying supervision and evaluation policies for possible revision, and planning the return-to-school orientation. Part of every orientation should be a review of performance standards and supervisory procedures. If particular performance standards are to be emphasized during the year, teachers should be notified. School leaders should never assume that teachers have a clear understanding of the supervision and evaluation system,[28] and special care, of course, needs to be taken to inform new teachers. Some school leaders even plan ongoing "induction classes" to help socialize new teachers to school and district expectations and procedures.

An additional planning activity for school leaders involves their own time management. Since time for supervision and evaluation typically is scarce, it may be prudent to develop a weekly schedule with designated times for teacher conferences, observations, and post-observation write-ups. Such a schedule permits school leaders to notify staff members at the beginning of the year of the times when they are apt to be away from their desks.

Supervision and Evaluation Planning Checklist

- Have spring evaluation conferences been used to set professional development goals for the coming year?
- Have all teacher evaluations been reviewed collectively in order to set staff-development goals for the coming year?
- Have any important revisions been made in district supervision and evaluation policies or in the teachers' contract?
- Have plans been made to review policies, procedures, and performance standards with teachers when school opens?
- Should particular performance standards be emphasized during the coming year?
- Has an inventory been made of resources available during the coming year for instructional improvement, professional development, and staff development?
- Have job descriptions been reviewed?
- Has a schedule that includes designated times for conferences, classroom observations, observation write-ups, etc., been developed for the coming year?

Goal Setting

In many districts supervisors and teachers meet annually to set goals. The goals pertain to individual professional development as well as targets established for the entire school. Care should be taken in the specification of goals, if the process is to be taken seriously. The Lake Oswego (Ore.) School District provides teachers and supervisors with a helpful set of guidelines concerning the writing of goals:

- Is the goal stated in explicit terms?
- Is the intent or purpose clear?
- Is the goal valid? (Does its attainment improve performance? Is it linked to performance standards?)
- Is the goal stated in observable and/or measurable terms so that data can be collected for feedback?
- Can the goal be achieved to a major degree within the year?
- Can means be provided for achieving the goal?
- Is the goal flexible? (If the goal cannot be reached, can an alternate course of action be easily provided?)

Goal setting is the component of supervision and evaluation systems that provides the greatest opportunity for accommodating individual differences among teachers. Supervisors can establish different goal expectations for elementary and secondary teachers or for new and experienced teachers. They may use the research on teacher development to create a differentiated set of expectations for teachers. Since new teachers tend to worry most about student control, goals for them might focus on classroom management. Goals for experienced teachers, on the other hand, could be more closely tied to student achievement. Another basis for differentiating among teacher goals could be district performance standards. New teachers might reasonably be expected to set goals related to demonstrating competence in basic performance standards. Goals for veteran teachers could go far beyond the basic performance standards to areas of special talent or virtuosity. When supervisors recognize teacher differences in the course of goal setting, they must avoid using the results of the process for making comparisons among teachers.[29] Comparisons are valid only when all teachers pursue the same goal.

When they engage in goal setting, supervisors may find that checklists of good teaching practices are useful supplements to lists of performance standards. Figure 7.1 represents one such checklist, derived from the research on teaching effectiveness, that was developed by Linda Simington, a Portland (Ore.) principal. Teachers review this checklist during goal setting to determine whether their daily practice conforms to Simington's vision of good teaching. Areas of noncompliance serve as possible focuses for goal setting.

To avoid a constant focus on teacher deficiencies in goal setting, wise supervisors provide periodic opportunities for teachers to concentrate on areas of particular strength. Allowing teachers to use annual goal setting to augment or expand on talents help prevent it from being perceived as a strictly remedial process.

TEACHER EFFECTIVENESS CHECKLIST: CLARENDON SCHOOL

Linda Simington — Principal

A. Appropriate Placement, Use of Instructional Time, Evaluation of Student Progress

1. I have carefully assessed test data (Stanford Diagnostic, Levels tests, teacher-made tests) and my observations, and have used that information as a guide for goal selection and group placement in my classroom.

2. I have completed by long-range plan using the continuum and CPS guide. I am using that plan to target monthly and weekly goals for my students. I have designed or selected a variety of evaluation procedures to check student progress on each goal selected and use that information to plan appropriate instruction for each student.

3. I keep accurate records of student progress. These records are used as a guide for lesson planning and the formation of skill groups.

4. I write weekly lesson plans which include: a balanced selection of objectives from major goal categories in my long-range plans, an emphasis on direct instruction, seatwork that reinforces skills previously taught through direct instruction and that children can perform with a high rate of success, skill maintenance activities, and evaluation procedures.

5. I have developed strategies to meet the instructional needs of those students who do not master objectives (e.g., flexible skill groups, individual tutoring, supplementary learning activities, homework) which is efficient and effective and does not penalize those children who are ready to progress to the next objective.

6. If some children continue to have difficulty after I have tried alternative approaches, I seek assistance from other staff members.

7. I carefully monitor students during direct instruction and seatwork activities to see that they are deeply engaged in their learning tasks and that those tasks are of the appropriate difficulty (tasks on which the students can have a high rate of success).

8. I organize instructional activities, materials, and classroom procedures so that children can and do move promptly and efficiently from task-to-task.

9. When planning activities in content areas, I am careful to provide opportunities for the application of basic skills in language arts and mathematics.

10. I assign appropriate homework assignments to reinforce skills or concepts taught in the classroom. I have a system for checking those assignments and recognizing students who complete them.

B. High, Personalized Expectations

1. I have high, but personally appropriate standards of achievement and behavior for each of my students.

2. I have high standards of performance for myself as a teacher. I am not satisfied until each of my students makes significant progress toward achievement and behavior goals.

3. My students recognize my expectations and show evidence of internalizing them. They have an "I can learn" attitude and generally appear to feel "good" about their ability to function successfully in school.

4. My students are frequently appraised of their performance in relation to academic and behavior goals and are recognized and rewarded for good progress.

5. I recognize that an effective school where every child can learn requires the individual and collective best efforts of every member of the staff. I have made a personal commitment to work with my colleagues to insure each child's success in his or her effort to meet academic and behavior goals.

Figure 7.1 Reprinted with permission of Linda Simington.

Before a goal-setting conference concludes, it is important that teacher and supervisor reach agreement on such matters as the evidence to be used to indicate that goals have been achieved and the person or persons responsible for determining when goals have been achieved. It is usually helpful to develop a time-line or schedule in which key events are noted in the process of accomplishing goals. Teachers may lose interest in goal setting if they feel that school leaders have not set aside time to monitor their progress carefully. In some cases, more than a year may be required to achieve ambitious goals. Finally, the resources required by the teacher to accomplish designated goals should be specified whenever possible.

Goal-Setting Checklist

- Has care been taken to set goals that are clear, valid, and measurable?
- Are sufficient resources available to help reach the goal?
- Has a schedule been developed that includes progress checks and a completion date?
- Do goals allow for individual differences among teachers?
- Do teachers play a major role in developing their professional growth goals?
- Are teachers and supervisors clear about the evidence that will be used to indicate successful accomplishment of goals?

Pre-observation Conferences

Supervisors may conduct classroom observations for various purposes, including (1) monitoring progress toward annual goals, (2) assessing competence on performance standards, (3) becoming familiar with new teachers, and (4) determining whether deficiencies have been corrected. Whatever the reason, both teacher and supervisor should use part of the pre-observation conference to clarify why the classroom visit is occurring.

The usefulness of pre-observation conferences may depend on several other factors besides the extent to which their purposes are clarified. For instance, the quality of information gathered by supervisors may vary, based on the time available for conferences and the questions asked. Supervisors often pass quickly over important issues, getting a distorted view of teacher concerns. It is usually preferable for supervisors to delve right in—to find out teacher concerns, key assumptions on which teachers operate, lesson plans and objectives, seating arrangements, what students have been doing prior to planned visits, and what students are expected to do afterwards. To make sure they cover these and other important topics, supervisors may wish to use a conference survey form or list of questions. Figure 7.2 is an example of one such form used by William Korach of Lake Oswego (Ore.) High School.

Another possible impediment to effective pre-observation conferences is the aforementioned tendency of some supervisors to manipulate teacher concerns to conform to issues with which they themselves are familiar or concerned. For example, a supervisor may know little about how to meet the individual learning needs of students, a major teacher concern based on observed off-task behavior. The supervisor redefines the issue as a classroom management problem, since he or she knows what to do when rules are broken. Altering teacher concerns in this manner can undermine supervisor credibility and detract from the perceived value of classroom observation. Supervisors must real-

Lake Oswego High School
Pre-Observation Information

by William Korach

Teacher:
Course:
Period:
Observer:
Date of Observation:

1. What learning (content, information, concept, skill, etc.) will the student acquire as a result of instruction?

2. At what cognitive level should the student be able to demonstrate the learning? (Knowledge, comprehension, application, analysis, synthesis, evaluation).

3. What will be the teacher's instructional strategy? (Method)

4. What materials will the student use during the learning activity?

5. What behavior will indicate the student has acquired the learning at the cognitive level intended?

6. How will the teacher determine the success of the lesson?

7. What degree of learning success will the teacher accept?

Figure 7.2   Reprinted with permission of William Korach.

ize that they do not need to know how to resolve every problem posed by teachers. In many situations, it is appropriate and even desirable simply to acknowledge the problem and collaboratively devise some way to learn more about it. In such instances, supervisor and teacher become co-investigators in search of instructional improvement.

An additional obstacle may be presented by supervisors who use pre-observation conferences exclusively to search for problems. Supervisors may identify too closely with the so-called "medical model," which calls on practitioners to diagnose problems and prescribe treatments. Many supervisors probably believe that their jobs are dependent on the existence of instructional (and other) problems. They may fear that failure to locate teacher problems will lead to inquiries regarding the need for supervisors. In reality, teachers do not have to have problems in order to grow and improve. On occasion, for instance, it may be valuable to devote pre-observation conferences to identifying what is working particularly *well* for a teacher. A variety of insights for classroom observation are possible by asking teachers to describe how their classes look when they operate ideally.

The general purpose of pre-observation conferences, as the name suggests, is to learn enough to permit the supervisor to collect information thoughtfully and systematically. Since teachers know more about the context in which they teach than supervisors, they should probably talk more during these conferences. Teachers also should help select aspects of their lessons on which to focus, methods and instruments for collecting data, and the date on which the observation will be conducted. Pre-observation conferences should not conclude until a time for a post-observation conference has been set.

Pre-observation Conference Checklist

- Has the purpose of the intended observation been clarified?
- Has sufficient time been set aside for the pre-observation conference?
- Would it be useful for the teacher to submit additional information in writing?
- Would it be useful to use a checklist of questions related to the teacher's concerns and classroom context?
- Has a seating chart with student names been obtained?
- Is the supervisor clear about the objectives of the lesson, the level of student performance, and other contextual matters?
- Has care been taken to permit the teacher to participate in selecting a focus and a time for the observation?
- Will special equipment, such as videotape cameras, be required for the observation?
- Has a time been designated for the post-observation conference?

Classroom Observation

If the guidelines for pre-observation conferences have been observed, the tasks of observing and collecting data will be less taxing. Nonetheless, it is difficult under the best of circumstances to monitor the behavior of a teacher and a number of students. Depending on the purpose of the observation, the supervisor may either zero in on a specific set of behaviors or try to apprehend as much of what is going on in the classroom as possible. In both cases, great care must be taken to avoid recording subjective judgments and opinions. The key to effective observations is the capacity to record descriptive data.

Collecting descriptive data is not easy. Impressions intrude in unexpected ways—this is shown by the words we use, by what we choose to stress, and by what we ignore. Research suggests that supervisors must be constantly on guard against personal biases.[30] Often without thinking, supervisors will put individuals into categories or stereotype them in some way. And once the supervisor has made a categorization, it tends to influence subsequent observations. He or she will attend to behavior that confirms the stereotype, and ignore or forget behavior that conflicts with it. A talented teacher whose performance declines may still receive positive observation write-ups, while another teacher who makes a genuine effort to improve may go unappreciated because of a poor reputation. To prevent stereotyping and other forms of subjective assessment, supervisors should practice collecting descriptive data using videotapes of teaching. Observation instruments also can minimize bias and opinion, as long as supervisors are familiar with the coding categories and symbols. Again, there is no substitute for practice.

While direct observations are usually the primary source of data, supervisors may also need to collect documents distributed prior to or during class and examples of student work. In some instances, supervisors may select several students with whom to "debrief" after class. How students perceive a lesson can be very important information for supervisors and teachers as they attempt to make sense of a given observation.

Supervisors sometimes find it useful to visit the same class several days in succession to assess continuity of instruction from one day to the next. Follow-up visits also give opportunities to determine if students understand material covered the previous day.

On occasion, supervisors may need to observe teachers in contexts other than classrooms. Parent conferences, faculty meetings, out-of-class supervision, and field trips are only some of the extra-classroom settings where formal observations can be useful.

Before concluding an observation, supervisors may leave a copy of their descriptive data with teachers. This can reduce teacher anxiety and give teachers time to analyze the data on their own, prior to the post-observation conference.

Classroom Observation Checklist

- Has care been taken to practice using observation instruments?
- Has care been taken to record only descriptive data?
- Is it necessary to collect supplementary data, such as documents related to the lesson and examples of student work?
- Should several students be interviewed after the lesson?
- Have arrangements been made to share observation data with teachers prior to post-observation conferences?

Post-observation Conference

Some post-observation conferences are reminiscent of two people driving along the highway in adjoining lanes and attempting to switch lanes. Both drivers at first speed up. Then both slow down. In each case they are both prevented from achieving their objective—switching lanes. They grow angrier and more frustrated at each other. But if only they could communicate with each other, they would realize that they could be helping each other. If one of them slows down while the other changes lanes, for example, then the other lane would be clear for the second driver.

In a similar way, teachers and supervisors sometimes block each other's way during post-observation conferences. Supervisors, for example, may feel they should be first to analyze data and make suggestions so that they can impress teachers with their knowledge and desire to help. Ironically, allowing teachers to initiate data analysis and interpretation ultimately may contribute more to professional growth. Only then may teachers begin to see themselves as capable individuals with insights on their own instructional improvement. Common sense suggests they are more likely to change behavior as a result of self-analysis than supervisory persuasion.

Teachers, for their part, may prevent well-intentioned supervisors from providing genuine assistance because of negative stereotypes *they* may have. By unfairly assuming that all supervisors are interested solely in rules and regulations, teachers can deprive themselves of the benefit of a valuable external perspective. They also may overlook the fact that most supervisors once were teachers and are likely to sympathize with teacher concerns over supervision and evaluation.

To ensure that post-observation conferences are as growth producing as possible, supervisors should make certain that teachers have the first opportunity to analyze and interpret data. As in the case of pre-observation conferences, it is reasonable to expect teachers to do most of the talking. It can be helpful to schedule conferences in comfortable and nonthreatening settings—it is probably best to avoid the supervisor's office. And obviously, the sooner the conference takes place after an observation, the more likely it is to make an impact.

While every post-observation conference is different, most should probably include a balance of positive comments and constructive criticism. Sometimes supervisors can ask teachers—even experienced ones—to explain *why* they used a particular technique or approach. Growth can result when we have to provide reasons for doing what we normally take for granted. Supervisors should come to post-observation conferences prepared to suggest resources that may be helpful to teachers as they follow through on recommendations. Occasionally, it may be appropriate for supervisors to share post-observation notes with students. This way, students can learn how *their* performance is perceived by an outsider.

No post-observation conference should conclude without a clear idea of follow-up activities. Post-observation conferences may serve as pre-observation conferences when an observed deficiency needs to be corrected. If the deficiency is a serious one, arrangements may be necessary for developing a plan of assistance. When analysis of data reveals no cause for concern, teachers should be free to suggest new areas of inquiry.

Post-observation Conference Checklist

- Has the conference been scheduled in a comfortable, nonthreatening location?
- Has the conference been scheduled as soon after the observation as possible?
- Is the supervisor careful to allow the teacher to analyze and interpret data first?
- Does the supervisor include positive comments as well as constructive criticism?
- Is the supervisor prepared to suggest resources to help the teacher improve?
- Are arrangements made for some form of follow-up activity?

Assistance

When it is necessary to place a teacher on a formal plan of assistance, supervisors should remain as understanding and supportive as possible. The interests of district patrons, however, must be of paramount concern. A plan of assistance is like a play in which everyone has a part. The parts are typically circumscribed by policy, contract, and statute. The supervisor must remember his or her obligation to the district. The union representative must act to protect the due process rights of the teacher. The teacher must make a genuine effort to improve performance. It is not in the best interests of the teaching profession or the district for procedural mistakes to permit an inadequate teacher to retain his or her job, despite the weight of evidence. Because of the great care required in cases of teacher assistance, it may be prudent to enlist the aid of a lawyer specializing in personnel decisions.

The first step in the assistance process is informing the teacher in writing of a change in employment status. This step indicates that the teacher is on probation and that a possible consequence of failure to correct deficiencies is dismissal. Once notification has occurred, the teacher and a supervisor may start negotiating a reasonable plan of assistance. The teacher may request that a union representative be present at these negotiations.

A plan of assistance should conform to a standard district format. While no format is universally appropriate, all plans probably should begin with a clear statement of deficiencies. Deficiencies should be expressed with reference to district or state performance standards, where they exist. Evidence of deficient performance and dates when evidence was collected also should be recorded, either in the plan or in an attachment. If previous attempts have been made to correct the deficiencies, these, too, should be described.

The next component of most plans should be a specific program of correction. Objectives should be identified, along with indications of how a determination will be made that they have been satisfactorily accomplished. Also to be specified are resources that are available, at district expense, to help the teacher achieve remedial objectives. Such resources may include specialists, workshops, and university courses as well as building-based supervisors. The final component of plans of assistance should be a schedule listing supervisory contacts that will be used for monitoring and a date by which deficiencies must be corrected. Since teachers may claim that insufficient time has been allocated for successful completion of plans of assistance, supervisors need to consider the schedule carefully. In some cases, it may be necessary to extend a plan from one school year to the next. It is incumbent on the supervisor and the district to demonstrate that they have acted in good faith and provided teachers on plans of assistance with a reasonable opportunity to correct deficiencies. The morale of entire faculties can be undermined when colleagues who are experiencing difficulties are treated unfairly by supervisors.

Plan of Assistance Checklist

- Has the teacher been notified in writing that he or she is being placed on a plan of assistance?
- Has a conference been scheduled for negotiating a plan of assistance?
- Has the teacher been permitted to invite a union representative?
- Has the plan of assistance been reviewed by district legal counsel?
- Does the plan of assistance specify the nature of the deficiencies and the level of performance necessary to correct them?
- Has a corrective program complete with district resources been specified?
- Have a schedule of checkpoints and a date of completion been designated?
- Does the plan include references to any previous efforts to correct the deficiencies?

Evaluation

People do not like to be taken for granted, and the evaluation process gives supervisors an opportunity to acknowledge teacher performance. Not all supervisors, of course, take full advantage of this opportunity. Some compose evaluations full of gratuitous praise and unsupported generalizations, while others seem to operate more on the rule of silence—"As long as you don't hear anything, assume you're doing fine." If evaluations of teacher performance are to be perceived as meaningful, they should be literate, specific, backed by evidence, and linked to some vision of teaching.

In most cases, evaluations must be written. Obviously, teachers are more apt to take evaluations seriously if they have been written carefully. Standardized forms and checklists save time and conform to district and state guidelines, but they lack the impact and personal touch of good prose. Also, it may be tempting, amidst the rush of activity at the close of the school year, to rely on school mail for the distribution of evaluations, but supervisors should try to find some occasion before teachers leave for summer vacation to sit down and discuss evaluation results. Such meetings provide excellent opportunities for preliminary goal setting for the coming year, too.

Evaluations for probationary teachers should refer to basic performance standards and job descriptions. For experienced teachers, however, it seems unnecessary to focus annually on such minimum expectations. It makes more sense to check performance standards every three to five years. During the intervening period, evaluations can concentrate on the results of professional goal setting and on the cultivation of special talents. The more that evaluations of experienced teachers take into account individual differences in background, assignments, talent, and aspirations, the more likely they are to foster continuing instructional improvement.

In instances where evaluations reveal unacceptable or questionable performance, it is particularly important to make specific reference to next steps. Teachers will want and deserve to know the nature of the evidence on which negative evaluations have been made as well as the possible consequences. Again, these issues are best addressed in person, even though such occasions may be taxing for both parties involved. Supervisors are advised to keep a written record of discussions during evaluation conferences.

Evaluation Checklist

- Has care been taken to compose an evaluation that is based on performance standards and empirical evidence?
- Has an effort been made to differentiate evaluations of probationary and experienced teachers?
- Do teachers have an opportunity to discuss evaluations in person with supervisors?
- In the case of negative evaluations, have possible consequences and next steps been specified?

Conclusion

As the preceding discussion indicates, good supervision and evaluation take time, effort, skill, and an even disposition. While it is tempting to look for shortcuts—particularly after years of experience—supervisors who wish to be regarded as instructional leaders should be firm. Any move that implies that supervision and evaluation are not of paramount importance can undermine the credibility and authority of school leaders. That many teachers today regard supervison and evaluation as a game one must play to mollify district officials and state authorities is as much a testament to the "benign neglect" of school leaders as it is a statement about teacher cynicism. Fortunately, there are enough schools where supervision and evaluation function as key elements in the process of instructional improvement to suggest that game playing, benign neglect, and cynicism need not be fixtures of school culture.

STUDY QUESTIONS

1. What attributes would you associate with effective instructors? How can you convey these attributes to teachers who are most likely to benefit from supervision and evaluation?

2. Keeping in mind the attributes of supervisors listed in this chapter, interview a school leader. How would this person assess his or her communication skills, credibility, technical skill, ability to inspire trust, and patience? Now ask a teacher who works with this school leader to make an assessment using the same attributes. Are there any discrepancies? Why?

3. Locate several first-year teachers and several experienced teachers. Ask them to indicate professional development goals that they are pursuing or would like to pursue. Are there any differences in the types of goals they choose?

4. Ask a teacher to describe the annual supervision and evaluation experience. What feelings are revealed? What suggestions does the teacher have for improving these processes?

5. Prepare an "interview schedule" containing questions you would ask a teacher during the course of a pre-observation conference.

NOTES

1. Milbrey Wallin McLaughlin, "Teacher Evaluation and School Improvement," *Teachers College Record,* Vol. 86, No. 1 (Fall 1984), pp. 193–207.

2. Shirley A. McFaul and James M. Cooper, "Peer Clinical Supervision: Theory vs. Reality," *Educational Leadership,* Vol. 41, No. 7 (April 1984), p. 7.

3. Kenneth Strike and Barry Bull, "Fairness and the Legal Context of Teacher Evaluation," *Handbook of Teacher Evaluation,* Jason Millman (Ed.) (Beverly Hills, Calif.: Sage, 1981), p. 339.

4. Findings from this study are summarized in Daniel L. Duke and Richard J. Stiggins, "Five Keys to Growth Through Teacher Evaluation" (Portland, Ore.: Northwest Regional Educational Laboratory, 1985).

5. On the basis of this field research an instrument entitled "A Review of Your Teacher Evaluation Experience" was developed. For further information, contact the author or Richard J. Stiggins, Center for Performance Assessment, Northwest Regional Educational Laboratory, Portland, Ore.

6. M. S. Knapp, *Toward the Study of Teacher Evaluation as an Organizational Process: A Review of Current Research and Practice* (Menlo Park, Calif.: SRI International, 1982), p. 5.

7. Arthur Blumberg, *Supervisors and Teachers: A Private Cold War,* 2nd ed. (Berkeley: McCutchan, 1980), p. 4.

8. Frances F. Fuller and Oliver H. Bown, "Becoming a Teacher," *Teacher Education,* Kevan Ryan (Ed.), The Seventy-fourth Yearbook of the National Society for the Study of Education (Chicago: The University of Chicago Press, 1975), pp. 36–39.

9. H. S. Pambookian, "Initial Level of Student Evaluation of Instruction as a Source of Influence on Instructor Change after Feedback," *Journal of Educational Psychology,* Vol 66, No. 1 (February 1974), pp. 52–56.

10. Arthur W. Combs, Donald L. Avila, and William W. Purkey, *Helping Relationships* (Boston: Allyn & Bacon, 1971), p. 289.

11. M. D. Wittrock and A. A. Lumsdaine, "Instructional Psychology," *Annual Review of Psychology,* Vol. 28 (1977), pp. 417–459.

12. Abraham H. Maslow, *Motivation and Personality,* 2nd. ed. (New York: Harper & Row, 1970), pp. 35–58.

13. Meredith Howe Jones, "Anatomy of an Evaluation," *Principal,* Vol. 61, No. 1 (September 1981), p. 52.

14. Robert L. Sutherland, "Can an Adult Change?" *The Teacher as a Person,* Luis F. S. Natalicio and Carl F. Hereford (Eds.), 2nd ed. (Dubuque, Iowa: Wm. C. Brown, 1971), pp. 84–86.

15. Fuller and Bown, "Becoming a Teacher," pp. 42–43.
16. Arthur W. Combs, Donald L. Avila, and William W. Purkey, *Helping Relationships* (Boston: Allyn & Bacon, 1971), p. 297.
17. Duke and Stiggins, "Five Keys to Growth Through Teacher Evaluation."
18. Barry C. Jentz and Joan W. Wofford, *Leadership and Learning* (New York: McGraw-Hill, 1979), pp. 123–161.
19. Thomas Gordon, *Leader Effectiveness Training* (New York: Bantam, 1977), pp. 55–74.
20. Andrew W. Halpin, "Muted Language," *The School Review,* Vol. 65, No. 1 (Spring 1960), pp. 85–104.
21. Judith Warren Little, "Finding the Limits and Possibilities of Instructional Leadership: Some Possibilities for Practical and Collaborative Work with Principals" (unpublished paper).
22. Richard J. Stiggins and Nancy J. Bridgeford, "Performance Assessment for Teacher Development," *Educational Evaluation and Policy Analysis,* Vol. 7, No. 1 (Spring 1985), p. 93.
23. John Goodlad, *A Place Called School* (New York: McGraw-Hill, 1984), p. 303.
24. Donald A. Schön, *The Reflective Practitioner* (New York: Basic Books, 1983), p. 327.
25. Daniel L. Duke and Richard J. Stiggins, "Five Keys to Growth Through Teacher Evaluation," p. 19.
26. Robert Donmoyer, "Cognitive Anthropology and Research on Effective Principals: Findings from a Study and Reflections on Its Methods," paper presented at the annual meeting of the American Education Research Association, 1984.
27. Judith Warren Little and Thomas D. Bird, "Is There Instructional Leadership in High Schools? First Findings from a Study of Secondary School Administrators and Their Influence on Teachers' Professional Norms," paper presented at the Annual Convention of the American Educational Research Association, 1984, p. 21.
28. In one of the few studies to examine this, it was found that principals believed teachers knew more about the supervision and evaluation system than teachers reported knowing. See June E. Thompson, Sanford M. Dornbusch, and W. Richard Scott, "Failures of Communication in the Evaluation of Teachers by Principals," Technical Report No. 43 (Stanford, Calif.: Stanford Center for Research and Development on Teaching, 1975), p. 7.
29. For a discussion of the limitations of evaluation based on goal setting, see Arthur E. Wise, Linda Darling-Hammond, Milbrey W. McLaughlin, and Harriet T. Bernstein, *Case Studies for Teacher Evaluation: A Study of Effective Practices* (Santa Monica, Calif.: Rand, 1984), p. 111.
30. Berkeley Rice, "Performance Review: The Job Nobody Likes," *Psychology Today,* Vol. 19, No. 9 (September 1985), p. 35.

CHAPTER 8

STAFF DEVELOPMENT— THE PROMOTION OF GROUP IMPROVEMENT

The preceding chapter focused on the processes—specifically supervision and evaluation—that promote the professional development of individuals. But there are occasions when school leaders must ensure that groups of staff members learn and grow together toward some common goal. Collective development presents certain challenges that do not exist when individuals are being helped. More time and resources are required with groups. Attention must be devoted to interpersonal relations and group dynamics, and logistical problems are greater, such as scheduling and locating meeting places. Finally, more effort is needed to monitor progress and provide supplementary or follow-up assistance.

Staff development is distinct from both school improvement and professional development. While school improvement focuses on changing "things"—school organization, rules, curriculum, and the like—staff development is concerned with changes in people. This may include changes in knowledge, behavior, understanding, and attitude. To maintain that staff development and school improvement are different is not, however, to claim that they are unrelated. Teachers may have to change in order for schools to improve. Schools may have to change in order for teachers to improve. Much of this book deals with creating organizational conditions that promote both kinds of improvement.

It may be helpful to think of staff development as a form of ongoing organizational socialization. All organizations, including schools, have formal and informal mechanisms by which employees are apprised of key expectations, values, and norms governing behavior. When staff development is linked tightly to school district goals and policies, and when it takes into account local organizational culture, it can serve to nurture a spirit of community and common interest. Failure to root staff development in the local culture can foster devisiveness and squander precious resources.

School leaders play a crucial role in staff development, but it is a role that seems to be evolving. In tracing the evolution of the principal's role in staff development, Judith Little points out that the early sixties found principals serving as "gatekeepers."[1] This role entailed such functions as approving ideas, preparing proposals, negotiating funding, and doing general supervision. Managerial tasks like these, however, have increasingly been displaced by leadership activities, as contemporary principals find themselves more frequently in the role of "change agents." This role calls for the promotion as well as the approval of ideas. Principals are expected to seek faculty commitment to staff development, receive training, conduct teacher training, adjust teacher schedules to facilitate cooperative learning, and report relevant research to the school community.

Staff development today obviously entails a major investment of time by school leaders. The need for this commitment reflects, in part, decades of experience with unproductive attempts to change teachers. Research has shown that school leaders must play an active role in initiating, guiding, and supporting staff development if it is to succeed.[2] After reviewing this research, this chapter will investigate several case studies of staff development and identify the key elements of staff-development plans.

HOW TEACHERS LEARN

In recent years a variety of models of staff development have been proposed by educational researchers. These models are derived from several different theoretical bases, including adult learning theory, concerns-based theory, and teaching-effectiveness research. This section will briefly review these three perspectives and present several illustrative models of staff development.

Adult Learning

Influenced heavily by recent scholarship on stages of adult development, adult learning theory holds that the factors associated with adult growth are somewhat different from those reported for nonadults. While relatively little experimental investigation has been undertaken in this area, researchers believe that adults are capable of continuing cognitive and moral development. A comprehensive review of the research suggests that teacher development can be encouraged by the following:

- Significant role-taking experiences
- Careful matching of role-taking experiences with teacher level of ability
- Careful and continuous guided reflection
- Guided integration of role-taking experiences and reflection
- Provision for personal support as well as challenge[3]

These suggestions imply that teachers, as well as other adults, may be less apt than younger learners to benefit from more passive learning modes, such as lectures and reading. Teachers lead complex lives with numerous competing demands and challenging responsibilities. Intended learnings that cannot be related directly to improved job performance or a better quality of life are likely to be given less attention and energy. As teachers start on growth-related programs, they are more apt than immature learners to require emotional support and encouragement. The perceived consequences of trying something new and failing are probably greater for adults than youngsters. Fear of failure can lead some adults to completely reject opportunities for growth or to deny that improvements are necessary. Adult learning theory suggests that school leaders should try to make it safe for teachers to try new ideas.

Concerns-based Approaches

A second approach to staff development grows out of the previously cited work of Frances Fuller. Closely related to the scholarship on adult learning, this research links teacher motivation to learn with teacher level of concern; in other words, teachers are more likely to learn things that are linked directly to areas of major personal concern. Fuller's contribution was to show empirically that teacher concerns were not completely idiosyncratic; concerns tend to be similar for teachers at similar stages of their professional careers.

Gene Hall and his associates built on the ideas of Fuller and developed a Concerns-Based Adoption Model (CBAM).[4] The model is both a representation of the change process as it occurs in educational settings and a guide for planning staff development and school improvement activities. The model suggests that successful change typically requires one or more persons to play the role of "change facilitator." A primary responsibility of a change facilitator is to determine how staff members and others feel about proposed changes. Their reactions can be classified according to a seven-part hierarchical scheme that Hall refers to as "Stages of Concern" (see Table 8.1).

Hall and his associates found that the extent to which people seize upon and want to use an innovative idea is directly related to their stage of concern. By carefully assessing a faculty's stages of concern, a change facilitator can determine whether or not the general climate is conducive to change. It makes

Table 8.1   Stages of Concern: Typical Expressions of Concern About the Innovation

	Stages of Concern	Expressions of Concern
Impact	6 Refocusing	I have some ideas about something that would work even better.
	5 Collaboration	I am concerned about relating what I am doing with what other instructors are doing.
Task	4 Consequence	How is my use affecting kids?
	3 Management	I seem to be spending all my time in getting material ready.
Self	2 Personal	How will using it affect me?
	1 Informational	I would like to know more about it.
	0 Awareness	I am not concerned about it (the innovation).

SOURCE: Gene E. Hall and Shirley M. Hord, *Change in Schools: Facilitating the Process* (In Press). With permission of the State University of New York Press.

little sense for school leaders to press for staff development or school improvement until the level of concern is sufficiently high to warrant the time and energy required.

Teaching Effectiveness

As discussed earlier, the so-called teaching-effectiveness research attempts to link statistically specific teacher behaviors to student outcomes. And as the research has identified influential behaviors, teacher educators have been called on to develop appropriate ways to train teachers. Some of the most comprehensive and widely used staff-development programs, such as Madeline Hunter's "Clinical Teaching" and Sam Kerman's "Teacher Expectations and Student Achievement," are based in part on the teaching-effectiveness studies.

As efforts to train teachers using teaching-effectiveness research have increased, a distinct body of research on staff development has begun to accumulate. In a review of this research, Georgea Sparks highlights ten findings on the delivery of staff-development services:

1. Select content that has been verified by research to improve student achievement.

2. Create a context of acceptance by involving teachers in decision making and providing both logistical and psychological administrative support.

3. Conduct training sessions (more than one) two or three weeks apart.

4. Include presentation, demonstration, practice, and feedback as workshop activities.

5. During training sessions, provide opportunities for small-group discussions of the application of new practices and sharing of ideas and concerns about effective instruction.

6. Between workshops, encourage teachers to visit each others' classrooms, preferably with a simple, objective, student-centered observation instrument. Provide opportunities for discussions of the observation.

7. Develop in teachers a philosophical acceptance of the new practices by presenting research and a rationale for the effectiveness of the techniques. Allow teachers to express doubts about or objections to the recommended methods in small groups. Let the other teachers convince the resisting teacher of the usefulness of the practices through "testimonies" of their use and effectiveness.

8. Lower teachers' perception of the cost of adopting a new practice through detailed discussions of the "nuts and bolts" of using the technique and teacher sharing of experiences with the technique.

9. Help teachers grow in their self-confidence and competence through encouraging them to try only one or two new practices after each workshop. Diagnosis of teacher strengths and weaknesses can help the trainer suggest changes that are likely to be successful—and, thus, reinforce future efforts to change.

10. For teaching practices that require very complex thinking skills, plan to take more time, provide more practice, and consider activities that develop conceptual flexibility.[5]

In case studies of two staff-development programs undertaken over a three-year period, Judith Little notes many of the same factors reported by Sparks.[6] In addition, however, she stresses the importance of collective participation and collegiality. Both staff-development programs Little wrote about were designed carefully, using recent research on effective teaching. Both provided well-conducted training sessions for teams of teachers. Teachers at each site had ample opportunity during training to discuss their concerns and to plan. In both cases, evaluations of the training were enthusiastic. Three years after these two programs started, however, one school had implemented a variety of new practices and stimulated considerable teacher growth, while teachers in the other school had ceased thinking about or using the recommended instructional practices. Interestingly, the latter group of teachers still had positive feelings about the staff-development program! Little's research reminds school leaders not to be deceived by the illusion of improvement.

What accounted for the different outcomes of the two staff-development programs, both of which had started off in such a promising manner? Little concluded that,

> ... staff development is most influential where it: (1) ensures collaboration adequate to produce shared understanding, shared investment, thoughtful development, and the fair, rigorous test of selected ideas; (2) requires collective participation in training *and* implementation; (3) is focused on crucial problems of curriculum and instruction; (4) is conducted often enough and long enough to ensure progressive gains in knowledge, skill, and confidence; and (5) is congruent with and contributes to professional habits and norms of collegiality and experimentation.[7]

Models

The accumulating body of scholarship on staff development has stimulated the creation of various models for the delivery of staff-development services. Table 8.2 presents the major elements of three such models.

These three models share a number of common features, including provisions for the assessment of teacher needs, practice of new techniques, and evaluation of staff-development outcomes. There are also important differences among the models. The Gall Model, for example, limits the focus of staff development to a narrow range of teacher behaviors associated with academic learning time, classroom management, and student assessment. The Orlich Model is the only one that explicitly provides for the advanced training of a cadre of volunteers who, in turn, direct staff development for all personnel. Based in part on Bloom's Mastery Learning Model, Stallings's Model calls for direct observation of teachers as part of both the preliminary assessment of needs and the post-training evaluation phase.

It is one thing to develop in writing a rational model of staff development and often quite another to actually deliver staff-development services. School leaders may therefore benefit from several case studies of schools and school systems that attempted to implement staff development in a systematic way.

Table 8.2   Staff Development Models

Gall Model	Orlich Model	Stallings Model
Content of Staff Development	Needs Assessment	Pretest
Focus on increasing time for academic instruction, student on-task behavior, monitoring of student performance	Seek strengths as well as weaknesses	Observe teachers
Delivery System	Awareness	Assess what is needed
Involve teachers in identification of concerns and trainers	Application	Start where they are
Build consensus	Arrange for sub-groups to practice new skills	Inform
Follow up on initial training	Implementation	Link theory, practice, and teacher experience
Organizational context	Provide training for *all* teachers	Provide practical examples
Group teachers with similar assignments	Maintenance	Organize and guide practice
Buffer teachers from other distracting activities	Evaluation	Provide conceptual units of behaviors to change
Governance Structure		Support and encourage behavior change
Involve teachers in planning		Assess and provide feedback
Provide incentives		Help integrate into scheme
Selection and Evaluation		Post test
Select a research-validated program		Observe teachers
Assess teacher implementation of new methods and student outcomes		Feedback to teachers
		Feedback to trainer

SOURCES: Meredith D. Gall, "Using Staff Development to Improve Schools," *R&D Perspectives*, Center for Educational Policy and Management, University of Oregon (Winter 1983).
Donald C. Orlich, "Establishing Effective In-service Programs by Taking . . . 'AAIM'," *The Clearing House*, Vol. 53, No. 1 (September 1979), pp. 53–55.
Jane Stallings, "What Research Has to Say to Administrators of Secondary Schools about Effective Teaching and Staff Development," paper presented to 1981 Conference "Creating Conditions for Effective Teaching," Eugene, Oregon.

STAFF DEVELOPMENT EXAMPLES

Opening a New School

In *Anatomy of Educational Innovation,* Louis Smith and Pat Keith provide a richly detailed picture of staff development at Kensington Elementary School. Their narrative of the creation of an open-space school in a midwestern suburb begins with a month-long summer workshop for the entire staff. This workshop was designed to mold the staff into a "smooth-working unit and to develop concrete teaching plans for the year."[8] A major portion of the book is an account of why these objectives were not fully realized.

Anatomy of Educational Innovation is really a series of cautionary observations regarding the planning and conducting of staff development. Among the reasons why the summer workshop was not as productive as intended was the failure of school leaders to develop a common language for examining teaching, children, and school organization. In addition, some workshop participants felt that, on occasion, the consultants involved in providing training in group dynamics overstepped their authority. This situation arose, in part, because the major impetus for change came from outside of Kensington. In his desire for a national showcase school, the superintendent had opted for what Smith and Keith call the "alternative of grandeur." Thus, Kensington's leaders and faculty lacked a clear sense of ownership in the project. They knew that the superintendent expected great things of Kensington, but they were uncertain about exactly what they were. And as it turned out, so too was the superintendent! School leaders were never able to communicate to teachers precisely what kind of innovative performance they desired.

Another problem with Kensington's staff-development program was its failure to take into account that the faculty consisted primarily of inexperienced teachers. School leaders felt it would be more productive to work with new teachers whose ideas about schooling had not yet become rigid—new teachers seemed to be more open to training, more confident, and more enthusiastic about innovation in general. School leaders soon discovered, however, that youthful inexperience also meant limited teaching skills, unimaginative teaching, difficulty handling children, and limited knowledge of sure-fire techniques.[9] As a result, it became increasingly difficult for school leaders to focus on innovations. Teachers were concerned about more immediate and fundamental issues. For example, they grew frustrated and anxious because students were not learning as well as they had anticipated.

The luxury of hindsight allows us to realize that just opening a new school is a major undertaking. It was unrealistic to expect to shape Kensington into a highly visible experiment in innovative instruction at the same time. The lesson of Kensington is that successful staff development must be sensitive to context and timing. The opening of a new school staffed by a largely inexperienced faculty calls for staff development that focuses on such basics as developing a common language for discussing instruction and generating common routines for managing instruction and student behavior. Once such fundamental concerns have been addressed, then the time may be right for exploring new ideas about the organization and delivery of instruction. Alternatively, district leaders can choose to hire a more experienced staff with a track record of successful innovation. As it turned out, the early history of staff development at Kensington is a chronicle of grand intentions gone awry.

The Clarendon Story

In contrast to Kensington is the experience of Clarendon Primary School in Portland, Oregon, and its principal, Linda Simington.[10] Clarendon was not a brand-new facility when Simington became principal, but it boasted a large, open-space core area and modern equipment. Located in a relatively poor urban neighborhood, Clarendon enrolled large numbers of children who qualified for free lunches and Chapter 1 assistance. Its standardized test scores were among the lowest in the district.

Simington was determined to raise the level of student achievement at Clarendon, and staff development became a major component of her strategy. The summer before assuming her position, she began talking individually with every staff member, getting to know their strengths as well as their concerns. She also reviewed all available test results to identify areas of particular need. With these data in hand, Simington generated a set of very specific instructional goals for the year. Several years later, looking back on her experience at Clarendon, she admitted that she set too many goals for that first year. Still, she had made it clear to the faculty that she had high expectations of them, their students, and their principal.

It took three years for Simington's staff-development efforts to yield results. An article in the Portland newspaper in 1984 announced that Clarendon students had dramatically reversed a sustained downward trend in achievement—Simington and her staff had effected an almost unprecedented turnaround in performance. What had made the difference?

Simington and her staff credit the increase in student achievement to a staff development plan that focused squarely on the district basic skills curriculum. Teachers were asked to identify curriculum objectives with which they were having difficulty. Simington then shared research showing that practically all students are capable of learning. She encouraged teachers to share ideas about how to teach to particularly troublesome objectives. She also made certain that everyone participated in the sharing process, realizing that it would be of little long-term value if staff members relied on a few superstars for instructional insights.

Gradually, the faculty's confidence in its collective ability began to grow. Simington continued to focus attention on curriculum and instruction. Rather than erect walls and create a conventional office, she placed her desk in the midst of the open-space instructional area, where she could see firsthand whether staff development was working. Students were asked whether they understood lessons. She did more than collect data, however. She insisted on teaching different units every year, and in the process was able to model both successful and unsuccessful instructional strategies. Allowing teachers to see her try something new and sometimes fail made it safer for them to experiment. In her daily informal contacts with teachers, Simington shared her own instructional problems, solicited advice, and offered some of her own. By the end of her first year at Clarendon, the entire staff was engaged in an ongoing discussion of how to improve instruction.

During the next year, Simington shifted the focus of staff-development activity from the school to the grade-level teaching team. This change reduced the amount of time teachers spent in relatively unproductive schoolwide faculty gatherings. Meeting with individual teams, Simington discussed test results, analyzed error patterns, and inquired about the progress of particular students. When problem areas surfaced, she personally helped to design improved lessons. She insisted that assistance plans be developed for every student having difficulty meeting basic curriculum objectives.

The Clarendon experience indicates that successful staff development need not involve exotic or expensive new programs, and also that it need not exist separately from the regular instructional program of the school. Sometimes, helping teachers to follow existing curriculum guidelines and to carefully monitor student progress can promote substantial teacher growth. Of course, it is doubtful that Clarendon's teachers could have accomplished all that they did without the tireless and committed instructional leadership of Simington. As she concisely puts it, "If I'm asking staff to do more, I've got to do more to help them." Ultimately, Simington's approach to staff development was simply to insist that instructional problems be addressed. Her capacity for follow-through—for never allowing an instructional concern to be raised and forgotten—encouraged others never to give up on a student and to keep searching until effective instructional strategies were discovered.

The Valley Educational Consortium

The Clarendon story demonstrates what one school can accomplish with a dedicated leader and concerned faculty. Some schools, however, may require outside assistance to undertake successful staff development. The Valley Educational Consortium (VEC), an innovative collaborative effort involving ten small school districts, three intermediate agencies, and one college, sponsored a project in Oregon's Willamette Valley which aimed at improving the quality of mathematics instruction in 15 elementary schools.[11]

The model for the VEC staff-development effort was the Missouri Mathematics Project, designed by Tom Good and Doug Grouws. Major elements of the VEC Mathematics Program for grades 1 through 8 included the following:

- Learning goals organized by grade level
- Test-item pools and other assessment procedures that teachers and administrators can use to monitor student progress toward goal attainment
- Computer programs for scoring, analyzing, and reporting test information
- Grade-level handbooks for teachers that provide guidelines for goal-based planning, assessment, and decision making

- Guidelines for assessing and reporting students' progress toward graduation competence requirements
- Goal-based program evaluation and reporting procedures
- Guidelines for choosing and using program-related standardized tests

Besides seeking to improve the quality of mathematics instruction and ultimately to raise student achievement, VEC researchers wished to show that by training principals in instructional leadership skills, the effectiveness of staff development can be enhanced. For the purpose of research, participating schools were divided into two groups. The first group required principals to be actively involved in training teachers. The second, or control, group called for minimal principal involvement in staff development. In the first group, principal participation consisted of attending a two-and-one-half-day training session for teachers, observing two complete mathematics lessons for each teacher, conducting pre-observation and post-observation conferences, and facilitating troubleshooting sessions with teachers in order to refine the instructional model.

As a result of the VEC staff-development project, student achievement gains for both the minimum-involvement and the high-involvement groups exceeded gains for those who were not exposed to the staff-development project at all. In addition, the high-involvement group exceeded gains made by the group with minimal principal participation. While the gains were not as impressive as researchers had desired, they suggested that instructional benefits can be obtained from carefully planned staff development and active instructional leadership, either by principals or district administrators. VEC researchers acknowledged the importance of basing staff development on *proven* instructional techniques and clear curriculum objectives. As with Clarendon, the VEC staff-development project was an integral part of the regular instructional program—not an activity perceived by participants as peripheral.

A District-wide Effort

As indicated earlier, it is sometimes difficult to tell where staff development ends and school improvement begins. The Achievement Goals Program (AGP) of San Diego (Calif.) City Schools combined elements of both teacher growth and organizational change in an effort to upgrade the quality of basic skills instruction for San Diego elementary-age students.[12]

Like the Valley Education Consortium program, the AGP was based on recent research. Studies of time on task, direct instruction, mastery learning, and classroom management were investigated by a task force made up of elementary school principals, teachers, and curriculum specialists. The focus of their efforts was to identify effective instructional practices in reading and mathematics for grades K through 6 and in vocabulary for grade 7. They were also concerned about providing productive learning opportunities for Spanish-speaking students, who made up a substantial portion of the San Diego school census.

Courter and Ward identify six major steps in the AGP. Initially, a cadre of teachers received district support to develop special materials to use in staff-development activities. Studying the research on effective instruction contributed to their own staff development. They then generated a common format for basic skills instruction in schools selected to participate in the AGP. This format was built around 12 annual group instruction units, each having ten daily segments. Students were tested after completing each unit. Those who demonstrated mastery joined in enrichment activities for one to three days, while others were retaught through use of direct instruction techniques. After a second test, any students who still failed to achieve mastery received remedial instruction at another time in the school day. As soon as 80 percent of a class achieved mastery, the teacher moved on to the next unit.

Once the instructional format and curriculum materials had been developed, school leaders prepared implementation plans, including specifications for staff development. Administrators first received their own staff development on how to create a school plan. Additionally, half a day a week during the summer before implementation, school principals and vice principals, together with central office staff, reviewed the AGP and cultivated a team spirit which would provide support to individuals as they embarked on the change process. The summer program culminated in a two-day seminar in August addressed by the president of the Board of Education.

Teacher staff development was the goal of the third step. Following the August seminar for school leaders, teachers from 14 participating schools attended a district workshop where they were exposed to the core research findings upon which the AGP was based and to the instructional format and curriculum materials developed during the preceding year. Opportunities were provided during the workshop for teachers and administrators from each school to meet and discuss such practical matters as scheduling for reading and mathematics, homework policy, and the role of teacher aides.

Step four involved technical support for teachers involved in implementing the AGP. Support came in several forms, including review units for teachers to use when starting the school year and special-resource teachers for every 15 AGP instructors. These peer advisors were available to any teachers who encountered difficulty implementing particular instructional strategies. They also provided reassurance, particularly during the first few weeks of the fall. The district provided additional technical support in the form of one permanent substitute teacher for each AGP school. The availability of a trained substitute allowed regular teachers to meet with their resource teacher or to undertake other forms of staff development on relatively short notice.

To monitor implementation progress, several groups met on a regular basis. Every two weeks, all resource teachers together with central office staff gathered to share information and troubleshoot. All AGP principals also met every two weeks to examine management issues related to program implementation. Both groups tried to deal with teacher concerns quickly and effectively.

The final step of the AGP process involved evaluation of student progress and program implementation. Mastery tests were administered after each unit, and results were charted for each classroom. Formal and informal classroom observations were conducted by school leaders to see that the instructional format was being faithfully followed. A district-wide AGP steering committee convened every two weeks to review program progress and to determine if additional staff development was needed.

As a result of its systematic and coordinated approach to staff development and school improvement, the AGP yielded impressive gains in student achievement after only one year.[13] San Diego's experience demonstrates that successful staff development may entail extensive teacher and administrator involvement in early planning, adequate resources for ongoing technical support, and a design solidly rooted in research. It is also noteworthy that the AGP was not launched until after a year of local instructional and curriculum development. There are few quick fixes where effective staff development is concerned.

Secondary Staff Development

Thus far, the examples of staff development have focused on elementary schools. Staff development for secondary teachers poses several special problems—which may explain the dearth of case studies in this area. One difficulty for those planning secondary staff-development activities is scheduling. Secondary schools generally involve more teachers and more complicated schedules than elementary schools. Because many secondary teachers are engaged in extracurricular activities, staff development cannot be easily shifted to after-school hours. Unless a day or some portion of a day is set aside exclusively for staff development, it is hard to ensure the presence of all faculty members. Some secondary school leaders resort to offering staff-development activities twice—once before school and again in the afternoon—to accommodate as many teachers as possible.

A second problem with staff development at the secondary level is posed by specialization. Secondary teachers typically identify more closely with subject matter areas than elementary teachers. The most meaningful staff development for them is often related to curriculum content. Instructional issues are preceived to vary from one subject matter area to the next. Outside of the most general information on teaching methods and certain schoolwide concerns such as discipline and promotion policies, there are few issues that can attract the attention or interest of an entire secondary school faculty. As a result, it may be more sensible for most secondary staff-development activities to occur at the department level.[14] The success of such enterprises naturally depends a great deal on the quality of department leadership.

STAFF DEVELOPMENT PLANS

Since staff development is an ongoing need for every school and since scarce resources and human limitations do not permit simultaneous growth in all areas of educational practice, it is reasonable to expect school leaders to create written plans to guide their decisions on the delivery of staff-development services. However, the preceding case studies, along with the review of research, suggest that no one staff-development plan can fit the needs of every school. A variety of factors must be considered, including district goals and commitments, school history and culture, and faculty quality and level of concern.

Diagnostic Question 2.1

Does a written plan exist for ongoing, systematic staff development?

While no particular staff-development plan is universally appropriate, all plans probably should address the following areas:

- Performance goals
- Rationale for performance goals
- Schedule of learning activities
- Inventory of staff-development resources
- Monitoring system

A brief look at each of these key components of staff-development plans will be helpful.

Performance Goals

Staff development implies a change in the knowledge, behavior, understanding, or attitude of groups of people. An obvious assumption underlying most staff-development efforts is that such change will alter on-the-job performance in a constructive way. Thus, a critical component of any staff-development plan is a clear set of goals regarding desired changes in teachers. Listed below are several examples of staff-development goals:

- Teachers will be able to identify the symptoms of behavior disorders and describe them in writing using district referral forms.
- Teachers will develop classroom management plans consisting of rules, consequences for breaking rules, and rewards for appropriate behavior.
- Teachers will be able to explain to parents the justification for the school's new policy on student writing.
- Teachers will describe the key elements of an effective school, based on recent research.

In his account of the failure of many school improvement efforts, Sarason notes that school leaders often have been unclear about how teachers must change in order to improve instruction.[15] For example, he points out that the goals of "New Math" curriculum development projects in the sixties were expressed in terms of changes in *student* understanding and achievement. Planners neglected to specify exactly how *teachers* would have to change in order for students to improve performance. They operated on the assumption that attendance at one National Science Foundation summer workshop would assure that teachers learned an entirely new approach to mathematics instruction. Among other things, planners failed to realize that people who have learned and practiced one set of skills and understandings must be given time to "unlearn" their old ways before setting off in new directions. They also failed to communicate to teachers beforehand what changes would be expected by summer's end. Had the planners done so, they might have learned about teacher misgivings and anxieties and subsequently allocated a longer period of time for staff development.

Diagnostic Question 2.1.1

Does the staff-development plan include a clear statement of expected changes in teacher knowledge, behavior, understanding, and attitude?

Rationale

It is one thing to call for changes in people's performance and quite another to explain why such changes are needed. A sound rationale for staff development, of course, cannot ensure teacher support. Even the most reasonable proposals may be tabled on occasion because individuals are already over-extended or sufficient resources are lacking. It is hard to imagine, however, that teachers would endorse any staff-development plan that lacked an explanation of why change is necessary.

Diagnostic Question 2.1.2

Does the staff-development plan include a rationale for proposed changes in teacher performance?

It is not difficult to understand why a convincing rationale is a key component of any staff-development plan. First, proposals for change are apt to be interpreted by some teachers as "votes of no confidence." They may reason that if the school were functioning well, change would not be needed. A carefully crafted rationale often can justify the need for change without discrediting or embarrassing those for whom it is intended. Changing public expectations, new research findings, instructional innovations, demographic shifts, district policy revisions, and new state or federal mandates are all legitimate reasons for change that are not necessarily based on the incompetence or failure of current staff members.

A second justification for a rationale is that staff development typically requires resources. The likelihood of securing resources from district officials or other funding sources is much greater if a persuasive rationale is included in the plan. Given the limited nature of resources for public schools, it is important for school leaders to indicate how expenditures related to staff development are likely to yield improved performance.

Schedule of Learning Activities

The heart of any staff-development plan is the set of experiences intended to produce changes in teacher performance. Research reviewed earlier suggests that these experiences should include ample opportunity for teachers to practice new skills and get constructive feedback. Follow-up activities are essential if new skills are to be maintained over time. Peer coaching has emerged as one promising vehicle for both guided practice and follow-up.

Diagnostic Question 2.1.3

Does the staff-development plan include a schedule of learning activities?

By specifying a schedule of learning activities, a staff-development plan can ensure that adequate time is reserved for practice and follow-up, as well as for initial instruction. Occasions for teachers to share their feelings and concerns about new methods can be set aside as well. While school leaders must be careful not to demand too much time for staff development, they also must avoid creating situations where teachers feel rushed. There are few instances where a single workshop is sufficient for teachers to learn new skills.

Inventory of Resources

Staff development requires resources, especially time. While teachers may be willing on occasion to donate time to planning or participating in staff-development activities, school leaders should not build their plans on the assumption that such contributions will continue. Funds need to be secured for things like hiring substitutes so that teachers can attend in-service activities and reimbursing teachers for involvement during noncontracted times. In some cases, districts provide funds to support teacher projects during the summer. But in others, promising staff-development efforts have aborted because school leaders neglected to ensure adequate resources after the initial startup period. Ideally, school districts would build an appropriation into their annual operating budgets so that school leaders would not have to expend valuable time each year convincing school boards of the need for staff development. Many districts simply earmark a certain number of dollars per teacher for growth-related activities.

Besides teachers' time, resources may be needed for special materials and equipment, travel to conferences or other schools, consultants, and tuition reimbursement. Some districts contract with local colleges and universities to provide training for a small group of school leaders who, in turn, conduct staff-development activities for their colleagues. Staff development need not be costly to be effective, but it almost certainly will require some additional funds.

Diagnostic Question 2.1.4

Does the staff-development plan include an inventory of resources needed to accomplish performance goals?

Monitoring System

To determine whether resources are being used wisely, some type of monitoring system should be included in each staff-development plan. A monitoring system may include formative and summative components. The formative component usually is designed to determine whether learning activities are being conducted as intended and whether participants are understanding the material they are being exposed to. The purpose of the summative component is to determine whether teachers have changed in desired ways and whether these changes have led to actual improvements in student achievement, classroom climate, and so on. The lackluster legacy of staff development in public schools makes the careful assessment of these efforts essential. Without high-quality evaluation data, it is impossible to understand why some activities succeed and others fail.

Diagnostic Question 2.1.5

Does the staff-development plan include a monitoring system?

STAFF DEVELOPMENT ISSUES

Even the best staff-development plans can be subverted by unforeseen problems. School leaders should try to anticipate possible threats to the success of their plans before launching staff-development efforts. Some predictable threats include teacher resistance, unprotected time, and professional jealousy.

Teacher Resistance

It is reasonable to expect that at least a few members of any relatively large faculty will be opposed to, or at least apathetic toward, any staff-development plan. Their concerns may be quite understandable. For instance, certain of them may be involved in too many activities already or they may be recovering from a period of intensive involvement. Others may fear that staff development will expose areas of ignorance or provide occasions for public embarrassment. Then there are those other concerns—somewhat less easy to have sympathy for, that arise from interpersonal animosities and unwarranted assumptions about the purposes of staff development. For whatever reasons, school leaders should not be surprised to discover pockets of resistance within their faculties.

This observation prompts a question often asked by school leaders: "How many supportive teachers are needed before it is worthwhile to launch a staff-development effort?" Judy Little cites one district that required its principals to confirm agreement with at least 75 percent of the teachers before committing their schools to a staff-development project.[16] While it is prudent to ensure that most teachers support a particular activity, school leaders are advised not to waste precious time and energy trying to persuade extremely reluctant teachers to participate. Even if they grudgingly consent to become involved in staff development, such people may inhibit the development of positive group feelings and jeopardize the success of the project.

One way to handle teachers who do not wish to participate in staff-development projects is to make the projects an experiment. For a period of time, those desiring to learn new skills can be given the opportunity to do so while others are allowed to opt out. After the initial phase of staff development, the instructional performances of participants and nonparticipants can be compared. If the former group demonstrates a higher level of performance, school leaders have a legitimate basis for compelling the involvement of nonparticipants.

Diagnostic Question 2.2

Has care been taken to involve in initial staff-development activities only those teachers who are receptive to them?

Unprotected time

Most teachers do not begin their careers opposed to staff development. If they grow suspicious or resistant, it is often because they have experience with projects that start with high hopes only to be displaced the next year by a new set of projects. Over the years, teachers learn to become anxious any time school leaders attend a conference for fear that they will bring back a load of new staff-development ideas! Each activity may be exciting and valuable, but people have limited amounts of energy and time. They may be unwilling to invest these scarce resources in new projects if they believe that school leaders will give them insufficient opportunity to achieve project goals.

The author once worked with a high school principal who was interested in providing her teachers with staff-development training related to the needs of reluctant learners. As part of the planning process, an inventory was taken of staff-development projects already under way at the school. The principal was astounded to discover 27 separate activities, ranging from "wellness" meetings every Thursday to clinical teaching workshops to textbook adoption committees. She wisely decided to postpone a new staff-development thrust until several existing projects had been completed.

Smith and Keith write about the importance of creating a "protected subculture" around new programs. They describe this process as one in which a group of teachers is isolated "from the usual pressures, restraints, and directives" that face them.[17] The success of Milwaukee's RISE Program, described in Chapter 5, can be attributed in part to a guarantee from the central office that participating schools would be protected from new mandates and projects for the three-year duration of the program. A critical role for school leaders, therefore, involves assuring teachers that they will be permitted to complete staff-development training and implement its results without being asked to meet unreasonable *new* expectations and demands.

Diagnostic Question 2.3

Has care been taken to protect teachers involved in staff development from additional demands on their time and energy?

Professional Jealousy

It was noted earlier that staff-development activities have the potential for undermining interpersonal relations among faculty members.[18] School leaders and teachers involved in early planning may come to be perceived as an "in group." Likewise, certain teachers may begin to believe that they are working harder on staff development than their colleagues. Also, staff development may concentrate on certain areas of the curriculum, causing teachers from other areas to feel neglected. Whatever the reason, school leaders need to anticipate possible morale problems resulting from staff development.

Preventing professional jealousy is often merely a matter of keeping people informed. It has already been pointed out that it may be unwise to involve all teachers in staff development at any given time, but this decision should not preclude widespread communication regarding the progress of planning and subsequent training. Favoritism is less likely to be charged when all teachers feel they know what is going on and have an opportunity to provide input. School leaders should also see that staff-development responsibilities are shared among many teachers, rather than a few of the best and brightest.

Diagnostic Question 2.4

Has care been taken to keep all teachers informed of staff-development activities?

Along with supervision and evaluation, staff-development activities are ones with which instructional leadership is most closely associated. As Chapter 5 pointed out, however, instructional improvement requires that other functions be undertaken on a regular basis. Instructional support and management is the next aspect of instructional leadership that will be discussed.

STUDY QUESTIONS

1. How would you design a staff-development plan, using the guidelines in this chapter, to address the need to teach students higher-order thinking skills?
2. How do you approach your own growth and development? Record in writing your feelings about staff-development activities in which you have participated. Under what conditions do you learn best? What factors inhibit your learning?
3. Can you detect differences in the level of concern of a group of teachers involved in a local staff-development project? Have each teacher discuss feelings about the project. Use the categories developed by Hall in Table 8.1 to classify each teacher's level of concern.
4. What are ways in which school leaders can grow collectively? Identify some contemporary models of staff development for administrators. Do they differ from models for teachers?
5. Contact several local principals and find out how much their school spends on staff development annually. Does their district have a policy on staff development?

NOTES

1. Judith Warren Little, *School Success and Staff Development* (Boulder, Colo.: Center for Research, Inc., 1981), Appendix A, p. 40.
2. Seymour B. Sarason, *The Culture of the School and the Problem of Change* (Boston: Allyn & Bacon, 1971).
3. Norman A. Sprinthall and Lois Thies-Sprinthall, "The Teacher as an Adult Learner: A Cognitive-Developmental View," *Staff Development,* Gary A. Griffin (Ed.), Eighty-second Yearbook of the National Society for the Study of Education, Part II (Chicago: University of Chicago Press, 1983), pp. 27–31.
4. Gene E. Hall and Shirley M. Hord, *Change in Schools: Facilitating the Process* (in press).
5. Georgea Mohlman Sparks, "Synthesis of Research on Staff Development for Effective Teaching," *Educational Leadership,* Vol. 41, No. 2 (November 1983), p. 71.
6. Judith Warren Little, "Seductive Images and Organizational Realities in Professional Development," *Teachers College Record,* Vol. 86, No. 1 (Fall 1984), pp. 84–102.
7. *Ibid.,* p. 93.
8. Louis M. Smith and Pat M. Keith, *Anatomy of Educational Innovation* (New York: John Wiley & Sons, 1981), p. 381.
9. *Ibid.,* p. 395.
10. I am indebted to Linda Simington and her staff for recounting in detail the staff-development program for Clarendon Primary School.
11. The description of the VEC project is drawn chiefly from Meredith D. Gall, *et al.,* "Involving the Principal in Teachers' Staff Development: Effects on the Quality of

Mathematics Instruction in Elementary School" (Eugene, Ore.: Research and Development Center for Educational Policy and Management, University of Oregon, 1984).

12. This account is derived primarily from R. Linden Courter and Beatrice A. Ward, "Staff Development for School Improvement," *Staff Development,* Gary A. Griffin (Ed.), The Eighty-second Yearbook of the National Society for the Study of Education, Part II (Chicago: University of Chicago Press, 1983).

13. *Ibid.,* pp. 203–207.

14. In smaller secondary schools, of course, formal departments may not exist. In such circumstances it may be useful to group together teachers in allied fields, such as mathematics and science, or language arts and foreign language.

15. Sarason, *The Culture of the School and the Problem of Change,* pp. 29–61.

16. Judith Warren Little, "Seductive Images and Organizational Realities in Professional Development," p. 89.

17. Louis M. Smith and Pat M. Keith, *Anatomy of Educational Innovation,* p. 374.

18. Daniel L. Duke, "Toward Responsible Innovation," *The Educational Forum,* Vol. 42, No. 3 (March 1978), pp. 358–359.

CHAPTER 9

INSTRUCTIONAL MANAGEMENT AND SUPPORT

When school leaders are not supervising and evaluating teachers or helping them to develop professionally, they may still contribute to instructional improvement. *Instructional management* refers to development of school policies and procedures for dealing with predictable or recurring instructional matters. *Instructional support* refers to efforts to establish and maintain school climates conducive to teacher and student growth. This chapter explores some examples of the kinds of instructional-management and instructional-support activities in which school leaders may engage.

INSTRUCTIONAL MANAGEMENT

Interest in instructional management has grown in part because of recent work stressing the importance of educational policy making. Originally, this work focused on policy-making primarily at federal and state levels, but concern over the nature of district and school policies has been increasing recently as well. Much of this concern derives from school-effectiveness studies that reveal substantial differences in student performance in schools and districts serving similar populations.

The number of people employed in instructional-management positions has increased over the years and become more differentiated. At the district level, for example, a variety of curriculum and instruction specialists often can be found. One study of instructional management in California, however, indicated that from 1930 to 1970 the growth of positions for business, finance, and personnel specialists exceeded that for curriculum and instruction specialists.[1] These noninstructional positions also were less vulnerable to budget adjustments and elimination. Brian Rowan, who conducted the study, speculated that instructional-management responsibilities at the district level shifted to school-level personnel. He goes on to write, "District administrative staffs have evolved principally to control financial transactions, personnel problems, and auxiliary student services."[2]

Among the first to acknowledge the important role of school-based instructional management was a group of researchers involved in a county-wide school-effectiveness project in California. Focusing on policy-making, they noted that individual schools typically have been regarded as "implementers," rather than "initiators," of policy. In their investigations, though, these scholar-practitioners discovered a variety of areas in which policies were made appropriately at the school level. Included in their list were the following:

- Policies on school function and structure
  — school purpose
  — student grouping
  — protection of instructional time
  — orderly environment
- Policies on student progress
  — homework
  — grading
  — monitoring progress
  — remediation
  — reporting progress
  — retention/promotion[3]

Concurrent with the work done by the California group, researchers at the Far West Regional Educational Laboratory also were exploring the area of school policy.[4] In their study of instructional management, this group identified various ways in which principals influence instruction. These included the control of teacher instructional time through setting schedules and minimizing interruptions, the determination of class size and makeup, and the assignment of students and teachers to particular groups or tracks.

To appreciate the scope of instructional management and the issues involved in it, this chapter will look at several key areas of school policy in greater detail, including academic standards, instructional time, student grouping, homework, attendance, and school discipline.

Academic Standards

Academic standards encompasses a wide area: graduation requirements, course prerequisites, student achievement necessary to earn course credit, and the like. In addition, there are a variety of closely related topics, such as diploma differentiation, retention and promotion procedures, grading systems, and processes for reporting student progress. While many observers assume that decision making about academic standards occurs exclusively at the district level or above, it is becoming apparent that school leaders play a crucial role in the process.

Michael Kirst has identified a set of key policy questions related to academic standards and curriculum content. Among the most pertinent to school leaders are the following:

Category I: Student Access and Availability of Courses
- What are the trends in enrollments for courses by student subgroups over five or ten years? Why have enrollments in some subjects increased or decreased?

- What courses are required for graduation? What courses are recommended? Are these graduation standards pervaded by minimum concepts?
- What are the criteria for student access to courses? Do students and others know these criteria? Do some students miss out on elements of the common curriculum because certain courses cannot fit into their schedules?
- When and how do students select or become assigned to courses, sequences, and tracks? ·

Category II: Nature of Courses and Course Content
- How consistent is course content across teachers . . . in terms of a) materials covered (texts, topics), b) number of assignments (reading, writing), and c) entrance and exit criteria?
- How do teachers and others assess adequacy of course content, difficulty, and achievement?
- Are courses sequential or otherwise articulated or coordinated?
- Are remediation, special assistance, and lower-track courses designed to provide students with skills for more advanced work? Or are they dead ends?[5]

Perhaps the most important set of policy issues for school leaders involves the curriculum content that students are expected to master to advance from one grade to the next and, ultimately, to graduate. Closely linked to these issues are decisions about the nature of content mastery. At what specific level of competence are students expected to perform in order to demonstrate mastery? How are performance judgments to be made? Can these judgments be appealed? Unless there is resolution of these issues related to what schools should teach and require students to learn, it is unlikely that efforts to improve instruction will be very productive.

In elementary schools, principals and grade-level leaders must consider the level of reading skill or language competence needed to advance from one grade to the next. Are other standards—such as desired levels of social maturity and mathematics skill—to be applied as well? In setting standards for any area, should school leaders be guided by national or local norms? Many elementary schools have established a variety of specific instructional objectives tied closely to a prescribed curriculum. Are students expected to accomplish a certain percentage of total instructional objectives? Are certain objectives more crucial for advancement than others? As is readily apparent, elementary school leaders are confronted by a withering array of sophisticated issues, each requiring careful analysis and deliberation.

Because of its larger size and departmentalized structure, the secondary school typically presents problems of greater magnitude than those found at the elementary level. In her description of six exemplary high schools, Sara Lightfoot captures the scope of problems related to academic standards:

A . . . source of distraction from intellectual matters in high schools lies in their multiple, often confused, purposes. The thickness of most high school catalogues points to their institutional ambiguity and competing agendas. Oftentimes little thought is given to the values and substance that should provide the core of the curriculum. Instead, the courses expand in response to shifting cultural priorities and the special faddish interests of the inhabitants, producing a vast smorgasbord of offerings that rarely have a coherent base. The 188 pages of the Brookline catalogue, for example, are filled with over 500 course descriptions listed under 15 departments. Oldtimers on the faculty worry about the proliferation of courses and the thoughtless expansion of options. More, they observe, does not necessarily mean better.[6]

While problems at the secondary level may be of greater magnitude, in many cases, than problems at the elementary level, secondary school leaders tend to be more constrained by externally developed policies than their elementary counterparts. They must take into account state and district graduation requirements (courses) and minimum competencies (skills), along with guidelines from accreditation bodies and college entrance requirements. Still, school leaders exercise a certain degree of discretion in the area of academic standards. For example, in recent years school leaders have determined that students must engage in significant writing activities in all courses, not just those in language arts. Decisions about which electives will be considered "college preparatory" have been made as part of a general trend toward reducing the number of elective courses available to students. Some schools have created alternative routes, such as "challenge exams," to advanced courses. Others permit upperclass students to take courses at local colleges.

How to establish appropriate standards for mainstreamed handicapped students has presented school leaders with particularly difficult problems. In a detailed analysis of the awarding of credit to learning disabled students, Julia Hall and Paul Gerber contend,

> The requirement of a prescribed number of Carnegie units and courses for high school graduation has posed some hardships on learning disabled students enrolled either full or part time in special curricula. In many cases, special education students cannot earn Carnegie unit credits for enrollment in special classes and so may fail to earn enough regular credits to graduate with a regular diploma. . . .[7]

Hall and Gerber explore whether a special diploma for special education students is desirable, and they conclude that it is not. Similar concerns can be raised for students receiving special diplomas in vocational education. The decision about which courses or learning experiences count toward a regular diploma has important implications in terms of a student's ability to move on to higher education or obtain employment.

Once course requirements and academic expectations have been determined, policies regarding grading and reporting need to be developed. Without such policies, students' welfare may be unreasonably jeopardized because of a teacher's arbitrary or idiosyncratic grading procedures. Researchers have long been aware of the unsystematic and at times discriminatory ways in which many teachers judge student performance.[8]

School policies should clarify such issues as the following:

- To what extent are students taking the same course from different teachers held accountable for differing amounts of work?
- To what extent are students taking the same course from different teachers subject to differing expectations and grading criteria?
- To what extent are grades based on merit factors?

- Is it appropriate to base part of a student's grade on effort, class behavior, attendance, or other nonmerit factors?
- To what extent should grades be used as a disciplinary mechanism?
- Should students be allowed to raise their grades through correction of mistakes, extra assignments, etc.?
- If students who receive relatively low grades are allowed to do additional work to raise their grades, should the same option be provided to students who receive higher grades?
- Should a student's final grade for the year be based on his or her level of performance at year's end, on the average level of performance over the year, or on some other calculation?

Once student performance has been graded, it needs to be reported. Policies are needed to determine who receives notification of which grades and how frequently. For example, most schools send report cards and progress notes home to parents and require parents to acknowledge their receipt in some way. Guidance counselors also are usually informed of student progress, and coaches too, if students are involved in extra-curricular activities. Other persons who work with the student, such as probation officers and child welfare workers, also may need to be notified.

The frequency with which report cards and progress reports are issued may actually have an impact on student performance. Some students who fail to monitor their grades or who easily fall behind in their work may benefit from relatively frequent notification. Unlike mailed reports, parent and student conferences provide an opportunity for direct exchanges of information about student progress. While such time-consuming contacts may not be necessary for most students, school policy may need to require regular conferences for those whose performance is marginal.

Student grades in high school are often used to compute grade-point averages, which in turn are used to rank students. Such rankings may be influential in determining admission to better colleges and universities. An issue for which policy may be needed concerns the compilation of student rankings. Should grade-point averages for noncollege-bound students be included? These students may take easier courses and therefore tend to receive higher grades. Placing noncollege-bound students in class rankings could jeopardize the standing of students applying to colleges.[9] Some high schools choose to give greater weight to a grade in a college preparatory course than the same grade in another course.

Once students have received final grades for courses or other learning experiences, decisions must be made concerning promotion/advancement or retention. Again, school policies are needed if the rights and welfare of students and the integrity of the educational system are to be protected. Questions that school leaders may need to address include the following:

- Should a student with a D grade (or its equivalent) be permitted to advance?
- Should promotion to the next grade level be contingent on a certain percentage or number of passing grades in different courses?
- Should limits be placed on the number of years a student can be retained?

Some school systems, like the one in Norfolk, Virginia, report that, when combined with intensive remediation efforts and other innovations, focused retention programs can succeed in raising student achievement sufficiently to permit return of the students to their regular classes.[10] In general, though, research has failed to produce convincing evidence that retained students ultimately perform better than promoted students.[11] The likelihood that retained students will benefit from retention seems least when they continue to receive the same kinds of instruction they have always received.

Diagnostic Question 3.1

Do policies exist regarding academic standards, grading and reporting of student performance, and retention/promotion decisions?

Instructional Time

One complaint that all educators seem to have in common is "We don't have enough time." There is not enough time to teach all the material of potential value to students. There is not enough time to provide every student with meaningful learning experiences. There is not enough time to address and correct every learning problem. Educators live in a world of scarce resources, and time is the dearest resource of all.

Because of the importance and scarcity of time, school leaders should see to it that policies are developed which increase the likelihood that time will be used wisely. Research confirms the need for such policies. In a comprehensive review of research on time and learning, Nancy Karweit reported that only about half the time in the school day is typically used for instruction.[12] In addition, she found that time allocations differed markedly among classrooms. The educational opportunities of students in classrooms where substantial proportions of available time are spent on noninstructional activities may be seriously jeopardized.

These are some areas that might benefit from policies designed to maximize instructional time:

- Classroom interruptions
  - intercom use
  - parent visits
  - assemblies
- Scheduling of extracurricular activities
- Access during class time to special resources
  - library
  - guidance counselors
- Administration of standardized tests
- Paperwork required of teachers

In one high school visited by the author, the principal raised awareness about the issue of instructional time by sponsoring a contest. Any teacher could invite him to class on a day when the teacher wished to be clocked. The goal was to lose the fewest minutes to noninstructional activities during a regular class period. The contest winner was an industrial arts teacher who conducted a lesson where less than a minute was lost in a 45-minute period!

Increasing the quantity of instructional time is no guarantee, of course, that the time will be used well. Pamala Noli writes of the steps she took as an elementary principal to improve both the quantity *and* the quality of instructional time. Among her policies were the following:

- The day was extended by 15 minutes.
- Two morning ten-minute recesses were combined into one 20-minute recess, thus reducing transition times.
- After-school home tutors were employed using CETA funds.
- Public address announcements were limited to the first or last ten minutes of the day.
- Simulations and role-playing activities were conducted early in the year so that children would not be drawn off-task by a classroom disruption.
- Efforts were made to reward on-task behavior.
- A sustained silent reading program was carried on every day from 12:40 to 1:00 by everyone in the school.
- Parent volunteers and cross-age tutors were used to help students assigned to independent seatwork or learning centers.
- Activity-oriented subjects such as science and drama were reserved for afternoons when students were less likely to use seat time productively.[13]

At the secondary level, additional policies may be required because of the fragmentation of the day into separate periods and the demands of extracurricular activities. For example, a policy providing for guidance offices and the school library to be open after school can reduce the number of students needing to leave class during regular school hours. A policy requiring students who leave school early for athletic events to make up missed classes before school or during free periods can reduce lost learning time for them.

Some high school teachers complain that standard classes do not provide sufficient time for students to undertake certain intensive learning activities such as might be required for science labs, vocational classes, and creative arts projects. School leaders may need to develop alternative schedules that permit flexible classes. One possibility is a *zero period* before school that can be combined with the regular first period class to double the amount of time available. Scheduling certain courses taken by the same students in blocks can allow teachers to decide among themselves when additional time may be needed to complete special projects. Some high schools have even adopted college-style schedules, which alter the length of classes over a multi-day cycle.[14] Figure 9.1 contains an example of such a schedule.

Increasing the quantity and quality of instructional time is more than just a matter of adjusting schedules and reducing interruptions. Closely related to the issue of time are such factors as class size and student grouping, homework, attendance, and discipline. Policies that cover these areas may contribute directly to more productive use of the time available for instruction.

Module	Day 1	Day 2	Day 3	Day 4	Day 5	Day 6
1	ENGLISH 10 Large Group		AMERICAN HISTORY Small Group	BIOLOGY	SPANISH II	
2		GEOMETRY				
3						
4						ENGLISH 10 Small Group
5		SPANISH II		AMERICAN HISTORY Small Group	BIOLOGY	
6						
7	GEOMETRY					GEOMETRY
8						
9		ENGLISH 10 Small Group	GEOMETRY		PHYSICAL EDUCATION	
10						BIOLOGY LAB
11	SPANISH II	LUNCH				
12		LUNCH	LUNCH		AMERICAN HISTORY	
13	LUNCH		LUNCH	LUNCH		
14	LUNCH	AMERICAN HISTORY Large	ENGLISH 10 Small Group	LUNCH		
15				GEOMETRY	LUNCH	LUNCH
16	BIOLOGY				LUNCH	LUNCH
17			SPANISH II			
18					ENGLISH 10	
19	PHYSICAL EDUCATION			SPANISH I		
20			PHYSICAL EDUCATION			SPANISH II
21		BIOLOGY LAB				
22					GEOMETRY	
23	AMERICAN HISTORY					
24						

Figure 9.1 Adapted from Richard A. Dempsey and Henry P. Traverso, *Scheduling the Secondary School* (Reston, Va: National Association of Secondary School Principals, 1983), p. 21. Reprinted with permission.

Diagnostic Question 3.2

Do policies exist regarding the quantity and quality of time available for instruction?

Student Grouping

Issues related to how students are grouped for instruction include class size limitations, pull-out programs, tracking, and within-class grouping. It is obvious that policies concerning the number and types of students assigned to classes bear directly on the effectiveness of instruction.

Many teacher contracts specify a maximum class size. This does not necessarily ensure compliance, however. The author visited one high school where each September, in order to preserve low-enrollment electives and advanced courses, the principal allowed other classes to exceed the contract maximum of 34 students. He was unperturbed by the dozens of grievances about class size that were filed against him because he knew that by October many students would have dropped out of school or moved away, thereby bringing most classes into compliance!

School leaders may ask, "Is there an ideal class size?" To some extent, of course, the answer can be expected to vary depending on the subject, the age and ability of the student, and the skills of the teacher. Within the range of 20 to 40 students, class size does not seem to make much of a difference in achievement, at least as measured by standardized tests.[15] Research indicates, however, that classes of 20 or fewer students do contribute to greater learning, particularly for students of lower ability.[16] School leaders should take note, though, that reducing class size is unlikely to make much difference in student learning if instructional strategies remain the same. To take full advantage of smaller classes, teachers must be prepared to provide more individual attention, monitor student progress more systematically, and carefully re-teach material that was not learned the first time.

One policy for reducing class size is to create special pull-out programs which remove certain types of students from regular classes for a portion of the day. Presumably, the needs of particular students can be addressed more effectively in separate settings with specially trained personnel. Pull-out programs have been developed for disadvantaged students (Chapter 1, migrant education), students with limited skills in English (ESL), handicapped students (resource rooms, remedial speech classes), and gifted students (TAG centers). Additional pull-out programs, found primarily in elementary schools, are for students desiring band and orchestra lessons. A potential problem of pull-out programs concerns the disruption caused by students leaving and entering class. Some students become confused over expectations from their regular teachers and their resource teachers. Teachers also complain that the integrity of their lessons is violated when students come and go during the day. Additional time is required to tell pull-out students about missed material. Furthermore, it is feared that students who miss regular lessons to receive remedial instruction lose touch with what their classmates are doing. As a result, it may become difficult for pull-out students to eventually rejoin their peers. Because of these and other concerns, a policy eliminating pull-out programs was established for schools in Milwaukee's highly touted RISE program.[17] Students requiring special assistance received it in their regular classes at designated times from visiting resource teachers.

Perhaps the most hotly debated issue concerning student grouping is the desirability of homogeneous grouping and tracking. Should students be placed in classes made up entirely of students of similar ability or interest? While educators often prefer to work with homogeneous groups, there are a variety of policy considerations that must be reviewed. Grouping practices may systematically discriminate against certain students, thereby perpetuating racial or other forms of segregation and deep social divisions. Research fails to demonstrate that homogeneous grouping is of long-term value to students of lower ability, though there are some indications that more able ones may benefit.[18] Several reform reports have attacked the creation of separate tracks (college preparatory, vocational, general diploma) in high schools on the grounds that students in noncollege-preparatory tracks tend to receive a less rigorous education and are not exposed to critical elements of their culture.[19]

Given the controversies surrounding the issue of how students should be grouped for instruction, what are school leaders to do? Robert Calfee and Roger Brown caution against simplistic policies for complex concerns:

> We are concerned about the all-or-none tone of many of the discussions of grouping. The high school is tracked or not. The primary school is "nongraded" or self-contained. Special education students are mainstreamed or not. Gifted students are in a "pullout" program or given "enrichment" in the regular classroom. We see value in programs that offer variety and flexibility in assignments to groups. The practical problems of implementing this recommendation are real ... We doubt that the extra effort will pay off in an immediate increase in the average performance of the group, but we see no other alternative for handling the differences in individuals who make up "The Group."[20]

For those who worry that pull-out programs and tracking have the potential for negative social—and possibly personal—consequences, but who also recognize the practical difficulties associated with instructing students of vastly different abilities, within-class grouping may be a viable alternative. Teachers can divide students in the same class on the basis of ability and permit them to pursue course objectives at a pace commensurate with their skill level. If within-class grouping is used, a policy may be needed permitting the adoption of optional textbooks for students at different reading levels. Also, a policy for handling parent or student requests for transfer to another group may be required.

One promising alternative to homogeneous within-class grouping is cooperative learning arrangements that place students of different abilities in the same instructional groups. Robert Slavin and his colleagues at Johns Hopkins have designed a variety of cooperative learning strategies, including Teams-Games-Tournament (TGT).[21] In TGT the teacher creates heterogeneous groups of four or five students. Teammates study new material and quiz each other in preparation for an end-of-the-week tournament. Tournament competition has students of similar ability from different teams participate in a variety of content-based games. Students earn points for their teams. Cooperative learning strategies have demonstrated that students of different abilities can learn effectively together as they pursue a common goal.

How students are grouped for instruction can have a major impact on how time during the regular school day is used. Homework, on the other hand, is a mechanism that increases the time students are engaged in learning without having to deal with complex issues like grouping.

Diagnostic Question 3.3

Do policies exist regarding the grouping of students for instruction?

Homework

Like increasing the amount of time available for instruction, simply requiring students to do more homework is unlikely to yield dramatic improvements in learning. There is also the possibility that such a policy may actually cause harm by reducing the time available for student recreation and domestic activities. It is important for school leaders first to clarify the purposes that homework is intended for before developing schoolwide homework policies.

Homework may be required for a variety of reasons, including the following:

- To provide practice in skill areas covered during regular classroom activity
- To expand upon concepts or topics introduced during regular classroom lessons
- To introduce new material that will be covered later in class
- To review material to be covered on quizzes or tests
- To clarify material that was not understood when it was introduced in class
- To obtain remedial assistance in skill areas
- To provide an opportunity to move through content at an accelerated rate
- To provide an opportunity for students and parents to work together
- To inform parents of what their children are learning at school
- To provide an opportunity for students to undertake projects requiring larger blocks of time than are available during school hours
- To serve as a form of punishment or discipline
- To develop independent work habits and skills
- To make up work missed during an absence

Certain purposes for homework seem more justified, of course, than others. For example, the value of homework as a form of disciplinary action is questionable. To use it as a punishment implies that it is something students should strive to avoid—hardly the message most educators wish to convey. Other purposes, for example, those associated with remediation, assume that resources are available at home to assist students. It makes little sense to request that students focus on poorly understood subject matter if their parents are unprepared to help them. Some schools have responded to this potential problem by creating after-school homework centers staffed by trained volunteers or teachers. Other schools offer "homework hotlines" that students or parents can call if assistance in completing assignments is required.

Once the purposes that homework is intended for have been agreed upon, it is necessary for policy developers to consider such matters as the evaluation of homework and expectations for completion. When used to practice new skills or to expand upon ideas introduced in class, homework should be corrected and returned quickly. Some teachers establish routines whereby students exchange and correct each other's homework, thus reducing their own workload and expediting the process. It is unlikely that students will take homework seriously unless it is carefully reviewed, evaluated, and integrated into subsequent lessons.

When developing homework policies, school leaders may need to address certain questions, including the following:

- Should homework be graded?
- If homework is to be graded, what provision should be made for monitoring cheating and plagiarism?
- What percentage, if any, of the final grade should be based on homework?
- Should all students in a class have to do the same homework?
- How far in advance should homework assignments be made?
- Should homework be assigned on weekends or holidays?
- Should students be able to work on homework at school?
- How long should absent students be given to make up homework?
- What should happen if students fail to turn in homework assignments?[22]

How much time students spend on homework is an issue frequently debated by educators and parents. It is probably important that a homework policy specify time expectations by grade level. In this way parents can be alerted to how much time their children should be devoting to homework. In order to focus student energies and protect them against unreasonable amounts of homework, some schools assign specific days for homework in different subject matter areas. For example, Monday and Wednesday nights may be reserved for English and Social Studies, Tuesday and Thursday nights for Science and Mathematics, and Mondays for tests (giving students the weekends for review).

Diagnostic Question 3.4

Do policies exist regarding the purposes and procedures for homework?

Attendance

Student absenteeism takes a double toll on instructional time, first because of the learning time lost during absences and second because of the time required by teachers to help students catch up. Absenteeism has been identified as *the* student behavior problem of the eighties.[23]

Absenteeism takes several forms, including truancy from school, absence from particular classes, and tardiness. High school students are estimated to miss approximately ten percent of their school days each year, and this rate may be doubled in many urban areas.[24] There are disturbing indications that absenteeism increases during times of retrenchment, when class sizes swell as a result of "reductions in force" and understaffed school faculties are unable to monitor absenteeism carefully.[25] For schools already facing budget reductions, increased student absenteeism may mean additional losses of revenue, since state education funds are typically allocated on the basis of attendance figures.

Among the policy issues related to absenteeism that need to be addressed by school leaders is how to define, differentiate, and verify absences. For example, should absence from school when a student is visiting a noncustodial parent or a college campus be regarded as a legitimate excuse? If a distinction is made between excused and unexcused absences, a system for assessing the legitimacy of written excuses must be established. Some schools have taken the position that it is impossible to determine the validity of every excuse. Either they check only those excuses that are most suspect or they abandon the distinction between excused and unexcused absences entirely. Other schools routinely contact parents to check on every absence or require parents to notify the school at the time of an absence. High schools run into difficulty when they must deal with absences of legally emancipated minors (students under 18 who no longer live under the custody of parents).

Once students arrive at school, another type of attendance problem arises. The phenomenon known variously as cutting, ditching, or skipping class has become a major headache for secondary schools. To combat the problem, policies have been created for recording class attendance. Rather than collecting attendance data once or twice a day, some secondary schools require teachers to report missing students at the beginning of every period. In this way, school personnel can check to see if students are in school but out of class.

What to do with truants and class cutters once they are apprehended is another policy issue. Educators have seriously questioned the value of suspending students who miss school for illegitimate reasons. Such punishment may actually be rewarding! Alternatives such as in-school suspension and Saturday school have gained popularity in recent years because they require students to make up illegal absences by remaining in school. Some schools also punish students who miss school or class without permission by not allowing them to make up missed assignments or by giving them a failing grade for class participation during absences. In certain instances, passing grades in courses and even graduation requirements are linked to minimum numbers of attendance days.

The merits of using grades as punishment for unexcused absences have been debated at length. Some argue that receiving a failing grade only increases the likelihood of further absenteeism. Students may feel there is no sense in trying if they are denied the opportunity to make up missed work. Other educators contend that it is parents rather than students who typically are at fault in cases of unexcused absences. These parents write phony excuses, give children responsibilities that prevent them from attending school, and fail to monitor their children's behavior closely. School policy may need to specify what legal actions administrators may take against parents or guardians of students who are consistently absent.

Yet another attendance-related policy issue concerns who is responsible for monitoring student absences. Many schools employ full-time attendance clerks to receive and verify written excuses. Other schools enlist community volunteers to phone the homes of students to check on absences. While truant officers are rarely employed these days to patrol the streets, schools may use community liaisons, school social workers, or school nurses to check on absences and contact parents of students who miss a great deal of school. Teachers also may be expected to contact the homes of absent students, at least initially. While this is an extra burden for teachers, it is generally believed that their intervention is more likely to be successful than that of others.

A final area requiring policy involves make-up work and missed assignments. Should students who know in advance that they will be absent be able to obtain assignments? Should work missed during absences always be made up? How long do students have to make up missed assignments? Is a special policy needed for tests that are missed? Is a special center for make-up work needed so that regular class time need not be taken up? These and other issues are linked to the effectiveness of the instructional program and should be addressed on a schoolwide basis if students are to be assured of fair and equitable treatment.

Diagnostic Question 3.5

Do policies exist regarding the definition and verification of student absenteeism and the consequences for unexcused absences?

School Discipline

If the research on school effectiveness agrees on anything, it is the direct relationship between orderly classrooms and school environments and good instruction. It stands to reason that learning will suffer when teachers must devote precious time and energy to classroom control and school discipline. Where major problems with disorderly student behavior are found, strained relations between teachers and school leaders also tend to exist. Each accuses the other of inconsistency and lack of support. Often, the real problem is the lack of clarity of policies regarding rules, consequences for disobedience, enforcement procedures, and related issues. Sometimes, there are no policies in the first place.

School leaders committed to maintaining orderly schools must attend to several key concerns, including the specification of rules for student conduct and consequences for disobedience. In addition, policies may be needed regarding how rules and consequences are determined, how students are made aware of rules and consequences, and who is expected to enforce rules.

That students benefit from knowing how they are expected to behave in class and elsewhere on campus is beyond dispute. But the form in which behavioral expectations are expressed may vary. Some educators prefer positive statements detailing how students should behave, while others choose to tell students what they must not do. Whatever form rules or expectations take, it is important that the list be kept short. Students are unable to remember lengthy discipline codes, and teachers have difficulty trying to enforce dozens of rules.[26]

A manageable set of six classroom rules for secondary students has been suggested by Ed Emmer and his associates:

1. Bring all needed materials to class.
2. Be in your seat and ready to work when the bell rings.
3. Respect and be polite to all people.
4. Do not talk or leave your desk when someone else is talking.
5. Respect other people's property.
6. Obey all school rules.[27]

For rules to be taken seriously by students, it is important that they not be designed exclusively for the convenience or protection of school employees. To ensure that areas of concern to students are also taken into account, students should be involved in developing and periodically evaluating classroom and school rules. There is evidence that student participation in rule making is associated with lower levels of school disorder.[28] Parent involvement also may be desirable, at least for elementary-age students.

Once rules have been established, it is necessary to consider the consequences for disobeying them. Again, student opinions can be useful. Students tend to know which sanctions are most effective. As with rules, the form that consequences take may vary. Some educators prefer punishments, while others recommend "logical consequences."[29] Among the variety of disciplinary actions available to educators are the following:

- Expulsion
- Suspension
- Corporal punishment
- Parental contact and involvement
- Contact with school officials
- Loss of privileges
- Detention
- Reduced grades
- Corrective classes
- Nonmonetary fines
- Warnings

School leaders must see to it that the advantages and disadvantages of these consequences are carefully examined and debated before they are adopted as policy. Some educators may prefer establishing a range of possible sanctions for particular offenses rather than prescribing one consequence. Flexibility in assigning consequences can be helpful, but it invites abuses. Interestingly, the courts have tended to review and criticize the consequences for rule breaking in school more than the rules themselves. Expulsion and long-term suspension procedures have been accused of depriving students of their Constitutional right to an education. School leaders also have been challenged on rule-enforcement practices that systematically discriminate against minority students.

Once rules and consequences have been determined, school leaders must develop policies designed to make students aware of them. It does little good to have rules if only teachers and administrators know about them. Many schools routinely post rules in prominent places and send copies home to parents. Individual teachers may attach their own lists of classroom expectations. To make sure students understand how they are expected to behave, it may even be desirable to teach rules to students and then test them. Students who demonstrate an awareness of school and classroom rules by passing the test can earn certain privileges. Younger students may benefit from seeing rules demonstrated or by role-playing appropriate behaviors.

Another area where policies can be useful is rule enforcement. What procedures should be followed when enforcing rules? Who is responsible for enforcement? Do students have the right to appeal disciplinary decisions? These and other questions must be addressed because school discipline has become a highly complex and carefully watched aspect of school life. A variety of staff members may be called upon to participate in handling student behavior problems. In addition to teachers and principals, schools may employ deans, special counselors, attendance officers, security guards, social workers, "crisis teachers," community liaisons, teacher aides, and psychologists. As the number of discipline-related roles increases, the likelihood of confusion over ultimate responsibility for resolving behavior problems grows as well.[30] Carefully developed policies spelling out the specific duties of various persons can help minimize confusion and improve effectiveness. To the same end, teachers should be encouraged to generate their own classroom management plans and keep copies of them on file in the office of the administrator to whom disciplinary referrals normally are made. This way, those who handle referrals can help reinforce the teachers' actions.

A final dimension of policy making in the area of school discipline is contingency planning. Veteran school leaders testify to the value of anticipating unusual problems and preparing appropriate responses. A false fire alarm or bomb scare may occur rarely, but having contingency plans for coping with such troublesome situations helps preserve a climate of order in the school. Among the infrequent situations for which plans may be needed are the appearance of strangers on campus, police requests to enter school and question students, locker searches, and group pranks.

Diagnostic Question 3.6

Do policies exist regarding the development and enforcement of school and classroom rules?

Closing Thoughts on Policies

It should be noted that the preceding section generally has avoided prescribing particular policies. It is difficult to claim that one policy is universally best—contexts and circumstances differ and so, too, must policies. To develop school policies without considering local history and organizational culture is to invite problems.

A second point that needs to be stressed is that no single policy is capable of turning an ineffective school into an effective one. It is the *comprehensiveness* of policies supporting good instruction—rather than the strength of any particular policy—that is most likely to support a climate conducive to continuing instructional improvement.

INSTRUCTIONAL SUPPORT

To promote productive school climates, school leaders can undertake other activities besides policy development. In fact, too heavy an emphasis on policies and procedures without accompanying efforts to recognize individual accomplishment and to foster group cohesiveness may actually undermine instructional improvement. What can school leaders do to cultivate climates that support learning and instruction?

In their study of secondary schools in London, England, Michael Rutter and his colleagues contend that a school's climate, or *ethos,* encompasses the norms and expectations that guide people's behavior.[31] Among the primary influences on student behavior that they identified were (1) staff attitudes toward students, (2) shared activities between staff and students, (3) student opportunities to exercise responsibility, and (4) opportunities for success and achievement.

How staff members feel about students is manifested both directly and indirectly. When students are ridiculed or embarrassed by teachers or when their assignments are not returned in a timely manner with appropriate evidence of teacher examination, students are unlikely to feel supported and cared for. Students value opportunities to express their concerns to teachers and to be listened to. In the London study, staff concern for students was demonstrated in a variety of ways, including the following:

- Upkeep of school facilities and furniture
- Student access to telephones
- Availability of refreshments
- Staff availability for individual consultation
- Frequent praise and encouragement for student effort[32]

Activities that are shared by staff and students help to foster a sense of common purpose. They also permit students to see adults in a different light, not as distant professionals who know the answers, but as collaborators and fellow learners. Extracurricular activities often give opportunities for such shared experience. So, too, do field trips and community projects.

Rutter and his colleagues found that student behavior and academic achievement were better in schools where a high proportion of students had the chance to hold some kind of position of responsibility.[33] At least one study has shown that students who experienced difficulties in conventional school settings learned to behave more appropriately in alternative schools where they were treated more like responsible adults.[34] Duke and Jones have identified a variety of school-based activities that call on students to exercise independent judgment and take responsibility for themselves and others.[35] These include opportunities to do the following:

- Establish and adjust classroom rules and procedures
- Establish and adjust consequences for disobedience
- Evaluate their own behavior
- Record and evaluate their own academic progress
- Develop plans for correcting their own behavior
- Participate in academic goal setting
- Select learning activities
- Work in groups
- Work independently in class
- Evaluate behavior of peers
- Participate in correcting peer behavior
- Establish rules for teacher conduct
- Provide feedback to teachers
- Participate in class meetings
- Evaluate school programs

A fourth element of school climate concerns the extent to which students feel a sense of accomplishment from classwork and other school activities. Although the experience of failure doubtless can be of value, those in the best position to take advantage of failure are students with substantial track records of success. Students are unlikely to feel good about themselves or their school if they are constantly being told or shown how inadequate they are. Recognition should focus on both individual and group success. Success need not mean only high levels of achievement in traditional subject matter areas. Students can be acknowledged for improvement, contributions to their school and community, artistic and athletic prowess, and leadership.

School leaders are in an important position to recognize and publicize student achievement of various kinds. A team of University of Oregon researchers came up with the following activities school leaders can undertake to show special recognition:

- Require student body to attend an annual awards assembly
- Display awards in a school trophy case
- Mail reports of student achievement to parents and community
- Announce scholarships won by students
- Send list of honor roll students to newspapers
- Get media coverage of special projects
- Ask teachers to submit weekly lists of student achievers to the principal
- Encourage local businesses to offer prizes for student achievement[36]

Recognition of staff, as well as student, accomplishment is crucial to the maintenance of productive school climates. Normally, teachers are recognized on an individual and relatively private basis. Recognition may come in the form of praise from a supervisor or peer, a change in assignment, or additional delegated responsibility. The impact of teacher recognition, however, cannot be fully understood by focusing only on the form that recognition takes. What is recognized also is of importance. The fact that individual rather than collective performance tends to be acknowledged by many school leaders may need to be examined.

Judith Little finds, for example, that there may be merit in rewarding teachers for group effort and collegiality.[37] She reports that principals who are instructional leaders reward teachers who demonstrate a capacity for working productively together with more opportunities to collaborate. Samuel Bacharach and Sharon Conley underscore the value of group recognition when they observe:

> . . . in the education of any given student, the contribution of an individual teacher cannot be differentiated from the contributions of all the others. Teaching is a cooperative endeavor. Each student is taught by a series of teachers, working within a school system. And each student's academic success or failure greatly depends on the capacity of the school system to encourage cooperation among these educators.[38]

Release time and resources for group projects can be valued forms of recognition to teachers. In many schools, recognition in the form of advanced classes and assignment to classes of talented students also is accorded to teachers who are regarded as the strongest instructors by school leaders. However, while it certainly is challenging to teach bright students, the challenge may pale in comparison to the job of helping students of low ability. School leaders should consider modifying local norms and expectations in ways that place the highest professional value on teaching the most difficult students. It is hard to imagine a group of physicians meeting to acknowledge the skills of those who treat the healthiest patients! Professionals earn their stripes, so to speak, by successfully tackling the toughest cases. They derive great personal satisfaction out of getting referrals from less experienced colleagues. School leaders may well reserve assignments of students requiring extensive help for those teachers generally regarded as most capable. Helping such students learn and develop should be recognized as one of the greatest accomplishments an educator can achieve and should be rewarded accordingly.

Besides recognition, research indicates several other factors that teachers associate with a positive work environment: large amounts of student learning, constructive principal-teacher relations, effective community-school interactions, and extensive teacher involvement in the formulation and execution of the educational progam.[39] School leaders are advised to remember that schools must be supportive and pleasant places for staff members as well as students.

Diagnostic Question 3.7

Have efforts been made to support a productive school climate through (1) recognition of student and teacher accomplishment, (2) student and teacher involvement in school decision making, and (3) opportunities for students to exercise meaningful responsibility?

STUDY QUESTIONS

1. What aspects of school climate can be observed by walking around a school building?
2. Interview a building principal. Request information on each of the policy areas specified in this chapter. Do formal policies exist? How were they arrived at?
3. How many different forms of teacher recognition can you identify? Which of these are most likely to be regarded by teachers as meaningful? Why?
4. How many different forms of student recognition can you identify? Which of these are most likely to be regarded by students as meaningful? Why?
5. Collect school-discipline plans from several schools. How do they compare in terms of rules, consequences, procedures, etc.?

NOTES

1. Brian Rowan, "Instructional Management in Historical Perspective: Evidence on Differentiation in School Districts," *Educational Administration Quarterly,* Vol. 18, No. 1 (Winter 1982), pp. 43–59.
2. *Ibid.,* p. 57.
3. Joseph F. Murphy, Marsha Weil, Philip Hallinger, and Alexis Mitman, "Academic Press: Translating High Expectations into School Policies and Classroom Practices," *Educational Leadership,* Vol. 40, No. 3 (December 1982), pp. 22–26.
4. S. T. Bossert, D. C. Dwyer, B. Rowan, and Ginny V. Lee, "The Instructional Role of the Principal," *Educational Administration Quarterly,* Vol. 18, No. 3 (Summer 1982), pp. 34–64.
5. Michael W. Kirst, "Policy Implications of Individual Differences and the Common Curriculum," *Individual Differences and the Common Curriculum,* Gary D. Fenstermacher and John I. Goodlad (Eds.), Eighty-second Yearbook of the National Society for the Study of Education, Part I (Chicago: University of Chicago Press, 1983), pp. 293–295.
6. Sara Lawrence Lightfoot, *The Good High School* (New York: Basic Books, 1983), p. 357.
7. Julia Hall and Paul Gerber, "The Awarding of Carnegie Units to Learning Disabled High School Students: A Policy Study," *Educational Evaluation and Policy Analysis,* Vol. 7, No. 3 (Fall 1985), p. 229.
8. Jeffrey Leiter and James S. Brown, "Determinants of Elementary School Grading," *Sociology of Education,* Vol. 58, No. 3 (July 1985), pp. 166–180; Gary Natriello and Sanford M. Dornbusch, *Teacher Evaluation Standards and Student Effort* (New York: Longman, 1984).
9. The questionable way this dilemma was handled in the school where I started my teaching career was to control the number of A's and B's that students in noncollege-preparatory courses could earn, therefore ensuring they would not occupy top ranks in large numbers!
10. Eddie D. Hall and Ann B. Madison, "A Step Beyond School Effectiveness Research: Planning, Implementing, Maintaining, and Evaluating a School Improvement Program," *The Effective School Report,* Vol. 3, No. 3 (March 1985), pp. 1–2.
11. James R. Johnson, "Synthesis of Research on Grade Retention and Social Promotion," *Educational Leadership,* Vol. 41, No. 8 (May 1984) pp. 66–68.
12. Nancy Karweit, "Time-on-Task Reconsidered: Synthesis of Research on Time and Learning," *Educational Leadership,* Vol. 41, No. 8 (May 1984), pp. 32–35.

13. Pamala Noli, "A Principal Implements BTES," *Time to Learn,* Carolyn Denham and Ann Lieberman (Eds.) (Sacramento: California Commission for Teacher Preparation and Licensure, 1980), pp. 219–221.
14. Richard A. Dempsey and Henry P. Traverso, *Scheduling the Secondary School* (Reston, Va.: NASSP, 1983), p. 21.
15. G. V. Glass and M. L. Smith, "Meta-analysis of Research on the Relationship of Class Size and Achievement," *Educational Evaluation and Policy Analysis,* Vol. 1, No. 1 (1978), pp. 2–16.
16. Educational Research Service, *Class Size: A Summary of Research* (Arlington, Va.: Educational Research Service, 1978).
17. Maureen McCormick-Larkin, "Ingredients of a Successful School Effectiveness Project," *Educational Leadership,* Vol. 42, No. 6 (March 1985), p. 37.
18. Robert Calfee and Roger Brown, "Grouping Students for Instruction," *Classroom Management,* Daniel L. Duke (Ed.), The Seventy-eighth Yearbook of the National Society for the Study of Education, Part II (Chicago: The University of Chicago Press, 1979), pp. 180–181.
19. Mortimer J. Adler, *The Paideia Proposal: An Educational Manifesto* (New York: Macmillan, 1982), and Ernest L. Boyer, *High School: A Report of Secondary Education in America* (New York: Harper & Row, 1983).
20. Robert Calfee and Roger Brown, "Grouping Students for Instruction," p. 181.
21. Robert Slavin, "Cooperative Learning," *Review of Educational Research,* Vol. 50, No. 3 (Fall 1980), pp. 315–342.
22. My appreciation to Joel Turvey of Beaverton (Ore.) School District for her contributions to this section.
23. Daniel L. Duke and Vernon F. Jones, "Two Decades of Discipline—Assessing the Development of an Educational Specialization," *Journal of Research and Development in Education,* Vol. 17, No. 4 (Summer 1984), p. 26.
24. John de Jung and Kenneth Duckworth, "New Study Looks at High School Absenteeism," *R & D Perspectives* (Summer/Fall 1985).
25. Daniel L. Duke and Jon S. Cohen, "Do Public Schools Have a Future? A Case Study of Retrenchment and Its Implications," *The Urban Review,* Vol. 15, No. 2 (1983), pp. 89–106.
26. Daniel L. Duke, *Managing Student Behavior Problems* (New York: Teachers College Press, 1980), pp. 55–58.
27. Edmund T. Emmer, *et al., Classroom Management for Secondary Teachers* (Englewood Cliffs, N. J.: Prentice-Hall, 1984), pp. 22–23.
28. Daniel L. Duke, *Managing Student Behavior Problems,* pp. 47–50.
29. Rudolf Dreikurs and Loren Grey, *A New Approach to Discipline: Logical Consequences* (New York: Hawthorn Books, 1968).
30. Daniel L. Duke and Adrienne M. Meckel, "Disciplinary Roles in American Schools," *British Journal of Teacher Education,* Vol. 6, No. 1 (January 1980), pp. 37–50.
31. Michael Rutter, Barbara Maughan, Peter Mortimore, and Janet Ouston, *Fifteen Thousand Hours* (Cambridge, Mass.: Harvard University Press, 1979), pp. 183–184.
32. *Ibid.,* pp. 195–196.
33. *Ibid.,* pp. 197–198.
34. Daniel L. Duke and Cheryl Perry, "Can Alternative Schools Succeed Where Benjamin Spock, Spiro Agnew, and B. F. Skinner Have Failed?" *Adolescence,* Vol. 13, No. 51 (Fall 1978), pp. 375–392.
35. Daniel L. Duke and Vernon F. Jones, "What Can Schools Do to Foster Student Responsibility?" *Theory Into Practice,* Vol. 24, No. 4 (Fall 1985), pp. 227–285.
36. James S. Russell, Thomas E. White, and Steven D. Maurer, "Effective and Ineffective Behaviors of Secondary School Principals Linked with School Effectiveness," presentation made at the annual convention of the American Educational Research Association, 1985.

37. Judith Warren Little, *School Success and Staff Development* (Boulder, Colo.: Center for Action Research, Inc., 1981).

38. Samuel B. Bacharach and Sharon C. Conley, "Educational Reform: A Managerial Agenda," *Phi Delta Kappan,* Vol. 67, No. 9 (May 1986), pp. 641–642.

39. For a comprehensive review of research on school climate, see Herbert J. Walberg (Ed.), *Improving Educational Standards and Productivity* (Berkeley: McCutchan, 1982), pp. 289–303.

CHAPTER 10

RESOURCE MANAGEMENT

Schools need money to operate. Funds are derived from a variety of sources, depending on the state and the locality. Many school systems rely on state legislatures, local property owners, and the federal government for revenue. School leaders exercise relatively little control over the funds their schools receive; educational appropriations are decided at other levels—state houses, Congress, voting booths, and district offices. Where school leaders can be influential, however, is in determining budgetary needs and deciding how funds will be spent. While authority in this area typically is limited by federal, state, and local policy as well as employee contract, it is incorrect to assume that school leaders exercise no discretion over the allocation of resources.

Resource management begins with an assessment of school needs and a determination of the funds needed to purchase the resources necessary to meet those needs. School leaders next must make certain that the Superintendent and other central office administrators (in large districts) are aware of their schools' resource requirements. When the funds available are insufficient to meet all the identified needs of a school, school leaders may be called on to see that priorities are established to assist in the allocation of limited resources. Most schools—particularly during times of declining enrollments—are unable to address every identified need in a totally satisfactory manner. Resource management during such times is a particularly crucial dimension of school leadership.

It may be useful to borrow the language of economists and think of schools in terms of inputs, throughputs, and outputs. To obtain desired outputs—for example, certain levels of student achievement or a specific percentage of students who graduate—it is necessary to invest inputs. Rebecca Barr and Robert Dreeben identify three critical inputs: students, instructional materials, and time.[1] While some researchers, such as James Coleman, have strongly suggested that school outputs are almost totally determined by the quality of students entering the schools, it is now widely acknowledged that what schools do with students influences both their development and achievement.[2] As Barr and Dreeben put it, "An organization runs on resources, and how it works depends on what happens to them."[3] *Throughput* is a term that describes what happens to inputs in the process of creating outputs. This area of responsibility will be referred to here as *resource management*.

If we can put aside students for the moment, the major resources that school leaders must manage include personnel, time, and learning materials. In addition, they may handle funds dedicated to instructional improvement. Depending on how these resources are allocated and managed, a school will serve the needs of all, some, or none of its students. This chapter will now take a closer look at how school leaders work with resources. The next chapter will cover the assessment of school needs and the monitoring of how well resources are utilized to meet those needs.

PERSONNEL

In Chapters 6, 7, and 8, suggestions were made concerning the development, supervision, and evaluation of instructional personnel. What was not discussed was the recruitment, selection, and assignment of personnel. These are central issues in resource management. Aside from students, teachers are a school's most valuable resource. Since public school leaders generally have little control over the students they serve, how they recruit, select, and assign teachers may be one of their most crucial resource-management functions. However well conceived or implemented, no system of teacher development, supervision, or evaluation is likely to compensate fully for poor judgment in the hiring and placement of teachers.

There is ample reason to expect the recruitment of talented new teachers to pose a serious challenge for school leaders. Influenced by relatively low starting salaries and the growth of nonteaching job opportunities for women, the number of college graduates preparing for careers in teaching has been steadily declining.[4] The demand for new teachers is projected to exceed the supply for the immediate future.[5] Faced with hundreds of unfilled positions, many large school districts have been forced to recruit in foreign countries such as Mexico and Ireland. And in certain subject matter areas, such as bilingual education, special education, physics, and computer education, teacher shortages are acute.[6]

Not only do school leaders confront a shortage of teachers, but also the teachers from whom they select may be less talented than their predecessors. The loss of bright women as a captive labor market has clearly contributed to this situation. Victor Vance and Phillip Schlechty analyzed the Scholastic Aptitude Test scores of 1,177 prospective teachers nationally and found that those electing to teach had a disproportionately large share of low scores and a disproportionately small share of high scores.[7] So great has become the concern over teacher competence that some states and school systems now require prospective teachers to pass tests of basic literacy!

Given the scarcity of talented prospective teachers, school leaders concerned with instructional quality must devote considerable energy to recruiting and selecting staff members. Recruitment may necessitate visits to teacher education programs and correspondence with promising graduates. School leaders also may need to look at persons who have not prepared for teaching careers, but who possess valuable subject matter expertise and the potential to be effective instructors. Some states, such as New Jersey, have modified teacher certification requirements to make it easier for these people to obtain positions.

Once a group of teacher candidates has been identified, school leaders must select the ones who best fit the needs of their schools. It seems too obvious to point out that great care should be taken in the selection process, but the profession has enough anecdotes about careless hiring decisions to warrant some words of caution. At the very minimum, selection should include phone calls to references, a personal interview, and demonstration teaching. Dale Bolton also notes the value of stress interviews, group interviews, and special written assignments.[8] A thorough selection process might entail a group interview with representative faculty members, students, and parents; a performance assessment of live or videotaped teaching; a review of a sample lesson plan; and an intensive interview with the principal. While time-consuming, such a process is less costly than the one required to deal with the consequences of a poor selection. If school leaders are unable to locate any suitable candidates, they may be better off postponing selection and hiring a substitute or temporary teacher until a qualified person is located.

Diagnostic Question 4.1

Do procedures exist to ensure the recruitment and selection of qualified instructional personnel?

Once qualified people have been hired, they must be assigned. This is important since the effectiveness of talented teachers can be reduced when they are mis-assigned. If a comprehensive study of teachers is accurate, thousands of teachers in the United States have been assigned to teach in areas for which they are not qualified or certified.[9] The impact of mis-assignment on students may be to jeopardize their chances of performing well at the next level of coursework. Thus, another important responsibility of a school leader is to determine what functions teachers do well and to make sure they have an opportunity to do them. In other words, a school leader must be a good talent scout.

Among the considerations that school leaders must take into account when assigning teachers are the following:

- What does the teacher perceive he or she does particularly well?
- Does the teacher get along with staff members with whom he or she will have frequent contact?
- Does the teacher have appropriate certification or demonstrated competence in the area of assignment?
- Does the teacher have the attitudes and expectations to be effective with the particular group of students served by the assigned position?
- Has the teacher participated in the assignment decision?

It can be assumed, of course, that situations will arise when school leaders will be unable to create a perfect match between teachers and assignments. In these instances, care must be taken to provide sufficient in-service professional development and emotional support to enable teachers to handle these less-than-ideal assignments. Peer coaches, retired teachers, consultants, department chairs, and other resource people may all be used. School leaders need to remain in close contact with mis-assigned teachers and those providing specialized assistance to them to ensure that students' welfare is not at risk.

In recent years, the assignment of teaching personnel has grown in complexity as a result of the increased numbers of teacher-specialists. Besides regular classroom teachers, it is not unusual to find reading and mathematics specialists, a variety of special education teachers, teachers of the gifted and talented, Chapter 1 teachers, bilingual teachers, English as a Second Language specialists, and child development specialists. These persons may work in regular classrooms or in separate resource rooms. Stephen Kerr has noted some of the problems that specialists pose for school leaders.[10] Several of his concerns are related to the issue of assignment. For example, where specialists must serve several schools, the daily schedule may have to be completely modified to accommodate their visits. Regular classroom teachers frequently resent these adjustments. In addition, specialists who do not work alongside regular teachers require students to be pulled from class. School leaders who wish to maintain good relations with regular teachers must try to schedule specialists in ways that minimize class disruptions for these teachers.

One elementary school that has experimented with new ways of assigning specialists is William Hatch School in Oak Park, Illinois.[11] Every morning a three-hour block of time is allocated for core academic subjects—language arts, reading, mathematics, and social studies. Students are placed in groups of 15 and are taught by both regular classroom teachers and specialists (reading specialist, art specialist, media specialist, counselor, etc.). In the afternoon, groups swell to 25 or more and specialists return to their areas of special responsibility. Afternoon classes cover art, science, music, and physical education. Pull-out programs for instrumental music, speech therapy, Chapter 1, and the learning disabled are conducted during this time as well. To accommodate more activities in the afternoon, the size of classes in art, music, and physical education has been increased to an average of 29 students.

By carefully considering the best way to assign specialists, Oak Park school leaders were able to reduce class sizes in core subjects from 25 to 15 students without adding to faculty. The time teachers spend with individual students has been increased and, with it, on-task behavior. Relations between regular teachers and specialists have improved as well. Specialists report gaining a better understanding of what their students are expected to do in other subject areas.

Diagnostic Question 4.2

Are instructional personnel assigned in ways that take advantage of their talents and contribute to the achievement of school-wide instructional goals?

TIME

Closely related to the assignment of instructional personnel is the allocation of time for instruction. Daily schedules must be built on the basis of which teachers are available during which times of the day. School leaders need to take into account requirements, often fixed by contract, for teachers to eat lunch and prepare for class. How the school day is subdivided for instructional purposes typically is a macro-level issue handled by school and district policies, state guidelines, and contract. Certain issues related to scheduling were addressed in the preceding chapter.

In this section the focus shifts to the micro level. Specifically, how is time allocated on a daily basis by teachers to particular subjects and particular students? It is at this level, more than the higher plane of district policy, that the quality of instruction is frequently determined. While school leaders cannot be in every classroom for every minute of the day, it is important for them to try to understand how class time is spent and to encourage teachers to allocate it in ways that best promote realization of school goals.

Let us consider first how time is allocated to various subjects. Being human, teachers are bound to have preferences for certain areas of the curriculum. When these preferences result in the neglect of other content areas, the instructional program and, ultimately, students are bound to be affected. Elliot Eisner has written about the "null curriculum,"[12] contending that what teachers do not teach may be as important as what they do teach. A history teacher, for example, who fails to note the cultural contributions of women may not consciously intend to perpetuate sexual stereotypes, but the outcome is likely to be just that. By failing to expose students to examples of female influence, the teacher unwittingly supports the belief that "men make history."

It generally has been assumed that student learning is directly related to exposure to instruction. For this reason, schools that serve large numbers of students who are deficient in basic skills often increase the time they must spend studying reading and mathematics. In Washington, D.C., junior high school students who are working below acceptable levels in these subjects, for example, must take two periods of reading and two periods of mathematics every day as part of a program called Intensive Junior High School Instruction.[13] Some researchers, however, wonder whether exposure to instruction influences learning uniformly across all subject matter areas. Abraham Daniels and Emil Haller question the justification for scheduling class periods of equal length for all subjects.[14] Their analysis of student achievement data in New York State suggests that, in certain content areas, learning may not be adversely affected by reducing the time allotted for instruction.

Besides controlling the time devoted to different areas of the curriculum, teachers can exert major influences on student learning by determining how much attention and assistance each student will receive. Just as teachers may have preferences for certain subjects, they may have preferences for certain students. Preferred students may be asked more questions, and they may receive more and higher-quality help. They may be given special opportunities to exercise responsibility, thereby boosting their self-esteem. If they appear to have misbehaved, they may be given the benefit of the doubt or released with only a warning.

A number of researchers have noted that students with whom teachers interact in such positive ways are most likely to be the students who eventually perform best in school. These researchers have also found that teachers tend to provide more attention and assistance for certain types of students—primarily, those who are more able and who are from higher social classes.[15] Ironically, then, many students who are in the greatest need of teachers' time and assistance are least apt to receive it. Such a finding raises serious questions about the value of schooling for less able and lower-social-class students. A major responsibility of conscientious school leaders must be to monitor the allocation of time in classrooms to determine whether needy students are receiving their fair share of teachers' time. It is also important that this time largely consist of constructive, rather than punitive, contacts.

Diagnostic Question 4.3

Is instructional time allocated to curriculum content and to individual students in ways that promote school goals and equity?

LEARNING MATERIALS

Anyone who has ever taught realizes the importance of learning materials. Outdated textbooks, books that are too easy or too difficult for students, and inadequate instructional supplies can contribute to frustration for both teachers and students as well as impede progress toward instructional objectives. School leaders must see that teachers have appropriate textbooks and other materials at the time when they are needed. It is of little instructional value for learning materials to arrive weeks after the lesson for which they were intended has concluded.

Considerable attention has been devoted to textbooks since the mid-seventies. Prior to that, criticisms about overreliance on hard-to-read textbooks and curriculum control by large publishers had resulted in a diversification of learning materials. Teachers discovered, however, that students often became lost without textbooks. Parents also seemed to appreciate textbooks, as if they symbolized academic rigor and organization. Pressure mounted for the development of new textbooks reflecting advances in knowledge and written in ways that invited student exploration. Contemporary curriculum development efforts often consist primarily of selecting a textbook—as if the textbook were the curriculum.

By 1985, 22 states had policies governing textbook adoption. The intent of these policies varies and includes at least nine distinct purposes:

1. To achieve statewide uniformity of curriculum
2. To ensure the selection of textbooks of the highest quality
3. To reduce textbook costs
4. To save time and work for local school districts
5. To provide for public participation in the adoption process
6. To provide structure and order to the adoption process
7. To ensure the periodic review and updating of textbooks
8. To control the marketing practices of the textbook publishing industry
9. To protect local school districts from textbook controversy[16]

The task of selecting textbooks obviously can be greater for school leaders in states that do not have textbook adoption policies. Even in states with such policies, however, school leaders must see that some process is in place for choosing textbooks from lists of acceptable possibilities and for evaluating the usefulness of the chosen books. Research indicates that where principals actually participate in the process of selecting textbooks, student achievement may be positively affected.[17] At the very least, principals who are involved in textbook selection may develop a better understanding of what teachers value in learning materials.

Connie Muther has provided a useful set of guidelines for school leaders engaged in textbook selection.[18] The process should begin with a clear description of course or program objectives. If clear objectives do not exist, it is the school leader's responsibilty to see that they are developed. Then, along with teacher representatives, the leader must define the role the textbook is to play. For instance, will the textbook be the total curriculum, a reference manual, or a basis for organizing information? Only after these tasks have been completed is it appropriate to begin examining alternative textbooks.

The value of devoting time and energy to textbook selection becomes apparent when it is realized that many schools are supplied with materials that are inappropriate for many students. Studies suggest that a majority of students in affluent schools may already know the content of the textbooks they will use.[19] Textbooks in low-income schools, on the other hand, may be so difficult that students learn virtually nothing from them.[20] There is little justification, aside from practical concerns like cost and teacher convenience, for using the same textbook for students of widely differing levels of ability. By seeing to it that appropriate textbooks or supplementary materials are available for students of different levels of ability, school leaders can contribute greatly to instructional improvement.

Diagnostic Question 4.4

Do procedures exist for selecting textbooks and other learning materials that are appropriate for students of different levels of ability?

Textbooks, of course, represent only one—albeit the largest—category of learning materials. School leaders also may become involved in the selection and distribution of workbooks, enrichment books, computers and software, films, filmstrips, library resources, and instructional equipment. Teachers depend on these materials to support or augment instruction. Although a great deal of money is spent annually on instructional materials, it is likely that what is spent falls short of what is needed.[21] In a random sample of nearly 1,000 U.S. principals, 43 percent indicated that they experienced problems with insufficient instructional resources.[22] A key function of school leaders, therefore, is deciding how best to allocate scarce resources. Spending thousands of dollars on one piece of science equipment may not be as critical as supplying hundreds of students with supplementary workbooks. Decisions such as these are never easy, but they are the stuff of which school leadership is made.

Leila Sussmann argues that some instructional innovations fail because school leaders underestimate the resources needed to sustain programmatic changes.[23] In case studies of open education experiments in elementary schools, she notes that school leaders created the impression that, with its high degree of individualized instruction, open education cost no more than traditional practices. It turned out to be a false impression, however, and though it served to entice people to support the innovation, in reality, individualization was very expensive in terms of materials. For example, books and other reading materials at different levels of difficulty had to be available for students so they could work effectively on their own. Sussmann concluded:

> Innovations like the open classroom and individualized instruction cost more than traditional teaching, not only during the implementation phase. They cost more after routinization as well. The needs for more adults in the classroom, more planning time for teachers, and more materials for the classroom are inescapable. If an attempt is made . . . to take the extra costs out of the hides of the teachers by getting them to commit their "own" time to the innovation, the commitment breaks down as soon as the novelty of the innovation has worn off, or the teachers become exhausted. Making impossibly heavy demands on teachers is not the way to solve the cost problem or to insure adequate implementation of a new program.[24]

Another important aspect of resource management involves anticipating teacher needs for materials and providing systems that ensure teachers will receive these materials in a timely fashion. Instruction can suffer and teachers may become disgruntled when red tape and poor planning prevent them from obtaining materials when they are needed. In one study of school effectiveness, the principal and his school cabinet devised a supply system that allowed teachers to pick up supplies immediately upon making a verbal request.[25] Such systems convey the idea that teacher instructional needs are important and deserve rapid administrative response.

Diagnostic Question 4.5

Does a system exist that ensures teachers receive instructional materials in a timely fashion?

RESOURCES TO SUPPORT INSTRUCTIONAL IMPROVEMENT

In addition to the resources previously mentioned, school leaders must see that funds are available to support instructional improvement. The discussion of teacher supervision, evaluation, and development in Chapters 6, 7, and 8 indicated that instructional improvement requires time and expertise—both of which are costly. As Sussmann stated previously, teachers must be provided sufficient time to plan and practice new programs. Funds may be required to hire substitute teachers to cover classes while teachers participate in staff- and professional-development activities and to reimburse teachers for involvement during noncontracted hours. When teachers are required to undertake remediation programs to correct deficiencies, the cost of workshops, special classes, and consultants typically must be borne by the school system. Also, many districts provide tuition reimbursement, sabbatical leave, and salary adjustments for teachers who pursue advanced graduate studies related to their responsibilities.

Additional expenditures related to instructional improvement may be required for videotape equipment and tapes for supervision and peer coaching, books and films for school professional libraries, and subscriptions to professional journals. Programs that recognize outstanding performance by selected teachers and students represent further costs, though these can sometimes be underwritten by local businesses and civic groups.

When school budgets must be reduced—as is often the case in localities facing declining enrollments and depressed economic conditions—funds for instructional improvement may be especially vulnerable to cuts. Ironically, instructional improvement may be even more critical during these times because schools are able to hire fewer new teachers. The following section examines the impact of fiscal retrenchment on the delivery of instructional services in an urban high school. School leaders who are confronted with the need to reduce expenses may find that the nature of resource management changes dramatically.

RUNNING FASTER TO STAY IN PLACE

When educators are faced with budget reductions, they really do feel they are "running faster to stay in place." They try to accomplish everything they have always accomplished, but with fewer resources. Their goal no longer is to improve, but simply to preserve the existing quality of instruction, and in pursuit of this goal, they often become fatigued and dispirited. School leaders have a particularly crucial role to play during times of retrenchment.

Let us consider the case of San Jose High School in the aftermath of California's Proposition 13. With passage of the proposition in 1978, severe limitations were placed on the ability of California school districts to generate revenues from local property taxes. The author studied the impact of budget cuts on San Jose High School over a two-year period.[26] Findings from the study indicated that the quality of instruction was adversely affected by the loss of resources—an outcome that proponents of Proposition 13 tended to discount.

At the time of the study, San Jose High was one of two inner-city high schools in the San Jose Unified School District. It had approximately 1,300 students, about 65 percent of Mexican origin. Most students came from families of low socioeconomic status. Before passage of Proposition 13, the school had focused the energies of staff members on raising student achievement in the basic skills, an effort that had begun to produce increases in standardized test scores. These accomplishments were effectively erased by the loss of resources accompanying the passage of Proposition 13.

What resources were lost? To sustain two annual budget reductions of roughly 10 percent each, San Jose High was forced to shorten its school day from six to five periods. The faculty was reduced by 14, representing a new loss of 44 class sections. These losses occurred primarily in nonmandated areas such as remedial reading, English as a Second Language, and electives. Twenty paraprofessionals were fired, and this compounded the problems created by teacher losses. Average class size jumped from 23 students to 30. Also lost were support personnel such as counselors, attendance clerks, and campus supervisors. Their responsibilities, as with the paraprofessionals, either were picked up by remaining staff or abandoned. Because of seniority regulations, talented teachers in various departments were "bumped" by more senior colleagues, even though these persons often lacked proper certification. For example, not one teacher in the mathematics department was certified in mathematics!

The impact of these and other losses on the instructional program at San Jose High is captured in Figure 10.1. The diagram shows that the loss of personnel can lead to the loss of instructional time which, in turn, can exert a disproportionately great impact on the achievement of lower-ability students. This downward spiral process starts even before staff members are released. When Proposition 13 passed (A), teacher morale (1) dropped, causing teachers to spend less time planning, working after school with students, and participating in noncontractual activities (2). Student achievement (3) declined within a year of the proposition's passage, before any personnel actually were lost. When 14 teachers were fired (B) the next year, the workload of those who remained increased (4) as class sizes grew. Again, teacher willingness to put forth extra effort (5) declined, precipitating another drop in student achievement (6). At this point, parental dissatisfaction (6.10) became evident with the withdrawals of more able students (6.11). Teachers, therefore, faced larger numbers of lower-ability students (6.13). Students, meanwhile, became increasingly disgruntled (6.20) as teachers found themselves less able to provide individualized attention. As student discontent grew, so too did discipline problems (6.21). More instructional time was taken up in classroom management (6.22), thereby reducing student exposure to instruction (6.23) and triggering a further drop in student achievement (6.24).

Those who doubt that budget reductions affect the quality of instruction need only reflect on the experience of San Jose High. The case study further

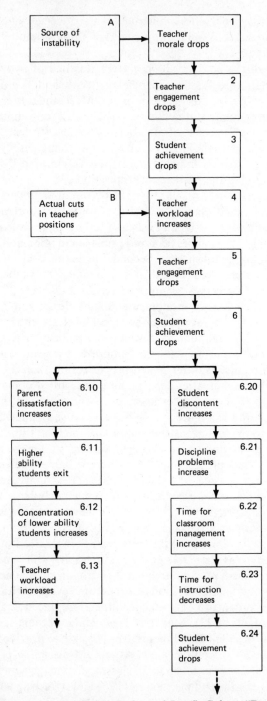

Figure 10.1   Adapted from Daniel L. Duke and Jon S. Cohen, "Do Schools Have a Future? A Case Study of Retrenchment and Its Implications, *"The Urban Review,* Vol. 15, No. 2, 1983, p. 100. Reprinted with permission.

suggests that lower-ability students may be more adversely affected by the loss of resources than other students. For example, teachers tended to focus their limited energies on students who attended school regularly and achieved the best results. Program cuts resulting in teacher losses tended most acutely to affect departments serving the largest numbers of lower-ability students. School leaders who must reduce expenses must consider ways to do so that minimize the likelihood of harming the "at risk" students who are most dependent on the schools.

A follow-up study of three New York City high schools revealed additional examples of the strain that retrenchment can place on the management of instructional resources.[27] When New York City's 1975 fiscal crisis hit, schools were plunged into years of budget trimming. Teachers reported having to use outdated textbooks or no textbooks at all. Teachers with textbooks were reluctant to allow students to take them home because funds to replace lost copies were lacking. Class sizes were allowed to exceed the 34-student limit established by contract, thereby generating demands for more desks and instructional resources. Unfortunately, funds to accommodate these demands were unavailable. Budgets for instructional equipment were particularly hard hit. At one point, a high school of 5,000 students had only one functioning 16-mm projector. Typing classes often lacked adequate numbers of typewriters and many of the typewriters that did exist were broken. Vocational-technical programs were unable to purchase up-to-date machines and tools. Budgets for supplies and repairs steadily lost pace with inflation.

What can school leaders do when they are faced with budget problems of the kind experienced by San Jose and New York City? Resource management during retrenchment is obviously different from resource management during periods of expansion. Roland Barth vividly captures the challenges of contemporary resource management for school leaders in the following passage:

> The school principal stands at the intersection of *needs* and *resources*. It is no longer possible to make a judicious match: resources are shrinking as needs expand. Todays principal somehow has to generate resources where there are none, and reduce needs as demands for services rise. And as principals try to mediate between growing needs and shrinking resources, we are faced with public demand that we account for our every act, a demand that is increasing as control over personnel, budget, and program diminishes.[28]

School leaders first must see that instructional priorities are established to guide the allocation of scarce resources. They must make decisions concerning how to sustain cuts. For example, is it better to make reductions selectively, targeting certain programs for large cuts or elimination, or to undertake across-the-board cuts in all programs.[29] Should personnel cuts dictate program reductions or vice versa?

Another key function of school leaders may be to raise public consciousness on the impact of budget reductions. When San Jose High was hit with two consecutive years of retrenchment, principal Basil Huffman asked his staff to specify exactly what services could no longer be provided as a result of lost resources. He realized that vague warnings about "the declining quality of schooling" were unlikely to be persuasive. The staff reported that they no longer had time to monitor student absences by phoning the homes of missing students, that staff members no longer were available to patrol the campus for strangers, and that only the most severe reading problems could be handled by reading specialists. Armed with his list of lost services, Huffman met with community representatives and the school board. His action generated sufficient concern that some of the lost resources were regained.

School leaders who are unable to regain resources through official channels may have to obtain supplementary resources in other ways. For example, they may solicit support from the local business community or foundations. To compensate for lost personnel, they may create corps of volunteers to work in classrooms and special programs. Some school programs, such as extracurricular activities, may need to generate resources through user fees. If user fees are charged, however, care must be taken to provide financial assistance to students whose parents cannot afford to pay the fees.

Of all the functions of school leadership during retrenchment, probably the most important is related to staff morale. The health of the instructional program may depend on the ability of school leaders to focus staff attention on long-range objectives and prevent them from becoming absorbed in day-to-day shortages and inconveniences occasioned by reductions. The capacity to inspire others in the midst of adversity is one of the most frequently cited attributes of leadership. While it is unlikely that such a capacity can be taught directly, school leaders must be made aware of the value of vision in helping staff members find meaning in their work during times of tight budgets and lost resources.

STUDY QUESTIONS

1. What are the sources of revenues for your school system? How are school budgets developed? How much discretion do principals exercise over the allocation of resources?

2. What questions would you ask all candidates for a teaching position in your school? What other sources of information would you rely on to make a decision about which teacher to hire?

3. How do teachers allocate their time to particular students? Observe in a classroom during a lesson in which the teacher is interacting with students. Determine how much time the teacher spends with each student and the nature of the contacts. Then, after class, ask the teacher to categorize each student by ability. Does the teacher tend to interact more often and more constructively with higher-ability students?

4. Locate a school system that has experienced budget reductions in recent years. In what areas were savings realized? How were services related to instruction affected?

NOTES

1. Rebecca Barr and Robert Dreeben, *How Schools Work* (Chicago: University of Chicago Press, 1983), pp. 56–57.
2. James S. Coleman, *et al., Equality of Educational Opportunity* (Washington, D.C.: U.S. Government Printing Office, 1966).
3. Barr and Dreeben, p. 56.
4. Daniel L. Duke, *Teaching—The Imperiled Profession* (Albany, N.Y.: State University of New York Press, 1984), pp. 10–20.
5. Valena White Plisko and Joyce D. Stern (Eds.), *The Condition of Education, 1985 Edition* (Washington, D.C.: National Center for Education Statistics, U.S. Government Printing Office, 1985), p. 137.
6. *Ibid*, p. 147.
7. Victor S. Vance and Phillip C. Schlechty, "The Distribution of Academic Ability in the Teaching Force: Policy Implication," *Phi Delta Kappan*, Vol. 64, No. 1 (September 1982), pp. 22–27.
8. Dale L. Bolton, *Selection and Evaluation of Teachers* (Berkeley: McCutchan, 1973), pp. 69–93.
9. "Making Do in the Classroom: A Report on the Misassignment of Teachers" (Washington, D.C.: Council for Basic Education, 1985).
10. Stephen T. Kerr, "Generalists Versus Specialists," *Organizational Behavior in Schools and School Districts*, Samuel B. Bacharach (Ed.) (New York: Praeger, 1981), pp. 365–370.
11. Howard Hawkinson, "Hatch School—Not at Risk," *Phi Delta Kappan*, Vol. 66, No. 3 (November 1984), pp. 181–182.
12. Elliot W. Eisner, *The Educational Imagination* (New York: Macmillan, 1979), pp. 83–84.
13. Sandra Lee Anderson, "Turning around Junior Highs in the District of Columbia," *Educational Leadership*, Vol. 40, No. 3 (December 1982), pp. 38–40.
14. Abraham F. Daniels and Emil J. Haller, "Exposure to Instruction, Surplus Time, and Student Achievement: A Local Replication of the Harnischfeger and Wiley Research," *Educational Administration Quarterly*, Vol. 17, No. 1 (Winter 1981), pp. 64–65.
15. Ray C. Rist, "Student Social Class and Teacher Expectations: The Self-fulfilling Prophecy in Ghetto Education," *Harvard Educational Review*, Vol. 40, No. 3 (August 1970), pp. 411–451.
16. Michael A. Tulley, "A Descriptive Study of the Intents of State-Level Textbook Adoption Processes," *Educational Evaluation and Policy Analysis*, Vol. 7, No. 3 (Fall 1985), p. 295.
17. Alfred C. Marcus, *et al.,* "Administrative Leadership in a Sample of Successful Schools from the National Evaluation of the Emergency School Aid Act," paper presented at the annual meeting of the American Educational Research Association, 1976.
18. Connie Muther, "What Every Textbook Evaluator Should Know," *Educational Leadership*, Vol. 42, No. 7 (April 1985), p. 5.
19. P. Kenneth Komoski, "Instructional Materials Will Not Improve Until We Change The System," *Educational Leadership*, Vol. 42, No. 7 (April 1985), p. 36.
20. *Ibid.*
21. It has been estimated that about one percent of the annual operating budgets of schools is devoted to instructional materials. See P. Kenneth Komoski, "Instructional Materials Will Not Improve Until We Change the System," p. 36.
22. Educational Research Service, "A Special Report: Polling the Principals," *Principal*, Vol. 64, No. 4 (March 1985), p. 62.
23. Leila Sussmann, *Tales Out of School* (Philadelphia: Temple University Press, 1977), pp. 223–224.

24. *Ibid.*, p. 224.
25. D. J. Fox, *et al.*, "More Effective Schools Program: Evaluation of ESEA Title I Projects in New York City, 1967–68" (New York: Center for Urban Education, 1968).
26. For an account and analysis of San Jose High's experiences, see Daniel L. Duke and Adrienne M. Meckel, "The Slow Death of a Public High School," *Phi Delta Kappan,* Vol. 61, No. 10 (June 1980), pp. 674–677; Daniel L. Duke and Jon S. Cohen, "Do Public Schools Have a Future? A Case Study of Retrenchment and Its Implications," *The Urban Review,* Vol. 15, No. 2 (1983), pp. 89–105.
27. Daniel L. Duke, Jon S. Cohen, and Roslyn Herman, "Running Faster to Stay in Place: Retrenchment in the New York City Schools," *Phi Delta Kappan,* Vol. 63, No. 1 (September 1981), pp. 13–17.
28. Roland Barth, *Run School Run* (Cambridge: Harvard University Press, 1980), p. 176.
29. The process of retrenchment decision making is discussed in greater detail in Daniel L. Duke, *Decision Making in an Era of Fiscal Instability* (Bloomington, Ind.: Phi Delta Kappa Educational Foundation, 1984).

CHAPTER 11

QUALITY CONTROL

The pursuit of quality instruction is the duty of all certified school staff, but it is up to school leaders to ensure that these efforts are undertaken in a responsible and systematic way. No organization as large and complex as most schools can be operated on the premise that all staff members automatically will conduct themselves in ways that serve the common good. Even if self-interest did not sometimes intrude on professional judgment, teachers still would need occasional monitoring. Any teacher, no matter how capable and well intentioned, can overlook important details, forget key goals, or neglect instructional concerns. The constant pressure on teachers to serve large numbers of students for small segments of time is by itself sufficient justification for monitoring.

Different terms can be used to describe the external monitoring of instructional activities. While *evaluation, supervision,* and *assessment* are frequently used, *quality control* is the preference of this book. A term borrowed from private industry, quality control refers to a variety of activities designed to determine the extent to which organizational goals are being achieved. In the case of schools, these activities may range from teacher observations to students tests to accreditation visits. More than simply the gathering of data on performance, quality control encompasses generating and implementing suggestions for improving performance as well as follow up to see if performance has actually improved. The primary concern of this chapter is the role that school leaders can play in instructional quality control.

Monitoring the quality of instruction, of course, requires school leaders to supervise and evaluate teacher performance. These aspects of instructional quality control have been addressed in detail in Chapters 6 and 7. Quality control also involves overseeing the assessment of student performance, evaluating curriculum and programs, assessing school effectiveness, and monitoring the success of school-improvement and staff-development efforts. These are the dimensions of quality control that will be focused on in this chapter. Before discussing them, however, it is necessary to review the variety of specific purposes of quality control.

WHY MONITOR QUALITY?

To say that quality-control activities are designed to ensure that school goals are achieved is to convey simplicity when complexity is the rule. Ensuring that

220 Dimensions of Leadership for Instructional Improvement

school goals are achieved may be the chief purpose of quality control, but there are at least four other important purposes:

- To determine whether, in the process of achieving school goals, undesired by-products also are achieved
- To provide information relevant to the promotion, retention, and remediation of individual students
- To determine whether special programs and projects have been implemented as originally intended
- To assess whether resources are being used efficiently and effectively

It is important for school leaders to realize, then, that quality control is intended to do more than just provide information. Information, in and of itself, accomplishes little. Microcomputers may have increased the capacity of school leaders to collect and store information, but advanced technology provides no guarantee that information will be used effectively. Only when it is analyzed and used to make decisions about students, subject matter, programs, personnel, and resources can there be a reasonable likelihood that instructional quality will be enhanced. Still, using data to make decisions does not guarantee that decisions will be understood or implemented. As a result, school leaders must be prepared to monitor performance to determine whether data-based decisions, in fact, have been acted upon. This key aspect of quality control is referred to as *follow-through.*

Diagnostic Question 5.1

Do provisions exist for monitoring the quality of instruction and instruction-related activities?

Diagnostic Question 5.2

Do provisions exist for making data-based decisions related to instructional quality and for ensuring that decisions are implemented?

School leaders who obtain instructional data but who either neglect to use it to make decisions or do not follow through to see that those decisions are implemented are unlikely to promote effective instruction. They may simply be creating the illusion of quality control, in the hopes that school personnel will perform adequately and the concerns of central office supervisors will be allayed.

Naftaly Glasman concludes that principals may tend to make little use of evaluation data because they themselves have played a relatively minor role in designing and conducting evaluations.[1] While it is unrealistic to expect all school leaders to personally collect all necessary data on student performance, curriculum and program implementation, school effectiveness, and the like, they *can* be actively involved in planning quality-control activities and interpreting data.

Diagnostic Question 5.3

Are school leaders involved in planning and interpreting the results of quality-control efforts?

Goal Setting

While quality-control efforts must address a variety of purposes, their chief purpose is to determine the extent to which goals are being achieved. It therefore stands to reason that quality-control efforts will be no better than the quality of the goals themselves. The quality of instructional goals will depend, to some extent, on the quality of school and district goals. One of the major responsibilities of school leaders is to see that school and instructional goals are well designed and well expressed. There are at least four important qualities that goals should have—clarity, reasonableness, coherence, and visibility.

Diagnostic Question 5.4

Has care been taken to establish school and instructional goals that are clear, reasonable, coherent, and well publicized?

Clear goals are goals that can be understood by those responsible for achieving them. They should be expressed with a minimum of jargon and with enough precision that people can assess progress toward goal achievement. It is preferable, for example, to have a goal that reads, "Teachers will identify two different ways of teaching the same concept, use both approaches, and compare learning outcomes," than "Teachers will expand their repertoire of teaching methods."

One way that school leaders can increase the likelihood that goals will be understood is to involve staff members in goal setting. A high level of staff participation increases their awareness of goals (thereby reducing the need for subsequent publicity) and the likelihood of staff support. Goals that are created and "owned" solely by school leaders are not likely to be as effective.

Two additional criteria of well-conceived goals are reasonableness and coherence. While goals should, of course, be challenging, they also should be achievable. Unrealistic goals are more likely to demoralize and frustrate than to inspire and focus energies. Part of the art of school leadership is being able to judge the reasonableness of goals. Goals that are linked to existing elements of school programs, or that derive from other goals are more likely to be perceived as reasonable than goals that arise out of nothing, unconnected to ongoing activities or current expectations. Ideally, for example, instructional objectives at the classroom level will derive from school curriculum goals which, in turn, will be tied to district and state goals related to anticipated learning outcomes. Where goal coherence is missing, teachers will be more likely to do whatever they like, possibly wasting valuable resources in the process.

ASSESSING STUDENT PERFORMANCE

The first level of quality control is the classroom; it involves determining the extent to which individual students are learning what they are expected to learn. Responsibility for class-level quality control resides primarily with teachers. One study of more than 100 elementary principals found that only 20 percent felt they had much direct influence on student achievement.[2] School leaders, however, *do* have important supporting roles to play in monitoring student performance.

For example, school leaders can share the results of externally mandated tests with teachers and conduct item analyses in which error patterns are sought. In a study of 88 California school districts, Glasman found that the vast majority of principals report sharing data on student achievement with teachers on a regular basis.[3] In addition, the principals felt that sharing data with teachers had a strong positive effect on student achievement.[4] This finding is supported by Pittsburgh's experience with the Monitoring Achievement in Pittsburgh (M.A.P) program.[5]

Glasman went on to note, however, that sharing student achievement data and analyzing results, by themselves, were unlikely to benefit individual students.[6] The school leader's quality-control duties also must include follow-through activities in which efforts are made to help teachers (1) re-teach students who performed poorly on tests, (2) develop improved lesson plans to prevent future problems, and (3) refine skills in assessing student performance.

Diagnostic Question 5.5

Have provisions been made to share on a regular basis with teachers the results of externally mandated tests and to see that results are incorporated into plans for instructional improvement?

In spite of all the publicity surrounding it, externally mandated testing makes up a relatively small portion of the total effort to monitor student progress toward instructional goals.[7] Since it is crucial to provide students with frequent feedback on their performance, school leaders must see that teachers use various means of performance assessment to supplement externally mandated tests. Performance assessment may range from teacher-made tests and quizzes to less formal types of performance assessment where students demonstrate skills and knowledge in the context of regular instruction. Stiggins and Bridgeford have observed that part of the reason teachers may not know much about good performance assessment practice is that it is rarely addressed in teacher preparation courses.[8] Therefore, school leaders may need to provide staff development opportunities for teachers to learn such things as how to design valid and reliable tests and how to observe student performance systematically during instruction. Stiggins recommends that both teachers and administrators receive training in the following areas:

- Clarifying the demands of the various purposes of assessment
- Selecting assessment methods to match purposes
- Designing or planning assessments that work
- Ensuring the quality of those assessments
- Building specific paper-and-pencil tests
- Constructing assessments based on judgment of performance
- Measuring specific basic communication skills
- Using modern technology in classroom assessment
- Promoting test-wiseness among students
- Measuring high-order thinking skills[9]

In a unique study of secondary student views of classroom evaluation, Gary Natriello identifies a variety of questionable assessment practices that lend support to Stiggins's recommendations.[10] Substantial percentages of the 65 students questioned indicated that they were:

- Assigned more things than they could satisfactorily complete
- Evaluated by more than one adult, where pleasing one of them meant displeasing the other
- Given poor evaluations for group work because some members of their groups were not doing well
- Given incorrect information about how their performance would be evaluated
- Not told how they were expected to perform
- Evaluated using standards that were much too high

Diagnostic Question 5.6

Are teachers aware of good performance-assessment practices and do they use this knowledge to assess student performance on a regular basis?

A study of teacher testing practices indicates that school leaders clearly could be doing more to monitor assessment practices and to provide assistance. In a national survey of principals and teachers, Herman and Dorr-Bremme found that school leaders tend not to require teachers to (1) turn in test scores and grades on classroom tests or assignments on a regular basis or (2) turn in copies of tests they have developed.[11] Furthermore, released time is not routinely provided for teachers to develop tests. Only about one in three teachers at the elementary level and one in five at the secondary level reported receiving training in the use of test results to improve instruction.

Partially because they have little training in evaluation and assessment, teachers may concentrate on monitoring student achievement for a narrow range of behaviors. One study, for instance, reported that teacher-made tests focused on lower-level skills requiring recall of terms, factual knowledge, rules, and principles.[12] While such tests are easier to construct and grade, they are not necessarily more meaningful. The ultimate goal of instruction should not be the mastery of facts, but the ability to apply factual knowledge. School leaders, therefore, may need to help teachers broaden the scope of their assessments to include higher-level skills.

Diagnostic Question 5.7

Are teacher assessments reviewed to assure that a broad range of student abilities is monitored?

Another area where school leaders can assist teachers in classroom quality control is the management of comprehensive instructional systems. Such systems usually call for the continuous monitoring of student progress. While continuous progress approaches are theoretically very attractive, in practice, they frequently entail extensive recordkeeping. Van Cleve Morris and his colleagues have provided a useful illustration of this problem based on Chicago's experience with mastery learning.[13]

Faced with discouraging results on achievement tests of Chicago students, school leaders decided to abolish grades one through eight and replace them with mixed-age groupings. Hundreds of reading skills were identified and organized into levels, and for each level of performance, a criterion-referenced test was developed. Decisions then were made about expected performances for each level.

Once the testing system had been created, teachers were trained to test and diagnose each student's reading level, generate learning plans for each student, and retest to determine if new skills had been learned. The entire system promised to individualize reading instruction and provide for the continuous monitoring of student progress.

The practical difficulties of operating such an elaborate instructional system were numerous. Because principals were expected to provide data on student mastery levels every ten weeks to the deputy superintendent, they began to pressure teachers to complete paperwork on time. The problem was compounded when a similar system for mathematics instruction was later introduced. Teachers began to complain about the arbitrary timing of tests and to question the validity of placing certain skills at particular levels of performance. They also voiced concern about the targets (numbers of students expected to progress to "on level" or "above level" performance) established by the central office for particular schools.

Despite the theoretical soundness of the mastery learning system, it was abandoned in Chicago in large part because of the management burden it placed on teachers. School leaders interested in developing continuous progress systems should be careful to limit the amount of noninstructional activity expected of teachers. One solution to the paperwork problem may be to centralize criterion-referenced testing. The Center School in New Canaan, Connecticut, for example, implemented a mastery learning program similar to Chicago's. However, when teachers there felt that individual students had mastered a particular skill, they referred them to the school's Testing and Evaluation Center to be tested.[14] A program coordinator then analyzed the test results and made a recommendation to the referring teacher—thus reducing the teacher's paperwork.

Diagnostic Question 5.8

Has care been taken not to require of teachers excessive amounts of paperwork and noninstructional activity?

School leaders can also assist teachers engaged in classroom-level quality-control efforts by seeing that teachers share student performance data with each other. For various reasons, teachers may not always exchange these data with colleagues, support personnel, or parents. But student performance data may provide important insights to teachers in succeeding grades, teachers in schools to which students transfer, and guidance counselors. Considerable time can be wasted retesting and diagnosing students simply because existing data have not been shared properly. Parents cannot be expected to support classroom instruction if they are not regularly apprised of their children's progress. The ways student progress is reported may also make it difficult for many parents to understand what to do. School leaders should investigate alternative methods for communicating student performance data to parents. One series of studies, for example, found that, along with teachers and administrators, parents preferred standardized achievement test reports that included "(1) samples of what a student could successfully read and (2) both self- and norm-comparisons."[15] Particularly when students have not performed well, progress reports should include suggestions of what can be done to correct deficiencies. A low numerical score or poor letter grade alone is more likely to create frustration and hopelessness than understanding. Progress reports can be self-defeating when they simply classify students.

Diagnostic Question 5.9

Have constructive and meaningful ways of sharing data on student progress been developed?

ASSESSING COURSE AND PROGRAM QUALITY

While school leaders play largely a supporting role when it comes to assessing student performance, their responsibilities are likely to increase when the focus shifts to the curriculum. Assessing the quality of courses and programs is necessary for instructional improvement, since effective instruction is more than sound pedagogical practice. Students may perform poorly on achievement tests because courses address inappropriate subject matter, texts and tests are not aligned, or course content is inadequately organized. Research on school effectiveness has found that principals in more effective schools appeared "to monitor more carefully to see that the curriculum actually met the achievement goals of the schools."[16]

Bob Gowan identifies five reasons for monitoring the quality of curriculum:

- Intrinsic value—Does the curriculum include the best thinking to date on a particular subject?
- Instrumental value—What is the curriculum good for, and for whom?
- Comparative value—Is one curriculum better than another?
- Idealization value—How can the existing curriculum be improved for students and teachers?
- Decision value—What decisions should be made regarding the curriculum? (The answer to this question derives from the answers to the four previous questions.)[17]

The chief responsibility of school leaders here is to see that mechanisms are in place for periodically monitoring the quality of curricula, courses, course materials, and special programs (such as Chapter 1, Talented and Gifted, and Migrant Education). It is probably unnecessary and definitely unrealistic for school leaders to plan on evaluating every course and program annually. Instead, they should develop multi-year evaluation cycles that provide for reviewing several different curricula each year. Where external funding is involved, however, annual program evaluations may be required by law.

Diagnostic Question 5.10

Do provisions exist for the periodic evaluation of curricula, course materials, and special programs?

How to go about monitoring the quality of curricula will likely vary from school to school, depending on state and district policies, resources available for evaluation, school size, and other factors. Still, there is a set of basic questions and issues that can be addressed during the course of any curriculum review. Some of these questions and issues have been incorporated into a systematic assessment process called the *instructional audit*. It is represented by the diagram in Figure 11.1.[18]

The instructional audit relies on a variety of information to answer four basic questions. To determine what a teacher intends to teach and what students are expected to learn, an "auditor" interviews the teacher and reviews lesson plans and materials *prior to* a learning experience (lesson, unit, course, etc.). Students then are given a pre-test to establish baseline data regarding knowledge of course content. Next, the "auditor" attempts to determine what the teacher actually teaches through classroom observations and review of student notes and course documents. Following the learning experience, students

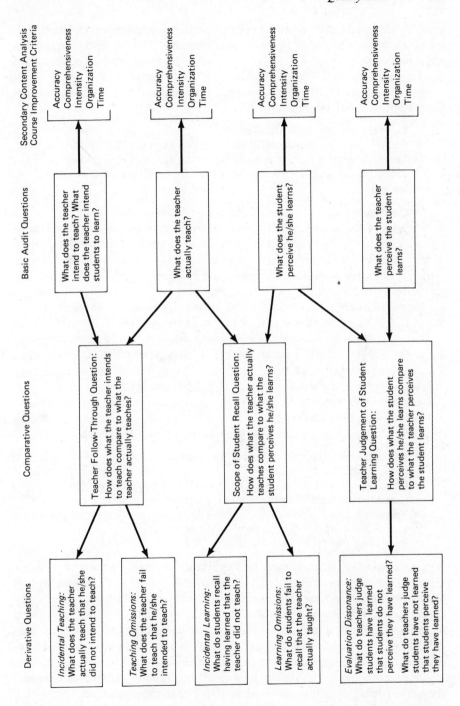

Figure 11.1 Adapted from Daniel L. Duke, "Data Curriculum Workers Need," in *Curriculum Theory* (Washington, D.C.: Association for Supervision and Curriculum Development, 1977), p. 46. Reprinted with permission.

are debriefed to find out what they perceived they learned. The teacher then is interviewed again to gather his or her perceptions of what students learned. Finally, students are given a post-test to obtain a written indication of the extent to which they learned what the teacher expected them to learn.

A learning experience that is well designed and skillfully delivered should yield audit data which indicate that:

- Teachers actually teach what they intend to teach
- Students perceive they learn what the teacher expected them to learn
- Teachers perceive that students learned what students perceive they learned
- Teachers and students perceive that students learned what students actually learned

Systematic assessments such as the instructional audit also should include an analysis of the accuracy, comprehensiveness, intensiveness, and organization of curriculum content as well as the time devoted to particular content items.[19] The quality of curriculum content has tended to be overlooked in recent years by educators intent on improving instructional practice. To separate curriculum quality from instructional improvement efforts, however, is to risk equipping teachers with the skills and knowledge to do an excellent job of teaching material that should not be taught in the first place. To monitor the quality of curriculum content on a regular basis, school leaders may need to enlist the aid of subject matter specialists, department heads, experienced teachers, and university scholars. In addition, national associations often have developed criteria and guidelines for judging the quality of various curricula. For example, the National Science Teachers Association offers sets of criteria for determining the excellence of various kinds of science offerings, including the following recommendations for programs advancing "science as inquiry:"

- Teachers who value inquiry, encourage such an orientation, and possess such skills themselves
- Classrooms in which science objects and events focus on investigation
- Curricula and units of instruction that give attention to science processes
- Teachers who act as role models in debating issues, admitting errors, examining values, and confronting their own ignorance
- Instruction that focuses on exploration rather than on coverage[20]

On certain occasions, it may be important for school leaders to evaluate learning experiences without specific guidelines or even foreknowledge of teacher expectations. One purpose of such "goal-free evaluations" (to use Michael Scriven's term) is to determine whether students acquire unintended learning as a result of such factors as how content is organized and what content is omitted.[21] Another purpose of goal-free evaluation may be to see whether curriculum goals are apparent to an uninformed observer.

Once mechanisms are in place for periodically monitoring curriculum quality, school leaders may be advised to check that the content of tests—both teacher-made and externally derived—corresponds to the content of courses and course materials. Such efforts are referred to generally as *curriculum alignment*. To George Behr, the essential question for persons engaged in curriculum alignment is "Are these test questions something . . . students have seen or practiced in their classroom work?"[22] Many evaluation experts strongly suspect that a major reason for poor student performance on tests is that students have not been exposed to the material on which they are tested. Curriculum alignment addresses this problem as well as several others related to instructional effectiveness.

In a major project conducted by the Los Angeles Unified School District and Southwest Regional Educational Laboratory, curriculum alignment efforts were believed to benefit the quality of instruction in a number of "racially isolated minority schools" by:

1. *Helping to eliminate underplacement and underpacing.* Minority students often do not succeed because they are placed too low and paced too slowly in instruction. Curriculum alignment activities include making instructional decisions on the basis of meaningful and appropriate assessment data.
2. *Helping to focus on essential skills.* Many skills in the curriculum can be learned in classrooms where the instruction is in a language other than English. Curriculum alignment helps keep instruction focused on these essential skills, regardless of language.
3. *Helping to establish priorities and manage time accordingly.* Racially isolated minority schools have many activities that compete for students' and teacher time. Curriculum alignment helps teachers establish their instructional priorities and plan instruction so that students spend sufficient time learning the essential skills.
4. *Helping to clarify school objectives.* Curriculum alignment brings school personnel together to review and develop school and grade-level plans for instruction.[23]

Diagnostic Question 5.11

Are regular efforts made to assure that curriculum content is aligned to the content of tests?

Learning experiences (like courses, units, and lessons) and instructional objectives presumably should not exist in isolation. They are linked, at least in theory, by learning sequences, hierarchies of objectives, and curriculum continua. One course often serves as a prerequisite for a more advanced course. Units build on previous units, lessons on previous lessons. When students move from one grade to another or transfer between classes, they often discover that teachers vary in the ways they sequence objectives and organize content. Since teachers may not regularly exchange information regarding instructional objectives and curriculum content on their own, school leaders may need to ensure that such sharing takes place on a regular basis. Among the purposes of sharing are the following:

- To assure that students at each level of instruction are exposed to the content they need in order to function successfully at the next level of instruction

- To identify areas of curriculum duplication across levels of instruction
- To determine if the degree of difficulty of instructional objectives is appropriate for each level of instruction
- To facilitate the transfer of students from one class to another within the same school
- To promote teacher interaction and awareness of curriculum across levels of instructions

Comprehensive curriculum assessment, or program evaluation, may call for a review of specific instructional objectives and tests at each grade level, an analysis of instructional activities, and a comparison of currently used and alternative curriculum materials. Such activities can lead to new textbook adoptions, revisions of graduation requirements, development of comprehensive systems for assessing student achievement, and re-allocation of district instructional resources. While larger districts typically employ curriculum specialists to conduct program evaluations, the presence of these staff experts should not preclude the active participation of school leaders in the processes of monitoring curriculum quality. Ultimately, these are the individuals most likely to determine whether or not the intended curriculum is actually implemented.

Diagnostic Question 5.12

Are course sequences and series of instructional objectives across grade levels periodically reviewed to determine compatibility and monitor duplication?

ASSESSING SCHOOL EFFECTIVENESS

If school-effectiveness research has made a contribution, it has been to demonstrate that student achievement is a function of more than the quality of instruction in individual classrooms. It is the capacity of many teachers in many classrooms to work together to accomplish school-wide goals that is often a distinguishing characteristic of more effective schools. Therefore, school leaders concerned about quality control should see to it that efforts are made periodically to assess the effectiveness of the entire school.

The nature of assessments of school effectiveness will vary, of course, with the stated goals of the school and the district. Many, however, derive in large part from the findings of school-effectiveness research. These assessments focus on such things as the percentage of the school day allocated to instruction, the percentage of instructional time that students are on-task, the nature of school discipline, and expectations for students. Other assessments draw on standards and guidelines developed by accreditation agencies and professional groups. For example, the National Association of Elementary School Principals has created 21 standards, each with quality indicators, for judging the quality of elementary schools.[24]

The Northwest Regional Educational Laboratory, among others, has developed a comprehensive profiling process that school leaders can use to gather data on school effectiveness. The process provides for the collection of data in the following areas:

I. Academic achievement
   A. Basic skills achievement
      1. Standardized, norm-referenced test
      2. Standardized, criterion-referenced test
      3. Progress tests from text series
      4. Grade promotion test
      5. Graduation competency test
   B. Problem-solving proficiency
   C. Life role proficiency
   D. General intellectual attainments
   E. Achievement in specific content areas
      1. Norm- or criterion-references test
      2. Structured performance test
      3. Semester or year-end test
      4. Awards from external sources
   F. Generalized competence

II. Student attitude
   A. Self-concept
   B. Attitude toward school
   C. Independence/locus of control

III. Social behavior
   A. Attendance
   B. Tardiness
   C. Cumulative dropout rate
   D. Code of conduct violations
   E. Vandalism[25]

An assessment as extensive as the profiling process outlined above can provide a great deal of information relevant to instructional improvement. Among other things, it can be of value in setting specific targets or goals for improvement. For example, when one Oregon high school used the Northwest Regional Educational Laboratory profiling process, it learned that 72 percent of its students skipped a class occasionally.[26] Comparison groups from neighboring Washington State and the entire United States reported lower percentages—60 percent and 43 percent, respectively. The Oregon students also missed more school days for reasons other than illness than students in the two comparison groups. With these data in hand, a team of school leaders from the high school established a school goal calling for a 50 percent reduction in student absences and tardies by the end of the following year. Among the research-based strategies selected by the team to achieve this ambitious goal were the development of clear attendance policies, efforts to make classes more inviting and friendly, improvements in the quality of instruction and teacher-student interactions, and a more expeditious process for disciplining students with unexcused absences.

The above assessment also revealed areas of student achievement in need of improvement. An analysis of California Achievement Test results for a four-year period indicated a pattern of achievement for ninth-, tenth-, and eleventh-grade students in the 50th and 60th percentile range for reading, language, spelling, and mathematics. An analysis of course selections showed that students lagged behind comparison groups in the percentage taking advanced courses like algebra, geometry, and elective science. These and other data led the team to set a second school goal, which read:

> By June 1985, student academic performance will improve by 10 percent, as measured by the California Achievement Test, percentage enrolled in "advanced" courses, percentage of time on task in the classroom, and success rate on tests and assignments.

To achieve this goal, a multi-faceted approach was developed: Teachers were trained to increase on-task behavior by students, curriculum goals and objectives were clarified, expectations for each lesson were specified by teachers, and local tests were designed so that approximately 95 percent of the students could score at least 80 percent. In addition, provisions were made to ensure that classes started and ended on time, that teachers re-taught poorly understood material, and that students were frequently recognized for academic success.

Assessments of school effectiveness may appear to require more resources than most schools have available, but it is important to remember that many schools already collect a great amount of data. Leigh Burstein has identified 38 different types of data that schools and districts routinely collect.[27] These include data on student demographics, expenditures, standardized test results, teacher-made and curriculum-embedded test results, course-taking patterns, student grades, absenteeism, disciplinary infractions, and community perceptions. More than two-thirds of the states have legislation requiring public high schools to measure student competence in the basic skills. In addition, most high schools conduct extensive self-studies to prepare for periodic accreditation visits. School leaders committed to assessing their school's effectiveness should take advantage of these existing data.

Diagnostic Question 5.13

Are mechanisms in place for periodically assessing school effectiveness and developing data-based school improvement goals?

JUDGING THE SUCCESS OF SCHOOL IMPROVEMENT

School leaders' responsibilities for quality control do not end when goals for improving school effectiveness have been established. They must monitor school improvement efforts and related staff-development activities to ensure that sufficient progress toward school goals is being made. Chapter 8 briefly discussed several issues related to the evaluation of school improvement and staff development. A more detailed analysis of the process can be found in an article written by the author and Lyn Corno, entitled "Evaluating Staff Development."[28]

In the article, an evaluation is planned for a hypothetical staff-development project intended to reduce student behavior problems in a school. The evaluation plan is presented in the form of a series of decisions to be made by a school leader and his or her staff. These decisions include the following:

- Who will be involved in planning the evaluation?
- What are the anticipated outcomes of the staff-development project?
- How will the anticipated outcomes be measured?
- How will unanticipated outcomes be measured?
- Will any nonoutcome data be collected?
- Who will collect the data?
- From whom will the data be collected?
- When will the data be collected?
- How can we be relatively certain that any observed differences were due to the staff-development project (as opposed to some other factor or factors)?
- How will the data be analyzed?
- How will the evaluation data be shared and used?

In attempting to answer such questions, school leaders obviously should seek the advice of others. The more staff members can be involved in planning and conducting evaluations of school improvement and staff development efforts, the greater the likelihood of getting their support for any adjustments or revisions that may be called for. Prudent school leaders have learned to expect such changes during the course of new projects.

School leaders involved in innovation also should attend to the timing of evaluations and to assessing exactly what has been implemented. Promising projects, for instance, can be evaluated prematurely—before any positive outcomes can be reasonably expected. The unfortunate result may be cancellation of a credible project and wasted resources. Also, a prescribed improvement program may not be implemented as it originally was designed—if it fails, it may be hard to determine whether the fault rests with improper implementation or with the prescription itself. Therefore, school leaders monitoring the quality of school-improvement and staff-development efforts need to assess *fidelity*—the extent to which new programs actually have been implemented according to plan.

Diagnostic Question 5.14

Do provisions exist for monitoring the quality of school-improvement and staff-development projects?

School leaders engaged in various assessment activities invariably confront a dilemma. One purpose of quality control is accountability, or seeing to it that public resources are being used responsibly and efficiently. A second purpose is improvement. This purpose is served best by using assessment data in formative ways to guide revisions in program design and adjustments in professional practice. It is difficult to serve both purposes equally well.[29] Concern for accountability invariably threatens to undermine the trust so critical to the improvement of practice. An exclusive focus on improvement may unwittingly protect malpractice and the squandering of resources. As we shall see in the concluding chapter, living with dilemmas like this is one of the challenges of remaining a school leader.

STUDY QUESTIONS

1. What, to you, are the most important purposes of evaluating student performance? Ask several students and teachers their opinion. Are certain purposes mutually exclusive?

2. What kinds of data would you like to have in order to assess the effectiveness of your school? How would you gather these data? (Have you specified what you mean by "school effectiveness?")

3. Are there ever circumstances when it is inappropriate to conduct evaluation activities?

4. Would you predict that quality-control efforts in private business would differ from those in public schools? What are your reasons?

5. How can data on student performance be meaningfully communicated to students and their parents? Design a format for a report card that includes the kind of information that can help students improve performance.

NOTES

1. Naftaly S. Glasman, "The School Principal as Evaluator," *Administrator's Notebook,* Vol. 31, No. 2.
2. Elizabeth G. Cohen, Russell H. Miller, Anneke Bredlo, and Kenneth Duckworth, "Principal Role and Teacher Morale under Varying Organizational Conditions" (Research Memorandum, Stanford Center for Research and Development on Teaching, undated), p. 5.
3. Naftaly S. Glasman, "Student Achievement and the School Principal," *Educational Evaluation and Policy Analysis,* Vol. 6, No. 3 (Fall 1984), pp. 291–292.
4. *Ibid.*
5. Paul G. LeMahieu, "The Effects on Achievement and Instructional Content of a Program of Student Monitoring Through Frequent Testing," *Educational Evaluation and Policy Analysis,* Vol. 6, No. 2 (Summer 1984), pp. 175–187.
6. Naftaly S. Glasman, *Evaluation-based Leadership* (in press), p. 148.
7. It has been estimated that, depending on grade level, from a third to three-quarters of assessments in classrooms are teacher-developed. See Joan L. Herman and Donald W. Dorr-Bremme, "Teachers and Testing: Implications of a National Study," paper presented at annual meeting of the American Educational Research Association, 1984.
8. Richard J. Stiggins and Nancy J. Bridgeford, "The Ecology of Classroom Assessment," *Journal of Educational Measurement,* Vol. 22, No. 4 (Winter 1985).

9. Richard J. Stiggins, "Improving Assessment Where It Means the Most: In the Classroom," *Educational Leadership*, Vol. 43, No. 2 (October 1985), p. 73.

10. Gary Natriello, "Problems in the Evaluation of Students and Student Disengagement from Secondary Schools," *Journal of Research and Development in Education*, Vol. 17, No. 4 (1984), p. 18.

11. Joan L. Herman and Donald W. Dorr-Bremme, "Teachers and Testing: Implications of a National Study," pp. 17-21.

12. *Ibid.*, p. 27.

13. Van Cleve Morris, *et al.*, *Principals in Action* (Columbus, Ohio: Charles E. Merrill, 1984), pp. 164-166.

14. Stephen E. Rubin and William G. Spady, "Achieving Excellence Through Outcome-Based Instructional Delivery," *Educational Leadership,* Vol. 41, No. 8 (May 1984), pp. 42-43.

15. Marian Jean Dreher and Harry Singer, "Making Standardized Tests Work for You," *Principal*, Vol. 63, No. 4 (March 1984), pp. 20-24.

16. Shirley A. Jackson, David M. Longsdon, and Nancy E. Taylor, "Instructional Leadership Behaviors," *Urban Education*, Vol. 18, No. 1 (April 1983), p. 66.

17. D. B. Gowan, "Two Philosophers View Education," *Educational Evaluation and Policy Analysis,* Vol. 2, No. 2 (Summer 1980), pp. 67-70.

18. Daniel L. Duke, "Data Curriculum Workers Need" in *Curriculum Theory* (Washington, D.C.: Association for Supervision and Curriculum Development, 1977); Daniel L. Duke, *When Teachers and Researchers Cooperate: The Challenge of Cooperative Professional Development* (Stanford, Calif.: Stanford Center for Research and Development in Teaching, 1977).

19. One alternative to the instructional audit is the process of *curriculum mapping*. See Fenwick W. English, *Quality Control in Curriculum Development* (Arlington, Va.; American Association of School Administrators, 1978). Other methods for evaluating curricula are presented in Arieh Lewy (Ed.) *Handbook of Curriculum Evaluation,* (New York: Longman, 1977).

20. John E. Penick and Robert E. Yager, "The Search for Excellence in Science Education" *Phi Delta Kappan*, Vol. 64, No. 9 (May 1983), p. 623.

21. George J. Posner and Alan N. Rudnitsky, *Course Design* (New York: Longman, 1978), pp. 157-161.

22. George Behr, "Test-wiseness: Using Test Information for Planning Instruction," paper presented at the Northwest Regional Educational Laboratory Conference on School Effectiveness, 1982.

23. *Ibid.*

24. *Standards of Quality Elementary Schools* (Reston, Va.: National Association of Elementary School Principals, 1984).

25. For information on the Northwest Regional Educational Laboratory Profiling Process, contact Bob Blum, Goal Based Education Program, NWEL, Portland, Ore. 97204.

26. My appreciation to Ken Servas, Assistant Superintendent of Centennial School District, for information on the high school assessment process.

27. Leigh Burstein, "The Use of Existing Data Bases in Program Evaluation and School Improvement," *Educational Evaluation and Program Analysis,* Vol. 6, No. 3 (Fall 1984), pp. 312-313.

28. Daniel L. Duke and Lyn Corno, "Evaluating Staff Development," *Staff Development/Organization Development,* Betty Dillon-Peterson (Ed.) (Alexandria, Va.: Association for Supervision and Curriculum Development, 1981), pp. 93-111.

29. The dilemma of accountability versus improvement is discussed with regard to teacher evaluation by Richard J. Stiggins in "Improving Assessment Where It Means the Most: In the Classroom."

CHAPTER 12

COORDINATION AND TROUBLESHOOTING

The chapters thus far in this section have highlighted leadership "situations," or clusters of functions, that are easily recognizable to most people connected with public schools—supervision, teacher evaluation, staff development, professional development, instructional support and management, resource management, quality control. The present chapter deals with two dimensions of school leadership that may be somewhat harder to "see." Coordination and troubleshooting encompass a variety of activities that cut across *all* the preceding areas; by definition, they do not exist apart from other leadership functions. School leaders must coordinate *something*—personnel, programs, schedules, projects, processes, and the like. They do not troubleshoot for the sake of troubleshooting, but in order to anticipate possible problems related to some specific area of activity. Coordination and troubleshooting could have been discussed in each of the previous chapters—and have been, to some extent. But because these two dimensions of leadership are so rarely singled out for special treatment, they need to be addressed separately.

COORDINATION

Research clearly indicates that effective school leaders devote more time to coordination than less effective ones.[1] But what, exactly, is coordination? One dictionary defines it as "harmonious adjustment or working together."[2] The word conveys a more specialized meaning to students of organizations; to them, it encompasses activities designed to reduce the need for organizational control. Control mechanisms—such as supervision, evaluation, rewards, and sanctions—may be required when individuals do not behave in ways that advance the interests of the organization. An alternative to control is to convince people that helping to achieve organizational goals is also in their *own* best interests. Efforts designed to stimulate cooperation or at least to keep units within an organization from working at cross-purposes all fit under the rubric of coordination activities.

Organizations like today's schools typically consist of many units, employees, and functions. In addition, schools exist within larger entities—school districts and communities. The complexity of these relationships increases the need for coordination, or what many theorists now call *linkage*. Richard Daft defines linkage as "the extent of coordination between organizational elements."[3] Several types of linkage have been identified.[4] *Bureaucratic linkages* are the "formal, enduring arrangements" such as roles, rules, procedures, and authority relations that enable organizations to operate. *Cultural linkages* encompass more subjective forces that bring organization members together—shared meanings, symbols, stories, and rituals. The potential value of these linkages for schools and school systems has been noted by scholars who characterize these organizations as "loosely coupled."[5] Karl Weick has noted how tenuously connected the components of school systems are, while Blumberg and Greenfield have made a similar observation about individual schools; they contend that "What occurs between a teacher and a principal relative to the teacher's work, for example, or what occurs between a teacher and his/her students, has no necessary relevance for events that develop elsewhere in the school."[6] Without linkages, there is little assurance that the actions of one teacher or department will serve to support the actions of another teacher or department. Linkages promote the interdependence and predictability so crucial to organizational effectiveness.

School leaders may use a variety of means to create linkages between people and programs, thereby ensuring a reasonable degree of coordination. First of all, school leaders can see to it that staff members regularly meet together. Furthermore, they can make certain these occasions are productive. Planning and decision making are two activities that offer great opportunities for the development of productive linkages. School leaders cannot ignore the quality of relationships between individual staff members either. Ultimately, it is the character of these relationships, more than the number of occasions when staff members and others meet together to plan or decide, that will determine the effectiveness of coordination efforts.

This section will next discuss the increasing need for school leaders to devote time and energy to coordination and the building of linkages. Then it will look at several areas of school activity where the need is particularly acute—school discipline, special education, and school improvement. The final segment examines various ways school leaders can facilitate coordination—through planning, productive meetings, shared decision making, and interpersonal relations.

THE GROWING NEED FOR COORDINATION

Educational historians tell us there was a time in the United States when educators and the public shared a common vision of schooling. Schools were small organizations, and few laws constrained the conduct of school leaders. Teachers were not represented by powerful unions, nor was the federal government a major force in shaping local educational policy. Those who worked in schools were relatively clear about the tasks before them.

Few in education today can remember this bygone era. Schools of the late twentieth century are usually complex entities with large numbers of students and employees. As schools have come to serve virtually all young people, their mission has lost some of its earlier clarity. Should contemporary schools serve the cause of excellence or equity? Can both causes be pursued with equal vigor? Are schools better suited to recreating the existing society or forging a new one? Today's schools have become a jousting ground for an array of special interest groups, each with its own vision of what causes schools should serve.

As the ranks of educators swelled to accommodate increased numbers of students, so, too, did the degree of differentiation in job titles and roles. The traditional domain of the teacher and the principal now hosts a variety of certified and classified specialists, ranging from assistant administrators in charge of discipline to speech therapists to cooks. As new roles have proliferated, lines of authority often have blurred. Relationships among people working in schools are no longer clear. These intra-school problems are compounded by the rise of district offices. With district offices have come district curriculum specialists, evaluation specialists, staff-development specialists, and the like, adding to the confusion about who is responsible for what.

Increased role differentiation reflects, to some extent, an increase in the technical complexity of schooling. Today it is impossible for a teacher or administrator to master all areas of the curriculum. Special education, with its mandated Individual Education Plans (I.E.P.'s) and diagnostic procedures, requires a variety of specially trained teachers and support staff. School administration and counseling similarly have grown in complexity. In larger secondary schools today, full-time positions may be reserved for an athletic director, resource room coordinator, activities director, and drug and alcohol counselor. The person who fills each position must know a variety of laws and regulations as well as the intricacies of scheduling and the functions of other public agencies. It is unlikely that any one person in a school can know all the rules, regulations, and procedures governing school operations.

In situations where no individual has sufficient technical expertise—or time—to supervise everyone else, coordination is critical to organizational effectiveness. As Elizabeth Cohen and her colleagues put it, greater organizational complexity necessitates greater coordination.[7] When school leaders fail to respond to increasing complexity with more attention to coordination, confusion is likely to result, along with a decline in morale and possible failure to achieve school goals. Teachers often react to such situations by "closing their doors" and acting on their own.

COORDINATION AND SCHOOL DISCIPLINE

Few areas of school life have experienced greater growth in complexity than school discipline. We need only consider the increase in job titles associated with some aspect of student behavior. Depending on the school system, we may find discipline-related functions being carried out by principals, vice principals, deans of students, regular classroom teachers, special "crisis" teachers, guidance counselors, school psychologists, school social workers, community liaisons, detention-room monitors, security guards, playground and cafeteria supervisors, and attendance clerks. Role confusion and conflict have been two results of this expansion of roles.[8] Another has been the growth of uncertainty concerning where one specialist's responsibilities end and another's begin. Yet another result has been more "buckpassing"—or sequences of referrals without substantive progress. If decisions are made eventually regarding student behavior problems, they are frequently subject to challenge.

The complexities of school discipline have been further increased by the growing involvement of external agencies. Child welfare services and juvenile justice offices frequently play roles in the resolution of school discipline cases. Schools and school systems currently live under the threat of lawsuits in these cases. The courts have been particularly willing to review the sanctions used by school personnel to punish rule breakers. And special interest groups—such as the Children's Defense League and the Civil Rights Commission—monitor suspensions, expulsions, and other sanctions for discriminatory practices. There is, in fact, considerable evidence to suggest that school disciplinary practices tend to single out minority youth for harsher treatment.

A case study of two California secondary schools trying to deal with student absenteeism illustrates the growing need for coordination in school discipline.[9] School personnel regarded attendance-related problems such as truancy, cutting class, tardiness, and leaving school without permission as serious causes for concern. Considerable time and effort were devoted to reducing these problems. During a nine-month period, one of the schools initiated a detention hall and a new policy for handling unexcused absences as well as an independent study program for chronically absent students. During the same period of time, the second school required teachers to deal with the first disciplinary contact after a student had an unexcused absence, employed plainclothes police to patrol campus for students cutting class, and began a policy of giving chronically truant students a second chance by erasing their first semester unexcused absences. After each intervention, attendance problems subsided briefly and then started to increase again. By year's end, personnel at both schools were growing frustrated and cynical.

To try to understand why the various efforts to reduce attendance problems had failed, the author and a colleague conducted an intensive year-long study, which included field observations and interviews with school personnel. The study focused on aspects of school organization that might be contributing to ineffective disciplinary practices. A variety of problems were identified—many reflecting a lack of coordination.

For example, attendance at both schools theoretically was monitored by a number of persons—teachers, assistant administrators, counselors and attendance clerks. No one, however, assumed a leadership role in coordinating the monitoring activities of all these people. They never met as a team, developed shared understandings of attendance policies, or reviewed difficult cases. Since communication among school personnel was infrequent, students were able to "play" one adult against another. To make matters worse, school personnel unilaterally created new policies but failed to inform each other of what these policies entailed. Inconsistent enforcement of attendance rules, therefore, was the rule—not the exception.

In the case of one school, the lack of coordination actually became mildly humorous. It seemed that every month or so, when concern over attendance finally reached a point of alarm, the administrators would conduct a "sweep" of the campus. All students found loitering were sent immediately to the detention center. Unfortunately, the administrators never bothered to check with the detention supervisor first. Had they done so, they would have discovered that he already had as many students "doing time" as there were desks. The supervisor had no choice but to turn away the additional students who, quite rightly, found it hard to take seriously such a poorly coordinated disciplinary system. This helped explain the persistence of attendance problems.

Another coordination problem involved the failure of school personnel receiving attendance-related referrals to notify teachers of any action taken. Teachers consequently wondered whether their referrals ever resulted in anything more than a student furlough from class. As a result, some teachers simply ceased making referrals at all. The study revealed that coordination is sometimes a function of helping staff members see that their efforts to follow policies and procedures are not a waste of time.

Other coordination problems that contributed to continued poor attendance in the two schools included:

- Lack of regular communication between attendance clerks and administrators
- Lack of teacher involvement in developing school rules and sanctions
- Lack of regular contact with the parents of chronically absent students
- Lack of daily sharing of information among school administrators

There is no reason to believe that the coordination problems found in this study are unique to those two schools. School personnel are generally very busy, and the likelihood that important information will not be shared is always great. Individuals may desire to meet together and coordinate their activities, but finding time during the school day is difficult. Thus, school leaders who are faced with such time pressures but are concerned about coordination are advised to develop systematic management plans for problem areas like school attendance.

Chapter 9 discussed in detail the value of school-discipline plans. Such plans require school leaders and staff members to share thoughts about expectations for student behavior, consequences for misconduct, and procedures for enforcing rules. It is quite telling that neither of the schools mentioned earlier had a school-discipline plan. Written plans alone cannot ensure coordination, of course, but they do provide a common reference point for discussion and action. A key responsibility of school leaders is seeing that such plans are developed and that, once developed, they do not simply gather dust. To be of benefit, the contents of management plans should be reviewed and evaluated regularly, with changes made as circumstances dictate.

COORDINATION AND SPECIAL EDUCATION

To say that life for school personnel changed dramatically following passage of Public Law 94-142 in 1975 is to risk understatement. Almost overnight, educators were called upon to set up complex mechanisms for defining, diagnosing, and treating students' handicapping conditions. Treatments had to be carefully documented. Regular classroom teachers were directed to work with handicapped students who previously had been served exclusively by special education teachers.

The need for coordination of special education services at the school level is evident for several reasons. For example, the process by which students are diagnosed as "handicapped" and assigned to classes may involve a number of people, including specialists, classroom teachers, school administrators, and parents. Dealing with handicapped youngsters in the context of regular classrooms requires adjustments in teachers' expectations, instructional arrangements, classroom management, and peer interactions. Classroom teachers are required to develop I.E.P.s, work closely with specialists and aides, and keep parents informed. To increase the likelihood of teacher cooperation, school leaders may have to ensure teacher involvement in the assessment and assignment process. This process can be a complicated one, entailing intensive reviews of students' case histories, parental contacts and signatures, formal evaluations and analyses, and detailed prescriptions.

The author had an opportunity recently to appreciate how complicated the process actually can be. For a full year he served as a part-time teacher aide in an urban elementary school. Early in the year, it became apparent that one young boy was having difficulty adjusting socially, academically, and emotionally. His case was referred to the School Appraisal Team (S.A.T.) on September 11 for review. The S.A.T. met once a week and always seemed to have a backlog of cases awaiting review. When a particular student came up for review, the teacher making the referral was expected to present the case. Since S.A.T. meetings were held after school, it was not always possible for teachers to be present. As a result, the boy in question was not discussed until October, when it was determined that a formal evaluation, complete with testing, should be undertaken. To initiate testing, however, the signature of a parent was required, and because of the school's difficulty in contacting the boy's mother, over a month was required to obtain the necessary signature.

The evaluation indicated extreme social immaturity, but no severe learning disorders. An I.E.P. was called for, but disagreement rose within the S.A.T. as to who should be responsible for writing it. Because several specialists on the team did not get along well, the task of writing the I.E.P. fell, by default, to the classroom teacher. She had never written an I.E.P. before. Eventually, the I.E.P. was completed, at which point the S.A.T. requested that the boy's mother come to school and review the plan. Since the teacher refused to meet during noncontracted time again, a meeting had to be arranged during the regular school day. After much difficulty, all S.A.T. members, the teacher, and the mother finally agreed to a meeting time. The day arrived, and the mother failed to appear. Finally, the school social worker drove to the mother's apartment and picked her up. The plan was reviewed and approved, but it was the middle of December!

A third of a school year had passed before the first intervention was made in this case. During this time, the boy's life in school continued to deteriorate, affecting not only his opportunity to learn, but those of his classmates. And he was just one of dozens of students waiting to be reviewed by the S.A.T. If the intent of Public Law 94-142 is to be realized, and the welfare of handicapped students is to be served, there is a tremendous need for coordination of school services.

In one in-depth study of special education assessment, Hugh Mehan and his colleagues discovered that some principals expedite the process by conducting informal screenings themselves.[10] By personally consulting with teachers about prospective referrals and conducting their own classroom observations, these principals are able to reduce the number of cases handled by their S.A.T.s, focus attention on the most severe cases, and improve the efficiency of the entire process.

Coordination also may help diminish the tendency of some special programs to compete with each other for resources, preferential treatment, and even students. The Mehan study cited above found examples of such competition between bilingual and special education programs.[11] Personnel associated with both programs wanted a balance of white and nonwhite students. Because there were few white students in bilingual education, when one was referred to special education from a bilingual classroom, it was difficult to obtain approval. When the welfare of individual students is subordinated to the special interests of program heads, it is time for school leaders to intervene.

The effective delivery of special education services may necessitate coordination between the school and external agencies as well as between programs within schools. The families of children requiring special education services often face a variety of other concerns as well; many of them are characterized by internal disruption and impoverishment. They are served by a variety of social welfare agencies, each requiring separate intake procedures, diagnostic processes, and regular contacts with social workers. And unfortunately, there is great potential for competition, both among these agencies themselves and with the school. Recognizing this problem, Harvey Clarizio and George McCoy have urged greater efforts to coordinate these special services:

> It becomes apparent that some organization and coordination of services is essential, for multiple agency contacts obviously increase the pressures on an already disabled family unit. There is also the matter of tying up the services of personnel already in short supply in duplications of intake interviews, home visits, and related diagnostic study. Not only is there misuse of specialist personnel, but the ac-

tual delivery of available services is impaired when there is no central coordination.[12]

School leaders may not always be the people in the best position to provide this central coordination, but they *can* see to it that issues related to duplication of services and inter-agency competition are raised and addressed. In addition, they can monitor the assessment and assignment process to make certain that cases are being reviewed and resolved quickly and fairly. Also, school leaders can make certain that personnel who are expected to implement I.E.P.s and related strategies are aware of their responsibilities.

COORDINATION AND SCHOOL IMPROVEMENT

Much has already been written in this book about the need for coordination during innovation. School leaders have been urged to involve staff members in planning for change, to keep staff members informed as change occurs, to make certain adequate resources to sustain change have been set aside, and to monitor closely the process of implementation. Recommendations such as these derive from a large body of research on educational innovation, much of it describing how various efforts to improve schools fail. Seymour Sarason, in fact, has concluded that the more things change in schools, the more they remain the same.[13]

If knowledge about how to innovate successfully exists, then why do school improvement efforts continually encounter problems? Many reasons, of course, can be found, and a number of them involve factors beyond the control or influence of school leaders. Certain reasons, however, can be traced to a lack of awareness on the part of school leaders about how to approach the coordination of change. For example, some leaders feel that they must personally preside over all school improvement. Even the ways they express the problems that need correction, as Sarason has noted, frequently assume that they—and they alone—must solve them.[14] These persons have not learned the value of delegating authority. Delegation extends "ownership" of change to more people and taps expertise that school leaders may not possess.

In their extensive research on school improvement, Gene Hall and Shirley Hord find that many successful innovations involve not only a supportive principal, but also a second "change facilitator" or "consigliere"—often another administrator—and even a third change facilitator—typically an enthusiastic classroom teacher.[15] It is easy to understand the value of dispersing responsibility for school improvement if we accept Hall and Hord's dictum that change is a process, not an event. As a process, change is ongoing, continuous. The daily requirements of successful innovation—frequent contacts with staff members, responses to requests for information, efforts to locate extra resources, and similar routine activities—would tax any single person's stamina. Coordination often boils down to seeing that these routine matters are handled expeditiously.

Sarason believes that school leaders may not appreciate the complexity of the change process.[16] This naiveté leads them to assume, for example, that staff members understand the nature of an innovation, why it is needed, and how it will be implemented. As Hall and Hord indicate, however, the level of understanding of a given innovation is likely to vary widely across a faculty.[17] Even when the innovation is understood, it may not be regarded positively. Patricia Brieschke has found that some teachers act as guardians of existing organizational norms.[18] They can be counted on to view any proposed change as a threat. One of the coordination tasks connected with school improvement, therefore, may be to create opportunities for staff members to voice their feelings about proposed innovations. School leaders are more likely to win support for change by acknowledging the legitimacy of these feelings than by pretending they do not exist.

As noted already, teachers sometimes agree on the value of an innovation but feel that the timing is bad. They may be involved in other projects or have recently completed an innovation. Consequently, the energy and enthusiasm needed to launch a new project may be wanting. Part of the value of coordination lies in determining whether school-improvement efforts have been scheduled in ways that make unreasonable demands on staff members. Crucial to the success of school improvement may be a long-range plan in which new projects are spaced at appropriate intervals and ample time is reserved for identifying problems, discussing proposed changes, receiving training, implementing changes, and assessing their impact.

DEVELOPING COORDINATION SKILLS

As suggested earlier, coordination is not a specific behavior, but rather an array of skills and predispostions that relate to virtually all activities a leader undertakes. School leaders interested in improving their ability to coordinate will find themselves retracing familiar territory. For instance, good planning is usually an essential component of coordination—also, skill in running meetings, decision making, and fostering productive interpersonal relations. While entire books can be written on each of these dimensions of coordination, and indeed have been, it may be valuable to take a brief look at how each relates to coordination and the building of linkages within schools and between schools and other entities.

Planning

When people plan together, they share important information about their aspirations, assumptions, and level of commitment. Such information can be invaluable to school leaders desiring to forge an organizational culture that is supportive of instructional improvement. School leaders who choose to conduct planning by themselves or with only a select group of confidants may ultimately find themselves struggling to win broad-based support and also to stifle rumors. In short, how a leader approaches planning can either reduce or increase the need for subsequent coordination. It is usually wise to involve many staff members in the planning process, and thereby use planning as an occasion to build school-wide understanding and cooperation, instead of suspicion and mistrust.

Diagnostic Question 6.1

Is planning used as an occasion to foster school-wide understanding and cooperation?

School leaders may engage in at least three types of planning—operational, contingency, and long-range. Operational planning covers the day-to-day activities involved in running schools, ranging from preparing for a student assembly to developing a staff-development program. Because the activities take place frequently over the course of the year, operational planning for any one of them should not require great amounts of time. It should be regarded chiefly as an opportunity for school leaders to obtain information from staff members closest to particular concerns.

Contingency planning involves preparing for the unexpected. The assumption underlying contingency planning is that surprise is the enemy of organizational effectiveness. School leaders try to anticipate events and problems that could threaten the safety and welfare of students and staff members. Such occurrences could include bomb scares, school closures due to weather conditions or other natural phenomena, budget shortfalls, boiler explosions or breakdowns, strikes by staff members, student boycotts, and demands by community groups to review school programs and personnel. Once a possible source of disruption has been identified, school leaders or their designees develop plans for responding quickly, thus minimizing problems.

Diagnostic Question 6.2

Have provisions been made for handling possible sources of disruption to school life?

Long-range planning in some ways presents the greatest challenge to school leaders, since they rarely know from year to year what resources will be available or what new expectations must be addressed. Ironically, though, it is this very uncertainty that makes long-range planning essential. Without annual— and, preferably, multi-year—plans, schools are completely at the mercy of the moment. Long-range plans alert policy makers and the public to a school's goals and resource needs. When groups convene to reflect on the future, there is a great potential for discord and wasted time. The success of these gatherings may often depend on the ability of school leaders to run meetings productively with concrete long-range plans in hand.

Meeting Skills

All of us have had the misfortune to sit through unproductive meetings. We know all too well that good intentions are not enough to ensure a favorable outcome. Poorly run meetings can destroy interpersonal relations, foster cynicism, and undermine coordination efforts. What can school leaders do to facilitate productive meetings?

In *Leader Effectiveness Training*, Thomas Gordon provides a wealth of common-sense tips for running meetings. For instance, he stresses the importance of clarifying the purpose of the meeting.[19] Participants should be clear about what is expected of them before the meeting starts. Among the possible purposes of meetings are the following:

- Brainstorming new ideas
- Decision making
- Planning and implementation strategies
- Sharing information
- Discussing and advising
- Evaluating

A carefully developed agenda can alert participants to the purpose or purposes of a meeting. For example, agenda items can be designed as action items (requiring decisions to be made), information items, or discussion items. If meetings seem to be filled with too many information items, school leaders may wish to consider a daily or weekly school newsletter to handle such material. People resent having to sit and listen to information they can easily read.

To make sure that meetings run smoothly, Gordon urges that groups establish ground rules for speaking.[20] Under some circumstances, it may even be useful to appoint a person to provide "process feedback" to the group.[21] This person can comment on the extent to which ground rules are being observed as well as note when certain individuals are dominating discussions or failing to share their views. Ultimately, however, it is the group leader's responsibility to draw out the reticent and limit the loquacious.

Additional ground rules may be required to cover attendance at meetings, decision making, and confidentiality. Few things undermine the morale of a group more than spotty attendance. Group members should determine in advance the priority to be attached to attending particular meetings. It may be useful to have provisions for designating alternates to attend in case of emergencies. Another aspect of meetings that should be clarified in advance is how decisions are to be made. The quality of a decision often depends on how it was made—by consensus, vote by a majority, or vote by a plurality. More will be said about decision making in the next section. Finally, group agreement is needed on how to handle sensitive information. Careless sharing outside of meetings of remarks made in confidence can jeopardize the effectiveness of groups, engender hostile feelings on the part of nongroup members, and raise the possibility of lawsuits.

Diagnostic Question 6.3

Have provisions been made for clarifying the purposes of school meetings and establishing ground rules to ensure their effectiveness?

The accurate recording of information is also necessary for effective meetings. For all but the most informal gatherings, minutes should be taken, copied, and reviewed by group members. In this way, a sense of group history is created, as well as an official record to be used in case of disputes. Without minutes approved at each meetng by group members, considerable time can be wasted in subsequent debate over decisions and discussions. The trust so crucial to group effectiveness may suffer in the process.

Decision Making

One of the major responsibilities of many groups is to make decisions. Since much of the work of coordination involves seeing that decisions that have been made are understood and implemented, it is in the best interests of school leaders to do whatever is necessary to improve the quality of decision-making processes. Groups are not naturally endowed with the ability to make good decisions. Considerable research on decision making has led to important insights on how to improve the quality of decisions.

First of all, the research tells us not to regard decision making as a simple, one-step process in which a preference is expressed—decision making really entails a variety of activities. A study of the work of several decision theorists revealed five relatively distinct phases of decision making:

- Deciding to decide
- Determining guidelines
- Gathering information
- Designing choices
- Expressing a preference[22]

To initiate the process, some person or persons must decide that a decision is needed. Often, this function is considered a key responsibility of leadership. Just because a decision is needed, however, does not mean that one can be made, particularly if other decisions are pending or resources are unavailable. Once an issue requiring a decision has been identified, it is important to establish guidelines to govern the process. By what point in time must a decision be made? Who will be involved in making the decision? How will the decision be made?

Perhaps the most time-consuming phases of decision making come next, when information must be gathered and alternative courses of action generated. In these phases, the benefits of shared decision making can best be seen. A lone decision maker typically cannot gather the same amount of information or generate the same range of alternatives as a group. The final, and often least taxing, phase of the decision-making process is the actual expression of a preference for one of the alternatives. By this point in the process, a group is likely to be clear about what needs to be done.

The model of decision making that emerges from the theoretical literature is, of course, a rational model, presuming a certain degree of logical and orderly behavior by those involved in the process. Case studies of actual decision making, however, suggest that deviations from the model are common. For example, clear guidelines for decision making are not always carefully specified in advance. As a result, participants in the process may be unsure about their role or about any constraints on their actions. In addition, time may not be set aside to gather sufficient information or to generate a variety of alternatives. In fact, it is not unusual for decision making to boil down to a choice between only two alternatives. The fewer the alternatives that are considered during decision making, the greater the likelihood of making a wrong decision. Thus, we can see that school leaders can do a great deal to improve the decision-making process, and thus help improve the decisions that eventually are made.

Irving Janis has conducted extensive studies of successful and unsuccessful decisions that have been reached by consensus.[23] From this research, he has come up with a series of useful suggestions for avoiding "groupthink," his term for the tendency of members of closely knit decision-making groups to be more concerned about maintaining their self-esteem vis-a-vis others in the group than about reaching the best decisions. Janis urges leaders to recognize the possible negative byproducts of forging too great a sense of solidarity among group members. To counteract "groupthink," Janis offers a variety of suggestions, including use of a designated devil's advocate to question the will of the group and a mandatory reconsideration of all decisions reached by consensus.

Diagnostic Question 6.4

Have steps been taken to monitor school decision-making processes and to assess the quality of decisions?

Earlier, it was argued that there were certain benefits to involving staff members in school decision making. High levels of staff involvement increase the amount of information available from people closest to instructional concerns. Further, the greater the number of staff members participating in decision making, the greater the likelihood of support for decisions and, hence, the less need for additional coordination. Still, despite the obvious advantages of shared decision making, school leaders may have difficulty enlisting the participation of teachers and other staff members.

Lortie has maintained that teachers regard useful only what directly benefits their own classrooms.[24] Since school decision making often seems remote from students and instruction, school leaders may sometimes have difficulty involving teachers. In addition, teachers may not be convinced that their involvement ensures influence. A case study of decision making in five California secondary schools showed a majority of teachers choosing not to participate in school decision making, despite numerous opportunities to do so.[25] Efforts to understand the reasons for this revealed a high degree of teacher skepticism about shared decision making:

> Typically, teachers perceived that the principal or central office personnel made the important decisions. Shared decision making was viewed as a formality or an attempt to create the illusion of teacher influence.[26]

Convincing teachers and other staff members that their involvement in decision making is genuinely desired and that it can have a positive impact on what happens in their classrooms presents a major challenge to school leaders. In facing it, school leaders must be prepared to acknowledge that there are decisions for which they alone are responsible, and also ones that have little to do with students and instruction. Such straightforwardness can help reduce teacher skepticism and pave the way toward effective shared decision making.

Diagnostic Question 6.5

Are staff members who are invited to participate in school decision making assured that they have real influence to improve life in classrooms?

Interpersonal Relations

Chapter 7 made the point that technical skills in supervision are no substitute for the ability to sustain trusting, productive relationships with staff members. The same can be said for coordination. Knowledge of planning, group dynamics, and decision making is necessary, but it is not sufficient to create and maintain schools where people know what they are supposed to do and do it. Ultimately, coordination is a matter of people listening to, understanding, and working closely with other people. No amount of careful planning and no set of procedures, however thorough, will eliminate the need for people in complex organizations like schools to share information and cooperate.

It may be useful to conceptualize a school—or any other organization, for that matter—as "a coalition of individuals, some of them organized into subcoalitions."[27] Applying this concept to schools, Mark Hanson identifies a variety of formally organized subcoalitions, such as standing committees and academic departments, and informally organized subcoalitions, including "equal educational opportunity" groups and "mini-teams" of teachers and aides.[27] Research indicates that "those school administrators who were most knowledgeable about the informal coalitions and could work *through* them instead of against them tended to have the most success in implementing new academic programs."[28] What these school leaders did, essentially, was to forge a large coalition out of several smaller subcoalitions.

Convincing people and groups that they stand to benefit from cooperating is not always simple. As already has been noted, years of declining school enrollments and fiscal instability have promoted a high level of competition among many staff members. Furthermore, growing differentiation and specialization in the teaching profession has created deep divisions between regular classroom teachers and specialists. Cultivating a sense of common purpose among staff members may require all the dramatic, as well as interpersonal, talents school leaders can muster. As students of organizational culture have noted, leaders foster cooperation by using rituals and ceremonies, telling stories, recounting myths, and invoking inspirational symbols.

The need to foster cooperation extends to the community as well. School leaders rarely are able to pursue school improvement without the support of parents and other community members. Building constructive relationships with the community may necessitate establishing parent advisory groups, school-business alliances, community volunteer programs, and regularly scheduled parent conferences. School newsletters, telephone hotlines, annual reports of student successes, and special assemblies for the community also can be helpful in forging linkages. School leaders must realize, however, that no single strategy is likely to work for everyone. A variety of approaches can be used for successful public relations programs.

Diagnostic Question 6.6

Are efforts made to promote a sense of common purpose among staff members, students, and community?

No manual has been written that tells school leaders all they need to know about interpersonal relations. It would be a mistake even to suggest that such a manual *could* be written. Interpersonal relations depend on too many ineffable factors—the authenticity of personalities, perceived integrity and sincerity, the special circumstances under which people first meet. School leaders ultimately can do little more than create conditions that facilitate interactions among people, indicate by personal example that they value such interactions, and communicate frequently and persuasively the expectation that pople will talk and work with each other.

TROUBLESHOOTING

It is tempting to see in the current research on school effectiveness a prescription for eliminating problems completely. But such an interpretation, of course, would be erroneous. Problems are endemic to complex organizations, and schools are no exception. Effective school leaders realize this and learn to anticipate and manage problems so that their impact is relatively slight. Sara Light-foot refers to this quality as an "orientation to imperfection," and she finds it to be an essential component of "good" schools:

> The search for "good" schools is elusive and disappointing if by goodness we mean something close to perfection. These portraits of good schools [in her book] reveal imperfections, uncertainties, and vulnerabilities in each of them. In fact, one could argue that a consciousness about imperfections, and the willingness to admit them and search for their origins and solutions, is one of the important ingredients of goodness in schools.[29]

The practice of *troubleshooting* complements an "orientation to imperfection" quite well. Troubleshooting encompasses all efforts designed to anticipate and subsequently minimize the impact of problems that threaten an organization's ability to achieve its goals. Many troubleshooting activities already have been mentioned in the preceding chapters on teacher evaluation and quality control; these include both formal and informal processes. Before describing additional troubleshooting processes, it may be useful to look briefly at the growing literature on problem solving in organizations.

RESEARCH ON PROBLEM SOLVING

Various students of organizations have studied the ways problems are discovered and resolved. Some of the most valuable scholarship in this area has been contributed by Donald Schön.[30] Schön has investigated how various professionals *find* problems to which to devote their attention. Since there are always more problems to deal with than time and energy permit, this process can be crucial to organizational effectiveness. Schön criticizes those who concentrate exclusively on problem solving and overlook the importance of what he terms "problem setting":

> But with this emphasis on problem solving, we ignore problem *setting*, the process by which we define the decision to be made, the needs to be achieved, the means which may be chosen. In real-world practice, problems do not present themselves to the practitioner as givens. They must be constructed from the materials of problematic situations which are puzzling, troubling, and uncertain.
>
> . . . When we set the problem, we select what we will treat as the "things" of the situation, we set the boundaries of our attention to it, and we impose upon it a coherence which allows us to say what is wrong and in what directions the situation needs to be changed. Problem setting is a process in which, interactively, we *name* the things to which we will attend and *frame* the context in which we will attend to them.[31]

The message for leaders here is clear. An important function of leadership is to identify and frame problems in ways that permit available resources to be used most productively. It is of little value to define problems for which the necessary personnel, materials, expertise, or time is lacking. Furthermore, leaders need to develop vocabularies that allow organization members to understand and discuss problems. Schön argues that the successful resolution of organizational problems is often blocked because people cannot talk about the problem coherently.

Schön's argument is supported by a recent study by Kenneth Leithwood and Mary Stager.[32] Looking for differences in the problem-solving processes used by "moderately" and "highly" effective principals, they found that highly effective principals are more likely to invest time in carefully defining the problems to which they devote time and energy. These individuals used explicit sorting procedures in their daily problem solving and were concerned about giving reasons in support of their priorities. Moderately effective principals relied on fewer sources of information for problem solving and tended to view most problems as "familiar or old."

Some scholars contend that the real challenge for leaders goes beyond problem setting. Ronald Fry and William Pasmore, for example, maintain that the ultimate contribution of leadership "lies in the ability to rise above the immediate situation, go beyond current definitions of problems, and think past current solutions toward new visions, new conceptions of issues, and new questions."[33] Warren Bennis likens the process to riding in a helicopter, rising above one's own situation in order to look at it from an entirely different vantage point.[34] Skillful leaders, then, may be those who can not only anticipate and "set" problems, but also redefine them as opportunities. Fry and Pasmore indicate that such creative work, or "frame-breaking," requires extensive reflection and collaboration.[35]

Let us now consider some specific ways in which school leaders can go about these processes of problem identification, problem setting, and problem redefinition—or what we call troubleshooting.

FORMAL TROUBLESHOOTING MECHANISMS

A key to successful troubleshooting is getting information from those closest to actual or potential problems. But how best to obtain it is often a difficult question for school leaders, who are frequently too removed from problems to have accurate firsthand data. Many leaders rely on regular meetings with advisory groups and trusted colleagues. But unless people feel safe sharing information on problems, such formal troubleshooting mechanisms are unlikely to be productive. It can be argued, in fact, that some leaders actually discourage troubleshooting by acting in ways that suggest teachers should handle their problems themselves. If teachers feel they will be judged less competent or regarded as nuisances for disclosing problems, they are apt to keep concerns to themselves. Problems that go unshared obviously are problems less likely to be resolved satisfactorily. School leaders are therefore advised to create conditions wherein teachers—and others, too—feel comfortable sharing problems, even those in which they may personally be at fault. To do this, leaders may need to acknowledge publicly that everyone experiences difficulties and to offer assurances that people will not be evaluated negatively for airing concerns. These actions may help eliminate some of the loneliness and isolation teachers often feel as well as contribute to effective organizational troubleshooting.

Diagnostic Question 6.7

Do conditions exist that facilitate the sharing of information concerning problems and potential problems?

Recent reports of successful Japanese management strategies have inspired school leaders to explore formal mechanisms for troubleshooting. For example, the idea of "quality circles," as discussed by William Ouchi in his best-seller *Theory Z*,[36] has been picked up by educators and adapted to school settings.[37] A quality circle is "a small group of employees (5 to 12) who voluntarily meet on a regular basis to identify, analyze, and solve various problems."[38] Ideally, members of each circle should interact to some degree on the job or at least share responsibility for certain organizational goals. A school may sponsor several quality circles, each meeting weekly for an hour.

Advocates of quality circles stress the need for participants to be trained in the language and techniques of the process. They also note that quality circles are not an alternative to conventional management. Larry Chase proposes an eight-step process to guide school leaders interested in implementing quality circles:

- Round-robin brainstorming
- Voting to achieve group consensus
- Cause-and-effect analysis
- Data collection
- Decision analysis
- Generating solutions
- Management presentation
- Evaluation[39]

Besides quality circles, schools may use a variety of other formal mechanisms for troubleshooting. These range from periodic community surveys and staff needs assessments to official ombudsmen to groups charged with specific troubleshooting responsibilities. Some school leaders, for example, meet weekly with department chairs, grade-level representatives, or student leaders to review recent events and identify possible problems on the horizon. Often troubleshooting groups are concerned with school discipline and student learning. Anticipating student problems before they become serious can be a vital dimension of effective instruction.

Diagnostic Question 6.8

Have formal mechanisms for troubleshooting student problems been established?

To ensure that troubleshooting groups do not degenerate into unconstructive "gripe sessions," it may be necessary to establish guidelines for their operation. One example of a set of guidelines comes from a book on how to operate grade-level teacher teams.[40] The purpose of these teams is to identify and assist students whose academic performance is slipping or whose social behavior is becoming a problem. The guidelines include the following:

- Specificity of discussion
  Discussions must involve references to specific students rather than broad statements, vague feelings, or anecdotes.
- Need for confidentiality
  All discussions must be kept in strictest confidence.
- Planning of specific actions
  For each student discussed during a troubleshooting session, a specific plan of action must be adopted before the session ends.
- Delegation of responsibility
  One person must assume responsibility for seeing that the plan of action is implemented.
- Regular feedback on cases
  The person responsible for seeing that the plan of action is implemented must report back to the group at the next session about its success.
- Documentation of proceedings
  Minutes should be taken of all troubleshooting session proceedings.[41]

While regularly scheduled meetings of various groups can provide school leaders with important information, effective troubleshooting sometimes involves less formal data-gathering strategies.

INFORMAL TROUBLESHOOTING MECHANISMS

One of the most productive methods of informal troubleshooting is touring the school—its corridors, meeting areas, and poorly supervised spaces. During such times, school leaders can be on the lookout for anything out of the ordinary. Principals who spend too much time in their offices may well be criticized by staff members, who believe that the presence of school leaders serves to discourage misconduct as well as provide early warnings of problems.

In a study of the daily activities of a group of Chicago principals, a team of researchers found that much of the principals' day was spent on the go:

> Much of the principal's movement around the school is a "search routine," maintaining a physical presence in the school and trying to anticipate trouble. A common observation by the principals is that this activity helps them gauge the school climate. A halls tour of just a few minutes, spending a few seconds listening to the sounds coming from each classroom, gives a quick reading of "what's going on," of how well the school has "settled down to its business," and of what the "mood of the student body seems to be today."[42]

Besides walking around, school leaders have developed a variety of creative ways to detect problems. Some maintain rumor hotlines or cultivate relationships with key students, staff members, and community persons in order to learn about concerns before they become crises. Others make a point of eating lunch in the faculty room or cafeteria to pick up valuable information. Some unique approaches to informal troubleshooting have been the following:

- An elementary principal moved his desk into the main entryway of the school so he could make personal contact with everyone arriving at the school.
- A director of guidance held before-school open houses in the cafeteria so she could be available for students who wanted to "chat" or who came to school with problems.
- An English Department chair asked students completing each English course to write a letter to the following year's students telling them what they needed to do to get good grades in the course.
- A high school vice principal held a debriefing session with selected substitute teachers to get their impressions of the school and the classes they covered.

Diagnostic Question 6.9

Are informal methods used on a regular basis to gather information regarding possible sources of trouble?

Conclusion

With this discussion of coordination and troubleshooting, we conclude the major portion of this textbook for school leaders. We have tried to indicate that effective schools—those characterized by continuous instructional improvement—are at least partially a function of the quality of school leadership. Furthermore, we have argued that school leadership is more than a set of techniques or competencies. The kind of leadership that promotes good instruction requires a vision of effective teaching, prudent time management, sound judgment, and an appreciation for community context and organizational culture. The world of the school leader is a world of complex situations, each demanding a variety of professional skills. In Chapters 6 through 12, we have tried to highlight the most critical clusters of skills and situations that school leaders dedicated to instructional improvement must deal with.

In the last part of the book, we step back and look at the life of school leaders, how they become school leaders and how they continue to be school leaders. By doing so, we suggest that an understanding of school leadership is incomplete without reflecting on what it means to be a school leader.

STUDY QUESTIONS

1. Make an inventory of different types of decisions made by school leaders. Which types of decisions should also involve teachers and for what reasons?
2. What kinds of coordination activities might be needed to (a) implement a new K-8 reading program and (b) develop a master schedule?

3. Observe a school meeting. In what ways could the meeting be run more effectively? What role did the principal (or another school leader) play?

4. Identify a recently made school decision. Use the five phases of decision making mentioned in this chapter to analyze how the decision was made. In what ways could the process have been improved?

5. Reflecting on your own school experience, identify situations where advance warning of problems would have averted major difficulties.

6. Read several case studies in Donald Schön's *The Reflective Practitioner*. How do professionals in fields other than education identify problems that need to be addressed?

7. Interview several school leaders. What formal and informal mechanisms do they use to stay abreast of emerging concerns?

NOTES

1. David J. Kroeze, "Effective Principals as Instructional Leaders: New Dimensions for Research," *Administrator's Notebook,* Vol. 30, No. 9, 1984, p. 2.

2. E. L. Thorndike and Clarence L. Barnhart, *Thorndike Barnhart Advanced Dictionary,* 2nd ed., (Glenview, Ill.: Scott, Foresman, 1974), p. 226.

3. Richard L. Daft, *Organization Theory and Design* (St. Paul, Minn.: West, 1983), p. 207.

4. William A. Firestone and Bruce L. Wilson, "Using Bureaucratic and Cultural Linkages to Improve Instruction: The Principal's Contribution," *Educational Administration Quarterly,* Vol. 21, No. 2 (Spring 1985), pp. 9–10.

5. Karl E. Weick, "Educational Organizations as Loosely Coupled Systems," *Administrative Science Quarterly,* Vol. 21, No. 1 (March 1976), pp. 1–19.

6. Arthur Blumberg and William Greenfield, *The Effective Principal* (Boston: Allyn & Bacon, 1980), pp. 241–242.

7. Elizabeth G. Cohen, Russell H. Miller, Anneke Bredo, and Kenneth Duckworth, "Principal Role and Teacher Morale under Varying Organizational Conditions," Research Memorandum (Stanford, Calif.: Stanford Center for Research and Development in Teaching, undated).

8. A detailed analysis of role-related problems can be found in Daniel L. Duke and Adrienne M. Meckel, "Disciplinary Roles in American Schools," *British Journal of Teacher Education,* Vol. 6, No. 1 (January 1980), pp. 37–50.

9. Daniel L. Duke and Adrienne M. Meckel, "Student Attendance Problems and School Organization: A Case Study," *Urban Education,* Vol. 15, No. 3 (October 1980), pp. 325–357.

10. Hugh Mehan, J. Lee Meihls, Alma Hertweck, and Margaret S. Crowdes, "Identifying Handicapped Students," *Organizational Behavior in Schools and School Districts,* Samuel B. Bacharach (Ed.) (New York: Praeger, 1981), p. 391.

11. *Ibid.,* pp. 396–398.

12. Harvey F. Clarizio and George F. McCoy, *Behavior Disorders in Children,* 2nd ed. (New York: Thomas Y. Crowell, 1976), p. 466.

13. Seymour B. Sarason, *The Culture of the School and the Problem of Change* (Boston: Allyn & Bacon, 1971), p. 213.

14. *Ibid.,* p. 117.

15. Gene E. Hall and Shirley M. Hord, *Facilitating the Change Process in Schools* (Albany, N.Y.: State University of New York Press, 1987), Chapter 9.

16. Sarason, *The Culture of the School and the Problem of Change,* p. 9.

17. Hall and Hord, *Facilitating the Change Process in Schools,* Chapter 4.
18. Patricia A. Brieschke, "A Case Study of Teacher Role Enactment in an Urban Elementary School," *Educational Administration Quarterly,* Vol. 19, No. 4 (Fall 1983), pp. 74–75.
19. Thomas Gordon, *Leader Effectiveness Training,* (New York: Bantam, 1977), pp. 118–126.
20. *Ibid.,* p. 131.
21. For a variety of helpful suggestions on how to improve meetings, see pages 232–284 of Richard A. Schmuck, Philip J. Runkel, Jane H. Arends, and Richard I. Arends, *The Second Handbook of Organization Development in Schools* (Palo Alto, Calif.: Mayfield, 1977).
22. Daniel L. Duke, Beverly K. Showers, and Michael Imber, "Studying Shared Decision Making in Schools," *Organizational Behavior in Schools and School Districts,* Samuel B. Bacharach (Ed.) (New York: Praeger, 1981), pp. 314–320.
23. Irving L. Janis, *Victims of Groupthink* (Boston: Houghton Mifflin, 1972).
24. Dan C. Lortie, *Schoolteacher* (Chicago: University of Chicago Press, 1975), pp. 162–186.
25. Daniel L. Duke, Beverly K. Showers, and Michael Imber, "Teachers and Shared Decision Making: The Costs and Benefits of Involvement," *Educational Administration Quarterly,* Vol. 16, No. 1 (Winter 1980), pp. 93–106.
26. *Ibid.,* p. 104.
27. E. Mark Hanson, *Educational Administration and Organizational Behavior,* 2nd ed. (Boston: Allyn & Bacon, 1985), pp. 104–109.
28. *Ibid.,* p. 109.
29. Sara Lawrence Lightfoot, *The Good High School* (New York: Basic Books, 1983), p. 309.
30. Donald A. Schön, *The Reflective Practitioner* (New York: Basic Books, 1983).
31. *Ibid.,* p. 40.
32. Kenneth A. Leithwood and Mary Stager, "Differences in Problem-solving Processes Used by Moderately and Highly Effective Principals." Paper presented at the Annual Meeting of the American Educational Research Association, 1986.
33. Ronald E. Fry and William A. Pasmore, "Strengthening Management Education," *The Executive Mind,* Suresh Srivastva and Associates (San Francisco: Jossey-Bass, 1984), p. 292.
34. Warren Bennis, "The Artform of Leadership," *The Executive Mind,* Suresh Srivastva and Associates (San Francisco: Jossey-Bass, 1984), pp. 1–15.
35. Fry and Pasmore, "Strengthening Management Education," pp. 292–293.
36. William Ouchi, *Theory Z* (Reading, Mass.: Addison-Wesley, 1981).
37. Larry Chase, "Quality Circles in Education," *Educational Leadership,* Vol. 40, No. 5 (February 1983), pp. 18–25.
38. *Ibid.,* p. 19.
39. *Ibid.,* pp. 20–22.
40. Daniel L. Duke, *Managing Student Behavior Problems* (New York: Teachers College Press, 1980), pp. 96–98.
41. *Ibid.*
42. Van Cleve Morris, Robert L. Crowson, Cynthia Porter-Gehrie, and Emanuel Hurwitz, *Principals in Action* (Columbus, Ohio: Charles E. Merrill, 1984), p. 78.

PART IV

THE PERSONAL DIMENSIONS OF SCHOOL LEADERSHIP

No textbook for school leaders would be complete without a discussion of how one becomes and remains a school leader. Leadership is certainly not just a matter of mastering a set of technical skills. The effectiveness of school leaders depends on many factors—personality, reputation, imagination, courage, credibility, luck, and dozens more. We cannot understand the influence of these factors without understanding the processes by which men and women learn to lead.

Chapter 13 will deal with the socialization of school leaders. Socialization probably begins when people are students and first sense how schools operate. The process continues through the period when they enter teaching—as most school leaders do—and decide to pursue careers as school leaders. Advanced training, selection, and induction into initial positions of leadership represent additional stages of socialization. The question that we will focus on in this chapter is: *What aspects of the processes by which school leaders are socialized contribute to or discourage the development of an orientation to instructional improvement?*

Learning to be a school leader is only part of the story, however. Those who have gone through the process maintain that the challenges of school leadership are numerous and relentless. Just because one is committed to school improvement is no guarantee that he or she will be able to act accordingly. A variety of challenges stand ready to subvert the "best laid plans" of every leader. We have chosen to concentrate in Chapter 14 on three challenges of particular importance to contemporary school leaders: the challenge of organizational complexity, the challenge of ethical ambiguity, and the challenge of personal and professional meaning. How school leaders confront these challenges may largely determine their ultimate effectiveness as instructional leaders.

CHAPTER 13

BECOMING A SCHOOL LEADER

School leaders do not emerge from training programs fully prepared and completely effective. Their development is a more involved and incremental process, beginning as early as their own elementary schooling and extending through their first years on the job as leaders. As much as anything else, becoming a school leader is an ongoing process of socialization. It encompasses personal experiences in school settings, formal job orientations, college and university courses, interactions with mentors and supervisors, and a variety of other occasions during which aspiring school leaders learn the norms and expectations of their profession and of the organizations in which they will practice. There is every reason to believe that the eventual effectiveness of every school leader is tied, at least in part, to their experiences during this socialization process. What is of special interest to us in this chapter are those aspects of the socialization process that serve either to promote or discourage the development of leadership for instructional improvement.

The chapter opens with an overview of the socialization process and its various dimensions, and goes on to describe in detail the different phases of socialization—early work experiences, training, selection, and first days in positions of leadership. The concluding section summarizes aspects of the socialization process that inhibit or contribute to the development of instructional leadership.

THE SOCIALIZATION PROCESS

Various theories are available to help us understand how people become school leaders. Behavior theory, for example, examines the external reinforcements that shape people as they become leaders. Psychoanalytic theory looks at their internal, often subconscious, motives. Since becoming a school leader typically occurs in a variety of social settings, social learning theory, with its emphasis on modeling and imitation, can be informative. To the extent that school leaders are shaped by specific sets of organizational expectations, role theory also may contribute to our understanding. Of all the different theories, however, socialization theory seems to have the greatest potential for revealing important dimensions of the process of becoming a school leader.

Socialization is defined as the process "through which an individual becomes integrated into a social group by learning the group's culture and his role in the group."[1] Socialization theory encompasses a variety of concepts related to how people learn socially appropriate values, attitudes, folkways, and roles. Among the concepts that are most immediately useful in helping us understand how people become school leaders are anticipatory socialization, professional (or occupational) socialization, and organizational socialization.

Anticipatory socialization concerns the "learning of the rights, obligations, expectations, and outlook of a social role preparatory to assuming it."[2] In the case of prospective school leaders, this process can begin while people are elementary students. Certainly the time spent teaching, prior to becoming a school leader, contributes important information about how schools operate. Blumberg and Greenfield conclude that what "was learned in that situation [as teacher] often tends to be repeated when a teacher becomes a principal."[3] Other important elements of anticipatory socialization include formal college training and participation in the recruitment and selection process. By the time people actually assume positions of school leadership, they are likely to have learned a great deal about how to act and what to expect as school leaders. In fact, it can be argued that failure to acquire this prior learning actually may prevent persons from being selected for positions of leadership. The most desirable candidates for leadership positions frequently are those who require the least additional socialization.

A second type of socialization also starts prior to assuming a leadership position.[4] Professional or occupational socialization refers to the "process by which persons learn and perform according to the norms, values, and behaviors held to be necessary for performing a particular professional role."[5] The initial place for professional socialization typically is a college or university training program. In this setting, aspiring professionals learn the importance of specialized knowledge (expertise), as well as the values and ethics that guide the use of this knowledge. Typically, aspirants also acquire a technical vocabulary, not readily understood by those outside the profession, to help them describe and explain what they do. The process of professional socialization continues after initial training, as practicing professionals become involved in professional organizations and interact with each other across organizations.

There is a problem in determining exactly which profession serves as the focus for the professional socialization of school leaders. Should educational administration be considered a separate profession—with its own norms, technical knowledge, ethics, and specialized language? Or are all educators—teachers, teacher leaders, and administrators alike—part of one unified profession? It is our view that educational administration has become a profession in its own right, though many would debate the desirability of this development. School leaders typically participate in a separate training process beyond their teacher training, belong to separate professional organizations, and recognize separate codes of ethics. The professionalization of school leadership has been helped along by the rise of collective bargaining and the spread of special certification requirements for school administrators. It should be noted, though, that many school leaders still identify closely with the teaching profession, continue to teach, and participate in the professional organizations of teachers.

A third type of socialization is organizational socialization, defined by Edgar Schein as the process by which one learns the knowledge, values, and behaviors required to perform a specific role within a particular organization.[6] Blumberg notes that organizational socialization is a process that recurs throughout a person's career, each time a person changes jobs within an organization or leaves one organization to join another.[7] The norms and expectations governing an organizational role are not necessarily the same as, or even compatible with, those of a role occupant's profession. For example, the ways school leaders learn to supervise instruction in university training programs may not match the procedures for supervision required by a particular school district. Discrepancies of this kind can create major role conflicts for professionals working in large organizations. If the findings of Mary Guy's study of professionals in hospital settings can be generalized to schools, organizational norms tend to displace professional norms.[8] Since the organization, rather than the profession, pays the professional's salary, this finding seems understandable.

Organizational socialization consists of both formal and informal processes by which people "learn the ropes." Formal processes include recruitment and selection, orientation, and performance evaluation. Informal processes range from chance encounters with veteran members of the organization to mentoring relationships. The following sections of this chapter will examine in more detail how school leaders experience these and other socialization processes.

TEACHING—EARLY STEPS TOWARD LEADERSHIP

The vast majority of school leaders spend some time as teachers. If their teaching experience is combined with the dozen or so years each spends attending elementary and secondary school, we can understand why most school leaders have already formed some very strong impressions of schools by the time they assume their first positions of leadership. Larry Cuban has noted this of school administration:

> Few organizations normally require their professionals to have been clients of the organization for at least twelve years and then to have served an apprenticeship for at least a decade before being permitted to practice . . . Save for the total environment of a religious order, few professions can match such a long, intense preparation for service.[9]

The number of years an individual serves as a teacher before becoming a school leader varies, of course, from person to person and location to location. A 1984 survey of 919 principals from all types of schools and all parts of the United States found that the average number of years of teaching experience was nine.[10] Male teachers taught for an average of eight years, while female teachers taught for an average of 12 years before becoming principals. Almost four in ten (38.2 percent) taught for ten years or more before becoming principals. Sometimes it is difficult to find precise points when persons cease to think of themselves as teachers and begin to regard themselves as school leaders. In part, this is because—by design or not—many people move gradually into positions of leadership. For example, a teacher may head up an important committee and thus gain recognition for organizational skill and peer influence—a part-time assignment as department chair or team leader may result. After several years as chair, the teacher may be asked to serve as a half-time dean of students or administrative assistant. Eventually, if he or she is perceived to have performed well, a full-time administrative position may be offered. Of this process, Cecil Miskel and Dorothy Cosgrove have written:

> As teachers volunteer for committees, handle discipline problems and spend extra time at school, the principal becomes a mentor, encouraging the teacher to pursue administrative certification and providing opportunities to become more visible at the district level.[11]

The role played by mentors, both in providing encouragement to would-be school leaders and transmitting organizational norms, is a critical one in the socialization process. In fact, the failure of male administrators to serve as mentors for female teachers has been used to explain why relatively few women occupy positions of school leadership.[12]

While the primary purpose of this chapter is to look at *how* individuals become school leaders, it is important to comment briefly on *who* become school leaders. Women make up roughly 70 percent of the K–12 teaching force, but fewer than one school administrator in ten is a woman.[13] There are alarming indications, in fact, that the percentage of female administrators has actually been decreasing.[14] Charol Shakeshaft offers 12 possible reasons why women are so dramatically underrepresented.[15] Her list includes the following:

- Poor self-image or lack of confidence
- Lack of aspiration or motivation
- Lack of support, encouragement, and counseling
- Family and home responsibilities
- Socialization and sex role stereotyping
- Lack of preparation or experience
- Lack of finances for continuing training
- Too few role models
- Lack of sponsorship or mentors
- Lack of a network
- Sex discrimination in hiring and promotion
- Biased curricular materials

Accurate figures on the number of minority school administrators are more difficult to obtain than those for women, but it is generally assumed that they also are underrepresented. In 1975 Samuel Ethridge estimated that 5,368 additional black principals would need to be hired in order for the percentage of black principals to equal the percentage of blacks in the total population.[16] It is likely that many of the reasons why there are so few women in positions of school leadership also apply to minorities.

Impact of Teaching Experience

Given that most school leaders come from the ranks of teachers, what is the influence of teaching experience on the quality of school leadership? Seymour Sarason is openly skeptical of the value of teaching experience, observing that being a leader of children does not necessarily prepare a person to be a leader of adults.[17] He goes on to point out that teachers are "loners" who rarely "feel part of a working group that discusses, plans, and helps make educational decisions." Furthermore, he notes that years of working in isolation cause teachers to absorb and accept cultural norms of individuality and the *status quo.*

The ranks of teachers do not appear likely to yield large numbers of school leaders who are committed to continuing instructional improvement, able to work well with adults, and capable of seeing school-wide needs. When teachers do seek to become school leaders, the aspects of school leadership that may attract them most may be the autonomy of the job and its status, not its potential for producing change.

While this depiction of teaching is obviously descriptive of many individuals, it overlooks the impact of teacher unionization. In school systems with powerful unions, teachers may have developed norms of cooperation that mitigate some of their legendary isolation and individualism. But here, too, the socialization of school leaders may be adversely affected. Teachers who regard each other as co-equal members of the same bargaining unit may be less likely to have a positive regard for careers in school leadership. Particularly if relations with school administrators have been adversarial, teachers may have grown to regard leaders with suspicion and even hostility.

Reasons for Moving

Even though many teachers may fail to look upon school leadership favorably, others continue to seek leadership positions. Though certain aspects of teaching contribute little to the anticipatory socialization of school leaders, other experiences can be of great value. For example, school leaders who have taught or who continue to teach are more likely to have credibility in the eyes of teachers. And mastery of the technical skills of teaching is bound to be beneficial to those who eventually become involved in supervision and evaluation. Perhaps the greatest value of teaching experience for school leaders, however, may be the insights gained about teachers: how they "make sense" of the world around them, what they regard as trivial and essential, and how they feel about their work.

Flora Ortiz notes that the decision to move into administration usually is made after the teacher is granted tenure.[18] This finding suggests that people typically do not aspire to be school leaders before becoming teachers. In one study of Chicago elementary principals, only 17 percent entered teaching in order to become administrators.[19] Men were more likely than women to have planned administrative careers prior to entering teaching. Why, then, do those who originally plan a teaching career decide to pursue positions as school leaders?

Most of the research on reasons for entering school administration has focused on women. This may reflect a tacit assumption that men eventually *expect* to leave teaching for administration. In other words, researchers have not been surprised or intrigued to find men leaving teaching to become school leaders. Only when women—who perhaps are presumed to enter teaching as a career—decide to move on do researchers take notice. In reality, of course, both men and women doubtless enter and leave teaching for a variety of reasons.

In a series of interviews with a national sample of female administrative aspirants, Sakre Edson discovered that some women decide to leave teaching for school-leadership positions *after* getting a taste of extra-classroom responsibility, such as a resource room teacher or counselor.[20] So these positions that may not originally have been sought as stepping stones to school leadership often serve to raise women's consciousness of school-wide issues and the challenges of leadership. Coaching athletic teams probably has served the same function traditionally for many male teachers.

Another reason why some women in Edson's study decided to enter administration was the need for a change in their lives, occasioned in many cases by the breakup of a marriage or the maturation of children. Also, after observing how male school leaders actually functioned, other women realized that they, too, were capable of performing these responsibilities. And many aspirants were driven by a desire to improve the quality of schooling for students—they felt they could make a greater impact as a school leader than as a teacher.

Besides these reasons, it is likely that the desire for greater status and a higher salary prompts a number of people—both men and women—to leave teaching. A survey of 1,094 school districts for the 1980–81 school year indicated that the average salary for teachers was $17,678, compared to $27,923 for elementary principals, $30,401 for junior high/middle school principals, and $32,231 for senior high principals.[21] The relative value of various positions, with the average teacher's salary serving at 1.00, is shown below:

Classroom teacher	1.00
Elementary assistant principal	1.31
Junior high/middle school assistant principal	1.47
Senior high assistant principal	1.54
Elementary principal	1.58
Junior high/middle school principal	1.72
Senior high principal	1.82[22]

General dissatisfaction with teaching can be an additional impetus for teachers to pursue careers in school administration. National surveys of teachers have revealed numerous work-related concerns, ranging from physical safety and large class sizes to inadequate supplies and fiscal instability.[23] Indications are that the teachers who leave the classroom are among the most talented in the profession, but it is unclear whether they are also the most dissatisfied or simply those with the greatest likelihood of finding other positions. Were the ranks of school administration to be filled primarily with disgruntled, burned-out ex-teachers, the prospects of inspired instructional leadership would be slight indeed. Fortunately, it appears that many who aspire to positions of school leadership, while often displeased with current conditions in teaching, retain a commitment to improve schools and the quality of instruction.

TRAINING

Once people decide that they want to seek positions of school leadership, they frequently enter formal preparation programs to obtain supervisory or administrative certification. In general, these programs are in colleges and universities but, on occasion, other agencies, such as state departments of education and local districts, may also participate in the pre-service training of school leaders. The curriculum includes such subjects as school law, school finance, supervision, evaluation, and school organization, and many states also require aspirants to complete a field-based practicum or internship.

Formal preparation for administrative certification is an important phase in the socialization of school leaders. It introduces them to the profession of educational administration and to the norms and expectations of school systems. Professional socialization typically results from exposure to course content and contact with professors, practitioners, and peers. Anticipatory organizational socialization also may take place as students undertake fieldwork and meet adjunct professors from local school systems. Educational administration students often feel pulled between the need to learn how schools actually function and the desire to acquire the skills necessary to improve schools.

While states vary considerably in the specific educational requirements for school leaders, most expect some post-bachelor's work. In the previously cited study of 919 principals, 96.3 percent held graduate degrees.[24] Many states go beyond general requirements for graduate work to specify courses, content areas, and even competencies for prospective school leaders.

The process by which students are selected for graduate programs in educational administration is a potentially important element in the socialization process. In most instances, however, little effort is made to screen applicants carefully or to deny admission to marginally qualified candidates. This increases the challenge for local school districts of selecting capable school leaders. Several states are beginning to require aspirants to demonstrate competence in areas of basic literacy prior to being accepted into graduate programs.

How graduate training impacts prospective school leaders is a source of great speculation. If we rely on the perceptions of those who have completed training, reactions are mixed. A randomly selected group of more than 1700 elementary school principals, surveyed by the National Association of Elementary School Principals in 1978, indicated that graduate work was a much less valuable part of their preparation than previous teaching experience.[25] While only 36 percent and 26.2 percent, respectively, stated that their graduate education and internship had been highly valuable, 84.8 percent cited their teaching experience as a major influence. There is also evidence that many high school principals question the value of their formal training programs.[26]

Training programs evoke a variety of feelings. Some school leaders, for example, express more qualms about *how* material was taught than *what* was taught. At least 70 percent of the high school administrators surveyed by the National Association of Secondary School Principals in 1978 felt that human relations, supervision of instruction, school management, curriculum and program development, and school law were "essential" courses.[27] Problems arise when these courses are taught by professors who have little up-to-date knowledge about how schools are run and who also are ineffective instructors. To address the problem about up-to-date knowledge, Oregon now requires educational administration programs to involve practicing school administrators as adjunct professors.

Other school leaders are concerned about the subject matter itself. Edwin Bridges argues that graduate leadership training programs fail to socialize individuals for the realities of leadership.[28] His indictment includes the following failures in "attitudinal" and "socio-technical" socialization:

- Graduate programs encourage prospective leaders to overestimate their potential for influence.
- Graduate programs do not prepare prospective leaders to cope with success or deal with disappointment.
- Graduate programs prepare prospective leaders to be "thinkers" rather than "doers."
- Graduate programs ignore the value of intuition, despite the fact that intuition may be critical to a leader's success.
- Graduate programs predispose leaders to avoid conflicts rather than teach them how to collaborate to resolve conflict.
- Graduate programs stress written skills despite the fact that leaders function in a "verbal" world.
- Graduate programs emphasize rational behavior, while effective leaders often must rely on their emotions.

There are many indications of efforts being made to improve the quality of preparation for school leaders. In addition to involving more practitioners in instrumental roles and revamping curricula, more fieldwork is being required. Supplementary training opportunities, including administrator academies and summer institutes, have been developed to provide ongoing assistance to school leaders after they have completed their initial certification programs. While such improvements are important, it still can be argued that the preparation of school leaders is far from ideal.

The process for selecting persons to pursue administrative certification is virtually nonexistent in many cases, partially because of budgetary problems faced by institutions of higher education. Since peers can play a key role in the socialization experience, nonselective admissions policies are not without consequence. Talented aspirants become cynical when they have to attend classes with marginally qualified colleagues.

While training programs have begun to place greater emphasis on the development of instructional expertise, it has tended to focus mainly on technical skills. Missing from the content of many certification courses are opportunities to develop professional judgment, set instructional priorities, interpret policies related to instruction, and promote school-wide improvement. These areas cannot be neatly defined by competencies and behavioral objectives. For these kinds of learning to take place, provisions for "unlearning" may first be needed.[29] In other words, prospective leaders may need to stop looking at instruction from a classroom perspective *before* they can acquire the broader vision and understanding required of a school leader.

If training programs can be successfully reoriented to the cultivation of instructional-leadership skills, there is then a risk that graduates will not be equipped with the knowledge and skills necessary to survive in many contemporary schools. School leaders committed to instructional improvement may find it difficult to flourish in school systems that place a relatively low value on the instructional expertise of administrators or on the continuous professional development of staff members. Bearing this sobering thought in mind, let us turn to the processes by which school systems select school leaders.

THE SELECTION OF SCHOOL LEADERS

The recruitment, screening, and selection of persons for positions of school leadership are important opportunities for school systems to expose candidates to local norms and expectations. Robert Dentler and Catherine Baltzell argue that "Principals draw their sense of mission in significant degree from their selection experience."[30] In this section, we look at how the process works and try to determine the extent to which it influences the development of instructional leadership.

In 1982 Dentler and Baltzell conducted the only national study so far of how principals are selected. They investigated ten randomly chosen, geographically diverse school districts with enrollments of 10,000 or more students. While variations naturally were found among the districts, the researchers discovered certain things in common:

1. Superintendents or a deputy or veteran personnel director controlled *every* facet of the PSP [Principal Selection Process]. However, the degree of control that these leaders were able to exercise was constrained by local norms, customs, notions of what a principal is "supposed to be," and traditions of "how we select principals here."
2. This control aimed at reconciling each appointment with many other aims and decision points, from facilities to enrollments to the mediation of teacher disputes. Educational leadership merits are only one—and not always the most important—consideration.
3. Teacher and parent impacts are minimal everywhere.

4. Women and minority candidates are increasing in volume and frequency of appointment, while the pool of white male applicants is drying up.
5. Candidates are appointed not only because they fit the needs of a particular school but also for their generalized fit to the image of a rotatable, all-purpose sort of administrative implementor of a superintendent's aims.
6. Although able principals were observed and interviewed everywhere, the processes that led to their selection could *not* be characterized generally as merit-based or equity-centered. While merit and equity could and did emerge, special *local* goals, aims and conditions very frequently determined the process.[31]

There is little evidence that either proven ability or perceived potential to exercise instructional leadership has been a key factor in the selection of principals. What *has* seemed to be important is administrative or quasi-administrative experience, particularly for secondary principals. Prospective principals with some administrative experience seem to perform better than those lacking it during pre-selection assessment activities.[32] In a study of the socialization of 45 principals in the Northwest, researchers found that only ten (22 percent) lacked pre-principal administrative experience.[33] The remaining 35 principals averaged 1.5 administrative positions prior to becoming principals; these included acting principal (2), administrative assistant (2), administrative intern (5), full-time assistant or vice principal (14), part-time assistant or vice principal (4), dean of students (2), department chair (6), coordinator or director (11), and head of alternative or summer school (6). In addition, practically all the principals had exercised leadership responsibilities when they were full-time teachers. These ranged from coaching (3) and committee chair (25) to teacher union positions (9) and team leader (19).

Administrative and teacher-leadership experiences are important sources of organizational and professional socialization. They indicate whether or not educators can work effectively with other adults. Typically, however, these preparatory experiences entail relatively routine managerial functions rather than instructional-improvement activities. William Greenfield points out, for example, that the vice principalship—one of the primary stepping stones to the principalship—is concerned chiefly with student supervision and organizational maintenance.[34] As a result, it should come as no surprise that some principals with previous administrative experience are unprepared to exercise instructional leadership.

With the increased interest in instructional improvement that has marked the eighties, it is possible that the principal selection process may begin to place greater emphasis on instructional leadership. In a 1983 case study of her own socialization to the principalship of a Utah junior high school, Ann Hart notes that her suburban community and central office administration expected principals to function as instructional leaders.[35] Since her own graduate training had stressed this role, she felt she was "environmentally right" for the job.

The future of principal selection is somewhat clouded, however, by problems with the recruitment and retention of talented teachers. As indicated earlier, the pool of prospective teachers shows many signs of diminishing in quantity and quality. Charles Achilles points out that this development has major implications for the field of educational administration, since school leaders typically are recruited from the ranks of teachers.[36] A cynic, of course, could argue that teacher recruitment problems will have little impact because school leaders are rarely selected on the basis of exceptional talent anyway. In fact, large urban districts and small rural districts do often fail to look seriously for administrators outside the district.[37] Criteria such as popularity, visibility, seniority, and personal relations with key officials often have carried greater weight in the selection of school leaders than professional competence—this situation has particularly disadvantaged qualified women candidates.

EARLY DAYS AS PRINCIPAL

The first days and months of the principalship are critical to the process of shaping school leaders. Precisely how long the induction period lasts for new principals is open to debate. One study indicates that the feeling of being a "rookie" varies across schools and reference groups.[38] Within a few months of assuming their posts, the majority of new principals felt accepted by students and community. By the end of the first year, most principals no longer felt like rookies. Only relations with the central office and with other district principals continued to be characterized by uncertainty.

While new principals are learning the ropes, they are subject to a variety of influences, both formal and informal. While very little research is available on the socialization of new principals, it would appear that formal influences play less of a critical role than informal ones. For example, in the study cited above, only four of 45 principals received any formal orientation to their new position.[39] Several quotes illustrate the casual nature of the induction process and the anxiety it can invoke:

- The most vivid memory of my first year is that I was called by the central office on a Friday and asked to assume the role of acting principal on August 1. This gave me a little less than three weeks for which to be ready to open school and welcome staff back.
- Standing in the office on Labor Day looking at the clock and wondering, "How in the hell do you ring the bell?" is perhaps my most vivid memory. It also sums up many of the things I encountered that were simple but were things I had not done before.[40]

Without a formal orientation, new principals soon begin to discover the things they did not learn in their educational administration courses. It is during this time that school leaders often form the impression of the uselessness of graduate training. Help is available to new principals, but it is generally of the informal, anecdotal variety. Assistance may come in two basic forms—technical expertise and emotional support.

When principals were asked to name the persons who provided them with support during the induction period, they mentioned a variety of people.[41] Most frequently cited were other principals in the same district (63 percent), central office personnel other than the superintendent (61 percent), the superintendent (37 percent), and teachers in the new principal's school (28 percent). Asked to rate the influence exerted on them by various persons and groups during the first year, they indicated a somewhat different ordering.[42] The major influences on new principals were teachers in the school, both as individuals and as a faculty. Others receiving high ratings were assistant administrators (for those who had them) and students. It appears, at least for this particular sample of principals, that influences on their behavior during the induction period derived primarily from sources within their schools, while emotional support came mainly from outside.

Organization theory suggests that evaluation serves as an important mechanism for formal socialization. In Wolcott's ethnographic study of Ed Bell, we learn that Ed's periodic evaluation conferences with the Director of Elementary Education were important opportunities for him to learn district expectations.[43] What kinds of expectations are conveyed to principals through the evaluation process?

This question was addressed indirectly by Kent Peterson in a study of 113 suburban elementary principals from 59 different districts.[44] Peterson asked his subjects to identify criteria that they felt seemed to be of importance when they were being evaluated by the central office. The largest percentage (64 percent) of principals mentioned public reaction (parent satisfaction), followed by teacher morale (48 percent), principal and teacher compliance with district rules and procedures (39 percent), and "not making waves" (33 percent). Student performance and instructional leadership were cited by 28 percent and 26 percent, respectively.

A study of principal evaluation in Oregon suggests that the primary purpose of the evaluation process is not generally regarded to be socialization.[45] Principals and their supervisers in 30 districts were asked what purposes principal evaluation actually serve and should serve. The two most frequently cited "actual" purposes were about equal: to provide public accountability (25 percent) and to promote professional development (25 percent). Over twice as many respondents felt, however, that evaluation *should* promote professional development (64 percent) as those who felt it *should* provide public accountability (26 percent). Few respondents indicated that principal evaluation should or actually does ensure uniform practices among principals.

The formal and informal mechanisms by which new principals are socialized convey an impression of variability and arbitrariness. New principals learn a great deal on the job from confronting situations for which they lack sufficient expertise or warning. It is most likely a complex variety of factors that explain why some deal at all effectively with these challenges: the reputation of a principal's predecessor, the circumstances under which he or she is selected to be principal, the availability of supportive individuals, the talents of the new principal, and the major problems facing the school. For example, someone who succeeds an unpopular principal may enjoy a "honeymoon" period when teachers go out of their way to be cooperative and supportive.

Accounts of the first days and months of the principalship indicate that issues of instructional leadership are not always at the forefront of new principals' thinking. In fact, novice school leaders are apt to be more concerned about learning standard operating procedures and determining whether or not they are accepted by teachers, peers, and supervisors. In his study of the process of becoming a principal, Greenfield reports four key areas of concern for new leaders: relations with teachers, relations with the community, relations with peers and superiors, and the establishment of routines "associated with organizational stability and the maintenance of smooth day-to-day school operations."[46] These areas of concern imply a hierarchy of needs reminiscent of the aforementioned work of Abraham Maslow. Faced with a new and potentially threatening situation, beginning principals understandably will tend to focus on gaining security and acceptance before they devote great energy to school or instructional improvement. Achieving security and acceptance is generally a matter of learning what people value and "how things are done around here." Those who rush too quickly to initiate change may discover they lack sufficient understanding and support to carry out their ideas.

Paul Kelleher provides a revealing case study of a "bad beginning as principal."[47] Reflecting afterwards on his experience as a new middle school principal, he recognized his failure to understand the local culture. Loaded with enthusiasm and good ideas, he neglected to take into account how his new school, district, and community differed from those he was leaving. Later, after his contract was not renewed, he realized that local ideas about schooling, children, and life itself contrasted sharply with those with which he was accustomed.

Among Kelleher's mistakes was his failure to acknowledge local norms for hiring, cafeteria operation, school discipline, and tracking. For example, he put together a staff of bright, liberal graduates of universities from a metropolitan area 50 miles from his new community. Most of the district's teachers, however, had grown up locally and attended the local state teachers college. Kelleher and his imported staff members did not understand parent expectations about student behavior and school discipline. Believing that young adolescents needed lunchtime to "let off steam," they loosened cafeteria procedures. As a result, the cafeteria was always a mess and in a perpetual state of disorder. This situation troubled local visitors to the school.

Kelleher's views on discipline also clashed with local norms. While his own notion of discipline reflected a former counselor's interest in understanding students' problems, community members believed in the value of punishment. A similar clash of values occurred in the area of tracking. Kelleher believed students should be grouped heterogeneously, while community members were accustomed to homogeneous grouping. Kelleher later wrote, "As I naively moved forward during my first school year with the plan to change the grouping policy, I did not realize that I was in fact suggesting a change in the social structure of the town."[48]

Kelleher's experience should not be interpreted as evidence that new school leaders may as well abandon any hope of changing schools. His story simply illustrates the fact that change always occurs in a context. Failure to understand this context diminishes the chances for successful change. Expressed in different terms, the process of taking over the leadership of a school can be thought of as a process of reciprocal influences. As the new leader tries to shape the school, the school and its community try to shape the new leader. If all parties take sufficient care to understand what each is trying to do and why, there is the possibility of compromise and, ultimately, improvement.

Greenfield captures the challenge of becoming a school leader in the following passage:

> How one might modify existing preparation practices to achieve the socialization outcomes associated with an instructional leadership conception of the administrator role (an innovative rather than a custodial socialization response), and do so in a manner that does not unduly violate the current school culture and existing norms in the administration reference group presents an interesting dilemma. If one is to succeed in changing aspects of a social or cultural system, one must first be well acquainted with the system, knowledgeable but not blinded by unexamined underlying assumptions and values. Furthermore, if one is to act on the system from within the system, one must gain access to and acceptance among those who control participation in the system. . . [49]

LEADER SOCIALIZATION AND INSTRUCTIONAL IMPROVEMENT

Aspiring instructional leaders should recognize that many aspects of the process by which they become leaders may not promote the cause of instructional improvement. Instructional improvement, for example, requires a positive orientation to new ideas and a facility for working with adults. Those selected as school leaders, however, are often people with extensive teaching experience—experience that frequently fosters a skeptical attitude toward change. To teachers, innovations often represent short-lived experiments intended more to advance the reputations of administrators than to improve the welfare of students and faculty. Years of working with young people in classrooms also is no guarantee that new leaders will be capable of effective interactions with adults.

Although training programs for school leaders are starting to place more emphasis on instructional leadership, aspiring school leaders do not always view their graduate education as useful. Many devalue the experience because it fails to address issues of practical and immediate significance. Others are critical because professors do not model instructional leadership and programs fail to screen out weak aspirants.

Analyses of the processes by which school leaders are recruited and selected indicate that little stress generally is placed on qualities of instructional leadership. While prior administrative experience may be valued in choosing school leaders, the experience typically involves student management and school operations rather than instructional supervision, curriculum development, or program evaluation. Those concerned about affirmative action continue to maintain that *who* one knows, not *what* one knows, plays a key role in determining who becomes a school leader. Statistics revealing small percentages of women and minorities in leadership roles support this claim.

Once on the job, new leaders frequently find themselves spending a great deal of time getting to know people and procedures. Their most immediate concern is likely to be gaining the acceptance of teachers, students, parents, and supervisors. Those who evaluate the performance of school leaders are less likely to look for evidence of instructional leadership than they are to see whether school operations run smoothly. Since innovation and improvement often involve destabilization and conflict, new leaders may be reluctant to press for change for fear of jeopardizing their position in the district.

Having pointed out various aspects of the socialization process that may discourage the emergence of instructional leadership, we still must acknowledge that school leaders committed to instructional improvement continue to appear. If they did not, this book would be impossible, for it has relied heavily on actual examples of instructional leadership. Our contention is that these exemplary individuals are exceptions and that they will remain exceptions until changes occur in schools and school systems. It is of little value for graduate programs to prepare school leaders skilled in instructional improvement if they cannot find jobs or if, locating employment, they discover that their skills are not highly valued. Contemporary educational leaders should give serious thought to altering the socialization process so that instructional leadership is nurtured and rewarded.

Among the changes in the socialization process that are most likely to foster instructional leadership are the following:

- Greater efforts to encourage teachers with strong instructional skills to become school leaders
- More practica, internships, and pre-principalship administrative opportunities that focus on instructional leadership
- Greater selectivity in admissions to educational administration programs
- Greater emphasis in the leader selection process on instructional-leadership skill or potential
- Job descriptions for school leaders (department chairs, assistant administrators, principals, etc.) that stress instructional improvement
- Orientations for new administrators that stress instructional improvement
- Leader evaluation systems that focus on instructional improvement
- Incentives for school leaders who foster instructional improvement
- Sanctions for school leaders who fail to promote instructional improvement
- Efforts to train teachers to expect leaders to function as instructional leaders

If we can succeed in providing large numbers of new school leaders who are committed to continuing instructional improvement and related goals, we still must confront a variety of issues related to their survival. No one has ever maintained that instructional leadership is easy. In the concluding chapter, we will consider what it takes to remain a school leader.

STUDY QUESTIONS

1. Review the requirements to become a school administrator in your state. What percentage of the requirements deal directly with instructional leadership?
2. Obtain copies of local school systems' forms for evaluating principals. To what extent do these forms stress instructional leadership? Interview several administrators to determine how they view their evaluation.
3. Reflect on your experience as a classroom teacher. In what ways has this experience affected the way you think about schools and school leaders?
4. When a new principal takes over, what are likely to be his or her major concerns? Verify your impressions by talking with several new principals.

NOTES

1. George A. Theodorson and Achilles G. Theodorson, *A Modern Dictionary of Sociology* (New York: Barnes & Noble, 1979), p. 396.
2. *Ibid.,* p. 397.
3. Arthur Blumberg and William Greenfield, *The Effective Principal* (Boston: Allyn & Bacon, 1980), p. 243.
4. It can be argued that this second type of socialization—professional socialization— is actually a form of anticipatory socialization under certain circumstances.
5. Arthur Blumberg, *Supervisors and Teachers: A Private Cold War,* 2nd ed. (Berkeley: McCutchen, 1980), p. 221.
6. Edgar Schein, "Organizational Socialization and the Profession of Management," *Industrial Management Review,* Vol. 9, No. 2 (Winter 1968), pp. 1–16.
7. Arthur Blumberg, *Supervisors and Teachers: A Private Cold War,* p. 223.
8. Mary E. Guy, *Professionals in Organizations* (New York: Praeger, 1985), pp. 176–183.
9. Larry Cuban, *Urban School Chiefs under Fire* (Chicago: University of Chicago Press, 1976), p. 166.
10. Educational Research Service, "A Special Report: Polling the Principals," p. 55.
11. Cecil Miskel and Dorothy Cosgrove, "Leader Succession in School Settings," paper presented at the annual meeting of the American Educational Research Association, 1984, p. 7.
12. Charol Shakeshaft, "Strategies for Overcoming the Barriers to Women in Educational Administration," *Handbook for Achieving Sex Equity through Education,* Susan S. Klein (Ed.), (Baltimore: The Johns Hopkins University Press, 1985), p. 128.
13. National Center for Educational Statistics, *The Condition of Education: A Statistical Report* (Washington, D.C.: National Center for Educational Statistics, 1979)
14. Charol Shakeshaft, "Strategies for Overcoming the Barrier to Women in Educational Administration," p. 125.
15. *Ibid.,* pp. 125–130.
16. Samuel B. Ethridge, "Impact of the 1954 Brown vs. Topeka Board of Education Decision on Black Educators," *The Negro Educational Review,* Vol. 30, No. 4 (October 1979), pp. 217–232.
17. Seymour B. Sarason, *The Culture of the School and the Problem of Change* (Boston: Allyn & Bacon, 1971), pp. 112–113.
18. Flora Ida Ortiz, "Midcareer Socialization of Educational Administrators," *Review of Educational Research,* Vol. 48, No. 1 (Winter 1978), p. 129.
19. Sandra Prolman, "Gender, Career Paths, and Administrative Perceptions," *Administrator's Notebook,* Vol. 30, No. 5 (1982), p. 3.

20. Sakre K. Edson, *Pushing the Limits: The Female Administrative Aspirant* (in press).
21. Educational Research Service, *ERS Composite Indicator of Changes in Average Salaries and Wages Paid in Public Schools: Update 1980–81* (Arlington, Va.: Educational Research Service, 1981), pp. 6–7.
22. *Ibid.*
23. Daniel L. Duke, *Teaching—The Imperiled Profession* (Albany, N.Y.: State University of New York Press, 1984).
24. Educational Research Service, "A Special Report: Polling the Principals," p. 56.
25. William L. Pharis and Sally Banks Zakariya, *The Elementary School Principalship in 1978: A Research Study* (Arlington, Va.: National Association of Elementary School Principals, 1979), p. 29.
26. Richard A. McCullough, "Toward a Description of the Occupational Ethos of the Senior High Principalship," paper presented at the Annual Meeting of the American Educational Research Association, 1981.
27. David R. Byrne, Susan A. Hines, and Lloyd E. McCleary, *The Senior High School Principalship,* Vol. I (Reston, Va.; National Association of Secondary School Principals, 1978), p. 10.
28. Edwin M. Bridges, "The Nature of Leadership," *Educational Administration: The Developing Decades,* Luvern L. Cunningham, Walter G. Hack, and Raphael O. Nystrand (Eds.) (Berkeley: McCutchan, 1977), pp. 202–231.
29. Sarason, *The Culture of the School and the Problem of Change,* p. 41.
30. Robert A. Dentler and D. Catherine Baltzell, "Improving Principal Selection: Possibilities and Clues for Change," paper presented at the Annual Meeting of the American Educational Research Association, 1983.
31. *Ibid.,* pp. 2–3.
32. Neal Schmitt, Raymond Noe, Ronni Meritt, Michael Fitzgerald, and Cathy Jorgensen, "Criterion-related and Content Validity of the NASSP Assessment Center" (East Lansing: Department of Psychology, Michigan State University, n.d.), p. 18.
33. Daniel L. Duke, Nancy S. Isaacson, Richard Sagor, and Patricia A. Schmuck, "Transition to Leadership: An Investigation of the First Year of the Principalship," paper presented at the Annual Convention of the American Educational Research Association, pp. 8–12.
34. William D. Greenfield, "Being and Becoming a Principal: Responses to Work Contexts and Socialization Processes," paper presented at the Annual Meeting of the American Educational Research Association, 1985, p. 43.
35. Ann Weaver Hart, "Leadership Succession as Social Validation—The View from Inside the Principalship," paper presented at the Annual Meeting of the American Educational Research Association, 1985, p. 31.
36. Charles M. Achilles, "Forecast: Stormy Weather Ahead in Educational Administration," *Issues in Education,* Vol. 2, No. 2 (Fall 1984), pp. 127–135.
37. Sheppard Ranborn, "Focus on Leader's Role Sparks Concern over Training, Selection," *Education Week* (Feb. 22, 1984), p. 8.
38. Duke, Isaacson, Sagor, and Schmuck, "Transition to Leadership: An Investigation of the First Year of the Principalship,"pp. 11–12.
39. *Ibid.,* p. 15.
40. *Ibid.*
41. *Ibid.,* pp. 15–17.
42. *Ibid.,* pp. 19–21.
43. Harry F. Wolcott, *The Man in the Principal's Office* (New York: Holt, Rinehart & Winston, 1973), pp. 212–216.
44. Kent D. Peterson, "Mechanisms of Administrative Control over Managers in Educational Organizations," *Administrative Science Quarterly,* Vol. 29, No. 4 (December 1984), p. 593.
45. Daniel L. Duke and Richard J. Stiggins, "Evaluating the Performance of Principals: A Descriptive Study," *Educational Administration Quarterly,* Vol. 21, No. 4 (Fall 1985), p. 74.

46. William D. Greenfield, "Being and Becoming a Principal Responses to Work Contexts and Socialization Processes," p. 42.
47. Paul Kelleher, "A Bad Beginning as Principal," *Entry,* Barry Jentz (Ed.) (New York: McGraw-Hill, 1982), pp. 75–86.
48. *Ibid.,* p. 84.
49. William D. Greenfield, "The Moral Socialization of School Administrators: Informal Role Learning Outcomes," *Educational Administration Quarterly,* Vol. 21, No. 4 (Fall 1985), p. 111.

CHAPTER 14

SUSTAINING EFFECTIVE SCHOOL LEADERSHIP

Effective school leadership does not develop overnight. As previous chapters have shown, school leaders must accumulate technical skills, acquire professional judgment, and come to understand the local culture. A leader who is effective in one school may not necessarily be effective in another. And schools must adjust to leaders just as leaders must adjust to schools. Even veteran school leaders must, to some extent, start all over again when they move to a different school. One study of principal succession indicates that student achievement in basic skills does not begin to change until the second year of a new principal's tenure.[1] A comprehensive review of the literature on principal succession, however, suggests that a curvilinear relationship may exist between the length of an administrator's incumbency and school effectiveness.[2] In other words, principals may not continually increase in effectiveness, at least not at the same school.

What are the forces that conspire to diminish the effectiveness of school leaders, even as they acquire more experience? This chapter investigates three particularly potent forces: organizational complexity, ethical ambiguity, and uncertainty regarding the meaning of work. The ability of school leaders to remain effective will likely be linked to how well they handle these issues.

THE COMPLEX WORLD OF THE SCHOOL

There may once have been a time when schools were uncomplicated and simple to understand, but today's school leader confronts a bewildering and enervating array of organizational complexities, ranging from official regulations to interpersonal dynamics. A number of researchers have examined the variety of problems school leaders must deal with.

Blumberg and Greenfield, for example, discovered three major problem areas in interviews with eight principals. Each problem area exerted a "negative emotional impact" on them as they tried to perform their jobs. The three problems areas were:

- The problem of the exceeding difficulty and accompanying frustration that is attached to the process of terminating a tenured teacher.

- The problem of power and/or powerlessness that they felt relative to their prerogatives inside and outside the school.
- The problem of the behavioral constraints that are put on the person of the principal by reason of the role expectations that are held for him/her by others.[3]

Lipham has expressed key problems in terms of dichotomies. He identified eight "impelling issues" for school leaders:

- Diversity vs. uniformity in educational goals
- Traditional vs. non-traditional values and attitudes
- Centralization vs. decentralization in organizational relationships
- Directiveness vs. supportiveness in leadership behavior
- Authoritative vs. participative decision-making processes
- Managerial vs. instructional tasks to be completed
- Programmed vs. adaptive approaches to change
- Interaction vs. insularity in relations with the environment[4]

What are the root causes of these major areas of concern for school leaders? Why have contemporary schools become steadily more complex? One group of researchers points to four trends that have contributed to the complexity.[5] First, until recently, schools have grown in size. As a result, school leaders must be responsible for more staff members and students. Face-to-face communications and coordination become more difficult as organizational size increases. Second, schools have grown more technologically complex. Examples range from the introduction of computers for instructional and administrative purposes to the variety of specialists required to staff special education programs. Structural complexity or interdependence represents a third trend. Schools must now accommodate a variety of different programs and staffing arrangements. Negotiating cooperative relations among programs and personnel is a constant concern for school leaders. Finally, the environments in which schools exist require leaders to interact regularly with a number of public and private agencies, citizen groups, and district officials.

Reflecting on the complexity facing leaders in all types of organizations, Edgar Schein contends that the two challenges that supersede all others are "external adaptation" and "internal integration."[6] Failure to deal effectively with these challenges can jeopardize the very survival of the organization. Let us look more closely at these challenges as they relate to schools.

External Adaptation

It was noted earlier that all organizations exist in a variety of contexts. Schools certainly are no exception. They must adapt to changing technology, demography, politics, and regulations—to name just a few of the more obvious external forces.

Technological changes affect schools in numerous ways. As advances are made in the sciences and applied to the world of work, demands are made for improvements in school curriculum. Some of these advances also pertain to the technical "core" of schooling—how students should be taught and how schools should be organized. The advent of computers provides a useful illustration.

Schools were compelled to add computer education to the curriculum even as they were exploring how to use computers to improve instruction and school management. An example of technological changes that could have an impact on schools in the future are medical advances in obstetrics and neonatal care. These advances promise to reduce dramatically the future incidence of congenital handicapping conditions. The result could mean a substantial shift of resources away from special education programs and a subsequent reorganization of instructional delivery systems in schools. Harvey Brooks has captured the complexities and demands of the technological challenge faced by contemporary educators and other professionals:

> The dilemma of the professional today lies in the fact that both ends of the gap he is expected to bridge with his profession are changing so rapidly: the body of knowledge that he must use and the expectations of the society that he must serve. Both these changes have their origin in the same common factor—technological change . . . The problem cannot be usefully phrased in terms of too much technology. Rather it is whether we can generate technological change fast enough to meet the expectations and demands that technology itself has generated. And the four professions—medicine, engineering, business management and education—must bear the brunt of responsibility for generating and managing this change. This places on the professional a requirement for adaptability that is unprecedented.[7]

Other challenges have been brought about by demographic changes. As the percentage of adults without children in school has increased, for example, schools have experienced greater difficulty generating local resources. School leaders find themselves devoting larger amounts of time to public relations and preparations for retrenchment. In addition, the character of families with school-age children is changing. Children are more likely than ever before to live in unsettled domestic circumstances. Students from divorced homes or "blended" families often need special assistance. School personnel must learn to deal with both custodial and noncustodial parents. As more mothers join fathers in working outside the home, schools find it harder to contact parents or involve them in school activities. The emergence of the "latchkey child" who returns from school to a parent-less home has become a problem not only for schools, but also for society in general. Such changes in the American family have confronted school personnel with an array of new responsibilities—from testifying in custody trials and monitoring child neglect and abuse to processing restraining orders and dealing with legally emancipated minors.

Other demographic changes are related to the racial and ethnic makeup of the school-age population. The large influx of Southeast Asian, Central American, Caribbean, and Mexican peoples during the past decade has forced school leaders to expand opportunities for non-English speakers. Home-school communications have become more difficult, and the need for curriculum adjustments that recognize cultural differences has increased. The fact that many recent immigrants live in impoverished conditions places additional strains on schools, as they attempt to provide for basic welfare as well as the educational needs of their new students.

Changes have taken place in the political environment of schools as well. Once regarded as "neutral turf," schools today serve as political battlegrounds for various special interest groups. Each group claims to represent the interests of youth. Caught in the midst of controversies over such issues as curriculum content, guidance and counseling programs, and the character of school personnel, school leaders find themselves trying to simultaneously protect the rights of students, employees, and the community. As the following section on ethical ambiguity indicates, the demands of such controversies divert attention and energy from instructional improvement.

School leaders also have had to engage directly in political activity in order to secure or protect adequate levels of support for public education. Groups of educators must actively lobby legislators for increased state aid as well as special programs. Prior to budget, bond issue, and levy elections, local taxpayers must be wooed. Even dealings between individual school leaders and members of local Boards of Education have become highly politicized. Board members often try to circumvent superintendents and deal directly with school leaders. School leaders who fail to understand the local political environment may discover they lack the support necessary to exercise authority.

A fourth challenge of external adaptation involves regulations, laws, and procedures governing school operations. Previous chapters have identified many of the constraints on school leaders that have resulted from federal and state legislation, court decisions, and collective bargaining agreements. Depending on the location, policies may restrict a school leader's ability to assign personnel, determine class size, introduce controversial topics into the curriculum, and allocate instructional resources. Blumberg and Greenfield found that school leaders faced with such constraints may experience a real sense of powerlessness.[8] However, adapting to regulations and laws is not simply a matter of recognizing that ultimate authority for school policies resides outside the school. How particular laws are interpreted may change as the political party in power changes. State agencies frequently revise regulations in the face of public and political pressure. Labor contracts are renegotiated every year or two. The constantly changing nature of legal, legislative, and contractual constraints is as much a challenge for school leaders as their existence in the first place.

Internal Integration

If the challenges of external adaptation were not a sufficient drain on time and energy, just keeping schools from fragmenting internally can be a demanding full-time job for school leaders. Like everyone else, school personnel sometimes experience powerful urges to pursue self-interest. Left unchecked, these tendencies can undermine school cohesiveness and effectiveness.

As schools have grown in size, in number of special programs, and in role differentiation, the potential for fragmentation has increased. The first part of Chapter 12 looked in depth at what school leaders can do to improve coordination and cooperation among programs and personnel. Two issues that were not addressed, though, concern the management of professionals in complex organizations and the isolation of leaders.

The cultures of professions rarely specify norms for behavior in organizations. The image of a professional is that of an individual practitioner. Professionals, of course, are expected to interact with each other, but such collegial relations are presumed to be of a consultative nature. Professionals are not trained to expect to be managed or led by other professionals. In reality, of course, there are few opportunities for certain professionals, like educators, to function as private practitioners. Because they must apply what they know in public, bureaucratic organizations governed by laws and policies, educators are subject to the supervision, evaluation, guidance, and direction of others. These "others," for the most part, are fellow educators who have moved up through the school hierarchy. Chapter 13 identified some issues related to recruiting school leaders from the ranks of teachers.

In a hospital, the director typically is not a physician. Directors tend to have been trained separately, in business schools or special hospital administration programs. As a result, hospital directors make little attempt to challenge the professional expertise of hospital physicians. School leaders, on the other hand, once were teachers. They are in a position to be professional as well as organizational leaders—or, in other words, they can exercise authority based on their professional expertise as well as their position in the school authority structure. This can be an advantage in promoting internal integration.

All the authority in the world, of course, cannot ensure that leaders will be fully accepted as members of the organizations they head. One of the ironies of leadership is that leaders often find themselves isolated amidst crowds of people. Phil Jackson writes poignantly about this situation, where it is "lonely at the top."[9] As professor-turned-principal, he himself felt like an actor on stage, cut off from the audience. When he analyzed why he felt this way, Jackson realized that school leaders are privy to large amounts of confidential information, information that cannot be shared without violating confidences and undermining trust. He also learned that "the sheer press of events squeezes out intimacy and relaxed casualness from situations where they might otherwise be enjoyed."[10] The harder school leaders work to ensure internal integration, the busier they are likely to become. And the busier they become, the more likely they are to be perceived by staff members as preoccupied, detached, and inaccessible. By working diligently to mobilize staff members into a cohesive unit, school leaders actually may risk becoming isolated themselves! An organization cannot be fully integrated until its leader or leaders are perceived to be part of the whole. Being able to bring people together without being left outside the group oneself is one of the greatest challenges of internal integration for school leaders.

ETHICAL AMBIGUITY

School leaders in the United States function not only in complex organizational settings, but also within a pluralistic society. And where consensus concerning the goals of public schooling is elusive, the lines between right and wrong tend to blur. School leaders constantly find themselves trying to resolve issues where *each* side may appear to be right—or wrong! Where are they to obtain guidance in handling value conflicts?

Some school leaders fall back on laws, regulations, and procedures. Though they may complain about such constraints on their discretionary authority, school leaders also find comfort in not having to resolve every dispute themselves. Despite the proliferation of school policies in recent years, cases still arise—and with great frequency, if we are to believe school leaders—for which there are no clear guidelines. These are occasions where professional judgment is required. Professional judgment, in turn, is presumably informed by professional ethics—these are principles that can be applied when two or more values are in conflict to help establish decision priorities.[11] Examples of such principles are justice, freedom, honesty, order, loyalty, equity, equality, and responsibility. In 1981 The American Association of School Administrators adopted a "Statement of Ethics for School Administrators" (Figure 14.1) that provides a useful starting point for thinking about ethics:[12]

STATEMENT OF ETHICS FOR SCHOOL ADMINISTRATORS

An educational administrator's professional behavior must conform to an ethical code. The code must be idealistic and at the same time practical, so that it can apply reasonably to all educational administrators. The administrator acknowledges that the schools belong to the public they serve for the purpose of providing educational opportunities to all. However, the administrator assumes the responsibility for providing professional leadership in the school and community. This responsibility requires the adminstrator to maintain standards of exemplary professional conduct. It must be recognized that the administrator's actions will be viewed and appraised by the community, professional associates, and students. To these ends, the administrator subscribes to the following statements of standards.

The educational administrator:

1. Makes the well-being of students the fundamental value of all decision making and actions.

2. Fulfills professional responsibilities with honesty and integrity.

3. Supports the principle of due process and protects the civil and human rights of all individuals.

4. Obeys local, state, and national laws and does not knowingly join or support organizations that advocate, directly or indirectly, the overthrow of the government.

5. Implements the governing board of education's policies and administrative rules and regulations.

6. Pursues appropriate measures to correct those laws, policies, and regulations that are not consistent with sound educational goals.

7. Avoids using positions for personal gain through political, social, religious, economic, or other influence.

8. Accepts academic degrees or professional certification only from duly accredited institutions.

9. Maintains the standards and seeks to improve the effectiveness of the profession through research and continuing professional development.

10. Honors all contracts until fulfillment, release, or dissolution mutually agreed upon by all parties to contract.

Figure 14.1   Reprinted with permission of the American Association of School Administrators.

Contemporary school leaders realize, however, that even codes of professional ethics cannot guarantee clear-cut decisions. Ethical principles may conflict with each other or be subject to multiple interpretations. Coping with ethical ambiguity is a major challenge for those hoping to remain effective school leaders.

There are myriad ethical quandaries, for instance, around the delivery of instructional services. What is the balance between the rights of individual students and those of groups of students? Can schools be equally committed to the principles of equity and excellence? School leaders know that it is easier to uphold these principles when resources are plentiful—when they are scarce, ethical conflicts are likely to increase because tough decisions must be made. Should valuable resources be allocated for the instruction of students who are unmotivated to learn and uncooperative? Should relatively large amounts of resources be used to help a relatively small number of students—as is the case in programs for severely handicapped students? Is there a point at which a school leader can tell a student that the school no longer can afford to try to help him or her?

Among the ethical dilemmas raised in previous sections of this book, those related to teacher performance have been particularly perplexing. What is to be done when the rights of staff members are pitted against the welfare of students? The toughest decisions many school leaders confront are those related to staff discipline and dismissal. By disposition and training, most school leaders probably are inclined to help staff membrs, to give them a second chance. At what point, though, do the interests of school and community supersede those of employees?

An elementary school principal in a suburban district on the West Coast provides a revealing account of the ethical dilemmas presented by one of her veteran teachers. Her story suggests how troubling and complex is the world of school leadership when values-related issues surface daily.[13.]

> I have an ethical dilemma which I am sure is not uncommon to most building administrators. I would like to discuss my feelings as an elementary principal who employs a marginal teacher.
>
> Mel is nearing retirement. When I arrived as the new administrator in the building and read his file, I learned that in his many years with the District, Mel had accumulated many honors, among them the designation as a "Master Teacher" fifteen years before. His file contained dozens of letters from parents praising his work with their children, from owners of local businesses thanking the school for business—education partnerships Mel had initiated, and from colleagues citing his pioneering efforts in the field of Energy Education, which provided the District a "lighthouse energy project" later to be replicated nationally. In Mel's file were also the formal evaluation papers submitted at the end of each school year; the more recently dated ones not nearly as glowing, but giving no clues that alarmed me.
>
> During my initial few weeks at the school, I picked up no hints from his colleagues that Mel would present me with any challenges. The shared perception seemed to be, "What would we all do without Mel?" Indeed, he seemed to spend his time running around taking care of anyone in need—including an overwhelmed neophyte principal. His humor was healing and refreshing; he appeared

to have many of the nurturing traits of a mother hen. Arriving by 7:30 A.M., he'd already be off to jump-start a teacher's car before the rest of us learned she'd called in for help. He would bring coffee to another who'd stayed late for a heavy parent-teacher conference the evening before in case comfort was necessary. Sometimes he'd assist the morning custodian moving furniture or hanging up the tether balls. And more often than not he'd have a kid (of the waif variety) "illegally" in his classroom to "help" him.

Then came the moment I first entered his classroom to observe his teaching. I returned a week later to make sure it hadn't been an off-day. Then I called Personnel. The Director didn't seem particularly surprised or upset at my concerns; his response was more in the nature of "there are so many out there who are worse—do what you can" and reminded me that Mel was eligible for retirement in two years. Don't sweat it, Principal; Fair Dismissal statutes and all that.

Mel's teaching can best be described as an ongoing monologue occasionally interrupted by a child's question or comment; sporadic activities during which he still talks; and lots of "kid noise," which he continually shushes. Students read a lot from textbooks as an entire class, each child reading aloud in turn, Mel interrupting often with impromptu anecdotes and "higher-order thinking questions." The chalkboard is filled with his scrawl from today, yesterday, and last week—I can't distinguish one from another—and his handwriting is almost illegible. The classroom, with stacks of boxes here, newspapers he recycles for the whole building there, and an overstuffed chair with the stuffing coming out in the corner, evokes in me a similar response to the one I get from my five-year-old's bedroom. Glancing at his open lesson plan book, provided it's visible under the piles on the desk, is a memorable experience. He *does* plan. He plans in great detail. If I can decipher what I see there, he takes a textbook teacher's guide lesson, mixes it with 28 years of accumulated teaching strategies, adds a current teaching fad or two (small group discussions, learning logs, an anticipatory set perhaps), and ends up with slightly organized anarchy. I did not know where to start diagnosing toward the goal of instructional improvement. It blew me away.

A more serious concern was Mel's behavior toward students when he was under stress. When angry at a child, he could become very abusive. The first confrontation he and I had on this issue was after he told a misbehaving child that he'd acted "like a horse's rear end." The second occasion was where Mel pulled a student from a line in the hallway and ordered him to do 20 push-ups as punishment for something. On both these occasions and on subsequent ones, Mel was contrite, admitted his error, and promised that nothing of this sort would recur. To my knowledge, this has been the case. I have been unable, however, to alter his yelling at kids and am convinced that the volume of his voice is due as much to a hearing impairment as it is to the stress inherent in confinement with 25 fourth-graders.

Mel's classroom organization and management system also represent problems. He organizes his students into teams and seats them in small groupings. The teams earn points for certain things—having homework turned in, being on-task, scoring well on spelling tests, helping each other, etc.—big on cooperative learning strategies. The kids love the system; the losers, however, are the low achievers who must face the humiliation of disgracing their peers daily in some way or another. Mel and I have been around and around on this issue. I have stopped short of forbidding him to organize the class in this manner because of the argument—supported by a contingent of parents—that the arrangement boosts a child's self-esteem more often than it is harmful. And guess what? His achievement test scores at the end of each year are as high, and often higher, than those of the other fourth-grade class. Mel attributes this to his cooperative learning arrangement.

Mel also manages children with humor, humor that often takes a toll on the fragile self-concept of a nine-year-old. When I asked him to administer a student questionnaire containing the question, "What does your teacher do that you like?" the most frequent answers were "He makes us laugh," and "He teases/plays with us." Yet the playful comment to a slightly overweight child, or the casual reference to a budding fourth-grade romance has had devastating consequences.

My dilemma surfaces most profoundly each summer when I assign students to specific teachers. Mel's teaching partner, Pat, is one of the most popular teachers in the building. She is also a very strong teacher. Parent requests for specific teachers roll in each spring. Each time, 100% of them will be for Pat. Mel will bounce through my office in mid-summer and ask, "How many thousands requested Pat *this* year?" Maybe he doesn't comprehend the complexities of this issue for me; maybe he does. When I have finalized the placement of fourth-graders into Mel's and Pat's classes, I have done so only after some difficult grappling with the following factors:

- The need to provide academically and socially heterogeneous groupings of students in both rooms.
- The best interests of those few seriously at-risk students (I assign them to Pat).
- Each child's third-grade experience and the potential placement in fifth grade.
- The best interests of Mel. Which children will he be most likely to assist in his special way? Which kids will bait him? Which students or parents will be so hostile that they further reduce his efficacy?
- The best interests of Pat. It is possible to stack her class with so many challenging students that it would make it impossible for her to teach well. The emotional drain on her from this arrangement is substantial. She and I have an unspoken understanding about student placement—her only comment to me has been, "I trust you."
- Politically powerful parents. Should a principal take special care of the children of the community elite (Local School Committee members, a past School Board member, the PTC officers)? Should placement of their kids with the best teachers be a natural "perk" for their high level of involvement and support for the school? The parents who take the most time to get to know all the teachers should be rewarded for their interest, right? Shouldn't the squeakiest wheels be granted their requests, thereby improving everyone's chances for a harmonious year?
- Students without politically powerful parents. I believe that a major role of a principal is advocate for children whose parents do not/cannot speak up for them. Maybe these parents are silent because they work swing shift and cannot participate actively in the school life of their children, maybe they are by nature trusting that a teacher is a teacher and you take what you get, or maybe they just do not care. Still one of my responsibilities is to sit in the other chair and plead the cases of these kids for the best educational experience possible.
- My interests as building principal. What price am I willing to pay in time and energy and stress for every student assigned to Mel's class? In which cases am I simply unwilling to set up a situation that could subsequently draw a substantial amount of my effectiveness away from other school-wide issues which deserve my attention?

I have found no resolution to these issues. It would be easier for me if Mel were worse, if he served no valid organizational function. Yet he does. He is one reason my school as a whole is strong. He takes care of hidden human needs. He cares for others in such a way that their more visible contributions are maximized. But the price I pay to sustain this teacher on my staff is high, and manifests itself in both subtle and not-so-subtle ways. I am scarred by my ordeal with a family who moved out of the District because of their child's experience in Mel's class. The situation evolves into an ethical dilemma when I take seriously the competing and conflicting interests of the variety of human beings I feel obligated to serve.

I mentally piece together this puzzle continually, rearranging the pieces to take advantage of small victories and to head off impending crises. I dream at night about cross-grade grouping strategies. I listen to kids and parents in silence when they describe the realities of life in Mel's classroom. I strategize with the Personnel Director to create the right temperature at which to ensure Mel's retirement this summer but not to cause him so much stress that the kids pay the toll. I clinch my teeth and make one small decision after another regarding kids and teaching and learning in that classroom, until I must appear either callous or oblivious to the ramifications of those decisions. I confront and back off, confront and back off, and my sense of professionalism is offended at every turn. When I share this feeling with my colleagues, I am assured that this is just part of the job. It is a part of the job that hurts.

This example illustrates the emotional energy demanded by just one ethical dilemma. School leaders confront multiple dilemmas on a daily basis. Those who claim they do not probably have refused to recognize the value conflicts inherent in the job of school leadership. Denial, however, is not the answer to ethical ambiguity.

. A number of issues are raised by the preceding story. Mel's students generally performed well on achievement tests. How far should a school principal be willing to go to support student achievement? Are there values greater than student achievement that should be acknowledged? Is it acceptable to treat students injuriously as long as they achieve instructional objectives? The fact that Mel helped so many people in the school—both students and staff members—compounded the principal's dilemma. Mel had become a crucial element in the school culture. Were his benefits sufficient to allow his mistreatment of certain students to be overlooked? Was it fair to reassign all the students who are ill-served by Mel to his colleague Pat?

It is important for school leaders to be aware of the value conflicts involved in school leadership and instructional improvement. Awareness, of course, will not necessarily make administrative life easier and, in many ways, life without conscious concern for values is simpler and less taxing. At the same time, though, life is apt to be less meaningful without values, and as we will see at the close of this textbook, school leaders can use their concern for values to help counteract the daily frustrations of school life.

THE MATTER OF MEANING

Organizational complexity and ethical ambiguity pose serious challenges to school leaders intent on remaining effective. Complexity can interfere with a leader's ability to spend time in ways he or she judges important, and frustration and cynicism can result from getting bogged down with rules, regulations, and procedures. Ethical ambiguity can cause leaders to lose sight of why they became educators in the first place; decisiveness yields to equivocation and uncertainty, and the whole experience of school leadership grows less meaningful.

Our contention is that a sense of meaningfulness in a leader's work is the best antidote for the problems of organizational complexity and ethical ambiguity. Knowing what it means to be a leader will not eliminate these problems, of course, but it can remind leaders of why they must continue to endure them rather than quit. Having said this, it should be admitted that cultivating and sustaining a sense of meaning can be difficult. Time is required for reflection, and time, as we've already said, is a leader's scarcest commodity. If meaning came easily, there would be fewer school leaders who *burn out* prematurely or restlessly search for better job opportunities.

There have been few empirical studies of the meaning of school leadership. Therefore, we must listen carefully to how school leaders talk about their work to find out the degree to which meaning is an issue for them. Ed Bell, the elementary principal studied intensively by Wolcott, was quoted as saying:

> Sometimes I ask myself, "I wonder just how important is all of this work I do?" It's not like bales of hay that you can count or sacks of oats. But I guess I've gotten used to it.[14]

Blumberg and Greenfield recount the concern of a principal in their study who felt strongly that graduation should be a meaningful experience.[15] We cannot help feeling that he was speaking for himself as well as his students.

> The problem that concerned George ... was not that the weather fouled up the outdoor graduation and necessitated a move inside to the gymnasium, but rather that graduating under less than idyllic conditions was just "not the way to conclude thirteen years of education." In other words, it was disturbing to George's personal sense of values to have it end this way. As he said, "if graduation is at all meaningful, let's do it right."

A bright young principal of a nationally recognized high school recently summed up the situation. With a doctorate, numerous consulting opportunities, talented colleagues in his school and district, and a salary close to $50,000, he seemed to have everything going for him. Yet he said something that suggested a profound uncertainty about the meaning of his work. "What do you do," he inquired, "when you realize you've outgrown the principalship at the same time you recognize that it's the best job in education?" Without a clear sense of meaning, success and status are unlikely to provide sufficient impetus to face the daily challenges of leadership with enthusiasm and commitment.

The assumptions on which this book are based provide some clues for thinking about the meaning of school leadership. Three assumptions are particularly important to consider:

- To sustain commitment and enthusiasm, a person's work should be meaningful.
- Most people who pursue careers in elementary and secondary schools are motivated, at least initially, by a desire to help young people learn to lead meaningful lives.

- The primary mechanisms for helping young people in school settings are effective instruction and good relationships between students and staff members.

If these assumptions are accepted, then it makes sense for school leaders to devote a major share of their time and energy to improving instruction and creating conditions that foster productive relationships between students and staff members; they should regard as one of their primary responsibilities helping staff members and, ultimately, students to find meaning in the work they do in school.

What we are arguing for is a concept of leadership that acknowledges the critical role of meaning in people's lives. In fact, the defining quality of leadership is "helping to bring meaning to the relationships between individuals and greater entities—communities, organizations, nations."[16] What it means to be a school leader is linked inextricably to helping others find meaning in *their* school experience. While recognition, reputation, and remuneration are important incentives for school leaders, inspiring others to commit to causes greater than their personal welfare is crucial to sustaining effective leadership.

School leaders are advised to consider what they do that diminishes as well as enhances the meaning of the school experience for others. Preceding chapters have contained numerous examples of ways that school leaders can undermine the meaningfulness of teaching. For example, concern over a few marginally competent teachers often causes school leaders to allow the entire teacher evaluation system to be driven by the need for accountability. In so doing, they sacrifice the pursuit of professional excellence—a goal more likely to capture the imagination of teachers than accountability. Another way school leaders detract from the meaning of teaching is by constantly stressing rules, regulations, and procedures. Such emphasis on the bureaucratic dimensions of schooling denies the value teachers place on their role as professionals and on their personal relationships with students and colleagues.

Phil Jackson observes that teachers are interested "in the well-being of individual students."[17] He goes on to note that, when asked to describe the satisfactions derived from their work, teachers tend to talk about what happens to individual students, not groups.[18] School leaders who overlook the fact that the structure of meaning for teachers is tied to individual students and who insist on thinking solely in terms of collective accomplishments are less likely to engender teacher commitment. Of course, they must be concerned with averages, ratios, and totals—the quality-control functions of their work require them to consider such statistics as average daily attendance, average student scores on tests, teacher-student ratios, and school enrollments. But these concerns should not cause school leaders to overlook the fact that teachers equate success with making a difference in the lives of individuals.

There is much that school leaders can do to enhance the meaningfulness of the school experience. Besides inquiring about particular students and taking an active interest in teachers' efforts to help them, school leaders can encourage teachers to learn and grow professionally. Teachers should feel safe to discuss their concerns with supervisors and peers and to experiment with new ideas without fear of criticism. When appropriate, school leaders can remind teachers and other staff members of their role in advancing the interests of youth and the welfare of society. Articulating a vision of schooling that helps teachers see how their individual contributions relate to the world around them can be a crucial dimension of effective leadership.

School leaders would do well to bear in mind that the pursuit of meaning is not an end in itself. In his book, *Existential Psychotherapy,* Irvin Yalom maintains that meaning is best thought of as a byproduct of *engagement.*[19] From becoming involved in collective action, people gain experience, perspective, and an understanding of others—consequently, they are less likely to dwell exclusively on themselves and their own condition.

A challenge, then, for school leaders is to engage teachers in collective activity without devaluing their inclination to see themselves as helping professionals who equate success with assisting individual students. Meaningful school experiences ultimately derive both from commitment to collective action and devotion to individual accomplishment.

In closing, a relatively obvious point perhaps needs to be underscored. If school leaders are to help others find meaning in the school experience, they themselves must be clear about what the school experience means. School leaders who, for example, try to help teachers improve instructionally at the same time that they convey uncertainty about their own level of commitment to the educational enterprise are not likely to be very convincing. School leadership for instructional improvement ultimately represents more than a concern for professional growth and career advancement. It constitutes a continuing affirmation of the value of youth. To devote time and energy to improving how and what the young are taught is to be dedicated to leaving the world not as it is found, but better.

STUDY QUESTIONS

1. What does a career in school leadership mean to you? Interview several retired school leaders and ask them what their work meant to them.

2. Based on your own experience in schools, can you cite examples of how they are becoming more complex? Why are these changes taking place?

3. Have you faced issues of ethical ambiguity in your own school experience? List several examples and compare them with the experience of an experienced school leader.

4. In her book entitled *In a Different Voice* (Harvard University Press), Carol Gilligan argues that men and women think about values and morality differently. Ask several male and female school leaders to talk about value conflicts they have encountered and how they handled them. Do you detect gender differences?

5. In what ways can school leaders help remove "barriers to meaning" for teachers?

NOTES

1. Brian Rowan and Charles E. Denk, "Management Succession, School Socioeconomic Context, and Basic Skills Achievement," *American Educational Research Journal,* Vol. 21, No. 3 (Fall 1984), pp. 517–537.

2. Cecil Miskel and Dorothy Cosgrove, "Leader Succession in School Settings," paper presented at the Annual Meeting of the American Educational Research Association, 1984, p. 27.
3. Arthur Blumberg and William Greenfield, *The Effective Principal* (Boston: Allyn & Bacon, 1980), pp. 212–227.
4. James M. Lipham, *Effective Principal, Effective School* (Reston, Va.: National Association of Secondary School Principals, 1981).
5. Elizabeth Cohen, Russell H. Miller, Anneke Bredo, and Kenneth Duckworth, "Principal Role and Teacher Morale under Varying Organizational Conditions," (Stanford, Calif.: Stanford Center for Research and Development in Teaching, n.d.), pp. 41–44.
6. Edgar Schein, *Organizational Culture and Leadership* (San Francisco: Jossey-Bass, 1985), p. 119.
7. Harvey Brooks, "The Dilemmas of Engineering Education," *IEEE Spectrum* (February 1967), p. 89.
8. Blumberg and Greenfield, *The Effective Principal,* p. 234.
9. Philip W. Jackson, "Lonely at the Top: Observations on the Genesis of Administrative Isolation," *School Review,* Vol. 85, No. 3 (May 1977), pp. 425–432.
10. *Ibid.,* p. 431.
11. Herman Mertins, Jr. (Ed.), *Professional Standards and Ethics* (Washington, D.C.: American Society for Public Administration, 1979), p. 21.
12. Ralph B. Kimbrough, *Ethics: A Course of Study for Educational Leaders* (Arlington, Va.: American Association of School Administrators, 1985), p. 82.
13. My appreciation to this principal for sharing the private account with me. Anonymity is necessary to protect the parties involved.
14. Harry F. Wolcott, *The Man in the Principal's Office* (New York: Holt, Rinehart & Winston, 1973), p. 310.
15. Blumberg and Greenfield, *The Effective Principal,* p. 165.
16. Daniel L. Duke, "The Aesthetics of Leadership," *Educational Administration Quarterly,* Vol. 21, No. 2 (Winter 1986), p. 13.
17. Philip W. Jackson, *Life in Classrooms* (New York: Holt, Rinehart and Winston, Inc., 1968), P. 133.
18. *Ibid.*
19. Irvin D. Yalom, *Existential Psychotherapy* (New York: Basic Books, 1980), p. 48.

APPENDIXES

GLOSSARY

Anticipatory socialization The learning of the rights, obligations, expectations, and outlook of a role preparatory to assuming it.

Classroom management The provisions and procedures needed to create and maintain environments where teaching and learning can occur.

Coordination Processes and procedures designed to reduce the need for organizational control by facilitating communications and fostering internal integration.

Curriculum alignment The process by which a correspondence is achieved between the content of tests and the content of curricula.

Follow-through The monitoring of performance to determine whether and to what extent data-based decisions actually have been implemented.

Instructional audit A systematic process for assessing the extent to which what is intended to be taught is actually taught.

Instructional improvement The continuous process of upgrading the quality of teaching, curriculum content, assessment, and instructional support.

Instructional management The development, implementation, and enforcement of policies and procedures for dealing with predictable or recurring instructional concerns.

Instructional support Any efforts designed to establish and maintain school climates conducive to teacher and student growth.

Organizational socialization The formal and informal mechanisms by which organization members learn the expectations, values, and norms of the organization.

Professional development Efforts to help people become better professionals, taking into account their idiosyncratic needs, talents, deficiencies, assignments, and aspirations.

Professional socialization The formal and informal mechanisms by which professionals learn the expectations, values, and norms of the profession.

Quality control The variety of activities designed to determine the extent to which organizational goals are achieved.

Resource management The process of allocating and monitoring the use of organizational resources to ensure the achievement of organizational goals.

School-discipline plan The formal policies specifying acceptable student behavior and the consequences for inappropriate behavior.

Staff development Efforts to help groups of teachers meet the organizational needs of their schools and school systems.

Teacher evaluation The process of determining the extent to which a teacher achieves and maintains specified performance standards.

Troubleshooting Processes and procedures designed to anticipate and minimize the impact of problems that threaten an organization's capacity to achieve its goals.

Vision An image of what is desirable that can be expressed in ways that inspire and motivate people to work toward improvement.

DUKE INSTRUCTIONAL IMPROVEMENT CHECKLIST

The questions contained in this diagnostic checklist can help school personnel determine whether conditions conducive to instructional improvement exist in their schools. Each question is based on an aspect of school or teaching effectiveness. The questions are intended to generate discussion related to instructional improvement. They do not yield a composite score by which schools can be ranked or rated.

SUPERVISION AND EVALUATION

1.1 Do supervision and evaluation systems serve the purposes of improvement as well as accountability?

1.2 Is the system of teacher supervision and evaluation based on a sound vision of teaching?

1.3 Do teachers play a key role in developing and periodically reviewing performance standards of effective teaching?

1.4 Are data on teaching performance drawn from a variety of sources?

1.5 Have provisions been made for the frequent collection of data on teaching performance?

1.6 Have provisions been made to periodically check the quality of data collected on teaching performance?

1.7 Are data on teaching performance shared, analyzed, and interpreted in a timely manner?

1.8 Are teachers permitted to analyze observation data before observers?

1.9 Are data on teaching performance analyzed in light of the latest research on effective practice?

1.10 Do provisions exist for helping individual teachers and groups of teachers improve their professional performance?

1.11 Are a variety of kinds of assistance available for teacher growth and development?

1.12 Has provision been made for placing teachers with serious deficiencies on formal plans of assistance?

1.13 Do school leaders exhibit skill in interpersonal communication, including active listening, appropriate nonverbal communication, and use of a "shared language"?

1.14 Are school leaders perceived by teachers as credible sources of knowledge regarding instructional improvement?

1.15 Do school leaders possess technical skill in conferencing, goal setting, instructional diagnosis, and classroom observation?

1.16 Are relations between teachers and school leaders characterized by trust and honesty?

1.17 Are school leaders able to approach supervision and evaluation with patience?

STAFF DEVELOPMENT

2.1 Does a written plan exist for ongoing, systematic staff development?

2.1.1 Does the staff-development plan include a clear statement of expected changes in teacher knowledge, behavior, understanding, and attitude?

2.1.2 Does the staff-development plan include a rationale for proposed changes in teacher performance?

2.1.3 Does the staff-development plan include a schedule of learning activities?

2.1.4 Does the staff-development plan include an inventory of resources needed to accomplish performance goals?

2.1.5 Does the staff-development plan include a monitoring system?

2.2 Has care been taken to involve in initial staff-development activities only those teachers who are receptive to them?

2.3 Has care been taken to protect teachers involved in staff development from additional demands on their time and energy?

2.4 Has care been taken to keep all teachers informed of staff-development activities?

INSTRUCTIONAL MANAGEMENT AND SUPPORT

3.1 Do policies exist regarding academic standards, grading and reporting of student performance, and retention/promotion decisions?

3.2 Do policies exist regarding the quantity and quality of time available for instruction?

3.3 Do policies exist regarding the grouping of students for instruction?

3.4 Do policies exist regarding the purposes and procedures for homework?

3.5 Do policies exist regarding the definition and verification of student absenteeism and the consequences for unexcused absences?

3.6 Do policies exist regarding the development and enforcement of school and classroom rules?

3.7 Have efforts been made to support a productive school climate through (1) recognition of student and teacher accomplishment, (2) student and teacher involvement in school decision making, and (3) opportunities for students to exercise meaningful responsibility?

RESOURCE MANAGEMENT

4.1 Do procedures exist to ensure the recruitment and selection of qualified instructional personnel?

4.2 Are instructional personnel assigned in ways that take advantage of their talents and contribute to the achievement of school-wide instructional goals?

4.3 Is instructional time allocated to curriculum content and to individual students in ways that promote school goals and equity?

4.4 Do procedures exist for selecting textbooks and other learning materials that are appropriate for students of different levels of ability?

4.5 Does a system exist that ensures teachers receive instructional materials in a timely fashion?

QUALITY CONTROL

5.1 Do provisions exist for monitoring the quality of instruction and instruction-related activities?

5.2 Do provisions exist for making data-based decisions related to instructional quality and for ensuring that decisions are implemented?

5.3 Are school leaders involved in planning and interpreting the results of quality-control efforts?

5.4 Has care been taken to establish school and instructional goals that are clear, reasonable, coherent, and well publicized?

5.5 Have provisions been made to share on a regular basis with teachers the results of externally mandated tests and to see that results are incorporated into plans for instructional improvement?

5.6 Are teachers aware of good performance-assessment practices and do they use this knowledge to assess student performance on a regular basis?

5.7 Are teacher assessments reviewed to assure that a broad range of student abilities is monitored?

5.8 Has care been taken not to require of teachers excessive amounts of paperwork and noninstructional activity?

5.9 Have constructive and meaningful ways of sharing data on student progress been developed?

5.10 Do provisions exist for the periodic evaluation of curricula, course materials, and special programs?

5.11 Are regular efforts made to assure that curriculum content is aligned to the content of tests?

5.12 Are course sequences and series of instructional objectives across grade levels periodically reviewed to determine compatibility and monitor duplication?

5.13 Are mechanisms in place for periodically assessing shool effectiveness and developing data-based school improvement goals?

5.14 Do provisions exist for monitoring the quality of school-improvement and staff-development projects?

COORDINATION AND TROUBLESHOOTING

6.1 Is planning used as an occasion to foster school-wide understanding and co-operation?

6.2 Have provisions been made for handling possible sources of disruption to school life?

6.3 Have provisions been made for clarifying the purposes of school meetings and establishing ground rules to ensure their effectiveness?

6.4 Have steps been taken to monitor school decision-making processes and to assess the quality of decisions?

6.5 Are staff members who are invited to participate in school decision making assured that they have real influence to improve life in classrooms?

6.6 Are efforts made to promote a sense of common purpose among staff members, students, and community?

6.7 Do conditions exist that facilitate the sharing of information concerning problems and potential problems?

6.8 Have formal mechanisms for troubleshooting student problems been established?

6.9 Are informal methods used on a regular basis to gather information regarding possible sources of trouble?

BIBLIOGRAPHY

Achilles, Charles M. "Forecast: Stormy Weather Ahead in Educational Administration," *Issues in Education,* Vol. 2, No. 2 (Fall 1984), pp. 127–135.

Adler, Mortimer J. *The Paideia Proposal: An Educational Manifesto.* New York: Macmillan, 1982.

———. *The Paideia Program: An Educational Syllabus.* New York: Macmillan, 1984.

Anderson, Sandra Lee. "Turning Around Junior Highs in the District of Columbia," *Educational Leadership,* Vol. 40, No. 3 (December 1982), pp. 38–40.

Argyris, Chris, and Donald A. Schön. *Theory in Practice: Increasing Professional Effectiveness.* San Francisco: Jossey-Bass, 1976.

Austin, David B., and Harry L. Brown. *Report of the Assistant Principalship.* Washington, D.C.: National Association of Secondary School Principals, 1970.

Bacharach, Samuel B., and Sharon C. Conley. "Educational Reform: A Managerial Agenda," *Phi Delta Kappan,* Vol. 67, No. 9 (May 1986), pp. 641–645.

Bacharach, Samuel, and Stephen Mitchell. "The Sources of Dissatisfaction in Educational Administration: A Role-Specific Analysis," *Educational Administration Quarterly,* Vol. 19, No. 1 (Winter 1983), pp. 101–128.

Barnes, Susan. *Synthesis of Selected Research on Teaching Findings.* Austin, Tex.: Research and Development Center for Teacher Education, 1981.

Barr, Rebecca, and Robert Dreeben. *How Schools Work.* Chicago: University of Chicago Press, 1983.

Barth, Roland. *Run School Run.* Cambridge: Harvard University Press, 1980.

Behr, George. "Test-wiseness: Using Test Information for Planning Instruction," paper presented at the Northwest Regional Educational Laboratory Conference on School Effectiveness, 1982.

Bennis, Warren. "The Artform of Leadership," *The Executive Mind.* Suresh Srivastva and Associates. San Francisco: Jossey-Bass, 1984.

Blumberg, Arthur. *Supervisiors & Teachers: A Private Cold War,* 2nd ed. Berkeley: McCutchan, 1980.

Blumberg, Arthur, and William Greenfield. *The Effective Principal.* Boston: Allyn & Bacon, 1980.

Bolton, Dale L. *Selection and Evaluation of Teachers.* Berkeley: McCutchan, 1973.

Borich, Gary D. *The Appraisal of Teaching.* Reading, Mass.: Addison-Wesley, 1977.

Bossert, S. T., D. C. Dwyer, B. Rowan, and Ginny V. Lee. "The Instructional Management Role of the Principal," *Educational Administration Quarterly,* Vol. 18, No. 3 (Summer 1982), pp. 34–64.

Boyer, Ernest L. *High School: A Report on Secondary Education in America.* New York: Harper & Row, 1983.

Bredeson, Paul V. "An Analysis of the Metaphorical Perspectives of School Principals," *Educational Administration Quarterly,* Vol. 21, No. 1 (Winter 1985), pp. 29–50.

Bridges, Edwin M. "The Nature of Leadership," *Educational Administration: The Developing Decades,* Luvern L. Cunningham, Walter G. Hack, and Raphael O. Nystrand (Eds.). Berkeley: McCutchan, 1977.

Bridges, Edwin M., and Barry Groves. *Managing the Incompetent Teacher.* Eugene, Ore.: ERIC Clearinghouse on Education Management, 1984.

Brieschke, Patricia A. "A Case Study of Teacher Role Enactment in an Urban Elementary School," *Educational Administration Quarterly,* Vol. 19, No. 4 (Fall 1983), pp. 59–83.

Brookover, Wilbur B., and Lawrence W. Lezotte. "Changes in School Characteristics Coincident with Changes in Student Achievement." East Lansing, Mich.: Institute for Research on Teaching, Michigan State University, May 1979.

Brooks, Harvey. "The Dilemmas of Engineering Education," *IEEE Spectrum* (February 1967), pp. 89–90.

Burns, James MacGregor. *The Power to Lead.* New York: Simon & Schuster, 1984.

Burstein, Leigh. "The Use of Existing Data Bases in Program Evaluation and School Improvement," *Educational Evaluation and Policy Analysis,* Vol. 6, No. 3 (Fall 1984), pp. 307–318.

Byrne, David R., Susan A. Hines, and Lloyd E. McCleary. *The Senior High School Principalship,* Vol. I. Reston, Va.: National Association of Secondary School Principals, 1978.

Calfee, Robert, and Roger Brown. "Grouping Students for Instruction," *Classroom Management,* Daniel L. Duke, (Ed.), The Seventy-eighth Yearbook of the National Society for the Study of Education. Chicago: University of Chicago Press, 1979.

Callahan, Raymond E. *Education and the Cult of Efficiency.* Chicago: University of Chicago Press, 1962.

Carol, Lila N., and LuVern L. Cunningham. "Views of Public Confidence in Education," *Issues in Education,* Vol. 2, No. 2 (Fall 1984), pp. 110–126.

Carroll, J. Gregory. "Faculty Self-evaluation," *Handbook of Teacher Evaluation,* Jason Millman (Ed.). Beverly Hills, Calif.: SAGE Publications, 1981.

Carroll, John B. "A Model of School Learning," *Teachers College Record,* Vol. 64, No. 4 (Spring 1963), pp. 723–733.

Chase, Larry. "Quality Circles in Education," *Educational Leadership,* Vol. 40, No. 5 (February 1983), pp. 18–25.

Clarizio, Harvey F., and George F. McCoy. *Behavior Disorders in Children,* 2nd ed. New York: Thomas Y. Crowell, 1976.

Cohen, Elizabeth G., Russel H. Miller, Anneke Bredo, and Kenneth Duckworth. "Principal Role and Teacher Morale under Varying Organizational Conditions." Stanford, Calif.: Stanford Center for Research and Development in Teaching, n.d.

Coleman, James S., et. al. *Equality of Educational Opportunity.* Washington, D.C.: U.S. Government Printing Office, 1966.

Combs, Arthur W., Donald L. Avila, and William W. Purkey. *Helping Relationships.* Boston: Allyn & Bacon, 1971.

Conant, James B. *The American High School Today.* New York: McGraw-Hill, 1959.

Cooper, James M. *Developing Skills for Instructional Supervision.* New York: Longman, 1984.

Council for Basic Education. "Making Do in the Classroom: A Report on the Misassignment of Teachers." Washington, D.C.: Council for Basic Education, 1985.

Courter, R. Linden, and Beatrice A. Ward. "Staff Development for School Improvement," *Staff Development,* Gary A. Griffin (Ed.), The Eighty-second Yearbook of the National Society for the Study of Education, Part II. Chicago: University of Chicago Press, 1983.

Crim, Alonzo A. "A Community of Believers," *Daedalus,* Vol. 110, No. 4 (Fall 1981), pp. 145–162.

Cuban, Larry. "Effective Schools: A Friendly But Cautionary Note," *Phi Delta Kappan,* Vol. 64, No. 10 (June 1983), pp. 695–696.

_____. *Urban School Chiefs Under Fire.* Chicago: University of Chicago Press, 1976.

Cyert, Richard M., and James G. March. *A Behavioral Theory of the Firm.* Englewood Cliffs, N.J.: Prentice-Hall, 1963.

Daft, Richard L. *Organizational Theory and Design.* St. Paul, Minn.: West, 1983.

Daniels, Abraham F., and Emil J. Haller. "Exposure to Instruction, Surplus Time, and Student Achievement: A Local Replication of the Harnischfeger and Wiley Research," *Educational Administration Quarterly,* Vol. 17, No. 1 (Winter 1981), pp. 48–68.

Daresh, John C., and Ching-Jen Liu. "High School Principals' Perceptions of Their Instructional Leadership Behavior," paper presented at the Annual Convention of the American Educational Research Association, 1985.

Darling-Hammond, Linda, Arthur E. Wise, and Sara R. Pease. "Teacher Evaluation in the Organizational Context: A Review of the Literature," *Review of Educational Research,* Vol. 53, No. 3 (Fall 1983), pp. 285–328.

De Jung, John, and Kenneth Duckworth. "New Study Looks at High School Absenteeism," *R&D Perspectives* (Summer/Fall 1985).

Deal, Terrence E., and Allan A. Kennedy. *Corporate Cultures.* Reading, Mass.: Addison-Wesley, 1982.

DeBevoise, Wynn. "Synthesis of Research on the Principal as Instructional Leader," *Educational Leadership,* Vol. 41, No. 5 (February 1984), pp. 14–20.

Dempsey, Richard A., and Henry P. Traverso. *Scheduling the Secondary School.* Reston, Va.: National Association of Secondary School Principals, 1983.

Denham, Carolyn, and Ann Lieberman. *Time to Learn.* Sacramento: California Commission for Teacher Preparation and Licensing, 1980.

Dentler, Robert A., and D. Catherine Baltzell. "Improving Principal Selection: Possibilities and Clues for Change," paper presented at the Annual Convention of the American Educational Research Association, 1983.

Donmoyer, Robert. "Cognitive Anthropology and Research on Effective Principals: Findings from a Study and Reflections on Its Methods," paper presented at the Annual Convention of the American Educational Research Association, 1984.

Dreher, Marian Jean, and Harry Singer. "Making Standardized Tests Work for You," *Principal,* Vol. 63, No. 4 (March 1984), pp. 20–24.

Dreikurs, Rudolf, and Loren Grey. *A New Approach to Discipline: Logical Consequences.* New York: Hawthorn Books, 1968.

Duke, Daniel L. "The Aesthetics of Leadership," *Educational Administration Quarterly,* Vol. 22, No. 1 (Winter 1986), pp. 7–27.

_____. (Ed.). *Classroom Management,* The Seventy-eighth Yearbook of the National Society for the Study of Education, Part II. Chicago: University of Chicago Press, 1979.

_____. "Data Curriculum Workers Need" in *Curriculum Theory.* Washington, D.C.: Association for Supervision and Curriculum Development, 1977.

_____. "Debriefing: A Tool for Curriculum Research and Course Improvement," *Journal of Curriculum Studies,* Vol. 9, No. 2 (1977), pp. 157–163.

_____. *Decision Making in an Era of Fiscal Instability.* Bloomington, Ind.: Phi Delta Kappa, 1984.

_____. *Managing Student Behavior Problems.* New York: Teachers College Press, 1980.

_____. *Teaching—The Imperiled Profession.* Albany, N.Y.: State University of New York Press, 1984.

_____. "Toward Responsible Innovation," *The Educational Forum,* Vol. 42, No. 3 (March 1978), pp. 351–372.

_____. *When Teachers and Researchers Cooperate: The Challenge of Collaborative Professional Development.* Stanford, Calif.: Stanford Center for Research and Development in Teaching, 1977.

Duke, Daniel L., and Jon S. Cohen. "Do Public Schools Have a Future? A Case Study of Retrenchment and Its Implications," *The Urban Review,* Vol. 15, No. 2 (1983), pp. 89–106.

Duke, Daniel L., Jon S. Cohen, and Roslyn Herman. "Running Faster to Stay in Place: New York City Schools Face Retrenchment," *Phi Delta Kappan,* Vol. 63, No. 1 (September 1981), pp. 13–17.

Duke, Daniel L., and Lyn Corno. "Evaluating Staff Development," *Staff Development/Organization Development,* Betty Dillon-Peterson (Ed.). Alexandria, Va.: Association for Supervision and Curriculum Development, 1981.

Duke, Daniel L., and Michael Imber. "Should Principals Be Required to Be Effective?" *School Organization,* Vol. 5, No. 2 (April/June 1985), pp. 125–146.

Duke, Daniel L., Nancy S. Isaacson, Richard Sagor, and Patricia Schmuck. "Transition to Leadership: An Investigation of the First Year of the Principalship," paper presented at the Annual Convention of the American Educational Research Association, 1985.

Duke, Daniel L., and Vernon F. Jones. "Two Decades of Discipline—Assessing the Development of an Educational Specialization," *Journal of Research and Development in Education,* Vol. 17, No. 4 (Summer 1984), pp. 25–35.

_____. "What Can Schools Do to Foster Student Responsibility?" *Theory into Practice,* Vol. 24, No. 4 (Fall 1985), pp. 277–285.

Duke, Daniel L., and Adrienne M. Meckel. "Disciplinary Roles in American Schools," *British Journal of Teacher Education,* Vol. 6, No. 1 (January 1980), pp. 37–50.

_____. "The Slow Death of a Public High School," *Phi Delta Kappan,* Vol. 61, No. 10 (June 1980), pp. 674–677.

_____. "Student Attendance Problems and School Organization: A Case Study," *Urban Education,* Vol. 15, No. 3 (October 1980), pp. 325–358.

Duke, Daniel L., and Cheryl Perry. "Can Alternative Schools Succeed Where Benjamin Spock, Spiro Agnew, and B. F. Skinner Have Failed?" *Adolescence,* Vol. 13, No. 51 (Fall 1978), pp. 375–392.

Duke, Daniel L., Beverly K. Showers, and Michael Imber. "Studying Shared Decision Making in Schools," *Organizational Behavior in Schools and School Districts,* Samuel B. Bacharach (Ed.). New York: Praeger, 1981.

_____. "Teachers and Shared Decision Making: The Costs and Benefits of Involvement," *Educational Administration Quarterly,* Vol. 16, No. 1 (Winter 1980), pp. 93–106.

Duke, Daniel L., and Richard J. Stiggins. "Evaluating the Performance of Principals—A Descriptive Study," *Educational Administration Quarterly,* Vol. 21, No. 4 (Fall 1985), pp. 71–98.

_____. *Five Keys to Growth Through Teacher Evaluation.* Portland, Ore.: Northwest Regional Educational Laboratory, 1985.

Duminuco, Vincent J. "Viewpoint," *The School Administrator* (March 1985), p. 80.

Edson, Sakre K. *Pushing the Limits: The Female Administrative Aspirant* (in press).

Education Commission of the States. *Action for Excellence.* N.c.: Education Commission of the States, 1983.

Education Research Service, *Class Size: A Summary of Research.* Arlington, Va.: Educational Research Service, 1978.

_____. *ERS Composite Indicator of Changes in Average Salaries and Wages Paid in Public Schools: Update 1980–81.* Arlington, Va.: Educational Research Service, 1981.

_____. "A Special Report: Polling the Principals," *Principal,* Vol. 64, No. 4 (March 1985), pp. 54–64.

Edmonds, Ronald. "Programs of School Improvement: An Overview," *Educational Leadership,* Vol. 40, No. 3 (December 1982), pp. 4–11.

Eisner, Elliot W. *The Educational Imagination.* New York: Macmillan, 1979.

Emmer, Edmund T., Carolyn M. Evertson, Julie P. Sanford, Barbara S. Clements, and Murray E. Worsham. *Classroom Management for Secondary Teachers.* Englewood Cliffs, N.J.: Prentice-Hall, 1984.

English, Fenwick W. *Quality Control in Curriculum Development.* Arlington, Va.: American Association of School Administrators, 1978.

Epstein, Joyce L. "A Question of Merit: Principals' and Parents' Evaluations of Teachers," paper presented at the Annual Convention of the American Educational Research Association, 1984.

Ethridge, Samuel B. "Impact of the 1954 Brown vs. Topeka Board of Education Decision on Black Educators," *The Negro Educational Review,* Vol. 30, No. 4 (October 1979), pp. 217–232.

Firestone, William A., and Bruce L. Wilson. "Using Bureaucratic and Cultural Linkages to Improve Instruction: The Principal's Contribution," *Educational Administration Quarterly,* Vol. 21, No. 2 (Spring 1985), pp. 7–30.

Fisher, Charles W., David C. Berliner, Nikola N. Filby, Richard Marliave, Leonard S. Cahen, and Marilyn M. Dishaw. "Teaching Behaviors, Academic Learning Time, and Student Achievement: An Overview," *Time to Learn,* Carolyn Denham and Ann Lieberman (Eds.). Sacramento, Calif.: California Commission for Teacher Preparation and Licensing, 1980.

Fox, D. J., L. Flaum, F. Hill, V. Barnes, and N. Shapiro. "More Effective Schools Program: Evaluation of ESEA Title I Projects in New York City, 1967–68." New York: Center for Urban Education, 1968.

Frechtling, J. A. "Alternative Methods for Determining Effectiveness: Congruence and Divergence," paper presented at the Annual Convention of the American Educational Research Association, 1982.

Fry, Ronald E., and William A. Pasmore. "Strengthening Management Education," *The Executive Mind,* Suresh Srivastva and Associates. San Francisco: Jossey-Bass, 1984.

Fuller, Frances F., and Oliver H. Bown. "Becoming a Teacher," *Teacher Education,* Kevin Ryan (Ed.). The Seventy-fourth Yearbook of the National Society for the Study of Education. Chicago: University of Chicago Press, 1975.

Fuller, Frances F., and B. A. Manning. "Self-confrontation Reviewed: A Conceptualization for Video Playback in Teacher Education," *Review of Educational Research,* Vol. 43, No. 4 (Fall 1973), pp. 469–528.

Gall, Meredith D. "Using Staff Development to Improve Schools," *R&D Perspectives,* Center for Educational Policy and Management, University of Oregon (Winter 1983).

Gall, Meredith D., Glen Fielding, Del Schalock, W. W. Charters, and Jerzy M. Wilc-
zynski. "Involving the Principal in Teachers' Staff Development: Effects on the
Quality of Mathematics Instruction in Elementary Schools." Eugene, Ore.: Research and Development Center for Educational Policy and Management, University of Oregon, 1984.

Gallagher, Karen S., Michael Riley, and Patrick Murphy. "The Instructional Management Behavior of the High School Principal," paper presented at the Annual Convention of the American Educational Research Association, 1985.

Gersten, Russell and Douglas Carnine. "Administrative and Supervisory Support
Functions for the Implementation of Effective Programs for Low Income Students," Eugene, Ore.: Center for Educational Policy and Management, University
of Oregon, 1981.

Gersten, Russell, Douglas Carnine, and Susan Green. "The Principal as Instructional
Leader: A Second Look," *Educational Leadership,* Vol. 40, No. 3 (December 1982),
pp. 47–49.

Glasman, Naftaly S. *Evaluation-based Leadership* (in press).

———. "The School Principal as Evaluator," *Administrator's Notebook,* Vol. 31, No. 2.

———. "Student Achievement and the School Principal," *Educational Evaluation and
Policy Analysis,* Vol. 6, No. 3 (Fall 1984), pp. 283–296.

Glass, Gene V., and M. L. Smith. "Meta-analysis of Research on the Relationship of
Class Size and Achievement," *Educational Evaluation and Policy Analysis,* Vol. 1,
No. 1 (1978), pp. 2–16.

Glatthorn, Allan A. *Differentiated Supervision.* Alexandria, Va.: Association for Supervision and Curriculum Development, 1984.

Glickman, Carl D. *Supervision of Instruction: A Developmental Approach.* Boston: Allyn
& Bacon, 1985.

Good, Thomas L., and Jere E. Brophy. *Looking in Classrooms,* 3rd ed. New York:
Harper & Row, 1984.

Good, Thomas L., and Douglas A. Grouws. "Teaching Effects: A Process-Product
Study in Fourth-Grade Mathematics Classrooms," *Journal of Teacher Education,*
Vol. 28 (May–June 1977), pp. 49–54.

Goodlad, John I. *A Place Called School.* New York: McGraw-Hill, 1984.

Gordon, Thomas. *Leader Effectiveness Training.* New York: Bantam, 1977.

Gouldner, Alvin. *Studies in Leadership.* New York: Harper & Brothers, 1950.

Gowan, D. Bob. "Two Philosophers View Education," *Educational Evaluation and Policy Analysis,* Vol. 2, No. 2 (Summer 1980), pp. 67–70.

Greenfield, William D. "Being and Becoming a Principal: Responses to Work Contexts
and Socialization Processes," paper presented at the Annual Convention of the
American Educational Research Association, 1985.

———. "The Moral Socialization of School Administrators: Informal Role Learning
Outcomes," *Educational Administration Quarterly,* Vol. 21, No. 4 (Fall 1985), pp.
99–119.

Guy, Mary E. *Professionals in Organizations.* New York: Praeger, 1985.

Haertel, Geneva D., Herbert J. Walberg, and Thomas Weinstein. "Psychological
Models of Educational Performance: A Theoretical Synthesis of Constructs," *Review of Educational Research,* Vol. 53, No. 1 (Spring 1983), pp. 75–91.

Hagar, James L., and L. E. Scarr. "Effective Schools—Effective Principals: How to Develop Both," *Educational Leadership,* Vol. 40, No. 5 (February 1983), pp. 38–40.

Hall, Eddie D., and Ann B. Madison. "A Step Beyond School Effectiveness Research:
Planning, Implementing, Maintaining, and Evaluating a School Improvement
Program," *The Effective School Report,* Vol.. 3, No. 3 (March 1985), pp. 1–2.

Hall, Gene E., and Shirley M. Hord. *Change in Schools: Facilitating the Process* (in press).

Hall, Gene E., and Susan F. Loucks, "Teacher Concerns as a Basis for Facilitating and Personalizing Staff Development," *Teachers College Record,* Vol. 80, No. 1 (September 1978), pp. 36–53.

Hall, Julia, and Paul Gerber. "The Awarding of Carnegie Units to Learning Disabled High School Students: A Policy Study," *Educational Evaluation and Policy Analysis,* Vol. 7, No. 3 (Fall 1985), pp. 229–235.

Hallinger, Philip. "Assessing the Instructional Management Behavior of Principals," paper presented at the Annual Convention of the American Educational Research Association, 1983.

Hallinger, Philip, and Joseph Murphy. "Instructional Leadership and School Socioeconomic Status: A Preliminary Investigation," *Administrator's Notebook,* Vol. 31, No. 5.

Hallinger, Philip, Joseph Murphy, Marsha Weil, Richard P. Mesa, and Alexis Mitman. "Identifying the Specific Practices, Behaviors for Principals," *NASSP Bulletin,* Vol. 67, No. 463 (May 1983), pp. 83–91.

Halpin, Andrew W. "Muted Language," *The School Review,* Vol. 65, No. 1 (Spring 1960), pp. 85–104.

Hamilton, Stephen F., and Albert Mamary. "Assessing the Effectiveness of Program Delivery," *NASSP Bulletin,* Vol. 67, No. 465 (October 1983), pp. 39–44.

Hampel, Robert L. "The American High School Today: James Bryant Conant's Reservations and Reconsiderations," *Phi Delta Kappan,* Vol. 64, No. 9 (May 1983), pp. 607–612.

Hannay, Lynne M., and Kelline W. Stevens. "The Indirect Instructional Leadership Role of a Principal," paper presented at the Annual Convention of the American Educational Research Association, 1984.

Hanson, E. Mark. *Educational Administration and Organizational Behavior,* 2nd ed. Boston: Allyn & Bacon, 1985.

Hart, Ann Weaver. "Leadership Succession as Social Validation: The View from Inside the Principalship," paper presented at the Annual Convention of the American Educational Research Association, 1985.

Hawkinson, Howard. "Hatch School—Not at Risk," *Phi Delta Kappan,* Vol. 66, No. 3 (November 1984), pp. 181–182.

Herman, Joan L., and Donald W. Dorr-Bremme. "Teachers and Testing: Implications from a National Study," paper presented at the Annual Convention of the American Educational Research Association, 1984.

Horowitz, R. "Effects of the Open Classroom," *Educational Environments and Effects: Evaluation, Policy, and Productivity,* Herbert J. Walberg (Ed.). Berkeley: McCutchan, 1979.

Hoyle, John R. "Programs in Educational Administration and the AASA Preparation Guidelines," *Educational Administration Quarterly,* Vol. 21, No. 1 (Winter 1985), pp. 71–93.

Hunter, Madeline. *Mastery Teaching.* El Segundo, Calif.: Tip, 1983.

_____. "What's Wrong with Madeline Hunter?" *Educational Leadership,* Vol. 42, No. 5 (February 1985), pp. 57–60.

Imber, Michael. "Increased Decision Making Involvement for Teachers: Ethical and Practical Considerations," *Journal of Educational Thought,* Vol. 17, No. 1 (April 1983), pp. 36–42.

Jackson, Philip W. *Life in Classrooms.* New York: Holt, Rinehart and Winston, Inc., 1968.

Jackson, Philip W. "Lonely at the Top: Observations on the Genesis of Administrative Isolation," *School Review,* Vol. 85, No. 3 (May 1977), pp. 425–432.

Jackson, Shirley A., David M. Logsdon, and Nancy E. Taylor. "Instructional Leadership Behaviors," *Urban Education,* Vol. 18, No. 1 (April 1983), pp. 59–70.

Janis, Irving L. *Victims of Groupthink.* Boston: Houghton Mifflin, 1972.

Jentz, Barry C., and Joan W. Wofford. *Leadership and Learning.* New York: McGraw-Hill, 1979.

Johnson, James R. "Synthesis of Research on Grade Retention and Social Promotion," *Educational Leadership,* Vol. 41, No. 8 (May 1984), pp. 66–68.

Johnston, J. Howard, and Larry C. Holt. "Data-based Instructional Supervision and Self-assessment," *NASSP Bulletin,* Vol. 67, No. 463 (May 1983), pp. 22–33.

Jones, Meredith Howe. "Anatomy of an Evaluation," *Principal,* Vol. 61, No. 1 (September 1981), pp. 48–52.

Joyce, Bruce, and Marsha Weil. *Models of Teaching.* Englewood Cliffs, N.J.: Prentice/Hall International, 1980.

Karweit, Nancy. "Time-on-task Reconsidered: Synthesis of Research on Time and Learning," *Educational Leadership,* Vol. 41, No. 8 (May 1984), pp. 32–35.

Kelleher, Paul. "A Bad Beginning as Principal," *Entry,* Barry Jentz (Ed.). New York: McGraw-Hill, 1982.

Kerr, Stephen T. "Generalists Versus Specialists," *Organizational Behavior in Schools and School Districts,* Samuel B. Bacharach (Ed.). New York: Praeger, 1981.

Kierstead, Janet. "Direct Instruction and Experiential Approaches: Are They Really Mutually Exclusive?" *Educational Leadership,* Vol. 42, No. 8 (May 1985), pp. 25–30.

Kimbrough, Ralph B. *Ethics: A Course of Study for Educational Leaders.* Arlington, Va.: American Association of School Administrators, 1985.

Kirst, Michael W. "Policy Implications of Individual Differences and the Common Curriculum," *Individual Differences and the Common Curriculum,* Gary D. Fenstermacher and John I. Goodlad (Eds.). The Eighty-second Yearbook of the National Society for the Study of Education, Part I. Chicago: University of Chicago Press, 1983.

Kmetz, John T., and Donald J. Willower. "Elementary School Principals' Work Behavior," *Educational Administration Quarterly,* Vol. 18, No. 4 (Fall 1982), pp. 62–78.

Knapp, M. S. "Toward the Study of Teacher Evaluation as an Organizational Process: A Review of Current Research and Practice." Menlo Park, Calif.: SRI International, 1982.

Komoski, P. Kenneth. "Instructional Materials Will Not Improve Until We Change the System," *Educational Leadership,* Vol. 42, No. 7 (April 1985), pp. 31–37.

Kroeze, David J. "Effective Principals as Instructional Leaders: New Directions for Research," *Administrator's Notebook,* Vol. 30, No. 9 (1984).

Leiter, Jeffrey, and James S. Brown. "Determinants of Elementary School Grading," *Sociology of Education,* Vol. 58, No. 3 (July 1985), pp. 166–180.

Leithwood, Kenneth A., and Mary Stager. "Differences in Problem-solving Processes Used by Moderately and Highly Effective Principals," paper presented at the Annual Meeting of the American Educational Research Association, 1986.

LeMahieu, Paul G. "The Effects on Achievement and Instructional Content of a Program of Student Monitoring through Frequent Testing," *Educational Evaluation and Policy Analysis,* Vol. 6, No. 2 (Summer 1984), pp. 175–187.

Lewy, Arieh (Ed.). *Handbook of Curriculum Evaluation.* New York: Longman, 1977.

Lightfoot, Sara Lawrence. *The Good High School.* New York: Basic Books, 1983.

Lipham, James M. *Effective Principal, Effective School.* Reston, Va.: National Association of Secondary School Principals, 1981.

_____. "Leadership of the Principal for Educational Improvement," paper presented at the Northwest Regional Educational Laboratory, 1982.

Lipham, James M., James A. Hoeh, and Robb E. Rankin. *The Principalship: Concepts, Competencies, and Cases.* New York: Longman, 1985.

Lipsitz, Joan. *Successful Schools for Young Adolescents.* New Brunswick, N.J.: Transaction, 1984.

Little, Judith Warren. "Finding the Limits and Possibilities of Instructional Leadership: Some Possibilities for Practical and Collaborative Work with Principals" (unpublished paper).

_____. *School Success and Staff Development.* Boulder, Colo.: Center for Action Research, Inc., 1981.

_____. "Seductive Images and Organizational Realities in Professional Development," *Teachers College Record,* Vol. 86, No. 1 (Fall 1984), pp. 84–102.

Little, Judith Warren, and Thomas D. Bird. "Is There Instructional Leadership in High Schools? First Findings from a Study of Secondary School Administrators and Their Influence on Teachers' Professional Norms," paper presented at the Annual Convention of the American Educational Research Association, 1984.

Lortie, Dan C. *Schoolteacher.* Chicago: University of Chicago Press, 1975.

Manatt, Richard. "Teacher Performance Evaluation—Practical Application of Research," Occasional Paper 82-1. Ames, Iowa: Iowa State University, 1982.

March, James G. "American Public School Administration: A Short Analysis," *School Review,* Vol. 86, No. 2 (February 1978), pp. 217–250.

Marcus, Alfred C., *et. al.* "Administrative Leadership in a Sample of Successful Schools from the National Evaluation of the Emergency School Aid Act," paper presented at the Annual Convention of the American Educational Research Association, 1976.

Martin, William J., and Donald Willower. "The Managerial Behavior of High School Principals," *Educational Administration Quarterly,* Vol. 17, No. 1 (Winter 1981), pp. 69–90.

Maslow, Abraham H. *Motivation and Personality,* 2nd ed. New York: Harper & Row, 1970.

Mazzarella, JoAnn. "Instructional Leadership: Profile of an Elementary School Principal," *Oregon School Study Council Bulletin,* Vol. 26, No. 3 (November 1982).

McCormack-Larkin, Maureen. "Ingredients of a Successful School Effectiveness Project," *Educational Leadership,* Vol. 42, No. 6 (March 1985), pp. 31–37.

McCormack-Larkin, Maureen, and William J. Kritek. "Milwaukee's Project RISE," *Educational Leadership,* Vol. 40, No. 3 (December 1982), pp. 16–21.

McCullough, Richard A. "Toward a Description of the Occupational Ethos of the Senior High School Principalship," paper presented at the Annual Convention of the American Educational Research Association, 1981.

McFaul, Shirley A., and James M. Cooper. "Peer Clinical Supervision: Theory vs. Reality," *Educational Leadership,* Vol. 41, No. 7 (April 1984), pp. 4–9.

McLaughlin, Milbrey Wallin. "Teacher Evaluation and School Improvement," *Teachers College Record,* Vol. 86, No. 1 (Fall 1984), pp. 193–207.

Mehan, Hugh, J. Lee Meihls, Alma Hertweck, and Margaret S. Crowdes. "Identifying Handicapped Students," *Organizational Behavior in Schools and School Districts,* Samuel B. Bacharach (Ed.). New York: Praeger, 1981.

Mertins, Herman (Ed.). *Professional Standards and Ethics.* Washington, D.C.: American Society for Public Administration, 1979.

Miskel, Cecil, and Dorothy Cosgrove. "Leader Succession in School Settings," paper presented at the Annual Convention of the American Educational Research Association, 1984.

Morris, Van Cleve, Robert L. Crowson, Cynthia Porter-Gehrie, and Emanuel Hurwitz. *Principals in Action.* Columbus, Ohio: Charles E. Merrill, 1984.

_____. *The Urban Principal.* Chicago: College of Education, University of Illinois at Chicago Circle, 1981.

Murphy, Joseph F., Marsha Weil, Philip Hallinger, and Alexis Mitman. "Academic Press: Translating High Expectations into School Policies and Classroom Practices," *Educational Leadership,* Vol. 40, No. 3 (December 1982), pp. 22–26.

Muther, Connie. "What Every Textbook Evaluator Should Know," *Educational Leadership,* Vol. 42, No. 7 (April 1985), pp. 4–8.

National Association of Elementary School Principals. *Standards for Quality Elementary Schools.* Reston, Va.: National Association of Elementary School Principals, 1984.

National Center for Educational Statistics. *The Condition of Education: A Statistical Report.* Washington, D.C.: National Center for Educational Statistics, 1979.

National Commission on Excellence in Education. *A Nation at Risk: The Imperative for Educational Reform.* Washington, D.C.: U.S. Government Printing Office, 1983.

National Education Association. *Teacher Opinion Poll.* Washington, D.C.: National Education Association, 1979.

Natriello, Gary. "Problems in the Evaluation of Students and Student Disengagement from Secondary Schools," *Journal of Research and Development in Education,* Vol. 17, No. 4 (1984), pp. 14–24.

Natriello, Gary, and Sanford M. Dornbusch. *Teacher Evaluation Standards and Student Effort.* New York: Longman, 1984.

Nixon, Richard M. *Leaders.* New York: Warner, 1982.

Noli, Pamela. "A Principal Implements BTES," *Time to Learn,* Carolyn Denham and Ann Lieberman (Eds.). Sacramento, Calif.: California Commission on Teacher Preparation and Licensure, 1980.

Orlich, Donald C. "Establishing Effective In-Service Programs by Taking . . . 'AAIM'," *The Clearing House,* Vol. 53, No. 1 (September 1979), pp. 53–55.

Ortiz, Flora Ida. "Midcareer Socialization of Educational Administrators," *Review of Educational Research,* Vol. 48, No. 1 (Winter 1978), pp. 121–132.

Ouchi, William. *Theory Z.* Reading, Mass: Addison-Wesley, 1981.

Pambookian, H. S. "Initial Level of Student Evaluation of Instruction as a Source of Influence on Instructor Change after Feedback," *Journal of Educational Psychology,* Vol. 66, No. 1 (February 1974), pp. 52–56.

Patterson, J. P. *A Descriptive Analysis of the Instructional Leadership Activities of Elementary Principals* (Doctoral dissertation, University of Oregon, 1977).

Penick, John E., and Robert E. Yager. "The Search for Excellence in Science Education," *Phi Delta Kappan,* Vol. 64, No. 9 (May 1983), pp. 621–624.

Peters, Thomas J., and Robert H. Waterman. *In Search of Excellence: Lessons from America's Best-Run Companies.* New York: Harper & Row, 1982.

Peterson, Kent D. "Mechanisms of Administrative Control over Managers in Educational Organizations," *Administrative Science Quarterly,* Vol. 29, No. 4 (December 1984), pp. 573–597.

Peterson, Penelope L., Susan R. Swing, Kevin D. Stark, and Gregory A. Waas. "Students' Cognitions and Time on Task during Mathematics Instruction," *American Educational Research Journal,* Vol. 21, No. 3 (Fall 1984), pp. 487–515.

Pharis, William L., and Sally Banks Zakariya. *The Elementary School Principalship in 1978: A Research Study.* Arlington, Va.: National Association of Elementary School Principals, 1979.

Phi Delta Kappa. *Why Do Some Urban Schools Succeed?* Bloomington, Ind.: Phi Delta Kappa, 1980.

Plisko, Valena White, and Joyce D. Stern. *The Condition of Education, 1985 Edition.* Washington, D.C.: U.S. Government Printing Office, 1985.

Popham, W. James. "The Evaluation of Teachers: A Mission Ahead of Its Measures," paper presented to the Annual Convention of the American Educational Research Association, 1985.

Posner, George J., and Alan N. Rudnitsky. *Course Design.* New York: Longman, 1978.

Prolman, Sandra. "Gender, Career Paths, and Administrative Perceptions," *Administrator's Notebook,* Vol. 30, No. 5 (1982).

Purkey, William Watson. *Self-Concept and School Achievement.* Englewood Cliffs, N.J.: Prentice-Hall, 1970.

Purkey, William Watson, and John M. Novak. *Inviting School Success,* 2nd ed. Belmont, Calif.: Wadsworth, 1984.

Ranbom, Sheppard. "Focus on Leader's Role Sparks Concern over Training, Selection," *Education Week* (Feb. 22, 1984), pp. 8–9.

Reich, Robert B. *The Next American Frontier.* New York: Times Books, 1983.

Report of the National Advisory Commission on Civil Disorders. New York: Bantam, 1968.

Rice, Berkeley. "Performance Review: The Job Nobody Likes," *Psychology Today,* Vol. 19, No. 9 (September 1985), pp. 30–36.

Rist, Ray C. "Student Social Class and Teacher Expectations: The Self-fulfilling Prophecy in Ghetto Education," *Harvard Educational Review,* Vol. 40, No. 3 (August 1970), pp. 411–451.

Rosenshine, Barak. "Teaching Functions in Instructional Programs," *The Elementary School Journal,* Vol. 83, No. 4 (1983), pp. 335–351.

Rowan, Brian. "Instructional Management in Historical Perspective: Evidence on Differentiation in School Districts," *Educational Administration Quarterly,* Vol. 18, No. 1 (Winter 1982), pp. 43–59.

Rowan, Brian, and Charles E. Denk. "Management Succession, School Socioeconomic Context, and Basic Skills Achievement," *American Educational Research Journal,* Vol. 21, No. 3 (Fall 1984), pp. 517–537.

Rowan, Brian, David Dwyer, and Steven Bossert. "Methodological Considerations in Studies of Effective Principals." San Francisco: Far West Laboratory for Educational Research and Development, 1984.

Rubin, Stephen E., and William G. Spady. "Achieving Excellence through Outcome-based Instructional Delivery," *Educational Leadership,* Vol. 41, No. 8 (May 1984), pp. 37–44.

Russell, James S., James E. White, and Steven D. Maurer. "Effective and Ineffective Behaviors of Secondary School Principals Linked with School Effectiveness," paper presented at the Annual Convention of the American Educational Research Association, 1985.

Rutherford, William L. "School Principals as Effective Leaders," *Phi Delta Kappan, Vol. 67, No. 1 (September 1985), pp. 31–34.*

Rutter, Michael, Barbara Maughan, Peter Mortimore, and Janet Ouston. Fifteen Thousand Hours. Cambridge, Mass.: Harvard University Press, 1979.

Sarason, Seymour B. *The Culture of the School and the Problem of Change.* Boston: Allyn & Bacon, 1971.

Schein, Edgar H. *Organizational Culture and Leadership.* San Francisco: Jossey-Bass, 1985.

———. "Organizational Socialization and the Profession of Management," *Industrial Management Review,* Vol. 9, No. 2 (Winter 1968), pp. 1–16.

Schmitt, Neal, Raymond Noe, Ronni Meritt, Michael Fitzgerald, and Cathy Jorgensen. "Criterion-related and Content Validity of the NASSP Assessment Center." East Lansing, Mich.: Department of Psychology, Michigan State University, n.d.

Schmuck, Richard A., Philip J. Runkel, Jane H. Arends, and Richard I. Arends. *The Second Handbook of Organization Development in Schools.* Palo Alto, Calif.: Mayfield, 1977.

Schön, Donald A. *The Reflective Practitioner.* New York: Basic Books, 1983.

Sergiovanni, Thomas J. *Handbook for Effective Department Leadership,* 2nd ed. Boston: Allyn & Bacon, 1984.

Shakeshaft, Charol. "Strategies for Overcoming Barriers to Women in Educational Administration," *Handbook for Achieving Sex Equity Through Education,* Susan S. Klein (Ed.). Baltimore: Johns Hopkins University Press, 1985.

Shoemaker, Joan, and Hugh W. Fraser. "What Principals Can Do: Some Implications from Studies of Effective Schooling," *Phi Delta Kappan,* Vol. 63, No. 3 (November 1981), pp. 178–182.

Showers, Beverly. "Teachers Coaching Teachers," *Educational Leadership,* Vol. 42, No. 7 (April 1985), pp. 43–48.

Slavin, Robert. "Cooperative Learning," *Review of Educational Research,* Vol. 50, No. 3 (Fall 1980), pp. 315–342.

Smith, Charles R., and Rodney Muth. "Instructional Leadership and School Effectiveness," paper presented at the Annual Convention of the American Educational Research Association, 1985.

Smith, Louis M., and Pat M. Keith. *Anatomy of Educational Innovation.* New York: John Wiley & Sons, 1971.

Sparks, Georgea Mohlman. "Synthesis of Research on Staff Development for Effective Teaching," *Educational Leadership,* Vol. 41, No. 2 (November 1983), pp. 65–72.

Sprinthall, Norman A., and Lois Thies-Sprinthall. "The Teacher as an Adult Learner: A Cognitive-Developmental View," *Staff Development,* Gary A. Griffin (Ed.). The Eighty-second Yearbook of the National Society for the Study of Education, Part II. Chicago: University of Chicago Press, 1983.

Squires, David A., William G. Huitt, and John K. Segars. *Effective Schools and Classrooms: A Research-Based Perspective.* Alexandria, Va.: Association for Supervision and Curriculum Development, 1984.

Stallings, Jane. "What Research Has to Say to Administrators of Secondary Schools about Effective Teaching and Staff Development," paper presented at the 1981 Conference, "Creating Conditions for Effective Teaching," Eugene, Ore.

Stallings, Jane, and D. Kaskowitz. *Follow Through Classroom Observation Evaluation 1972–1973.* Menlo Park, Calif.: Stanford Research Institute, 1974.

Stiggins, Richard J. "Improving Assessment Where It Means the Most: In the Classroom," *Educational Leadership,* Vol. 43, No. 2 (October 1985), pp. 69–74.

Stiggins, Richard J., and Nancy J. Bridgeford. "The Ecology of Classroom Assessment," *Journal of Educational Measurement,* Vol. 22, No. 4 (Winter 1985), pp. 271–286.

———. "Performance Assessment for Teacher Development," *Educational Evaluation and Policy Analysis,* Vol. 7, No. 1 (Spring 1985), pp. 85–97.

Strike, Kenneth, and Barry Bull. "Fairness and the Legal Context of Teacher Evaluation," *Handbook of Teacher Evaluation*, Jason Millman (Ed.). Beverly Hills, Calif.: Sage, 1981.

Sussman, Leila. *Tales out of School*. Philadelphia: Temple University Press, 1977.

Sutherland, Robert L. "Can an Adult Change?" *The Teacher as a Person*, 2nd Ed., Luiz F. S. Natalicio and Carl F. Hereford (Eds.). Dubuque, Iowa: Wm. C. Brown, 1971.

Sweeney, James. "Research Synthesis on Effective School Leadership," *Educational Leadership*, Vol. 39, No. 5 (February 1982), pp. 346–352.

Taylor, Frederick W. *Scientific Management*. New York: Harper, 1911.

Teacher Education Conference Board. *The Effective Teacher*. Albany, N.Y.: Teacher Education Conference Board, 1981.

Theodorson, George A., and Achilles G. Theodorson. *A Modern Dictionary of Sociology*. New York: Barnes & Noble, 1979.

Thompson, June E., Sanford M. Dornbusch, and Richard W. Scott. "Failures of Communication in the Evaluation of Teachers by Principals," Technical Report No. 43. Stanford, Calif.: Stanford Center for Research and Development on Teaching, 1975.

Tom, Alan R. *Teaching as a Moral Craft*. New York: Longman, 1984.

Tulley, Michael A. "A Descriptive Study of the Intents of State-level Textbook Adoption Processes," *Educational Evaluation and Policy Analysis*, Vol. 7, No. 3 (Fall 1985), pp. 289–308.

Tyack, David B., and Robert Cummings. "Leadership in American Public Schools before 1954," *Educational Administration: The Developing Decades*, LuVern L. Cunningham, Walter G. Hack, and Raphael O. Nystrand (Eds.). Berkeley: McCutchan, 1977.

Tyack, David B., and Elisabeth Hansot. *Managers of Virtue*. New York: Basic Books, 1982.

Valentine, Jerry, Donald C. Clark, Neal C. Nickerson, and James W. Keefe. *The Middle Level Principalship*, Vol. I, A Survey of Middle Level Principals and Programs. Reston, Va.: National Association of Secondary School Principals, 1981.

Valentine, Jerry, and Thomas E. Moeller. "The Relationship between Programmatic Characteristics of Middle Level Schools and the Competencies of the Principals of Those Schools," (unpublished paper).

Vance, Victor S., and Phillip C. Schlechty. "The Distribution of Academic Ability in the Teaching Force: Policy Implication," *Phi Delta Kappan*, Vol. 64, No. 1 (September 1982), pp. 22–27.

Walberg, Herbert J. "Educational Climates," *Improving Educational Standards and Productivity*, Herbert J. Walberg (Ed.). Berkeley: McCutchan, 1982.

Wayson, William W., et. al. *Handbook for Developing Schools with Good Discipline*. Bloomington, Ind.: Phi Delta Kappa, 1982.

Weaver, Frances, and Jeffry Gordon. "Staff Development Needs of Department Heads," *Educational Leadership*, Vol. 36, No. 8 (May 1979), pp. 578–580.

Weick, Karl E. "Educational Organizations as Loosely Coupled Systems," *Administrative Science Quarterly*, Vol. 21, No. 1 (March 1976), pp. 1–19.

Weisberg, Alan. *Five Urban High Schools*. Palo Alto, Calif.: Bay Area Research Group, 1981.

Wise, Arthur E., Linda Darling-Hammond, Milbrey W. McLaughlin, and Harriet T. Bernstein. *Case Studies for Teacher Evaluation: A Study of Effective Practices*. Santa Monica, Calif.: Rand, 1984.

Wittrock, M. D., and A. A. Lumsdaine. "Instructional Psychology," *Annual Review of Psychology*, Vol. 28 (1977), pp. 417–459.

Wlodkowski, Raymond J. *Enhancing Adult Motivation to Learn.* San Francisco: Jossey-Bass, 1985.

Wolcott, Harry F. *The Man in the Principal's Office.* New York: Holt, Rinehart & Winston, 1973.

Yalom, Irvin D. *Existential Psychology.* New York: Basic Books, 1980.

Yukl, Gary A. *Leadership in Organizations.* Englewood Cliffs, N.J.: Prentice-Hall, 1981.

Zappulla, E. *Evaluating Administrative Performance: Current Trends and Techniques.* Belmont, Calif.: Star, 1983.

INDEX

Instructional feedback, 63
Instructional improvement, 1, 6, 13, 18, 27, 47–48, 50, 57, 66, 70, 82, 87, 117, 131, 138, 148, 158, 198, 205, 210, 212, 222, 225–226, 228, 231, 244, 255, 259, 261, 270, 273, 274–275
Instructional leadership, 4–7, 42, 44, 48–49, 51, 70, 72–84, 89, 90, 93, 94, 99, 105, 147, 159, 169, 171, 200, 255, 260, 261, 267, 269–270, 272, 273, 275
Instructional Leadership Behavior Questionnaire, 78
Instructional Leadership Survey, 77
Instructional management, 74–77, 81–84, 182–198
Instructional Management Rating Scale, 74–75, 77
Instructional objectives, 62, 63, 67, 77, 122, 184, 221–222, 229–230
Instructional planning, 62–67, 169–171
Instructional support, 81–84, 182, 198–200
Internal integration, 282–283
Interpersonal relations, 144–145, 162, 179, 244, 246–247, 248, 249–250, 268
Invitational teaching, 60–62

Janis, Irving, 248
Job satisfaction, 16

Kirst, Michael, 183–184

Leadership, 5, 12, 27, 51, 99, 144, 148, 216, 250, 251, 252, 264, 268, 283, 291
Lesson plans, 62, 67, 112–113, 119, 129, 152, 206, 222, 226
Lezotte, Lawrence, 17, 25, 72–73
Lightfoot, Sara Lawrence, 13, 87, 184–185, 251
Linkage, 237, 244, 250
Lipham, James M., 21–22, 280
Lipsitz, Joan, 87, 93
Little, Judith, 79–80, 122, 145, 147, 162–163, 166, 178, 200
Loose coupling, 25, 132, 237
Lortie, Dan, 248–249

Los Angeles Unified School District, 229
Loyalty, 18, 39

Management, 12, 43, 50–51, 163, 253, 270
Management by objectives, 14–15
March, James, 12, 50–51
Maslow, Abraham, 141, 273
Mastery learning, 63–64, 166, 171–173, 224–225
Meaning, 11, 23, 111, 139, 158, 216, 224, 289
Milwaukee (WI) Public Schools, 90–93, 179, 190
Miskel, Cecil, 264, 279
Monitoring Achievement in Pittsburgh, 222
Motivational teaching, 60–62

National Advisory Commission on Civil Disorders, 3
National Association of Elementary School Principals, 230, 267–268
National Association of Secondary School Principals, 43, 47, 268
National Commission on Excellence in Education, 3, 50
National Science Teachers Association, 228
New York City schools, 215
Nixon, Richard M., 13
Northwest Regional Educational Laboratory, 113, 230–231
Null curriculum, 208

Observation of teaching, 42–43, 45, 57, 110–123, 154–155
Observation instruments, 110–123, 155 criteria for judging, 122–123
Open education, 211
Organizational complexity, 33
Organizational culture, 87, 93, 98, 159, 162, 197, 244, 250, 262, 265, 289

Paideia Program, 4, 58–60
Parent evaluation, 119, 272